*Australian
Women
in Papua
New Guinea*

Australian Women in Papua New Guinea

Colonial Passages 1920–1960

Chilla Bulbeck
Division of Humanities
Griffith University

CAMBRIDGE
UNIVERSITY PRESS

For Isabel, and her children, Paquita and Newell, who shared her New Guinea.

Published by Press Syndicate of the University of Cambridge
The Pitt Building, Trumpington Street, Cambridge CB2 1RP, UK
40 West 20th Street, New York, NY 10011–4211, USA
10 Stamford Road, Oakleigh, Melbourne, Victoria 3166, Australia

© Cambridge University Press 1992
First published 1992

Printed in Hong Kong by Colorcraft

National Library of Australia cataloguing in publication data
Bulbeck, Chilla, 1951–
Australian women in Papua New Guinea: colonial passages 1920–
1960.
Bibliography.
Includes index.
ISBN 0 521 41285 4.
1. White women – Papua New Guinea – History – 20th century. 2.
Women colonists – Papua New Guinea – History – 20th century. 3.
Sex role – Papua New Guinea – History – 20th century. 4. Papua
New Guinea – Race relations. I. Title.
305.488240953

Library of Congress cataloguing in publication data
Bulbeck, Chilla, 1951–
Australian women in Papua New Guinea : colonial passages,
1920–1960 / Chilla Bulbeck.
Includes bibliographical references and index.
ISBN 0-521-41285-4
1. White women—Papua New Guinea—Social conditions. 2. Papua New
Guinea—Race relations. 3. Papua New Guinea—Social conditions.
I. Title.
HQ1866.5.B85   1992   91-37965
305.48'80340953—dc20   CIP

A catalogue record for this book is available from the British Library.

ISBN 0 521 41285 4 hardback

Contents

Photographs

Acknowledgements

My greatest debt is to Dr Deane Fergie, without whose support and ideas this book would not have come into existence. Initially Deane and I planned to write this book together. Deane conducted a number of the interviews both in Australia and New Ireland, transcribed materials at the National Library and, most importantly, provided the ideas which underpin this book's rationale and structure. Unfortunately other commitments prevented Deane from carrying on with the project, but she has maintained her interest in its completion. I am deeply grateful for her friendship and discussions in the six years between our meeting and the completion of *Australian Women in Papua New Guinea*.

For the expatriate women who so generously gave of their time, hospitality and memories, I hope this book will be a fitting memento of their time in Papua New Guinea. I would also like to thank those women or their relatives who allowed me to reproduce their written memoirs; the staff of the Manuscripts Room at the National Library and the Australian Archives for their assistance; and Hank Nelson and Judy Davis' relatives who allowed me to incorporate the research and insights from Judy Davis' unfinished doctoral dissertation. I am grateful for photographs from Joyce Walker's collection, Ann Deland's collection, and that of Marjorie Murphy, many of which were taken by her husband John Murphy.

Janice Mitchell, my secretary and more, has continued to keep the disorder which threatens my life at bay. I wish to express my gratitude to the team at Cambridge University Press for their professional and friendly support, especially Deidre Missingham, for her careful editing, and Robin Derricourt, who perceived the germ of a good book in my first drafts, provided me with helpful readers' reports, and has shown a commitment to producing a book that reflects the messages of the written text.

One of the expatriate women whose memories form the basis of the text was my grandmother, Isabel Platten, whose completed life was celebrated on International Women's Day in March 1991. I was fortunate to come closer to my grandmother through writing this book; in return she has brought me closer to my extended family. Their ongoing interest and support reflected both their talents and enthusiasm for what became a family project.

Annalisa Platten offered me a splendid crayon sketch of my grandmother's favourite home at Halis in New Ireland which unfortunately could not be used. Bronwyn Platten, with her fine sense of the political messages of images, directed me to a careful selection of Gil Platten's photographs of New Ireland. Alison Main spent many hours taking photographs and compiling a composite photograph of me and my grandmother, which the state of computer technology prevented us from using.

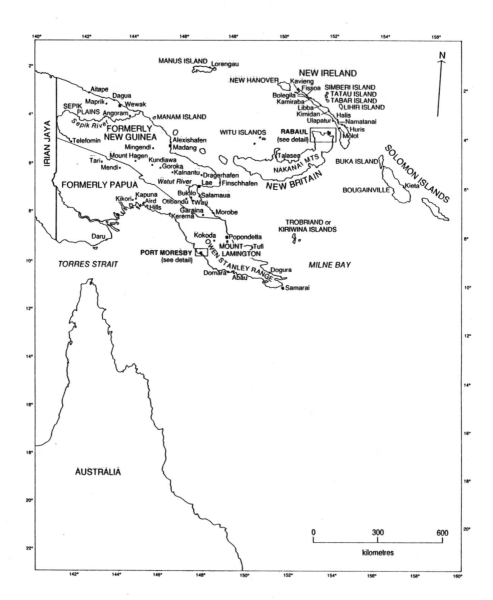

Papua New Guinea

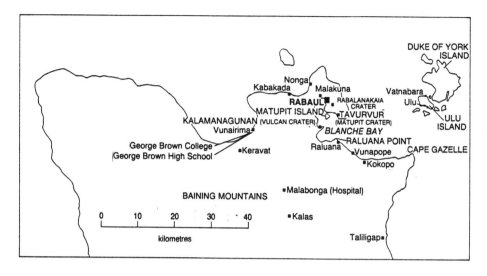

Detail of Rabaul area

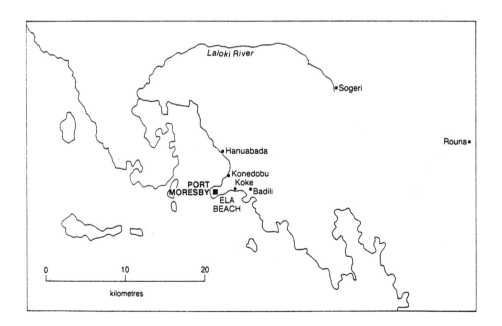

Detail of Port Moresby area

Abbreviations

AAMWS   Australian Army Medical Women's Service
ADO   Assistant District Officer
ANGAU   Australian and New Guinea Administration Unit
CMS   Church Missionary Society
CWA   Country Women's Association
DC   District Commissioner
DO   District Officer
EMA   European Medical Assistant
LMS   London Missionary Society
MBE   Member of the British Empire (British system of honours)
MCH   Maternal and Child Health Division (of Department of Health)
MO   Medical Officer
MSC   Missionarius Sacratissimi Cordis (Missionary of the Most Sacred Heart)
SPC   South Pacific Council (of the United Nations)
RSL   Returned Services League
VAD   Volunteer Aid Detachment

Introduction

Papua New Guinea was seen by men and women alike as a 'man's country'. Nevertheless there were 670 white women in Papua in 1921, almost 2000 white women in the country in 1933, and over 10 000 white women had lived in the Territory by the eve of Australian withdrawal in 1975.[1] The great majority of women went to the Territory because jobs took their husbands there, although more single women came after the 1950s as teachers, nurses and other government workers. 'Defined in terms of her relationships with various other people the white woman was overwhelmingly the wife, mother and missus.'[2] Helen McLeod, the wife of a District Officer between 1948 and 1958 says 'In colonial administration a wife is married to her husband who is married to his job'.[3] Even so, wives' experiences in the Territory were not a replica of their husbands' experiences. Wives had different concerns—household management, mother-hood—and different perspectives. In contrast with their husbands, they were more often partially disinterested bystanders and more likely to work with or at least talk to indigenous women. A number of women also went to Papua New Guinea unaccompanied by husbands, mainly as missionaries, but also as nurses, teachers, clerical and administrative workers.

Helen Callaway notes that women figure not at all in official memoirs, or appear anonymously as 'my wife' or 'the wife of'.[4] Papua New Guinea, too, has its official history, stitched together from government archives and the memoirs and biographies of administrators, male missionaries and planters. This history focusses on the colonial phenomenon. Implicitly or otherwise, Australia's performance is measured against some notion of 'good' culture contact. The focus of attention is thus race relations rather than gender relations. Sir Paul Hasluck's *A Time for Building* is a notorious example of an official history which pays scant attention to women (of any colour).[5] Hasluck devoted four pages to 'women's issues' and included them in 'A Mixed Bag of Social Questions'.

Records of women's experiences in Papua New Guinea are largely absent from the official narrative. Instead, women's stories are contained in a handful of white women's memoirs and the ephemera of mission booklets, often written for the immediate task of raising money or recruits at home. Wives have told the story of their husband's work, but also of their own adaptation to life in Papua New Guinea. Such books range from Dame Rachel Cleland's discussion of an administrator and his wife to Helen McLeod's story of a District Officer's wife.[6] There are a scattering of autobiographies of unaccompanied women, for example by the naturalist Evelyn Cheeseman or Doris Booth's exploits on the Bulolo goldfields in her husband's absence.[7]

More recently, a number of academic works have sought to tell of white women's experiences in the colonies of India, Africa, Fiji and Papua New Guinea.[8] Drawing on the perspectives of feminist scholarship, these books place a new inflection on white women's colonial experiences. They speak of white women's philanthropic work, whether in mission or plantation; they describe the restricted range of roles for women in a colony and women's negotiation of these roles; they identify the tensions between family concerns and the colonial enterprise; and they discuss the relations between white and indigenous women. In constructing this alternative history for women in the colonies, female writers have been forced to interrogate an earlier (and usually male) claim that white women, and not men, were the more racist members of colonial society. By some accounts, not only were white women more intolerant and ignorant of the colonial enterprise, their attitudes cost Britain its empire, and Australia its chance of creating a civilised Papua New Guinea. Chapter 8 takes up this debate, measuring it against the experiences of white women in Papua New Guinea.

This book is based on the experiences of nineteen women who spent time in Papua New Guinea between 1920 and 1960, a period between the hard pioneering of the firstcomers and the more rapid and regular influx of government workers from the 1960s. Some women lived in Papua New Guinea before the Second World War, and some after. Isabel Platten and Pat Murray arrived in the 1920s and returned to the Territory after the war. Women from the three major areas of colonial society—mission, government and private enterprise—are represented; and there are women who went to Papua New Guinea with husbands or family and women who chose to go on their own initiative.

The primary sources consist of edited transcripts of interviews conducted by Chilla Bulbeck and Deane Fergie and manuscripts held at the National

Library. Some interview transcripts are supplemented by diary extracts, letters, or a substantial revision of the interview materials written by the interviewee. The author's grandmother, Isabel Platten, wrote her story as a series of letters to her grand-daughter. The documentary sources held by the National Library consist of letters, diaries, speeches and records of interviews. The different documentary sources have their own interest. The varying textures of letters written to close family members, interviews given to a mere acquaintance, and speeches written for public consumption add variety to the reminiscences reproduced in this book. I have sought to preserve the individual voices of these women while also incorporating their story into the larger tale of Papua New Guinea's white history. To this end, each woman is introduced as she appears, and Appendix 1 contains biographical notes and sources for each woman. Deane Fergie and I also conducted interviews with several New Ireland New Guineans. Unfortunately, despite our attempts to include them, indigenous women spoke little during these interviews.

While male-oriented colonial histories have been told with no reference to women's history, the narrative told here is placed against the backdrop of official colonial affairs. The combination of an official and a personal register is not without its difficulties. Not all colony-building events significantly affected the lives of women concerned for their children's welfare, in the face of the domestic traumas of isolation and constant movement. Thus Judy Davis notes that men, but not women, identified their postings chronologically: 'it mattered how long [you were at an outstation], but it didn't matter when'.[9] This book is organised to reveal the apparent timelessness of some experiences these women shared, often determined more by geography than chronology, while also noting evolutionary changes in other aspects of their lives.

Chapter 1 introduces the women as birds of passage, between the two worlds of Australia and Papua or New Guinea. For those travelling to the tropics, their own first impressions are contrasted with the tropical romances and travelogues which propelled them northwards. More women will be introduced as they share the experience of a hasty passage home ahead of the Japanese troops at Christmas in 1941. Chapter 2 discusses the different colonial societies which receive white women: government, mission or private enterprise. While the destination of white women was significant, their status was also an important influence on their lives in the Territory. Chapter 3 compares the lives of wives and mothers with those of women who came as workers. This chapter explores some of the concerns common to all women in a colony, indeed anywhere: domestic management. But it also draws out the different experiences for single women and women who came as 'relative creatures', particularly in a discussion of that segment of colonial society to which most women came, the mission. Chapter 4 examines the third major determinant of white women's lives—whether they were thrown up on their own resources on an isolated outstation or participated in the social life of a colonial town, where their major contact with indigenous people was with their domestic staff. For readers who are largely interested in the interviewees' own experiences, these four chapters adopt that focus.

The remaining chapters write expatriate women's stories into the official history of colonial rule and the more recent analyses of white women's relationship to that rule. Chapters 5 and 6 explore the racial question, focussing on the oft-stated claim that the Second World War was a major watershed in race relations. In some ways, these chapters return to the register of official history, discussing the dominant perspectives of government, mission and private enterprise on the correct 'handling of the natives'. Missions brought 'the word'; plantation owners required land and labour; government sought order in a balancing of white demands and indigenous needs. Chapter 5 discusses political battles concerning the use of force, the alienation of land and the provision of labour for white enterprise. Chapter 6 focusses on the post-war period, exploring the role of missions and government in changing indigenous cultures, largely through the expansion of education. These chapters deal with matters of official history, but white women's experiences and reflections are woven into the account, often as a minor thread.

In contrast with official histories, the gender axis is central to this book. Chapters 7 and 8 focus on the specific issues of race and gender in the colonial setting. Chapter 7 argues that there was a circumscribed place for everyone in Papua New Guinean society, defined by both race and gender. Because white men were located at the top of the hierarchy, they can be said to have a 'position'. For white women and black men there are tensions in their subordinate position in terms of one marker but their dominant position in terms of the other: thus black men are still men but constructed as inferior to white women. These tensions find their major expression in outbreaks of hysteria concerning miscegenation.

Chapter 8 discusses the intrusion of white women into the male colonial world and the relations between European and Papua New Guinean women. Of all those who have lived in colonial societies, the voices of indigenous women are the most muffled. Even today, few ·speak with their own voice, and this book is unfortunately no exception. It tells the story of Papua New Guinean women only as white women have seen it. Chapter 8 also analyses the multitude of claims that women singlehandedly brought down

Empires, and thwarted civilising missions around the globe. The study of Papua New Guinea adds support to Callaway's argument that women did indeed ruin male empires, in their role as the softer face of colonialism.[10]

Some of the accounts are tales of action, for example Joyce Walker's experience as a nursing sister with the Methodist Mission at Mendi, told in Chapter 4. Other women reflect on the colonial experience, what it meant for them and also for the Papua New Guineans they knew; for example Isabel Platten (a missionary's wife), Mary Pulsford (an agricultural officer's wife) and Pat Andersen (a missionary's wife). Some married women faced conflicts between their husband's work and their own felt needs, describing an acute choice between the demands and desires of motherhood and the claims of the mission—for example, Grace Young and Isabel Platten. Marjorie Murphy, whose husband rose to District Commissioner, comments wistfully on the restriction of her horizons once her first child was born. Some accounts, such as those of Pat Murray and Ann Deland, deal with the conflicts between the missions, the planters and the administration. Joan Refshauge, who became second-in-command of a government department before she retired, deals with the difficulties a woman doctor faced in a man's world.

Some women, for example Ann Deland and Mollie Parer, discuss Papua New Guineans only as servants. Others, such as Pat Murray, Daphney Bridgland and Mary Pulsford, argue that relations with employees were far more complex than a simple cash-nexus. For mission workers particularly, their attention is focussed on Papua New Guineans rather than the rest of the white community, sometimes revealing strong and abiding friendships (Dorothy Pederick and Jean Mannering, for example).

The accounts also reveal the shape of daily life: running a household when provisions came infrequently; entertaining oneself when no other white woman lived close by; travelling where there were no made roads; running a hospital, school or plantation. Crises punctuated daily life and brought home to these women their exposure to potential death from snake-bite or infection; and the risks of delivering babies away from hospitals. The patterns of daily life were ruptured and changed by wider events. For planters living in Papua New Guinea in the late 1920s, the Depression significantly reduced their living standards. For missionaries, however, with access to home-grown food, the effects of the Depression were cushioned. The evacuation of women and children ahead of the Japanese invasion of New Guinea in December 1941 brought many of these women together. The nurses and other mission workers who stayed behind became prisoners of war in Japan (Dorothy Beale, for example).

Almost every woman with both pre-war and post-war experience of Papua

New Guinea sees the war as a great divide. Sisters Aquilonia Ax and Bohdana Voros, as well as a number of other women both inside and beyond the mission, comment on the devastation of the war and their austere lifestyles while buildings were being constructed, clothes and furniture made. Only two ministers of the Methodist Mission in New Guinea, Gil Platten and Rodger Brown, survived the war to return to mission work. The administration of the two colonies was brought under a single authority and civil servants were now posted to 'the other side' in an attempt to eradicate the old rivalries. A number of accounts, for example those of Dixie Rigby and Prudence Frank, point to the changed attitudes of Papua New Guineans after the war. Generally the blurring of status boundaries is not approved by the 'befores' (or B4s), those who were in the colony before the War.

Living in Papua New Guinea was also an adventure in politics. Administering the Territory was Australia's major colonial experience. All Australians have the experience of living in an ex-colony; very few have had the experience of being on the 'other side of the colonial fence', of being among the colonisers. None of these women participated directly in colonial rule as judges, *kiaps*, or district officers, but neither did any work actively for Independence during this period. There were no revolutionary Annie Besants in Papua New Guinea. None the less, some women were active participants in the delivery of education and health care, and some worked to improve the status of indigenous women.

While life in Papua New Guinea, for whites and for many Papua New Guineans, changed after the Second World War, it was Independence which irrevocably altered race relations in the country. Of those accounts that discuss changing race relations, all but two (those of Mary Pulsford and Pat Andersen), look back wistfully to the colonial days. Whatever one thinks of Australians as colonisers, the experiences these women had will never be repeated. It is trite to say that every life is unique, but these women shared a particular moment in Australian history. Few Australians have experienced the excitement, difficulties, and pleasures of living amongst a people with a completely different culture. By the time and at the places most of these women arrived, 'pacification' was complete and they were free without fear or anxiety to explore the benefits of culture contact. For some this meant little more than servants. For most, however, it meant at least a few friendships with Papua New Guineans. For all, it meant an abiding interest in a close neighbour and a time now passed into history.

1

Passages to Papua New Guinea

Although a few white Australian women have been born in Papua New Guinea and indeed spent all or most of their lives there, the great majority lived in the Territory for only a few years. For most expatriate women, Papua New Guinea was a passage in their lives, a brief moment, usually of their adulthood, after growing up and before growing old. Fewer women took passage to the Territory of their own initiative than went with husbands, or in some cases with parents. Nevertheless, going to Papua New Guinea was still a choice to relocate in another country. All those women who went before the Second World War also shared a passage out of Papua and New Guinea, the evacuation of women and children as the Japanese invaded. This chapter explores these passages to and from the Territory, comparing them with the adventure travels, tropical romances and mission tracts which had lured them northwards.

First impressions

> Mum says what she remembered most of all when waiting on the wharf at Kavieng for stuff to come off the ship, she smelled this weird horrible smell: 'What's that dreadful smell?' And this man beside her, Bill Garnett who planted Kamiraba later, said 'Madam, you're smelling money'. (Stale sweepings of copra in the shed!)

For Pat Murray's mother this was a pungent irony. She had convinced her husband to leave their Queensland property and buy an expropriated German plantation in New Guinea. One night she had found an advertisement for

7

the properties in an old newspaper: 'The next morning she said to Dad "Have a look at this. For God's sake let's go somewhere where we can get some black labour again" '. As Pat Murray admits, this is a 'very unfashionable thought' now, if not then.[1]

The Australian expropriation of German New Guinea plantations was a farflung element of the government's post-war soldier settlement scheme. A series of books produced in 1925, 1926 and 1927 described three groups of expropriated properties, and featured seductive pictures with captions such as: 'The Wonderful Witu Group: the envy of planters, the magnet of copra buyers'.[2] There were homilies for business life in a colony: 'Where native material is plentiful substantial labourers' houses are constructed at a small cost'; 'By fair dealing the confidence of the native is gained and the plantation of native copra stimulated'.[3] Pat Murray's father bought one of the third group, and the family arrived in New Ireland in 1927.

Thus are the lives of expatriate women wound around the events of war and politics. Even so, expatriate women's lives had their own particular register. War, Depression, unification, and changing government policies concerning the 'treatment of the natives' all had their impact on these women's experiences in the Territory. But their lives were also lived at a more personal level, not only in terms of a sharper focus on family or nearby village, but also in the specificity of each woman's biography. This chapter commences that balancing act between affairs of state and affairs of the heart, between public politics and private options, which structures this book. The women who people this narrative are introduced against the backdrop of the society and tales of adventure which drew them northwards.

Both of Pat Murray's parents spent many of their childhood years in British colonies. They met in India where Pat's father was in the Indian Army, and married in 1919. Their first two children, Jim, who was killed during the Second World War, and Pat, born in 1922, arrived before they came to Australia, to a sheep property of two soldier settlement blocks, in southern Queensland. From there they moved to a plantation, Bolegila, in New Ireland on 13 December 1927. In 1951 Pat married Peter and they ran their own plantation. Apart from her schooling in Australia and the war years, Pat lived in New Guinea until she and her husband returned to Australia, settling in Newcastle in 1982.

For Pat Murray the day of arrival as a small child evoked all her fantasies of the alien and colourful people of the Territory, commonly called 'kanakas' by the whites who lived in Papua New Guinea before the war:

> My first solid memories are of Kavieng. We went up in the *Marsina*,
> a very small ship. First port of call was Samarai, we didn't go to

Moresby in those days. A lot of ships didn't, Moresby wasn't very important, it was only a little place. And I can remember seeing the kanakas for the first time. In those days the Papuans used to wear their hair in an enormous bush. There were all these fellows racing around on the wharf doing things in red lap laps. And to this day I can remember thinking to myself 'Yes that is what it would be like'.

First impressions were all the stronger following the long sea journey undertaken by pre-war travellers. In 1920 ten or more days were spent at sea; by 1946 the Territory was a day's flight away. The sea journey allowed more time for adjustment, and forged friendships between white expatriate families. Before the war Pat Murray's return trip from school to Kavieng in New Ireland took a fortnight. Four of the eight weeks of her school holidays were spent at sea. In the 1950s, travelling by air, Pat's children returned home in two days at the most.

Port Moresby, the administrative centre of Papua, was a small poor place even in 1927, reflecting the languid, under-financed Australian administration. In 1910, Port Moresby and Samarai were described as 'two small towns of a few score inhabitants apiece'.[4] In contrast, Rabaul, which was the administrative centre of New Guinea, was quite a colonial town. The German administration had been far more energetic, supervising a larger number of plantations and much more vigorous trading and missionary activities. Trading was so extensive that the profits supported the likes of 'Queen Emma of the South Seas', Emma Eliza (Coe) Parkinson (1850–1913), who was the daughter of an American consul to Samoa and a chiefly Samoan woman. Educated in Sydney and the United States, Emma helped her father manage his business affairs; she married and had a number of love affairs before moving to Mioko Island east of Rabaul with an Australian schooner trader and hotel owner, Tom Farrell, in 1876. The couple established plantations in the entrance to Rabaul Harbour on the Gazelle Peninsula. Emma formed a friendship with the Rev. George Brown, who pioneered the Methodist Mission in New Guinea. Queen Emma became famous for extravagant entertainment and living, attended by a consort of cousins dressed in beautiful gowns, and bathing in champagne. In 1907 Emma Parkinson sold her New Guinea assets for one million United States dollars and, suffering from diabetes, entered a Frankfurt clinic.[5] Rabaul's social life reflected the growing wealth of the surrounding German plantations, expropriated by the Australians following the First World War. Marnie Bassett, a guest at Government House in 1921, describes a round of outings, dinner parties and dances.[6]

The less advanced social life of Port Moresby revolved around the two pubs and the club. Drunkenness and fights were common at the 'bottom pub' also called the 'slaughter yard' or the 'dead house'. At the 'top pub' gentlemen and men ate at separate tables and a greater decorum was preserved.[7] Doris Groves, a young missionary teacher, socialised at the club, where a religious air prevailed: 'billiards, singing, chatting, getting to know each other, followed by supper and Evening Prayers, when all the native people on the station came and joined us'.[8]

Prudence Frank, like Pat Murray, also had a second-generation association with the Territory, her mother having lived in Papua. She was born in 1907 in Cooktown in Queensland. Her cousin was 'Ma' (Flora) Stewart of the Hotel Cecil, Lae in New Guinea. In 1922 and 1923 Prudence obtained the Superior Public School Certificate (Commercial Classes). In 1925 she travelled to Port Moresby, washing clothes for single men during the Depression, but later becoming the confidential secretary to Captain Fitch, the Managing Director of Steamships Trading Company Limited. In 1938 she married Kendall Frank, a wireless operator with Amalgamated Wireless, then Overseas Telecommunications:

> Our breakfast room was used as the studio. Curtains were hung on the walls for acoustics. My piano was used in the broadcasts of local talent by children and adults. Our orchestra consisted of cornet, Ken Frank, violinist, Rev. Harry Matthews, and myself as pianiste. Mr Tommy O'Dea, pilot for Guinea Airways, an operatic tenor, was one of our vocalists. I took my turn to do the broadcasting.[9]

A series of almost chance accidents turned Doris Groves away from her comfortable government job to embrace the rigours and poverty of missionary work. Her interest was sparked when the Acting Secretary of the London Missionary Society (LMS) called for mission workers during a church service. She feared losing her job to an ex-serviceman returning from the First World War, but knew that a missionary's salary was much lower than a teacher's. Doris Groves (then Smith) was interviewed by the Society's Secretary, Rev. G. J. Williams. She relates the episode in an unpublished draft of her experiences in Papua:

> After some polite conversation he asked me had I thought things over, and what decision had I come to? I said that I had decided to accept the position. He then barked these questions at me: Why had I decided to go? Was it because I was a teacher? I wanted to do good? or in a spirit of adventure? I thought for a few moments, and then said 'I think all three'. 'What do you mean?' he rapped out. I answered:

1. 'If I wasn't a trained teacher I wouldn't be qualified to go.
2. If I didn't want to do good I wouldn't think of going.
3. And if it were not in a spirit of adventure I wouldn't be game to go'. His whole manner changed and he put out his hand to shake mine and said 'You'll do me and the mission' so my future fate was sealed.[10]

Doris Groves arrived in Port Moresby in December 1921. She was met by lines of decorated canoes and hundreds of 'natives' from the villages of Kanabada, Hanuabada and Elevala:

> Most of the men clothed only by what was called the G string—
> a small piece of material (banana leaves or bark or in some cases
> calico) worn between the legs and attached to a plaited belt around
> the waist, and the women were bare to the waist and wearing skirts
> made of grass or in some cases stranded pandanus . . .

Then Doris Groves was required to make physical contact with this alien people:

> All came forward to greet me and shake hands—some with bodies
> on which the whole skin appeared to be peeling off—this was a
> condition called 'Grillie', others with large suppurating sores called
> 'Yaws'. Mr Clark must have noticed me shrink a little as I shook
> their hands—so he said 'Don't worry Miss Doris, there is plenty
> of Lifebuoy soap up at the mission house, and you must get used
> to using it'.

Although Doris Groves arrived as a mission teacher, she was later to join the government teaching service. In 1925 Doris left the LMS and took up an appointment at a government school at Malakuna near Rabaul, where she was in charge of the Junior School. Bill Groves also taught at this school, and they married in the same year. In 1926 they returned to Victoria, Bill to teach and Doris to raise a family of three children. After the Second World War Bill became Director of Education in the Territory until his retirement. Doris Groves became involved in extensive philanthropic work in Port Moresby.

Marjorie Murphy's New Guinea adventure was in part a flight from an unhappy romance. She was offered a job by the managing director of Colyer Watson in 1940. Her written reminiscences balance the humidity and stench of copra against the tropical difference of Rabaul:

> I was a passenger to Rabaul on the China Navigation vessel *Tanda*.
> Blanche Bay and the beautiful harbour with the two volcanoes—

Matupit one side and Vulcan the other, took my breath away. The dreadful humidity and smell of copra in the tin roofed Customs Shed, however, gave me some misgivings. I wondered if I would be able to work in the heat. Tick Spensely collected me, dropped off my gear at the Rabaul Hotel where I was to board and after lunch, took me for a tour of the town. I fell in love with its wide tree-lined streets and old German-type houses high off the ground with wide verandahs all around and the colourful plants and flowers in the gardens.

For young women with some money pre-war Rabaul offered dances, pictures, dinner parties and cocktail parties, a dramatic Society called the Betel Club, while canoe races 'with white captains and native crews were held on Saturday afternoons'. [Marjorie Murphy]

Isabel Platten, the young wife of a poor Methodist minister, was unimpressed with Rabaul when she arrived in 1927. The wide tree-lined streets prevented breezes from entering her house, and the beautiful dark panelling in the houses encouraged mosquitoes to breed, while kerosene lamps, made necessary by the lack of electricity, added to the suffocating heat. Isabel Platten was unable to stretch her husband's mission salary to the lifestyle expected of white people:

Gil had to be decked out in what was the uniform for all males— long white trousers, long-sleeved white shirts, white socks and polished black shoes—and for any formal occasion a white coat. Much of this was made by Chinese tailors. Another financial burden. Fortunately the mission allowed us an overdraft free of interest.

As with all administrative towns Rabaul was an expensive place to be, so it was soon obvious to me, a trained book-keeper, that something had to be done about our expenses. But there was little, if any, way I could see to cut costs. There was no electricity and kerosene-fuelled domestic refrigeration had to wait more than a decade before its time had come. We did have an ice-chest and ice was purchased at one shilling a block. That came to 30 or 31 shillings a month. Folk on mission stations managed without such a luxury so the ice got the chop.

Isabel Platten describes a status-conscious society where even calling cards were used. The etiquette of calling cards was as much a mystery to new arrivals in other colonial towns as it was to Isabel Platten. One young caller in Nigeria in 1927 was sharply informed that there was to be no communication with the residents when calling cards were left. After dropping his card, he leaned over the fence to talk to the mistress of the house who was gardening. She admonished him: 'In Kaduna when we are calling we do not speak'.[11] Isabel Platten remembers:

> It wasn't until many years later when I read much on India that I realised how much our small port of the Pacific was being run on similar lines. This also explained the strange visiting card cult. Before we left Sydney we were told to get cards printed for each of us. We were told that when visiting we were to leave three cards, one bearing my name and where I lived and two bearing Gil's name, his status and address. The trouble was we were never sure where to leave them. In India there was a container on the front gate especially for them. Everyone knew everyone else in Rabaul so we were perplexed about the reason for dropping cards. Almost asking people to invite you into their homes. Gil probably used his cards as an introduction to newcomers. Mine lay in a drawer of my sewing machine for years gathering oil.

Ann Deland, the wife of Dr Charles Deland, lived in Bougainville and Vanikoro in the Solomon Islands between 1926 and 1931. For her the round of social engagements was an imposition, as she notes in a letter home:

> When I got home there was a boy waiting with a note from Mrs Widdup—an invitation to afternoon tea. There was nothing for it but to go. These afternoon teas are weekly affairs; the women all take it in turns and, as I don't go out to the evening parties, I can't get out of the afternoon affairs. I would not mind if we could take our sewing, and sew and talk, but we spend the afternoon doing wretched competitions which I simply loathe.
>
> The week is a full one: Tennis on Wednesday and Saturday, the women's party on Thursday. As you would imagine, I would prefer to do something useful; one wouldn't mind if it were for some purpose . . .
>
> And so the weeks fill up, some of the women are always complaining that there is nothing to do here. I find there are too many distractions, and it is quite difficult to get my sewing done. When Ray is at home, a couple of hours in the morning are used up with his lessons. He loves them and would spend more time at them, but I don't want to push him.[12]

According to Daphney Bridgland, who arrived after the war, hats and gloves were required for social occasions. She suggests of the pre-war social scene:

> There was a great deal of jealousy between the Mandate of New

Guinea administration and the Papuan one. I believe that even when travelling south on the ships they wouldn't speak to one another, or have very little to do with one another socially. Great competitions—the women used to order their gowns from Europe, I suppose they got a lead on that from Queen Emma. Dinner was never served before half past ten or eleven at night. We starved the first time we went out to dinner, no-one warned us . . .

They had their social standards before the war. It was a very restrictive social code. The social standards in Rabaul, particularly, were based on military guidelines. It was still strict for the first few years after the war, but very gradually things began to change . . . One of the first big tea parties I went to—Dorry [Doris] Groves took me to it—the ladies all wore gloves.

Women and children first: the 1942 evacuation

After the Japanese attacked Pearl Harbour, various rumours and alarms circulated in Papua New Guinea:

I can see Kevin in between one of his flights. He was lying on the bed listening to the wireless. I said 'What are you so serious about, Kevin?' He was a very, very nice man. He said 'Pearl Harbour'. I said 'What does that mean?' He said 'It means we might all have to get out'. 'Oh' I said 'We wouldn't'. He said 'I wouldn't be surprised'. I went to the kitchen and I said to Nance 'Kevin's telling me terrible news'. She ran into the bedroom. He was just lying on the bed. It was a very casual way of living up there. That was December, about the 18th. [Mollie Parer]

Mollie Parer (Yates) was born in Melbourne and went to New Guinea in 1933 as Bob Parer's bride, where she lived on the goldfields for five years. In the late 1930s she moved to Wewak when her husband started a freezer business there, chartering food supplies and storing them in a freezer works. In 1939 the *Bulolo* which brought in the food supplies for the business was commandeered by the Allies and Bob went prospecting in Bougainville. Mollie and the children stayed in Wewak. Her brother-in-law, Kevin Parer, encouraged her to come and stay with his family in Wau. It was from there that she was evacuated, eventually arriving in Melbourne.

The Parer family have a long association with New Guinea, mainly as mission workers and business entrepreneurs. Ray Parer went to New Guinea in the 1920s where he pioneered aviation, particularly to the goldfields near Wau. In New Guinea Ray Parer took out a miner's right in the Upper Watut and this financed his various flying concerns; his unwillingness to charge unlucky miners being a major cause of their financial failure. Ray Parer, and his brothers, Bob and Kevin, lived in Wewak during the 1930s. Damien Parer, a cousin, captured the Second World War on film, including the battles along the Kokoda trail and the work of the Papuan bearers. So numerous and well-known were the Parers in New Guinea that they were likened to a 'tribe'. Marjorie Murphy recalls: 'There seemed to be Parers all over New Guinea. When we were going to Otibandu John said to one of the ADOs (Horrie Nile, now Sir Horace) "Any last minute instructions?" "Yes, get on out there and push back the Kukakukas and make room for the Parers" '.

The administration believed that the Japanese would bomb Rabaul and the other towns, perhaps send ashore a marine party to destroy airports, ports, and radio stations, and leave. The administration's plans were to send the civilian population bush during this period, with enough provisions to last the week or so of Japanese presence:

> The assumption was that once all the facilities were put out of action that was all we'd see of the war, apart from blockading. Kavieng fell before Singapore, and people tend to forget that. There were two or three different plans of action worked out which I knew pretty well at the time because I was the District Office confidential typist and I had to type out umpteen copies of them. [Pat Murray]

As there were not enough commercially made rucksacks for the Kavieng population's stay in the bush, Pat's mother made her family some 'flee-bags' as she called them, out of brightly-coloured chair canvas. Some of the missionaries believed they would be allowed to carry on God's work even if there were a Japanese invasion; some were scornful: a 'What can the Japs do to us?' attitude as Isabel Platten put it. Returning from Synod in October, Gil Platten planned his own retreat into the southern mountains of New Ireland.

When the evacuation of the women and children was finally organised, there had been Japanese air activity over the Territory for some time. Pat Murray remembers a Japanese aeroplane which came so low over Kavieng that she could see the pilot's face. The women were brought to Rabaul or Port Moresby, by air, road or boat.

Jean Mannering first went to New Guinea in August 1940 as the wife of the Rev. John Poole, living on a small mission station at Kalas in the Baining Mountains. Jean was evacuated with the European women and children from Rabaul in December 1941; her husband lost his life when the *Montevideo Maru* was torpedoed. Jean was awoken by a police boy at midnight to say that she must be packed and ready for a truck to take her to Rabaul two days' hence. Her parishioners came with gifts of eggs, taro, pawpaws and bananas. The school boys carried the Mannerings' luggage the five miles down to Malabonga Hospital, whence a bumpy truck ride took them to Rabaul, although they had to walk up the slippery hills as the truck could not climb them loaded:

> All the white women from the district were gathering in Rabaul to board the boats. The volcano was erupting with pumice. The women were crowded in the mission houses and other houses in Rabaul. We had to get our documents for leaving and then all the women went on board; two boats filled up with women. I was on the *MacDui*, it was absolutely crowded. They even had mattresses in the music room on the floor for people to sleep on. The women with children had to dry their napkins and clothes in the passage ways . . . My mother and father didn't know I'd left New Guinea until I walked in the door.

The *Katoomba* which was fitted up with temporary sleeping for 800 women and children, sailed to Australia from Port Moresby. Prudence Frank describes the boat journey:

> We received our evacuation notice to board the *Katoomba* on 18th December, 1941. We were allowed to take one suitcase. We all thought the authorities were mad and we would be back in three weeks. I put flowers in the vases, put out my best cut glass on the morning table, bedspreads etc. We were later told to stay in our homes till the wardens came for us as Japan had announced over the radio that the women and children were leaving Port Moresby. We were later taken to the ship, there were also Europeans from Singapore on board. The *Adelaide* escorted us from Port Moresby until we entered the Great Barrier Reef as the Japanese Raiders were about. We slept on the deck even though some of us had cabins because it was too hot below. All we had to look forward to was the bar to be opened. We would all queue up.

Mollie Parer describes Moresby and the trip down:

> The next 'plane arrived [in Moresby] and it was the women from all over the Territory, from the labour wards, and they weren't allowed even to bring their nappies. Just imagine it. Some were

vomiting, some were sick, and some were trying to write a note to their husbands and giving it to the pilot: 'Would you please give this to my husband'. They were crying, oh it was dreadful.

It was a frightening voyage because the captain told us to wear life jackets all the time as he said there would be raids and mines and so forth. We went a roundabout way and I think we went near Thursday Island. On Christmas Day 1941 the captain lined up all the children and gave each one a shilling and a bottle of soft drink.

Marjorie Murphy and two other young women were left in Port Moresby until Christmas Day, because the administration chose to evacuate German missionaries ahead of them. Marjorie Murphy protested to a Mr Frame:

We said 'What are you doing? We are left here, just the three of us' and Frame said 'Look, you heard what they did last night'. These troops had not exactly rioted but they'd got a bit out of hand. They were a bit mad because the baker didn't have any pies, they smashed his window. Frame said 'Can you see what would happen if we brought German missionaries in here?' The next day we did get away, in a Dragon I think, as far as Cairns. Then from Cairns to Melbourne by train.

Marjorie Murphy was particularly keen to escape the sexual harassment of the troops:

But we had to be careful because of the many soldiers stationed in Moresby at that time. With the sun behind you, you'd walk into the hotel, and they would whistle, and call 'Go out and come in again' because they could see through our dresses. So we were being very careful.

Some women left Rabaul in the *MacDui* but those who lived on New Ireland outside Kavieng were unable to reach Rabaul in time. Pat Murray describes the evacuation in a letter she wrote to her brother shortly after leaving New Guinea. The women were to gather at Ulapatur near Namatanai. Heavy rain and a strong north-westerly buffetted the family as they drove to Ulapatur in open trucks, where the *Paulus*, a Catholic Mission boat, was to pick them up:

When we got to Ulapatur there was no sign of a boat and the weather was terrible. The schooner simply couldn't get there and was hiding out at the Duke of Yorks. We sat and waited for it, all day from 10 o'clock to 5 p.m. we sat. There were 27 women,

13 kids and assorted husbands and other menfolk. And the accommodation was one copra shed, empty but rather leaky, and two very old leaky sak sak boys' houses. Also the Catholic mission house to which the father invited anyone and everyone but it was on the very top of a frightfully steep climb of well over 100 feet (and pelting rain and slippery with mud too). So most of us didn't tackle it. We had quite a lot of kaikai with us, sandwiches, biscuits and so on, and the Kong who runs Ulapatur plantation kept up an almost continuous supply of boiling water for tea so we didn't do too badly. But we were so wet. The kids were marvellous, there wasn't a single howl out of the whole 13 and none of them even quarrelled. Five were tiny babies and even they didn't cry.

Isabel Platten, one of the twenty-seven women, remembers:

We sat miserably on this miserable beach in the rain. The only people who had thought to bring any tea or sandwiches were Connie Brereton and me. So we shared with all the other women and their youngsters. They were all planters. It was with a sense of relief we learned that we would not be travelling that day. We went back to our own homes to cook Christmas dinners and have a precious few more days with our husbands.

Those who did not live close by bedded down at Joe Kenny's pub in Namatanai, and returned to Ulapatur at 4 am the next day. The weather cleared, but only temporarily and by 8 am it was clear the storm had set in for the day at least:

So we went back to Namatanai again and this time Kenny more or less expected us. He just said to his cook 'Kukim kaikai bilong ol'. The ADO was in touch with Rabaul and was told the transport in Rabaul couldn't wait for us and as the weather might continue like that indefinitely we were all to go home pending further notice. (The government secretary in Rabaul said to Greg Benham, the Patrol Officer, on the phone 'What's wrong with all these damn women, are they all scared or what? The women from here have gone and the weather's just as bad over here. What's wrong with them there?' Greg said 'Look sir, I keep trying to tell you, there are no bloody boats. They can't swim to Rabaul'. 'Don't you swear on the air, Benham!'). [Pat Murray]

Pat Murray's family were told to return to Namatanai by 9 pm on Christmas night. The evacuees spent their time organising a belated Christmas party with the handful of Independent Company troops stationed in Namatanai. The next day the New Ireland women finally made their escape, as Pat Murray's letter recounts: 'On Saturday morning we set off for Ulapatur for the third and last time. The weather was fine and the *Paulus* was waiting, also the *Teresa*'.

Because they had missed the *MacDui*, Isabel Platten and Pat Murray were flown down to Cairns, where they joined Marjorie Murphy and many other women on the long train trip down the coast. According to Pat Murray there were good meals at convenient stopping places, VADs (Volunteer Aid Detachment) on the trains and nurses and doctors at some of the stations. The Red Cross and Country Women's Association met the women at various stations with refreshment, changes of clothing, and, at Rockhampton and Gympie, took the babies off for a bath:

> They dashed up to all the carriages as we pulled in: 'Any babies?' Grabbed the babies and small children and rushed them off to be bathed, dressed in clean clothes, fed and returned to their parents. John was very amused when Norman Ashby was carried off (Norman Ashby was actually seven, but he was very small; he looked about four). John thought it was hilarious. But Norman gave him a look and said 'I'm getting a bath out of this, don't worry'. The poor kids were very startled and almost all yelled loudly. A few took it complacently but you can imagine the uproar. There were about 90 of them. The German babies were the most inconsolable as they couldn't understand a word the poor girls said when they attempted to calm them down.

A number of women lost all their possessions as a result of the evacuation. Mollie Parer tells her story:

> At first we were told we were going to Salamaua and could bring our personal possessions. The second advice told us we would fly to Port Moresby early next day and to bring only forty pounds and I think fifteen pounds for each child. Kevin got special permission to fly his wife and her three children and me and my four to Moresby. I took Lactogen and things like that. We had to look round the home: 'Surely we're not going to leave it all behind'. But we had to, everything left behind, photos particularly. Because the weight of say a piece of silver would be the weight of a baby in the 'plane.
>
> The morning came and Auntie Teresa was staying with her daughter Mrs Owen, who had seven children. Doreen Owen was Damien's sister. Auntie Teresa had given her only daughter most of her silver.

I can just see the shelf all around, all sterling as it used to be in those days, and Auntie Teresa was going out the door. She was going to take a dear little sterling silver jardinière, it was at the door. She picked it up and someone said 'Everything's got to be weighed'.

Our first lady in Wewak, Lynette Townsend, was already down in Melbourne because her husband had finished his time there. Later she said to me 'I felt so guilty that I hadn't lost any of my possessions. I felt I couldn't see you'. She just kept ringing me up all the time and sending me parcels. She didn't want to see me. She said one of her friends had a breakdown over the evacuation.

Dixie Rigby, a patrol officer's wife, tells a similar story:

When Reg got back Japan had already invaded. He was in Lae and the Japs just simply swept right across and got as far as Lae. They walked out of Lae across to the hills above Moresby and relief parties were sent out to them. Everything that we had was destroyed, scorched earth policy. They pushed them into the sea, our refrigerators and beautiful china. We lost everything and we didn't have anything. Reg walked out in a pair of trousers and a shirt, a tin mug and a razor. Everything personal we lost. I was rather disturbed about that because in 1937 we'd gone back to England, and we went to Germany for a holiday. And we were there when all these 'Guns before butter' and things like that. But my mother had given me some very beautiful china and glass, which I took back to New Guinea, and it all went.

John Murphy packed Marjorie's case for her:

John kept coming to me and he said 'Don't worry, I'll pack all your trousseau, I'll pack everything. The *Neptune* is coming in to Salamaua and I'll label it down to you'. He stacked camphor wood boxes with our stuff. Then he came to me 'These are very valuable patrol reports. You'd better take them out, they'll be handy for the army'. So in go the patrol reports. And then the Pidgin-English dictionary. So I've got about that much in the suitcase, so I put in a sweater and my golf shoes and that was all. I remember being very very calm until I went down to the garden and I'd had a hell of a time trying to grow parsnips and now I was growing parsnips. And I said to John 'I won't be here to eat the parsnips'. I remember howling about that. Women are silly aren't they?

Isabel Platten's story had a happier ending.

Being refugees meant, of course, we had between us one suitcase
of clothes and very little money . . .

   To our delighted surprise one day a consignment of cases arrived.
Gil had packed much of our personal effects, including household
linen and, best of all, my sewing machine. Word had come to him
that a Burns Philp ship would be calling and would take on any
personal luggage. The ship took our luggage to Port Moresby, dumped
it on the wharf there where it rested quite a while until another
ship picked it up and got it to Sydney. Some way or other it eventually
arrived, intact, on my doorstep. To me one of the minor miracles
of war-time and a tremendous help to the household.

The mission sisters stayed behind with the men. Many were captured as
prisoners of war, spending the war in Japan. The men who were captured
were killed by allied fire on the *Montevideo Maru*, on their way to Japan.
Until their capture, the mission sisters continued their medical work, adapting
themselves to the circumstances:

> Dec 1941 women and children were sent from New Guinea: all
> the native people in residence at Vunairima were sent to their villages
> except the New Ireland people. Revs McArthur, Pearson and Trevitt
> were trying to arrange transport for them but not able. We closed
> the Stewart Hospital to people except for those living on the station,
> as it was too much of a target for the Japanese planes flying over
> us very low, every afternoon. We built an emergency hospital at
> Malmabeon in a concealed area where we had a supply of things
> and intended to put any patients there if nec. but tried to keep
> them in their homes and went out every day and met the people
> (in fever areas) and treated them, it was considered better for them
> not to congregate at any place for long. Howard Pearson always
> drove me. We did this till the Japanese invasion . . .[13]

Jean Mannering lost her husband on the *Montevideo Maru*:

> The Methodist missionaries decided they should stay with the natives.
> When some of the soldiers were escaping they wanted my husband
> to go with them. But he felt he had to stay with the people. Then
> my husband and two other missionaries walked down to give
> themselves up to the Japanese, when they knew the Japanese were
> coming up to where the house was. They were all put in a camp
> and they worked on the wharves in Rabaul until they were put
> on the *Montevideo Maru* to be taken to Japan, the one that was
> torpedoed off the Philippines. Rev. Gil Platten and Rev. Rodger

Brown escaped, but they were the only two missionaries who did, the others were lost on the boat.

The Chinese in Kavieng, as elsewhere, were not evacuated to Australia:

> After they invaded in January 1942, the Japs rounded up the Europeans and put them in the Kavieng gaol, and gave them a pretty hard time, pretty rough treatment, and not much to eat and no contact. A lot of the Chinese were sending in stuff to them to help them. What they used to do was make little packages and stick them under the bottom of the lavatory pans, which was the only way into the camp. Apparently they were caught at it and poor old Leslie Foon Kong and Wong Fong were both tortured and killed by the Japs for helping Europeans. Dreadful business. [Pat Murray]

New beginnings: after the war

A number of Methodist sisters and wives—Joyce Walker, Grace Young and Jean Mannering among them—travelled together on the first ship that carried white women back to the Territory after the Second World War:

> I went up with Kath Brown on the *Duntroon*. We left Sydney on the 12th November 1946. I think it took us three weeks to get there. We went via Port Moresby, Lae, Finschhafen to Rabaul. On the ship were also other missionaries, Dorothy Beale, Jean Mannering, Jean Christopher, Mary Woolnough and a number of buyers who were going to Papua New Guinea for the Commonwealth Disposals Commission Auction Sales. [Grace Young]

In 1946 Grace Young joined her husband Gordon, the Army Chaplain in Rabaul. Included in his duties was conducting services for the Japanese in the War Criminal Compound. He joined the Methodist Mission some months later, his army contacts and experiences helping with the purchase of vehicles and the mission boat, the *Talai*. They were stationed at Ulu in the Duke of Yorks, Gordon's job consisting mainly of skippering the *Talai* and managing the mission-owned coconut plantation. In 1948 they returned to Sydney for a short period. The Youngs took over the Namatanai circuit when Gil was appointed to George Brown College in 1949.

Jean Mannering describes the devastation caused by the war:

> Rabaul had been pounded so thoroughly, they even had to resurvey it to find out where the streets went; it was just rubble. The Japanese

bombed Rabaul and the Australians bombed it and the Americans bombed it. And it kept getting bombed all through the war years. When I went back, there was no wharf left. Our boat pulled in against an old wreck that was half on the shore, and that acted as the wharf for some time. All around the place there were wrecks of ships, wrecked vehicles, it was just a mess of rubble.

The Papua New Guineans were very happy to see the Australians come back after the war, because they'd had a very bad time under the Japanese, particularly the people in New Britain and the Duke of Yorks. The Japanese had burned down their churches and burned their hymn books and Bibles and forbidden them to have meetings of any kind. Some of them had been beheaded and they were tortured and filled up with water and jumped on; strung up by their toes. The Japs would come and take their gardens and the people would have to go and hide in caves. They said they'd never have lived only God made nut trees bear out of season and they just had to try and survive on that. All their little children died during the war years because they couldn't cook food for them, the Japs wouldn't let them light fires. So when we went back after the war we noticed a big gap, there were no children from about eight years down, except a few new babies. I sat and talked with lots of these women. One woman told me how she had four children and she just had to sit and watch them die one after the other . . . Saimon Gaius buried his two little boys. Then when John was born about a year later, that's their eldest that's alive now, they called him John To Warmari, because he was a love gift after losing the other two.

The Catholic Missions suffered as much as the Methodist:

The mission as I found it bore still all the marks of a cruel war. We had lost 54 sisters in a tragic way—37 in the strafing of a Japanese warship by Allied 'planes and later in Japanese captivity in Hollandia through hunger and disease. A group of 17 died on a Japanese warship, being shot and thrown into the sea. The mission lost in this way its two Bishops, many priests and Brothers. Other denominations and civilians lost members too but less because smaller in number.

All housing was of the most primitive construction for everyone. Food was a problem since we had as yet no livestock of our own. In some ways we lived directly from the bush—bread being a notable exception. Next to nothing could be bought in Madang at first but all gradually changed—though it took many years. Housing, food supplies sent in from the Highlands, getting our own livestock. I used to get during the very lean years 50 cases from the Provincial Motherhouse in Techny USA and valuable medical supplies from the Catholic Medical Mission Board in New York. However the Australian government soon began to provide good adequate medical supplies to all hospitals making them less dependent on overseas help. [Sister Aquilonia Ax]

Sister Aquilonia Ax corrected me when I asked her why she 'chose' to go to Papua New Guinea in 1947. A Sister does not choose her destiny, but rather has an obligation to obey the church's decrees, even when aged 50 and not in good health. Sister Aquilonia was born in a small German village, and worked with the International Congregation of the Missionary Sisters of the Holy Spirit in Holland and the United States, where she obtained postgraduate qualifications. In 1948 she was appointed Provincial Superior of the New Guinea mission with its headquarters in Alexishaven. She was responsible for the sisters and their work from Lae to Aitape, from coastal to highland stations.

It was often the tropical tales told in church or mission literature that drew women overseas. Sister Bohdana Voros felt the lure of alien worlds and mission work even as a child: 'I felt drawn to the tropics where the conditions were primitive and the spiritual need of the natives great.'

Sister Bohdana Voros was born in Czechoslovakia in 1911. She went to New Guinea with the Sisters of the Holy Spirit in 1947, teaching for five years in Alexishafen, then in nearby Madang for three years, at Manam Island for six years, and the Sepik for seven years. In 1968 she became the head teacher at Alexishafen and trained the local sisters of St Therese, retiring in 1977 due to ill health.

Many of the women who went as Sisters to Papua New Guinea responded to a calling. Both Joyce Walker and Dorothy Pederick, who joined the Methodist Mission, had been entranced by missionary work from Sunday School days. But only women with the appropriate training were welcome after the war. Joyce Walker supplemented her triple-certificate nursing qualifications with additional courses in tropical medicine and anthropology; Dorothy Pederick moved from Perth to Melbourne to do the midwifery course the mission required. Both Joyce Walker and Dorothy Pederick grew up on farms, and believe this made them practical and adaptable to the mission's spartan lifestyle.

All the nurses slept in tents when they first arrived, while houses and hospitals were being built. They used packing cases for furniture and:

We bought jeeps; you could buy a jeep for twenty-five pounds in those days and it was beaut to run around in. There were a lot of army comfort funds, Red Cross supplies, in dugouts on mission sites. So we got all the army medical gear together we could and we loaded our jeeps up and we got through some supplies from the Director of Health, Dr Gunther. They let us have arsenical compound which was an ampoule injection, six injections once a week given intravenously over six weeks would cure yaws which was rampant in those days. The Japs had neglected all medical procedures and nobody in the Territory, indigenous people, had had any medical help. So they were just a mass of yaws and ulcers and malaria and all sorts of diseases.

We'd load up our jeep and we'd go out and sit in a village, get a room from one of the native people. We'd put our mats down and live with them for a few weeks until our jeep load of supplies ran out. It would be six weeks because we'd have to give them an injection a week intravenously for yaws. By the time all our treatment was done and our jeep needed replenishing we'd go back to our tent and load up again and out we'd go again. We did that for many months until there was trafficking in the Pacific. After about a year, we were able to get more supplies, and no longer had to live on native foods, pork and beans and dehydrated foods left behind in underground stores by the army. [Joyce Walker]

Evacuated during the war, Prudence Frank returned soon after:

I received a letter from Canberra in 1945 asking me if I would like to return to the Territory. I accepted and arrived in Port Moresby early November. I was the fifth white woman to return. We lived in a hostel and went by jeep to the mess for meals. Our food mainly consisted of bully beef and silver fish (herrings). I was placed with Mr Melrose, Government Secretary, later being transferred to Government House to work for Colonel J.K. Murray. He was a gentleman of military stature with a sincere desire to better the life of native people.

Single women made their own decisions, perhaps guided by God, prompted by friends, or pushed by failed love affairs. Married women almost always went to the Territory because husbands chose to go. Pat Andersen reflects on the absence, not only of choice, but even of the idea that she might have a say, when her husband decided to go to Papua:

In 1948 my husband Neville said he wanted to go to Papua with the London Missionary Society. They were looking for a doctor who could start a hospital out in the Delta country west of Port Moresby . . . We'd not been married very long. I was mixed in my feelings towards going—I think I went at least partly because I was married to my husband. That's what wives did in those days. I don't think I'd made him aware of that. I think I just went, but it was certainly exciting. It was new country, it was frontier country, it was quite a different sort of experience from life here.

Pat Andersen completed a social work degree in the early 1940s, but had to give up her work while at Kikori in the Delta country. She gave birth to two children in Papua before the family returned to Australia in 1953.

The romance of the tropics

Pat Murray thinks to herself when she first sees Papuans on the wharf at Samarai: 'Yes, that is what it would be like'. Dea Birkett's 'Victorian Lady Explorers' also experienced a sense of *déjà vu* on arrival: impressions of 'complete familiarity' 'I knew the place so well' 'yet more fantastic and delicious than our baby minds could ever have imagined'.[14] In 1988 the visitors to a museum in Norwich could see a replica of a Victorian drawing room which displayed an empire brought back home, domesticated but still alluringly mysterious. Under glass covers were groups of colourful stuffed birds; another case captured and held still the beauty of butterflies and the strangeness of insects; the walls were adorned with spears and other weapons. The shelves were full of travellers' tales. Preparation for the tropical experience was in these ways made possible from the 'plethora of visual and written images of exotic places and peoples'.[15] Whether nurtured on mission literature or tropical romances, whether lured by travelogues or scientific treatises, expatriate women carried a rich ideological baggage to their new life. The romance of the tropics was a blend of adventure, beauty, and danger: all of which signalled difference.

But there would be more than one difference. If somewhat prepared for the difference between life in Australia and life in Papua New Guinea, these women were rarely prepared for the difference between their imaginings and the mundane actualities. Evelyn Cheeseman tells the story of one such woman, the lonely malaria-weakened Mrs Field, wife of a small plantation owner. Although a university career had been planned for her, the 'lure of the South Seas changed her destiny, fostered by books, magazines and films . . . it was the same story that I heard from most of the settlers' wives'. Mrs Field's reality was to be different. She intensely disliked the 'view inland of the mountains covered with their splendid forest' and the 'whispering' of the palm fronds.[16] One of Papua New Guinea's most assiduous propagandists, Beatrice Grimshaw, by contrast with Mrs Field, domesticates the exotic beauty of the Highlands in her description of a coffee planter's house:

There were no pictures on the wall, but you could always have one—much better than anything Corot or Turner could have done for you—by simply swinging wide one of the oblong bamboo-plait shutters and instantly painting on the wall a matchless landscape study.[17]

On this, and other plantations, even the economic products of New Guinea are beautiful, thus ensuring a happy coincidence of 'district after district emerg[ing] from savagery to civilisation *and beauty*'.[18]

Dixie Rigby, the wife of a patrol officer, comments:

> When I first arrived in Wewak I have never seen anything that could be so likened to the dawn of time as Wewak was, the beauty, the quality. We had the hills, the mountains, the woods, the forests and you had the sea. I've never forgotten those beautiful sunrises and sunsets we had. And to wake up at first light and see the dawn coming up. I never felt so near to paradise. The quality of the beauty there, the serene peace and quiet of it all, it was marvellous.

Daisy Symonds speaks of her walks with Mary McLean in the cool of the evening in India, enjoying the 'fields of waving green paddy' and the 'most gorgeous sunsets'.[19] Past a flame tree, Ann Deland could see the mountains:

> Those mountains—almost always they were violet in the distance, but at sunrise and sundown there was a curious clarity of light which showed an amazing amount of detail, usually lost in the violet shadows. That strange morning and evening light has never ceased to fascinate me.[20]

Doris Groves describes the road from Malakuna to Rabaul before the arrival of the motor car as 'brilliantly lit by myriads of fireflies—pulsating in and out in the breeze'.[21] Pat Andersen refutes the common claim that the Delta country was monotonous:

> The Wami River that we were on was quite a big river . . . at night just before dark the whole place would be lit up with a special glow which you don't get anywhere else. It was luminous and it was lovely. If you were in a canoe at night, it was beautifully peaceful, and you'd get phosphorous along the bottom of the canoe,

phosphorous on the paddles. On the river banks, huge banks of trees with fireflies in them would all wink on and off. It was fabulous.

Many more people gained their images of the tropics and its peoples from novels and travelogues than from the texts of Social Darwinism, to be discussed in Chapters 5 and 7. In the 1890s, Rudyard Kipling, Joseph Conrad and Henry Lawson 'reached maturity and found their respective literary voices'.[22] If Kipling brought India home to the mother country, Conrad became the 'Kipling of the Malay Archipelago'; 'He has annexed the Malay Peninsula for us'. Likewise Henry Lawson was to be described as 'the Australian Kipling'.[23] Sunderland argues that these were not the voices of self-satisfied imperial rule, which had been irretrievably lost following the Indian Mutiny of 1857, the Maori Wars of the 1860s, the Taiping Rebellion and the Jamaica Uprising of 1865. These writers represented a 'fantastic invasion' from the wilderness at the Empire's rim, questioning the moral certainties of imperial rule.[24]

Beatrice Grimshaw, a prodigious writer, has been described as the Kipling of Papua, 'a dusty, lower middle class, Australian version of the British Raj'.[25] Susan Gardner locates Grimshaw in a tradition which includes Rudyard Kipling, R.M. Ballantyne and Robert Louis Stevenson (who lived with his wife Fanny Stevenson, also a writer, in Samoa in the 1890s), as well as female writers such as Isak Dinesen, Doris Lessing and Nadine Gordimer.[26] Grimshaw's *When the Red Gods Call* was published by Mills and Boon, and the title comes from a Kipling poem. It was both a popular women's romance set in an exotic land and a vehicle for disseminating the values of imperialism. Grimshaw's novels told readers how to understand the intersection of race and sexual relations; she confirmed the superiority of the white gentleman. Black men peopled these stories as either wild savages or faithful, childlike servants; black women performed only a sexual role.

As educational vehicles in days when boys and girls received very different sexual trainings, tropical fictions fell into two distinct genres. Boys grew up on adventure stories, but girls and women were moulded by love stories. Thus Ann B. Murphy compares *Huckleberry Finn* and *Little Women* as the two great stories of American self-discovery. Huck's journey is an escape from the constraints of civilisation and dependency on women. His first escape is down river, but his final escape is 'lighting out for the "Territory" ', the frontier.[27] Jo March, by contrast, is immured in connectedness and dependency on her mother. The resolution of her journey requires that she stay in a domestic space, although her professor husband allows her the separate identity of a writer. The end of women's adventures is marriage, at home as well as in the colonies.

Rider Haggard, a popular turn of the century colonial adventure fiction writer, wrote for 'all the big and little boys'.[28] For Haggard, as for Mark Twain, escape from cultural/feminine constraints and initiation into manhood occurs through the male camaraderie of a shared physically dangerous adventure. Haggard assures his readers in the first chapter of *King Solomon's Mines*, 'I can safely say there is not a single petticoat in the whole history'.[29] Black women play a minor role, and usually lay down their lives to protect the purity of the white hero who falls in love with them.

C. Fenn's *Bunyip Land*, an Australian boys' adventure story set in New Guinea, describes the passage to manhood of Joe the protagonist, joined by three companions, Jack, a working-class lad, Jimmy, 'a native gentleman', and a doctor friend of the family.[30] They overcome or escape the threats of blackbirders, crocodiles, foaming seas, and headhunting savages to free Joe's plant-collecting father and return him to civilisation.

Tested by a fight with a crocodile, Jack worries that he will never have a beard and muscles, never be a man. Joe cheers him with the news that the doctor said 'he is sure he should never have borne it so bravely as you'.[31] Later Jack asserts that the myth that grown men are never afraid and that knights slayed several enemies a day was just 'gammon', lies.[32] Jack grows to six foot in adulthood, no longer worried about his puny physique. Joe's adventures convince him: 'Yesterday I was a boy, now I am a man'. On the return voyage, the captain says to Joe, 'Well, you have growed'.[33]

Joe at one point remembers wistfully the 'peaceful life at home' and the 'gentle face that bent over to kiss me when I was half asleep'.[34] This reminds the reader that the women, absent from the tale of adventure, are in their proper place, keeping the home fires burning. The story moves on, beyond its 'natural' conclusion at the end of the adventure. Joe goes to England for his education and returns to find Jimmy 'just as he was when I left home, faithful and boyish and winning'.[35] Thus, although Jimmy is a 'native gentleman' and the boys free South Sea Islanders captured illegally for the Queensland labour trade, blacks stay in their rightful place: they never outgrow their childlike ways. Similarly, while Jack achieves a working-class manhood in muscular strength, Joe achieves a middle-class manhood in education.

Errol Flynn, in his biography *My Wicked Wicked Ways*, is less coy about his relations with women; but then he is not writing for boys, big or small. He describes the swashbuckling adventures of a white male who conquers, albeit in different ways, the raw materials, local men and women of Papua New Guinea. During the course of his adventures, Flynn has sexual relations with three indigenous women, described principally in terms of their physical attributes. Maura had 'a waist you could span with your two hands. Naturally my ambition was to spend as much time spanning it as I could'. Flynn later discovers 'physically a female is a female the world over'.[36]

In the tropical romances written by and for women, the white women did not stay home; they went searching for their own adventure—a marriage based on love which also, but incidentally, brought economic security (nothing much had changed since Jane Austen). In the 1890s Beatrice Grimshaw (1870–1953) escaped both marriage and 'a career': low-paid jobs eked out in a 'dessicated' spinsterhood.[37] She convinced a shipping company to pay for her passage from Britain if she 'could assure them of certain newspaper commissions'.[38] She lived in Papua between 1907 and 1934, in 1908 being commissioned by the Australian Prime Minister Alfred Deakin to publicise Papua as a suitable destination for settlers with capital. She became a close friend of the Lieutenant-Governor, Hubert Murray, a grass widower, whose wife suffered ill-health in the tropics, taking the children to visit him only during school holidays.[39] Murray and Grimshaw were both Catholics, 'possessed a keen sense of humour, physical stamina, and vivid ability to paint thumbnail sketches of the eccentricities who dotted Papua'.[40] Murray's friendship helped sustain Grimshaw's ambiguous status as a single self-supporting female.

Although the tropics called, their song was heard predominantly by wastrels and those duty bound like Indian Civil servants, who must not like it too much:

As for the Pacific Islands, they were, and still are to most people a section of the world inhabited by beachcombers, blackbirders, bad lots, missionaries who are equally sanctimonious and depraved, and native beauties invariably and delightfully immoral.[41]

Grimshaw sought to correct this impression in her writings. In her semi-autobiographical *Isles of Adventure*, and her propaganda piece *The New New Guinea*, Grimshaw outlines the values that define the careers of her fictional characters. 'Her literary universe is peopled with distinct character types, whose moral qualities can be keyed with precision to whether they have "white blood" in their veins, and how much'.[42] For example:

For the well-bred man who because of his breeding will turn a hand to anything, and because of his racial pride will never say die, for the man of youth and strength and common sense, and the woman who will "do without" and see him through—Papua is the country.[43]

Good breeding ensured that the 'sheer pleasure in handling elemental things' would not result in degradation through manual labour.[44] Rather, the 'pleasure of breaking in a new country' is contrasted with the effeminacy of the delicate, the over-sophisticated and the idle who stay at home in London.[45] In Grimshaw's novels, true class origins were often initially disguised, their revelation being a mechanism which drives the narrative. Cohabiting with 'coloured women' was a betrayal of race; on the whole men preferred to marry. Grimshaw heaps scorn upon the wife who excuses herself from her husband's side because of health or the needs of her children.[46]

Although Grimshaw herself did not marry, her heroines always do, but for love. This higher commitment brings in its wake the discovery of the man's 'true' gentlemanly background. Thus race will out, and a true heroine recognises breeding even if disguised by social circumstances. Grimshaw could hardly be described as a feminist, even though it is clear from her writings that feminist ideas had considerable currency when she wrote. She asserted, 'We are not as clever as men—let the equality brigade shriek if they like . . . but neither are we as stupid—God forbid!'.[47] Welch, one of her characters, notes that a man who studies inferior animals can understand women, although 'it's as well the suffragists can't hear me; I should be treated as a crowd of secretary birds would treat a cobra'.[48]

She believed that fears of miscegenation were largely overplayed, although women who were careless and did not keep a revolver:

are answerable for a good deal. In very rare cases, there may have been direct encouragement. But it may be said on the whole that the white woman in the Western Pacific is about as likely to be attracted by a native man as to commit murder.[49]

Natives were grateful for employment and so did not attack white men.[50] The native also is 'extremely susceptible to the claims of etiquette, good manners, conventions of all sorts'.[51] They were thus educable; for example, a group of native women would no doubt succumb to 'feminine vanity' when they discovered the magic of a mirror she gave them.[52] Grimshaw endorsed the popular perspectives of social Darwinism, describing a hierarchy of the races. The Polynesians were superior to the Melanesians who were wicked, murderous, culturally rude, capricious, and 'nearer to monkeys than to human beings in aspect'.[53] One maintained white superiority before blacks, by not showing fear or being humiliated. Otherwise they were simply not there, did 'not count as human beings' or 'count as nothing' when lovers seek to be alone.[54] Black women appear occasionally as beasts of burden, or stereotypes—'Mrs Frizzyhead' 'Mrs Flatface', 'Mrs Blackleg'—but far more often as the tempting seductress, who threatens to destroy a good man.[55]

In *When the Red Gods Call*, the hero Hugh Lynd has forsaken his gentlemanly background by becoming an adventurer 'of no class, no country, no home, and no future' and by marrying a mission-educated girl, Kari.[56] 'When a white man marries a native girl, he commits the unforgiveable sin—folly'.[57] Furthermore, he does not contemplate the horrors of miscegenation until Kari miscarries:

[The] thought of a little half-caste boy or girl—a child with woolly hair and flat nose, that would nevertheless bear my own likeness—worse might look like my dear dead mother, or my father—was almost revolting to me.[58]

Lynd is spared this fate when a skipper, Sanderson, abducts Kari while Lynd is away in town. Lynd pursues Sanderson and kills him, while Kari puts out to sea and is drowned. Lynd returns to town where he has already met Stephanie, the Governor's daughter. It is expected that she will marry Carolen, who later becomes the Chief Magistrate. Certainly she is in a class above the 'proletariat', men like Lynd who are allowed onto the Governor's verandah to share an evening drink, but not into the dining room to share the evening meal. Stephanie's maidservant and Guria, Hugh's servant, fall in love and marry. They provide both the black parallel love story to the central white romance, and the mechanism whereby Lynd arranges a pre-dawn tryst with Stephanie. She floats down to meet him in a cloud of muslin, coyly says 'no' when she means 'yes', and finally makes her 'yes' plain. The Governor yields to Stephanie's pleas, promises to make Lynd Resident Magistrate at Samarai and the marriage is arranged. Meanwhile Carolen discovers that Lynd is a murderer and the widower of a black woman and arrests him. Stephanie flees to England, where she admits to a preacher that Hugh's marriage to a native girl was the chief cause of her desertion. Chastened, she returns to Papua and searches for Lynd, who has disappeared into the Gulf country. They are reunited, settle on a plantation and raise a family.

This story parallels that of A.C.G. Hastings' *Gone Native*, set in Africa and published in 1928. The beautiful and gracious Monica, unmarried sister of the magistrate, falls in love with a taciturn hero who is a 'gentleman by birth'. Monica nurses him through a delirium caused by spear wounds and is rewarded by his declaration of love.[59]

Hugh is luckier than the hero of *Queen Vaiti*, published in 1920, who must die because of his love for a Polynesian.[60] The most 'native' of Grimshaw's white heroes, Simon, who was raised by Papuans until he was 16, still respects his race and would not give the care of his children to a woman with 'one dark drop in her veins'. The 'dark drop' also talked in the character of girls who were 'not especially interested in boys'.[61] On the whole, only lower caste men married black women. Men who 'went native' died, leaving heroines free to marry their true loves; women who married bigamously (even if unintentionally) might also pay the price, for example death in childbirth.[62]

Heroes were also shiveringly strong. The 'bravest man in Papua', when asked what he had done with the cannibals who ate some of his mining mates, did not answer, but his eyes:

suddenly narrowed and turned hard as flint. Out of them looked, in that instant, the tameless spirit of the wilderness; the lightning flash of stark masculinity that dazzles a woman's soul and makes it cower away.[63]

In Grimshaw's *My Lady Far-Away*, twice married gold-digger Martha Lyle, a bird of paradise ('beautiful, hard—greedy') becomes engaged to Royden, and they set out in search of Royden's uncle whose (disputed) existence stands between Royden and a baronetcy.[64] In the wilds of Papua, Martha plays with the 'fierce passions of the savages about her'. Royden shows a moment's empathy with these black men: 'loving her more than ever, he had never liked her less'.[65] A graceful and (apparently) native youth, Antares, asks the travellers to heal his sick father, who is the missing uncle. Martha 'guessed it pretty soon', is captured, and the natives are only appeased if the uncle marries Martha. Following the wedding, the uncle dies suddenly. Martha is now Lady Wilsden and Royden is Lord Wilsden. As a man may not marry his father's brother's wife, the two cannot be wed.

It is now discovered that Antares is really Stella, the daughter of the dead uncle. Stella's naive innocence, fidelity and lack of vanity is praised: 'who never tricked, or lied, or posed, who knew no fear, save fear of bloodshed, who was beautiful—and didn't know it—passionate and pure'.[66] This is contrasted unfavourably with Martha, and other products of civilisation, 'holding promises lightly, whenever they conflicted with desire'.[67] Although Stella would seem to share an affinity with Welch, the snake-collector who guided the two title seekers into the interior, it is Royden who wins her love. She, like Welch, can handle snakes with confidence; Martha cannot. Martha frightens a snake and is sent below to lie down, musing it is men's 'remedy for everything, from a bill to a baby'.[68] It is civilised women, and not naive maidens, who have a shrewd estimate of sexual exchange rates.

The opposition between good and evil is not only drawn along the lines of blood, but also along a fissure between nature and decadent civilisation. Thus Royden must cross over from the fortune-seeker to be true to his title; but he must also question his English precepts. His landowning instincts are opposed to the Eden-like wildness of his uncle's retreat: 'Nevertheless it appealed to something that lay below those instincts . . . primitive, fierce, not to be resisted'.[69] Martha never makes this transition, and uses her title to remarry and live in what little contentment such a scheming woman can achieve.

Welch must be content with *My Lady Far-Away*, Papua herself with her magic and charm. According to Rebecca Scott, although Rider Haggard's stories are bereft of white women, the land itself substitutes for the female form—luring, trapping, and dazzling the explorers.[70] Africa is a wild and fickle woman, but she yields her treasure to those with the manhood to overcome her resistance. Sexual fantasies and fears are displaced rather than excluded. Grimshaw more often saw Papua as defeating those who would conquer her: 'a woman, dark and savage, with cruel beautiful eyes and bloodstained mouth'.[71] Doris Booth, a miner at Bulolo for several years, also evokes both the beauty—'orchids shyly raise their beautiful heads' — and terror of the tropics—a 'grinning skull' a 'blood-red creeper'.[72] The beauty, however, is paramount: 'in my heart is peace'. The otherness of the tropics was sometimes a 'terrible beauty' providing both fear and fascination. The women in the present study knew the fickleness of this beauty; they lived through volcanoes, earthquakes, snake bites from death adders, potential blindness from the poison of millipedes, and crawling between logs thrown across flooded rivers.

Daphney Bridgland, a planter's wife, records the eruption of Popendetta, which covered her garden on the other side of the Owen-Stanley Ranges with pumice and darkened the sky. She also found herself at the centre of an earthquake in Rabarua:

> When you're in force six or force five and the epicentre is right there, it is the most terrifying experience. The one we had at Rabarua scared the wits out of me. Our floor was solid concrete, very thick concrete and heavily reinforced with steel rods through it . . . the noise was absolutely terrifying, the noise was all around us. I was in bed, I'd just come home from Rabaul . . . It was just so terrifying. My husband threw himself across me to hold us on the beds. The beds, everything, was being tossed right up in the air. I heard someone screaming, I didn't realise it was me. Then my husband went away to rescue some of his precious recording equipment. When he came back, he wanted to go back a second time and get something else, I grabbed him, I wouldn't let him go. In the morning through that thick concrete base that our house was built on, there was a big star of cracks right at the foot of my bed.

Isabel Platten's description of the eruption of Vulcan in 1937, which claimed many lives, is tinged with awe for the extraordinary power of nature:

> Our return to New Guinea was remarkably spectacular. As we slowly steamed into Rabaul Harbour we passed Vulcan Island and Gil told

the story of its appearance about 60 years earlier, which is recorded in Rev. Brown's autobiography. Gil also 'gilded the lily' a little by explaining to the tourists how likely it was that one day Vulcan would explode again; some of them looked very sceptical . . .

[The next day] Friday 29th was a busy day, unpacking and settling in. Every so often I thought I sensed earth tremors, but dismissed the thought. Next day, May 30th, was a special day because the headmaster of the College was to be married in Rabaul. The bride-to-be had travelled from Sydney with us and had asked Gil if he would 'give her away'. On our way to Rabaul we called at Kabakada to pick up the bride and her matron-of-honour. Along the verandah a table had been laid for the wedding feast. As I waited I noticed how strange were the tremors. They were now constant and the verandah undulated. It was uncanny.

Then to Rabaul, and the wedding was conducted by Rev. Frank Lewis, the Chairman of the district. During the service we heard loud explosive noises. Some thought it was thunder! Ceremony over and we moved outside and I said 'Look at that strange cloud'. Then someone said 'That is not a cloud, it is an eruption'. Everyone stood still as the implications of this sank in. Then we all got into the cars and went down to the waterfront to get a good look. And I am glad we did, the risk was well worth the experience of seeing so spectacularly awesome an event of our planet. But as we gazed with uneasy eyes at a mountain of pumice ash pouring out of the sea we looked up and noticed the top part was already beginning to fall towards us. It was time to leave. I was put into one of the cars by Gil but he remained with the Chairman who insisted on returning to Malakuna, which was right in the path of the densest oncoming cloud.

Our party got as far as Kabakada. The festive table, now covered in pumice dust, made a sad note. Soon it was pitch dark, the massive clouds of pumice had blotted out the sun. We got back into the cars, deciding to try to get to Vunairima, but we were not far along the road when we found it was impassable. Fronds from coconut trees and branches from other trees covered it completely. By now the friction of all this matter in the atmosphere was causing a terrific lightning storm over the volcano and spreading away from it. 'Fireballs' danced among the coconut trees. The pumice was now wet, and had the consistency of wet cement. My main fear was that we would have an accident, such as broken bones, and no-one could come to our aid.

But people did come to aid us over the debris. Quite suddenly I felt a hand on my arm and was being guided firmly, but gently, over the littered road. Nearby village natives, hearing us struggling along the road, had come to help us. That gentle hand gave me the sense of security I needed. We passed out from fallen trees on to clear road and were soon at Vunairima. We went to the house where the sisters lived, and into their well-lit lounge-room and we all burst out laughing. We could not see ourselves, we didn't need to; we looked as though we were cast in cement and only two red eyes peered through all the greyness.

Next day we were shocked at the devastation that confronted us. Gone were the lawns and flowers, and trees were leafless. What we saw was a stark land seemingly cast in cement. Everything we touched was gritty; every breeze that blew scattered the gritty mess everywhere. It was horrible. We did not know what had happened to the group Gil was with so it was with relief and joy when he arrived at Vunairima during the morning and we knew all were safe. With sadness we heard many hundreds of natives had died; many had gone into a church—all were buried. Photos taken later show only the roof of the church above ground level.

It wasn't long before the rains washed away the worst of the grime and soon the lawns grew again; leaves were on our trees and flowers blossomed more beautifully than ever.

But there were aspects of living in the tropics which would never find their way into fiction, aspects like boredom and depression:

I do remember at times when it had been a wet day and you'd get a dripping sort of afternoon and you'd look out over the forest and the grey skies and so on, and there were some birds in the forest which used to have the most mournful sort of calls. It really wasn't a good antidote for homesickness at all. [Mary Pulsford, wife of an agricultural extension officer at Urip village]

Battles with cockroaches, rats, moulds and insects are not of the same order as battles with crocodiles, wild pigs and cannibals: 'One of the things that you begin to think when you live on an outstation, is that human beings are by no means the pinnacle of evolution or the most efficient living thing on planet earth'. [Mary Pulsford] Patricia Grimshaw lived in Papua and travelled its interior, in conditions at least as rough as those confronting women after 1920. But the stuff of romance is not pumice-covered women, defeat by hordes of insects, or seemingly endless rain.

The romance of the tropics is about the dangerous allure of the alien, where rules are not always known, and where both the inhabitants and the astounding scenery serve as mechanisms for a plot that reinforces white domination and sexual temptation. Expatriate women sometimes alluded to this register, their breath taken away by astonishing scenery or frightening experiences, or their privileged position as witnesses of unique times. Dixie Rigby describes Wewak as the 'dawn of time'; Annie Deland will always remember 'that strange morning and evening light'.

But these women do not cast themselves as beautiful heroines in amazing tales. Even in moments of life-threatening danger, a streak of humour runs through their stories. At Higituru following the war, Marjorie Murphy sat up in bed one night:

> I sat up, couldn't get my breath. There'd been a millipede on the pillow and I'd turned over and it had squirted in my eye . . . John grabbed me and spat in my eye! The Medical Assistant said that was the best thing he could have done. Luckily I had some eye lotion, but I looked as though I had a moustache because all the ammonia [squirted by the millipede] came down my nose and burned over my lip.

The night that Mary Pulsford arrived in Urip village in 1953 she trod on a death adder. She was rushed back to her house on a stretcher and eventually to Wewak hospital, again on a stretcher:

> I felt terribly embarrassed and frustrated. I thought 'How extra-ordinary, I walked up here yesterday. Here I am lying flat on my back watching the leaves go past in the trees, and all the village people who are carrying me or accompanying us running alongside, chattering away. What a way to start.' I rather felt as if I had let my husband down by treading on a snake.

Susan Blake suggests that such ironic self-portraits occur when writers can see themselves from another's perspective, when they wonder how 'they look to colonials . . . and readers back home'.[73] She claims that such ironies and self-reflections are uncharacteristic of travellers' tales told by men, who instead focus on 'big game romances' and other tales of conquering the land and its people.[74] Even more out of character with the tropical romance, these women experienced the mundane and irritating, and told domestic tales of everyday events. The shape of their days was determined not so much by the date as by their destination: whether outstation or town, and whether mission, government or private enterprise. The next three chapters focus on the lives of expatriate women in the Territory. Chapter 2 introduces the three major white communities of the Territory; Chapter 3 explores the differences between the roles of mother and worker in the Territory; and Chapter 4 discusses the differences between living 'in town' mainly Rabaul or Port Moresby, and living 'down the road', on an outstation, for instance.

2

Different Destinations

The German Government annexed New Guinea in 1884; it was administered by the German New Guinea Company and largely for the benefit of plantation owners. Papua was 'annexed' in 1883 by the Queensland colonial government, a nervous response to German activity so close to its borders. It was only in 1884 that the British government formally and reluctantly 'protected' Papua under the name of British New Guinea. In 1906 British New Guinea, renamed Papua, came under Australian administration, with the proclamation of the Papua Act. Pre-war Australian administration of Papua was dominated by J.H.P. (later Sir Hubert) Murray, who became Acting Administrator in 1907, and was Lieutenant Governor until his death in 1940. Murray has been described as 'ahead of his time at the beginning, quaintly old-fashioned at the end . . . always hampered by lack of funds and the Australian government's monumental indifference to Papuan affairs'.[1] Beatrice Grimshaw in 1910 describes the resources of Murray's neophyte administration as 'almost laughably inadequate—two resident Magistrates, thirty-four armed native constables, a couple of whaleboats, and two small ketches'.[2]

In September 1914 the Australian Naval and Military Expeditionary Force accepted the surrender of German forces on New Britain. The military administration was replaced by a civil administration under Brigadier-General Evan Wisdom in 1921. After the Second World War the administration of Papua and New Guinea was combined, with headquarters in Port Moresby.

Plantations were concentrated in New Guinea where adaptation of the local people to white ways was more extensive. The lingua franca of New Guinea became pidgin and of Papua Police Motu, the trade language of the people living around Port Moresby (and therefore of little use in communication with other peoples). The white colonists clung to the coasts and were concentrated in the towns and surrounding areas which had been expropriated for plantations. They were vastly outnumbered by the indigenous population. In 1921 there were approximately 1300 Europeans in Papua, in 1938 there were 3500 Europeans in New Guinea. The last pre-war figures enumerate 1500 white Europeans in Papua, 4500 in New Guinea and an indigenous population of between 2.5 and 3 million.[3]

Colonial societies are most obviously divided along the cleavage of race. Race is a shorthand term for the gulf between the ruler and the ruled, western 'civilisation' and local 'barbarism', the comparatively wealthy and the poor, the apparently educated and the 'ignorant'. The effects of this chasm, operating more or less consistently at the economic, political and cultural levels, mediate all other relations in a colonial society. Thus even within the white community the three major groups were differentiated by their attitudes to and treatment of the Papua New Guineans, their 'reason for being there'.[4]

In Papua New Guinea, as in most colonies, there were three significant groups. The business sector consisted largely of plantation owners, managers of plantations owned by the large shipping companies, traders, miners, and hotel owners. The mission sector consisted of preachers, teachers, medical personnel and support staff; some were ordained and some were lay workers. The government sector included a wide range of occupations from Administrator (New Guinea) or Lieutenant-Governor (Papua) and District Officer (New Guinea) or Resident Magistrate (Papua), to patrol officer (*kiap*), agricultural extension officer, medical staff, as well as clerical and trades positions. Because of these different reasons for being there, the lives of expatriate women were influenced by the white community they joined. This chapter introduces those three different communities, both as they are represented in official histories and as the white women experienced them.

Government

The Germans developed the '*luluai* system' to extend control over a large area with very few administrative personnel. This was adopted by the Australians when they took over New Guinea after the First World War; the system was also used in Papua. In India princes were obvious rulers, even to the British; in the Territory the Australians were not always successful in identifying or winning over the village leader, particularly if they chose the *luluai* after a hasty visit to the village. Many villages too were not ruled by a single 'big man' but by a group of elders.[5]

The *luluai* was given a peaked hat and a silver-headed stick and the right to retain 10 per cent of the head taxes collected in the village. In return he was to arbitrate in minor disputes, supervise road building, sanitary care and the collection of the annual head tax, and furnish men for the government labour recruiters. By the 1950s the *luluai* was fitted out with a hat, a lap-lap, a belt and knife, but his duties remained essentially the same: he was responsible to the patrol officer for trouble in the village. In the Highlands he was sometimes taken on patrol to other areas, thus increasing his prestige through association with white officers and some knowledge of their ways.[6] He was assisted by a *tultul* who acted as an interpreter. The *tultul*'s mediating role between the two languages meant he often became a force of change in the village, and a spokesman for those who had some contact with the white world, for example as labourers on plantations. A *doktaboi* in charge of health care, was also appointed.[7] From 1959 Local Government Councils were gradually established to replace *luluais*, and Aid Post Orderlies replaced medical *tultuls*.[8] These changes sometimes caused divisions in village communities. Young radical men used the word *kiap* to stand for alien and authoritarian rule, but the older men recalled a just firm government.[9] The deposed *luluai*'s loss of status following the appointment of village councils was particularly poignant:

A blanket was placed on the ground. Then forty or fifty elderly men, who had given many years of devoted service, wearing their sign of office, their 'hats' slowly filed past, and each in turn threw his hat onto the blanket.[10]

Sometimes there were hostile outbursts:

What sort of fashion is this? We village constables have toiled away for years for the government, and now we are being thrown away like rubbish, and all we get are these silly pieces of paper which we can't read anyway.[11]

The base camp system was a response both to limited budgets and to the mountainous topography. The District Officer divided his district into various categories, and access by whites to the so-called 'uncontrolled areas' was limited. These areas were gradually brought under control through the base camp system. Patrols worked from a base camp established near the geographical centre of the region.[12] Thus Joyce Walker, when a mission sister in Mendi, required an escort to move beyond a mile's radius from the base camp. Doctor Joan Refshauge too, although unwillingly, was required to enter the villages under police escort. Marjorie Murphy, against official policy, went with her husband on patrol into uncontrolled areas.

Once an area was deemed 'controlled' a magistrate was appointed and he was the:

sole personification of the government: policeman, explorer, road-builder, health inspector, social worker and prison warder; even in court where he deals with most of the 'lesser offences' against the law, and civil disputes between Papuans, he acts as prosecutor, defence counsel, judge and jury.[13]

Well into the 1960s the Magistrate had no special training and he was invariably white. Beneath the magistrate were the village constables and the native police.

Until 1951 the Papuan Administration was undertaken by the Lieutenant-Governor with the assistance of the Legislative Council, an appointed body of white men. The Lieutenant-Governor and the Legislative Council met as the Executive Council and forwarded its recommendations to the Australian government for ratification. In New Guinea the Administrator forwarded Ordinances passed by the Legislative Council to the Governor-General of Australia, either recommending or withholding his assent or reserving the Ordinance for the Governor-General's pleasure.[14] Generally speaking Ordinances and day-to-day administration were accepted by the Australian Government but there were both heated and muted battles over specific issues, for instance the execution of a Papuan convicted under the White Women's Protection Ordinance. In 1951 the Legislative Council became the Legislative Assembly, with three Papua New Guinean appointees. In the succeeding years a handful of women sat in the Assembly. In 1960 half the Legislative Assembly was made up of Papua New Guineans. In the main, throughout most of the period examined in this book, administration was a non-democratic all-white affair. Although the lowest ranks of village representatives were indigenous, they were appointed by white men and had little real power. The changes which commenced in 1951, with the appointment of Papua New Guineans to the Legislative Assembly, reflected that new attitudes to race relations slowly gained ascendancy. The seeds were sown in the Second World War but their fruition required both new administrative policies and more widespread education for the indigenous people. This is the subject of Chapters 5, 6 and 7.

Dixie Rigby, whose husband was a patrol officer between 1925 and the outbreak of war, describes the life:

> you were supposed to be on duty 24 hours of the day, 365 days of the year and for that you got three months' paid holiday on full pay which we thought was marvellous. But the whole point was that you were always on duty but you couldn't expect more money to be on duty. Money never entered into our heads. We were doing something we wanted to do; we felt it was valuable, and I still think it was very valuable.
>
> You had a certain number of duties to perform on patrol. When

we first went up there the patrol officers and Assistant District Officers had to spend at least nine months in that 21 months of service [on patrol]. But you could go in your own time. Reg was always in charge of a station so he could set his own time. The officer had a few broad lines laid out. Other than that, you could do what you thought was best for the natives. Different patrol officers or whoever was in charge of a station would have different views about what should be done. We'd go along to one place where the officer in charge felt they should plant more coconuts, another one where they decided they liked roads and so on. You couldn't always lay down a line of conduct. All your duties devolved on the well-being of the native.[15]

Dixie Rigby, born in England, joined the Women's Auxiliary Army Corps (WAAC) in 1916 and served in France in 1917. In 1919 she emigrated to Australia, meeting her husband Reg in 1923. She interested Reg in New Guinea and he went up in 1925 as a patrol officer, shortly after they married. Dixie became pregnant with John and stayed in Australia until 1928, before joining Reg in Rabaul, after his first leave. As Reg was 'not in favour of taking children up there' John went to boarding school in Australia. Reg moved to Aitape, the headquarters of the Sepik District, and Dixie went out with him on his first patrol. Reg was in the Sepik area for twelve years, during which time he became an Assistant District Officer, and then District Commissioner. Michael Somare's father was one of Reg Rigby's sergeants and Julius Chan's father was one of the first Chinese Dixie met in New Guinea. The Rigbys left New Guinea in 1955, when Reg retired.

Marjorie Murphy left an unhappy romance behind her when she went to Rabaul in 1940. She soon met John, a patrol officer, and they were married. After their first leave in Australia together, John was posted to Otibandu on the Watut River. This was an uncontrolled area, but Marjorie accompanied John on his patrols. During the war John worked in intelligence and was captured by the Japanese. He and six Americans were the only survivors of the prisoner-of-war camp in Rabaul. Marjorie was officially informed that John was missing; but she discovered that he had been captured when, coming home from her work at the bank one day, she picked up the Queensland newspaper, the *Courier Mail*. Across the front page was a headline: 'Japs claim capture of Australian spy'.

After the war, John was posted to Higaturu, but before leaving Samarai was promoted to Acting District Officer. A few years later the apparently extinct volcano, Lamington, erupted and everyone on Higaturu station was killed. By this time the Murphys were in Aitape, following a posting at Wewak. In 1948 and 1949 they went on leave and their son Kerry was born. They were stationed in Rabaul between 1950 and 1955, John as Acting District Commissioner for a time. Dale, their daughter, was born in 1955. John spent four years as District Commissioner in Daru, and then nine years in Kerema, before the Murphys retired to Brisbane in 1969.

Marjorie Murphy describes one aspect of John's duties as District Administrator:

> Because the two backward and neglected districts were Western Papua (Daru) and the Gulf District (Kikori), the Administrator, Sir Donald Cleland, sent John down to discover what could be done. He was away six weeks while I was at Boroko with the two children. John was then posted to Daru.
>
> When we arrived in Daru, Mrs so-and-so wasn't talking to someone else, everybody was unhappy and wondered what they'd done to blot their copybook to be sent to such a place. So John said 'We'll have a club'. Then we decided to raise money to buy furniture for it by having a revue, because most people can do something. I and a couple of lasses about my size, who had similar tulle evening dresses, were to do a dance while someone sang and so on. Anyway we had so much fun going round to the various houses practising that everyone was talking to everyone else. Suddenly we woke up we had no audience—we were all in the revue! No audience because the native people were not permitted to join clubs or drink in those days. But we had it just the same.

In 1960 the Murphys moved to Kerema:

> The headquarters of the Gulf District were transferred from Kikori to Kerema and when we arrived there, there was not even a wharf or road. Our gear came ashore in a raft. If it had been rough weather, we would have lost everything. When we left there we had an airfield, a High School, a wharf, private enterprise with an Hotel and Department Store, Bakery, and a Chinese Store, a concrete brick Catholic Church and of course a club. We also had 'Radio Kerema' which broadcast local and national news with appropriate programs for local consumption.

Both Dixie Rigby and Marjorie Murphy, sometimes after a lapse of time, followed their husbands' careers around the Territory as they rose from patrol officer, to District Officer, to District Commissioner.

Apart from working on missions, the most common occupation for women in Papua New Guinea was stenographer or typist,[16] a job which Marjorie Murphy performed on occasions after her marriage. Prudence Frank made her career with this skill, and was responsible for training Papuans for clerical work. From the 1950s the government expanded its role in education and health care; and more single women came to the Territory as teachers and nurses, supplementing the work of wives already in the Territory.

In 1969 Col. J.K. Murray reflected that 'education and public health were the basis on which the rest of that pyramid [of advancement] could be built'.[17] Improving the health of the people had always been an objective of the administration and the missions, the former using *doktabois* in the villages, the latter sending medical sisters and doctors. Until the Second World War, the bulk of local health care delivery was carried out by missions, although the administration offered subsidies for such work. In Papua the subsidies came from the native taxation fund.[18]

Initially the practice of tropical medicine mimicked racist segregation, relying on quarantine and confinement, for example of tuberculosis and leprosy cases. However, such practices were not popular with the indigenous people. To win the support of villagers, Sir Raphael Cilento recommended that medical officers concentrate on cases where there was likely to be a spectacular and ready cure, paying especial attention to the children of chieftains.[19] The application of 'miracle drugs' especially M&B 914 which cured yaws, guaranteed medical patrols an enthusiastic reception after 1922.[20] Despite their initial resistance, it is clear that the Mendi Highlands people came to appreciate Joyce Walker's work, as discussed in Chapter Four. It is also clear that one of the much noted differences between the Japanese and the Australians was the latter's concern for the health of the people. Sios Tabunamagin,[21] noted this, as did Aisoli Salin.[22] From 1933 there was limited medical training for Papua New Guinean men, but Cilento scotched the idea of a medical school in Rabaul.

After the war Dr John Gunther, 'hard-crusted, soft-hearted, not frightened of alcohol or anything else' took up the Directorship of Health.[23] He scrounged materials and supplies left over from the war, and convinced many orderlies to stay on as European Medical Assistants. He deplored the Australian government's refusal to allow him to appoint Chinese doctors, and appointed medically qualified refugees from central Europe whose qualifications were not recognised in Australia. His major campaigns were against malaria, tuberculosis and leprosy. The early results fell away as resistance to drugs developed. 'By 1956, when he ceased to be Director, Gunther had created what may have been one of the finest medical services of that era in a tropical dependency.'[24] His success was enhanced by a military campaign style which marshalled men, money and resources and the almost unquestioning respect for medical work shared by the administration and the villagers.

Donald Denoon claims that while infant welfare was a preoccupation of the medical administration, women's health was never a serious issue. Indeed infant and maternal welfare work was known in Hanuabada near Port Moresby as 'baby-weigh'.[25] The first specialist in maternal and child health was Joan Refshauge, who had been born into a family which valued education above all else.[26] Dr Joan Refshauge was not only a medical doctor, but also obtained a Master of Science, a Diploma of Education and a Diploma of Public Health. In 1947, after teaching and medical work in a number of Australian institutions, she was given a temporary appointment with the Department of Public Health in Port Moresby.

Joan Refshauge describes the poor conditions under which she started work in Papua.[27] Because of the lack of appropriate instruments, she sometimes used her finger, for example, to perform an abortion. There was no wire netting on the theatre windows, so operations were performed in suffocating heat with the windows closed. She was required to do dental extractions, based on a single fortuitous lesson from a dentist in Mildura, and even veterinary work. The situation improved gradually, due in no small measure to Gunther's vision and willingness to impose it. However, in 1953 Matron Taffy Jones wrote to Dr Refshauge, who was in Sydney to sit an examination:

Now I would like you to do me a favour please. Will you get at one of the drug houses 1 doz. packets of needles as enclosed sample. You will see it is the sort used for Procaine Penicillin. Told you in my last letter that I was going to do mass treatment of Yaws in Duke of Yorks, with approval of Port Moresby of course. United Nations of South Pacific want the information on treatment by penicillin. Well Moresby sent tons of it, but when I asked Dr Pike to ask on phone for the right needles they did not have any. They have none here either. Have been out once with intramuscular needles which turned out to be quite unsuitable for mass treatment . . . Rang up Thorb in Moresby because she knows exactly the right sort of needles we use at the hospital there. She could only get six, half of Irwin's stock.[28]

Following her divorce in 1948, Joan Refshauge became a permanent appointment, serving continuously until her retirement in 1963 as Assistant Director of Infant Child and Maternal Health, the most senior female administrator in Papua New Guinea. During that time Dr Refshauge built a network of maternal and child health services throughout the country, produced large numbers of practical and self-reliant nurses and conducted countless tours of inspection. As an example of the scope of her work, in 1959 there were twelve administration centres, thirteen European clinics, three Asiatic clinics, nine permanent 'Native' clinics and several mobile clinics. Only two clinics were administered by indigenous women, a New

Guinean and a Papuan. There were also 116 missions doing medical work under subsidy. During that year 18 000 adults, 3000 antenatal cases and 60 000 infants were cared for at the Native clinics. As a result of these clinics, Dr Refshauge argued that the infant mortality rate had dropped from as high as 500 in 1000 in some untouched areas to around 42 in 1000 in Port Moresby, although this was still twice the infant mortality rate for Australia.[29]

In the area of health, especially after the Second World War, there was potential for conflict between the government and the missions. Joan Refshauge was sensitive to this, stressing the greater knowledge of local 'customs, food patterns and conditions' on the part of the mission workers and accepting the occasional 'misunderstanding' between the two sets of workers. She was also committed to the highest practicable level of health for Papua New Guineans, and advocated preventative medicine:

> Briefly the aim of the Infant and Maternal Welfare Section of the Public Health Department is to work in co-operation with the Christian Missions for the benefit of the people. The endeavour is to lower both the infant and maternal mortality, to encourage widespread personal, domestic and village hygiene, and to build healthy children for healthy adulthood. Perhaps I may be permitted to give in more detail the scope of the work.
>
> Medical work today prefers the practice of preventive medicine as opposed to the practice of curative medicine. In this Territory it includes both though the accent is gradually being transferred to preventive medicine. Again health no longer means physical fitness or a freedom from disease, but is a state of complete physical, mental and social wellbeing. By our endeavour to build healthy adults then we mean adults who enjoy total health.[30]

In 1964 Dr Refshauge was awarded the Cilento Medal for the advancement of the local population in the Tropics of Australia. Dr Refshauge was the first woman to win the medal, which had been conferred only six times in the previous thirty years. Raphael Cilento wrote:

The trustees, of whom I am one, feel that there is no person more fitting upon whom it could be bestowed than yourself, in recognition of your work for 15 years amongst women and children in Papua and New Guinea'.[31]

Dr Refshauge died in 1979 at the age of 72 years.

It was not only the indigenous population who relied on the work of nurses and doctors. Taffy Jones is remembered with affection.

I met all of the women when Child Welfare came to give us all vaccinations for lung conditions. Taffy Jones was the welfare sister in Moresby. They turned her down to join the Army because they said she had flat feet. She escaped by walking out over the Owen-Stanleys, I think it was, during the Second World War. She was admired and loved by everyone. Nowhere was too difficult for her to go if there were babies to look after who needed her care. [Daphney Bridgland]

Private Enterprise

Before the Second World War, between a third and a half of the European couples living in New Guinea ran plantations; very few overseers had wives. However, many of the plantations, especially the smaller ones, had only one European, a man, in residence.[32] According to Daphney Bridgland running a plantation was a multi-skilled job:

If you are a plantation manager you are everything. You represent the law practically, the health of everyone is in your care. You had to feed, house, clothe and see to medical attention of every person on the plantation. You need to be able to build a house, to wire a house, to do the plumbing for the place. You need to be a mechanic, mostly a diesel mechanic which is not easy, and you need car mechanics. You need to be everything, you need to be able to weld and to do all carpenters' jobs.

Daphney Bridgland's husband was employed by the Department of Agriculture, Stock and Fisheries when she married him and moved to Sogeri in 1950. In 1952 Leon took up supervision of the Lowlands Agricultural Experimental Station at Keravat near Rabaul. In 1959 he left the government to run an Agricultural Advisory Service. Leon later became the manager of a group of plantations in the Rabaul area. Daphney Bridgland was not as lucky as Pat Andersen, who later returned to social work and the use of her degree. Daphney had trained at the Melbourne Conservatorium but was never to fulfill her wish of becoming a professional opera singer.

Wives usually performed many tasks inside and outside the home. They did medical work, helped with the books, ordered the food for the whole plantation, and ran the trade store.[33] Pat Murray describes the division of labour among the family members on her parents' plantation:

There was so much to be done that we'd divided the labour in our household. I used to take charge of the copra line and book work and pay and all that sort of thing. Di used to ride round on the horse and watch over the grass cutting and maintenance and she also looked after the animals. John used to do all the mechanical work and Dad was rebuilding the house and generally supervising and ordering the whole operation. Mum used to do the household necessities and the medicines.

Even as children, Pat and her brother had jobs on the plantation. They distributed the medicines, administered emergency first aid when their parents were absent from the plantation, issued rations to the workers—and kept the copra shippers honest:

> Then we had one other little job which came up periodically, on boat day when we were shipping copra off the beach. In those days most of the New Ireland copra was taken off the beach, until a year or two before the War. The supercargo, who was a sort of purser or what have you, his job was to weigh the copra on the beach and make out the weighbills for the ship thereby acknowledging how much copra had gone aboard and what weight. There was a rather iniquitous system in operation, whether officially or unofficially I've never known, whereby the ship's officers split the proceeds of any copra at out turn that wasn't accounted for on the ingoing weights. Well naturally this led to a lot of shenanigan and these supercargoes used to try to slip a few bags past the scale without recording them and this happened frequently. Jim and I used to stand by the scale and watch the supercargo who must have got frightfully fed up with us but obviously couldn't tell us to run away and play. They used to weigh two bags at a time, and the supercargo would give the boy a wave to indicate take the bags through. And every now and again, he'd wave his hand when he obviously hadn't written anything down. And this is when we'd pounce and say 'Mr so and so, you haven't written that one yet'. And he'd say 'Yes I have'. And we could read the scales and we used to look at his book, and it was extremely unlikely that the weight would be exactly the same on the previous two bags. So he was had cold any time we cared to challenge it. As a result we didn't lose much that way.

Plantation owners, especially those mortgaged to one of the big shipping companies, suffered dreadfully during the Depression. Pat Murray reports the poor treatment meted out by the shipping companies Burns Philp and Carpenters to plantation owners in the Depression:

> We just cut back on the plantation, we were all hamstrung, we

couldn't just leave it. Practically everybody who bought these
expropriated properties was stuck because you had to put down
a deposit . . . Very few people had the amount of money that was
necessary to put down the deposit. BPs and Carpenters said 'You
bloody beaut' and they offered to lend people what they needed
to make up their deposits . . . You signed a trading agreement that
you would only sell your copra through your particular company,
say Carpenters. You would buy all your supplies, all your insurance
through them. You could only buy supplies elsewhere if they couldn't
supply. And you had to use their ships, you had to do everything
through them. You were robbed blind, because the firms worked
together. You were no better off with one than the other, and
they'd decide what you could buy. They'd vet your orders, I'm
not kidding, I know my mother used to get furious.

We lived in the copra shed. Dad had put a roof frame on it
with the idea of putting iron on it, couldn't afford the iron, so
temporarily he put *sak sak* [palm fronds]. You think back to a *sak
sak* roof at that pitch, you can imagine what happened when it
rained. The roof used to leak like a sieve, despite the fact the
sak sak was put on very close, weighted down and all the rest of
it.

Anyway Mum used to write the orders and she wrote in that
she wanted two tons of iron or whatever quantity it was. Now
if you wanted anything like that you had to explain what it was
for, so she said 'Iron for the house'. 'Unnecessary': twice they knocked
it back. Then one day Mum wrote in and said 'Iron for the copra
shed' and it came on the next ship. This was a family with four
young children growing up. She'd send in orders, ordinary household
orders 'four tins of assorted jam' 'three bottles of worcestershire
sauce'. 'Unnecessary' they'd cross out things like pickles and that,
they were considered luxuries.

It got so bad with the firms, that in 1940 they decided they
would not give any cash at all for copra, you could buy goods from
them, but they wouldn't give any cash at all . . .

By this time Pat Murray was postmistress and secretary to the District Officer
in Kavieng. Because her parents had no cash, Pat paid for the stamps for
their letters.

What happened was the Australian Government (under pressure)
finally decided to have a Copra Board, a Control Board they called
it, after the War broke out. It was only just before we were evacuated,

in 1941, that the Copra Control Board actually came into operation. We sent away one shipment of copra under it before we left. We got something unbelievable, like sixteen pounds a ton. The War had made it happen. The War came, copra was needed, fats were needed, and that's why they had to ensure that the plantations could keep going.

Following the war, the shipping companies claimed their debts which had built up during the war—'interest on interest on interest'. [Pat Murray] During this period the plantations were controlled by the Japanese and the shipping was controlled by the government, so no planters in New Guinea were producing or selling copra. Pat's father offered a cheque for one-tenth of the account in complete satisfaction of his debt. The company accepted the offer, and other planters followed his lead. Pat's father was so scarred by this experience that he 'never bought a bloody thing from Carpenters, he rigidly refused to buy from them at all. He used to buy from BPs or the Chinese or anyone'. [Pat Murray]

The discovery of gold during the Depression lured many struggling planters and other hopeful fortune-seekers to the fields. Pat's family mined for gold at Tugi Tugi on Tabar. They had not staked a claim because Pat's father felt there was too little gold for the many people who would be lured by publicising the find. However one day a patrol officer, McDonald, came with a summons and discovered what was happening:

> The boys came up with a day's wash-up in the dish, and Dad was signalling them to go away. McDonald all full of bounce and understandable curiosity said 'Oh, what's that?' and Dad said 'Prospecting' or something like that. Before he could stop him, McDonald got up and took a look and there he saw smeared across the bottom of this dish about two and half ounces of very clean gold.
>
> Apparently when McDonald got to Namatanai, he went to the pub and he said he'd just come back from Tabar. And someone said 'How are those mad goldminers over there, have they declared gold yet?' And he looked at his watch and said 'Well, I left at ten o'clock and nothing had been done then'. And they looked at one another and they took off as one man to get picks and shovel and whatnot and were on their way. Dad guessed this would happen so as soon as McDonald went he said 'I'd better catch this boat back to Kavieng and go in and declare'. Because if you don't, someone else can declare and get all the reward claims. He said 'Start pegging first thing Monday morning' and they (Dad, Col

Mackellar and Charlie Petterson) sat down and worked out where to peg.

So there was Col Mackellar, Charlie, my mother and me—I was eleven—armed with a compass going through the bush with a boy and a shovel and a bush knife. There were eleven claims to peg. But what we were doing was running the outside perimeter and we'd divide up more or less at our leisure. Well we finally closed, we came together with our pegs, a little bit of shouting and yelling, and adjusting ourselves and we got there. We finished that up at about three o'clock in the afternoon . . . Mum had long hair at the time and her hairpins fell out and her hair fell down her back. I had long plaits and my plaits came undone and my hair was flying all over the place and I tied it back with bushrope (vine).

When we came together there was this big old log and Charlie was sitting on it having an asthma attack and Col was sitting on it massaging the leg that he had a tropical ulcer on. Mum was sitting on the other end of it trying to do something with her hair and I was down on my hands and knees digging a direction trench from the peg. Suddenly this vision burst through the bush, long white trousers, white shirt, white topee: Dick Heap. And when he saw us he said 'Oh my goodness'. He was most contrite and upset that he had caused a panic. He said 'You should have let us know. We could have waited until you were ready'. A more gentlemanly goldminer you never met in your life. It doesn't normally work that way . . .

Tabar became a hive of activity. Percy Blandon was sent from Wau as Mining Warden and Pat gave dish washing lessons—'We had a terrific lot of fun':

Across the hill from us, Bill McGregor had his camp. Bill McGregor was a keen ham radio man. I don't know how much mining he did, but he spent most of his time listening to the test match. And every now and again somebody would say 'Oh, Bill's got something'. And he'd come out and wave a lap lap, and when he saw a few people listening to him he'd yell '44 not out, so and so bowled so and so, 21'. This was yelled across the valley and picked up by people and you could hear voices relaying it up the valley; it used to go all the way round the camp what the cricket score was.

The goldfields of Bulolo and Edie Creek were more lucrative than those on Tabar. Although women were not allowed to take up mining licences,[34]

Doris Booth was responsible for the 'sick lines' and training the indigenous labourers while she and her husband were at Bulolo.[35] When her husband moved to Edie, Doris Booth sent supplies up to him and managed the Bulolo workforce.[36] Molly Parer lived with her husband at the Black Cat mine between Wau and Salamaua, and later at Watut for four years from 1933:

> I didn't see a black or white woman for eight months, and the hut had a dirt floor. I was not unhappy. I was with my husband and I wanted to be with him. He was goldmining and that was interesting. We'd send the natives in with our letters and they'd come back with all the food and periodicals. I had an aunt in Melbourne and she'd never stop sending me things. No work to do of course; I don't know how I filled in the time but I did.

Mission

For single people like Marjorie Murphy, Rabaul provided an entertaining social life, as well as a picturesque setting. Mission workers were both the poor and suspect relations in white towns: poor because of their low salaries, suspect because of their close relations with and defence of Papua New Guineans. Isabel Platten soon became aware that mission salaries could not support the colonial lifestyle of Rabaul in the late 1920s. She was much happier when Gil was posted to Halis near Namatanai (on New Ireland) in 1929:

> We passed through the Government sub-station of Namatanai and two miles farther on we came to Halis. For the first time in my life I had come to a place I would love so totally that time spent away from it would be painful. Settling in took time and Gil found there was much to do to get the station in order. Halis is on a plateau, and from it our view of the Coral Sea was spectacular. Lihir Island was not far away to our east. Tabar Island was further north. Halis was beautiful then but improvements would be made, until it would have a reputation as being exceptionally beautiful. Our Namatanai government friends would bring their own more important visitors to see us and I remember one such remarking 'I have heard of island paradise but this is the first time I have seen one'.

Newell was born in 1928 while Isabel was still in Rabaul; Paquita was born in 1931 at Halis. After two years in Perth between 1935 and 1937,

Gil was appointed to George Brown College in Vunairima to train the senior teachers as ordained ministers. The Plattens returned to Halis in 1939. Gil Platten and Rodger Brown were the only two Methodist ministers to escape when the Japanese invaded New Guinea. Gil returned to Halis in 1946 and Isabel joined him in 1947. In 1949, Gil became Chairman of the District and Principal of George Brown College, moving to Rabaul. Shortly afterwards, due to financial difficulties, Gil resigned from the Mission. He wrote to Bill Groves, the Director of Education, who appointed him as the vocational teacher at Sogeri High School, near Port Moresby. In 1949 Gil and Isabel moved to Sos on Tabar, as part of a government project to enquire into depopulation on the Tabar Islands. This was shelved following a change of government, and Gil remained as a teacher. He taught in Garaina and Kainantu before retiring in 1958, when the couple returned to Adelaide.

No longer living in a mission-minded world, it may be hard to imagine how men and women could leave job and home, sometimes for ever, to brave the dangers of malaria and other tropical diseases, the privations of the most basic accommodation, and the obligation to minister to a people they had never met but who were often reputedly ferocious cannibals. By the turn of the century David Livingstone and others had given missionaries a new status, while the lure of distant lands added romance to their work. The free education for LMS (London Missionary Society) entrants offered upward mobility, while mission salaries were up to twice that of a manual worker or clerk.[37] Women who chose to be missionaries may have responded to a prevalent theme in nineteenth-century feminism that women's special task was to take their domestic virtues into the public world, to combine 'female liberation with domestic piety'.[38]

Diane Langmore's study of missionaries in Papua before 1920 reveals that the death rate was lowest among the Protestants, who lived in solid, well-equipped houses with ample provisions and medication.[39] The Sacred Heart missionaries lived in primitive huts made from bush materials, with an inadequate diet and provisions. Many came from peasant families in Brittany or Normandy in France, and most died—either early or late— in Papua. The death rate for the Anglicans lay between these two groups, perhaps because they shared something of the Roman Catholic dedication to God's work where prudence would dictate retreat. Women were considered particularly prone to nervous ailments and hysteria, an advisor to the Anglican Mission saying that a woman was commonly regarded as 'a uterus surrounded by protoplasm'.[40] However, women's length of service was little different from men's, shorter in the Methodist Mission (4.7 years compared with 7.7 years, but partly because of the requirement to resign on marriage) and longer in the Catholic Mission (at 23.9 years compared with 17.4 for the men). The longest serving of all the missionaries in this period was Sister Clothilde Carroll who arrived in 1900 and remained until her death at the age of 90 in 1966.[41] The Anglicans sent a good proportion of professional men and women, teachers and trained nurses. The Protestant denominations were drawn from the artisan and clerical classes, as well as the unskilled. Farming backgrounds were also quite common.

By the 1940s in New Guinea the Roman Catholic staff of 550 far out-numbered the combined total of the other denominations.[42] In both New Guinea and Papua the missions had more or less accepted spheres of influence from the 1890s. This arrangement reduced the friction between the missions, and the options (although possibly also the confusion) of the local people, and allowed for greater efficiency of service delivery. In New Guinea the German administration forced a zoning system on reluctant missionaries. In the Solomon Islands a Marist said 'if the Protestants wish to have peace with us, let them go where we are not' supplying their catechists in Bougainville with bicycles in order to outstrip the Methodists around the district.[43] Bishop Navarre complained of the 'opposition of the people, especially the free-thinkers, meddling of the protestants and sometimes of the civil authorities' which stood in the way of the Sacred Heart Society's work.[44] In Papua the Catholic Mission refused to admit any limitations to their endeavours. The 'spheres of influence' policy never received legislative confirmation, although it was underwritten by the practice of selectively granting land only to the mission operating in each area. With the entry of the Seventh Day Adventist mission, which had not been party to the original carve-up, the Papuan administration refused to continue this practice.[45]

Both Sister Aquilonia Ax and Grace Young report good relations between their respective missions and the Lutheran mission. Grace Young stayed at the Lutheran Mission in Ogelbeng while waiting to enter Mendi, while Sister Aquilonia's staff attended the Lutheran hospital when sick:

> As to the question of relationships with other denominations, in the Madang area our closest associations were with the Lutheran Missionaries in and around Madang. Our closest were Dr Brown and his wife who had a rather large hospital near Madang with a wing for European patients. All sisters who needed medical attention went there. They were welcome, respected, lovingly and medically efficiently cared for. Not everyone in all religious groups have right attitudes. The right of religious convictions I claim for myself I must in justice and charity grant to others.

Conversion energies were often focussed on village leaders. Medical cures operated as a powerful inducement to conversion, although counteracted by the requirement to forego the labour and status brought by multiple wives.[46] Mission intervention also occurred at the weakest link in indigenous society, taking in those members who would otherwise be killed or ostracised; thus the Methodist sisters and Catholic nuns reared thousands of motherless babies. Marists focussed their missionary work on the young, even buying girls and boys regularly for labour, as pupils and as a ready-made congregation when founding a new station.[47] Babies were saved from infanticide and children from domestic violence; widows were saved from the death which customarily followed that of their husband.[48] Benjamin Butcher, a London Missionary Society medical missionary in Papua between 1905 and 1938, retrieved a baby abandoned in a village which had been subjected to a government raid. Several days later the parents arrived, covered in the mud of mourning, and reclaimed their child:

> It seemed to me all wrong when once I took the little one so clean and sweet and laid her in the unclean arms of the mother, who, without a single word or look of gratitude, clasped her to her mud-stained breast.[49]

Both this contrast of the dirty 'mud-stained' mother with the baby cleansed by Christian hands, and Butcher's hope to give the baby a chance 'as had come to none other of her people' reveals the belief in the superiority of white religion.[50] Such a belief propelled Christian missionaries into 'savage' lands, although not all missionaries found their beliefs unchallenged by life in Papua New Guinea, as Chapter Seven explores.

Homo hierarchicus: *Status relations in the white colony*

Helen Callaway captures the minute but pervasive gradations of status in colonial Nigeria with the term *homo hierarchicus*.[51] It covers both distinctions within groups—between officers and men, colonial administrators and technical officers—and between groups. The missionary and mercantile groups were more likely to come from lower-middle-class backgrounds and have received inferior education. Only the independently minded, and 'of course the missionaries and single women' did not join the club, or the appropriate club where there was one for each type of European—civil servants, military men, and businessmen.[52] These class differences were exacerbated by national differences—many missionaries and traders were not even British! Similarly in Papua New Guinea Lutheran missionaries came from Germany while many of the Catholic missionaries came from Europe. Forms of address, seating arrangements, procession into the dining room and even toilet queues were determined by the rank order of husbands' seniority. In colonial Papua New Guinea the housing on the hill was for senior government personnel;

men only joined their inferiors to share a drink or the playing field, women joined theirs for charitable works. Single men travelled second class, but single women, whatever the hardship, were expected to maintain their status by travelling first class.[53]

In India the soldiers' wives were 'to be pitied'; they were inexperienced country girls who shopped in local bazaars. If an officer was killed, his widow's return passage to Britain was provided by the government; soldiers' widows were left stranded in India. The civil wives were languid and ladylike, while the military wives were more affected and showily dressed.[54] 'Women of the regiment', women married to members of Britain's army in Victorian times, were incorporated into a satellite class structure. It was expected that officers' wives would take an interest in the domestic rectitude of soldiers' wives, who were punished (even to the extent of being turned out of barracks) for drunkenness, abusive language, and having men other than their husbands in their quarters.[55] Such behaviour was uncommon among wives in colonial society by the turn of the century, indicating the successful spread of middle-class values.

Helen Callaway notes that in West Africa in 1925, there was a mission side of the boat and a government side, while traders belonged to neither side.[56] Each group kept to itself. Administration families in Papua New Guinea report an 'unwritten rule' which decreed they should not become too friendly with missionaries or planters.[57] Jens Lyng describes the conversations between a wowserish spinster missionary (Miss Sharp) and the men on board a boat sailing among the Duke of York Islands.[58] Miss Sharp is ridiculed for condemning war as the invention of men, drink as the product of the devil, and one of the men for keeping 'quite a harem of black women'. He replies that the respect and admiration of the local people was gained by possessing many wives.

In the face of such stereotypes, it is little wonder that Isabel Platten kept her missionary identity a secret when travelling, hoping that after a few days people would accept her on her own terms:

> The general attitude between non-religious people and missionaries was never good. For example, I would never tell anybody when I was travelling on a ship that I was the wife of a missionary until we'd been out three or four days, and then I might let it drop. By that time I'd been taken for what I was. Otherwise you wouldn't get within six feet of them. They were very antagonistic to us, except when they knew you personally.

Nevertheless, Isabel Platten formed friendships with a nearby plantation family and several government wives.

Nearest to Halis were the Breretons, they were six miles south. The Breretons were to become life-long friends. The government officials moved around from station to station so friendships, though strong, were not as longlasting, except, perhaps, with Dixie Rigby and Ruth Pickwell. I used to get on tremendously well with the government people and the planters, even if I couldn't with all the missionaries. When we visited we wore old heavy shoes which we took off at the bottom of the steps, coming up in our lighter shoes. Only anybody without any sense would wear their muddy shoes inside. So there would be rows of old muddy shoes on the verandahs.

Heather Searle describes the hierarchy among the 'plahnters'. A man may be located by: 'Oh, they're working for X, but he's a plahnting family and her father is a plahnter for Y'.[59] Daphney Bridgland, as a government worker's wife, felt that plantation people looked down on her:

The plantation people were really very socially inclined. There were twenty white women in the Laloki River valley. We were just lowly government personnel. I did first meet some of the plantation people because Lorna Courteny-Smith had lived next door to the lass my husband had previously been engaged to. So Lorna was rather anxious to meet me. We were invited to Kontaki, but normally government personnel weren't invited to dinner parties of people who lived on plantations.

On the other hand, Pat Murray argues that the ostracism came from the government people:

I've never known any plantation people who were anti-kiap in the way the kiaps were anti-us. It started right back in the late '20s. In the early stages, plantation people were doing well, they were making money and all the rest of it. It was jealousy.

There were reasons, too, in the methods of administration that produced tensions between planters and government people. Local planters lobbied their District Officer for improved services but before anything was finalised he would be moved and the white community had to start again:

You'd get issues that come up in all communities, like getting a road fixed or getting a better bridge built somewhere, and the local planters' association and various interested bodies would get together and sort of say 'We'll go and see the D.O.' A delegation of say two or three planters and a couple of missionaries perhaps might go and see the D.O. and have a conference with him about say getting a jetty built somewhere or a bridge repaired. The D.O. would say 'Yes that's fine, we'll put it on the list' and all this would be lined up. And then lo and behold he'd be posted to Madang or something and the next bloke would have a whole different approach, new broom, and that was what used to drive people nuts. You'd have to turn around and get to know him all over again. You've also got the problem of the personality clashes in the government. One bloke taking over from another might take over from a bloke he loathed the sight of and he'd scrap everything just on principle.

Daphney Bridgland points out that the government decreed that the agricultural extension officers were to provide their services exclusively to the villagers. If strictly adhered to, this rule no doubt caused friction in the white community. Her husband 'did help all the planters that he could'.

It was very often the attitude towards the Papua New Guinean that determined alliances and divisions within the white community. In this way relations with the 'outside', the indigenous people, refracted relations on the 'inside', the internal dynamics of the white colony. Each group had certain beliefs concerning the 'correct' handling of the indigenous people, flavoured by their reason for being in the colony—conversion, order, or profit-making. According to Oala Oala-Rarua, 'the aims and attitudes of these three groups of Europeans were so different from each other that the territory became a battleground for their opposing ambitions; this utterly confused their native followers and admirers'.[60]

Missionaries very often could not afford to adopt the lifestyle required by colonial standards; sometimes their vows or commitments forbade it. But the missionaries were also under constant attack for their particular relationship with the indigenous people, captured in McAuley's six stereotypes.[61] Five of these focus purely on the relationship between missionary and potential convert: brave converter of the savage, champion of native rights, kill-joy in an island Eden, bigot and fanatic, demoraliser of native society. Only one stereotype aligns the missionary within the 'sinister trio' of capitalist imperialism, providing a camouflage behind which trader and official operate.

Missionaries in Papua deplored the traders for their commercial and sexual exploitation of the Papuans, while traders resented missions setting up trade stores and undercutting prices.[62] Missionaries were attacked as wowsers who forbade the local girls uninhibited relationships and introduced sexual guilt where none had been.[63] Miners were accused of drunkenness, sexual debauchery and undercutting the influence of civilisation.[64] Jens Lyng argues that the traders, 'feeling that sooner or later they would be hampered in their actions by the dictates of civilized life, fell upon the natives like hungry wolves—cheating, kidnapping, bullying and butchering'.[65] Clearly all these caricatures locate both the narrators and the subject of their attack in the web of race relations.

Settlers, miners and traders also remembered the care received from missionaries or their wives in times of illness. However, the Yodda diggers in 1903 directed that their testimonial go to the two female nurses who had helped them, and not the Anglican mission itself.[66] Doris Groves was charged reduced rates by the hotel owners when she was stranded on Samarai in 1924 for three weeks:

> I knew that I did not have enough money with me to pay 3 weeks' hotel expenses, and there was no way I could get it from Moresby in time. I need not have worried for the licencee's wife was the sister of friends of mine in Moresby and evidently knew that as a missionary I did not have a large income, and, when I came to pay my bill, it was greatly reduced and within my means.

According to some accounts, the British Colonial Service consisted of 'men who regarded colonialism as a venture in applied philanthropy—not as an enterprise designed to maximise profits'.[67] Dixie Rigby distinguishes 'ordinary civilians' from government officials: 'the native was our job'. However Callaway suggests there was an intermingling of altruism and egoism in the colonial venture.[68] Public service carried status that conferred both moral prestige and political power.

It was the supervision of labour contracts by government officers that earned them the epithets 'nigger-lover' [Dixie Rigby] or 'boong-lover'[69]:

> Our job in New Guinea was for the natives. We found some of the plantation people would get very annoyed with us. Actually they'd call you a nigger lover because my husband was there to uphold the law and his work was to help the native . . . as against the industry and the big plantation people. Theirs was making a living and getting money. [Dixie Rigby]

While government officials often conceived of their role in terms of preventing the exploitation of local labour, the planters had a different conception of exploitation. They felt that they had provided skills to Papua New Guineans and developed plantations which were later sold to local people. '(P)lanters have never been recognised for what they did in the pacification of New

Guinea and enhancing its economic status.'[70] Beatrice Grimshaw was also a staunch defender of the 'reclaiming and improving' of the natives carried out by the planters.[71] Government officials rarely invested in the country:

> Now these people as the years went by, they had plenty of time to invest in Australia. There was hardly a soul that didn't have a house down here. Every blasted bob, or 99.9% that the plantation community got, went back into the country, and we were exploiting the country, according to them. [Pat Murray]

On the other hand, government people bought plantations in New Guinea, while they 'were still in government service, of course they weren't supposed to. But at the same time the mealymouthed lot called us exploiters'. [Pat Murray]

At another level, the white community was united in the colonial enterprise. Few white people in Papua New Guinea could help feeling superior. Their structural location—bringing the Word, order, education, health care, the chance for economic improvement—made a commitment to equality of treatment almost impossible. Joe Leahy, a mixed-race son of Michael Leahy, says:

The white bossed the local people and pushed them around. The best belonged to the mastas . . . They never had any friends among the local people. They never ate together. They were up here and the locals down here. It was the same for all white people—miners, missionaries, planters or kiaps.[72]

Differences between the three communities were sometimes more apparent than real. The missions ran plantations, and in much the same manner as did Burns Philp and Carpenters.[73] The Rev. Dr Ralph Wiltgenen provides a justification for mission-based private enterprise: the missions needed money but the people were poor.[74] Furthermore 'missions have the obligation to help the native tame his wild nature, overcome idleness, and learn order and obedience'. Non-mission Europeans also applauded the missionary for converting the 'savage' into either a 'comical nigger' or 'harmless child'[75]:

On the principle that if you want to take a knife from an infant you should offer him an orange, you must give a savage something better if you wish to take away his headhunting. According to unbiased opinion, Christian teaching is, apparently, the answer to the problem.[76]

The significant role of missionaries in colonisation is aptly summarised by the common saying: 'When the white man came he owned the Bible and the colored man the land. In time the white man became the owner of the land and his colored brother owned the Bible'.[77]

In colonial societies where the indigenous people had a complex class structure, there was more room for ambiguities at the intersection of race and class relations. Race could overdetermine class in the formation of friendships. Lady Gordon became friends with a chiefly Fijian woman, Adi Kuila, writing 'she is such a lady'. Adi Kuila recognised her equal standing with Lady Gordon: 'you are a lady, like me'. On the other hand, Lady Gordon said of her nurse who looked down on all 'natives . . . as an inferior race': 'I don't like to tell her that these ladies are my equals, which she is not!'[78] British women worked with educated Indian women between the 1890s and 1930s, revealing that the 'boundaries of race but not class may be crossed in the imperial context'.[79] In Hawaii in the 1840s the female chiefs dandled 'slight American brides on their knees in an affectionate mood, like pets'.[80] The white women endured this humiliation in the hope that conversions would ensue.

Where indigenous societies had wealthy and powerful rulers, Indian Rajahs employed white governesses and white women formed friendships with chiefly families. The governesses and other white women who worked for British or Indian princely families, were close 'to the limits of what society considered permissible'.[81] Governesses in white families might eat lunch with the family including the children, but would seldom come to dinner or be invited to dances and parties.[82]

Significant class distinctions did not mark the village societies of Papua New Guinea. Moreover, the white community was not as hierarchically ordered as the Anglo-Indian community, or even the white community in Fiji. Nevertheless, although race superiority inflected all other distinctions, there were murmurings of class-based tensions concerning the right of all whites to dominate Papua New Guineans.

Flora Annie Steel argued that the 'Indian household can no more be governed peacefully without dignity and prestige than an Indian empire' and that a lady must repress her 'intense desire to hit' a servant who misbehaved.[83] Not all mistresses of white households were 'ladies', and attempts were made to regulate a mistress's behaviour with gossip and advice. Lower-class women, it was claimed, did not have the breeding or experience required to handle servants (did not deserve servants). Lower-class women compensated for their insecurity by asking too much of their servants, stressing too loudly the status distinction, which in fact was not wide enough for comfort:

Young kiaps came back from leave with 'a nice little shop girl' or one of the first girls they came to . . . Some of them were overwhelmed with native servants and instead of using a native servant with dignity they were ordering them around all day.[84]

Georgina Seton from the Solomon Islands criticised the 'suburban type of woman married to a clerk' who was 'charmed by the idea of servants'.[85]

Rowley claimed that having a servant 'turns the heads of silly men and women', mainly transients who spent only a short time in the Territory.[86] Similarly, 'men of moderate means who could not afford a servant even if they could find one' were bad employers of labour, oscillating between 'extremes of harshness and familiarity'. This failed to elicit 'that agreeable courtesy of manner' which was expected in servants.[87]

Like all whites, missionaries were expected to have servants but often could not afford them. Neither Jean Mannering nor Isabel Platten misunderstood the significance of servants as a marker of white status; however, they focus on the practicalities:

> In those days every wife of a missionary was supposed to have two native boys to help her in the house. Ours didn't know any English and they'd never been in a European house before. I'd never kept house before and I didn't know their language, so it would have been a lot easier to do the work myself. [Jean Mannering]
>
> No servants came with the house and we needed at least three. We had no idea how to go about hiring any. An appeal to one of our mission folk eventually brought us a pair of unlikely lads. They had had no training at all. Somehow we battled along together but we had a lot to learn. Though their monthly wage was only six shillings, they were also fed and clothed . . . Each servant was bought and given a box, blanket, cooking utensils and several lap-laps. We also had to feed them which sometimes seemed to cost more than what it cost ourselves. For two almost penniless young people this was an extra burden. [Isabel Platten]

The different attitudes of the three white communities toward Papua New Guineans are explored in relation to the particular policies of land and labour regulation and education in Chapters 5 and 6. Before that task is undertaken, a more detailed examination of the different lives of white women in Papua New Guinea occupies the next two chapters. Few men went to any colony as the dependants of another person. This was the common experience of white women; and their dependant relationship considerably influenced their life in the colony, as Chapter 3 explores. Another major factor shaping expatriate women's lives was whether they lived on an outstation or in town. This will be considered in Chapter 4.

3

White Women in Papua New Guinea: Relative Creatures?

The men who conquer the feminine landscape of Africa overpower a 'ravished dark woman'.[1] But there are also real women in the tropics, though they too are often characterised as dark and untameable. The myths of the Amazons are re-invoked to align the female 'Wild Women' of the New World with the land in which they live: both a feminine temptation and challenge to the masculinity of white male explorers and settlers. This myth keeps the white civilised woman at home, lest she too descends to the level of the savage woman, to the level of nature.[2] Thus the mother country stands for the safe and confining 'home' and the colonies for a farflung exterior world yet to be tamed by white men.

Claudia Knapman suggests the 'imagery of the Empire was feminine' characterised by Britannia and ruled by Queen Victoria (in all her prudery).[3] But the Empire was feminine in two distinct registers. The cloistered mother country, represented by the purity of middle-class white women, was contrasted with the untamed seductiveness of the frontier, represented by the animal passions of the 'Wild Women'. Thus expectant mothers retired home to deliver their babies in safety; wives, defeated by the rigours of frontier life, also retreated. In 1887 Lawes noted that 'only five ladies have attempted to live in British New Guinea. Of these two died, and the third is just leaving—now so reduced by fever that her only hope of life is in getting away'.[4] Captain C.A.W. Monckton, a resident magistrate in British Papua, voiced a widespread belief when he claimed that white women need 'a cool and bracing climate' and, unlike white men, were incapable of any exertion in the tropics.[5]

A man's 'ability to dress as he pleased, drink as much as he liked and be easy in his morals' spoke a freedom denied middle-class gentlemen at home.[6] The edge of empire was not only a 'man's country' but a 'bachelor's paradise'. With the sudden shrinking of Britain's imperial sway, a masculine 'imaginative space' was lost to those seeking escape from the artificial confines of 'civilisation'.[7] The arrival of white women, at least in significant numbers, polluted the masculine frontier and questioned the courage required to live and work there. It was not in the 'tame' civilisation of the cities but the dangerous 'wilds' of the back country where 'true manhood was forged'.[8]

A safe cloak was thus required for white women who ventured into the wilderness. Unescorted lady travellers, while few in number, travelled under the guise of eccentric gentlemen. But most women came as protected dependants, most particularly as wives. The majority of single women who came to the colonies came as mission workers; they were made dependants of missionary men in God's male-headed family.

The role of a wife

It was sometimes claimed that single women went to the colonies to 'catch a husband'. Thus the boats sailing to India before the 1930s were called 'fishing fleets'.[9] Nevertheless, most women went to the colonies as 'relative creatures' as the wife, mother, or child of someone else:

> You weren't accepted on your own merit. You were graded by the job your husband held. Managers didn't mix with the other men's wives much at all. If you were a manager's wife or you owned a plantation or a company you were automatically accepted into that group of people. No questions asked. [Daphney Bridgland]

If the wife or child of someone else, a woman possibly had little influence on the decision to relocate in the tropics; if a mother, the shape of her days was largely determined by the claims of childcare. A number of women comment that their lives changed utterly after the birth of their first child. Women without children joined more frequently in the social life beyond the boundaries of the home. Women who went to Papua New Guinea on their own account, especially mission workers, had more direct and unmediated relations with indigenous people, some of which led to strong friendships.

Most of the married respondents accepted unquestioningly the obligation of a wife to follow her husband's job. Mary Pulsford commented unfavourably on wives who arrived, were 'horrified' to discover what the Territory was like and refused to stay, forcing their husbands to resign:

> I think I was clear before I married my husband that was where

he wanted to be. If I was going to marry him I'd have to be able to cope with it too. I went there with the attitude that I was going to be able to cope with it. I was a bit worried as to just—it was so different—whether I would have what it took to make a go of it. But in fact I found it a very enriching experience to live there.

In the view of one of Callaway's informants, 'there were two types of wives: those who could stick it, and those who couldn't'.[10] 'Sticking it' grinning and bearing it, describes the lives of many uprooted wives. Another wife said, 'I didn't enjoy Nigeria, I put up with it'.[11] As a supernumerary Pat Andersen had to construct a role for herself:

Nev was running a hospital and I really had to find a role. In a place as isolated as Kapuna the only Europeans were at the sawmill on the other side of the river. I didn't know any of the local language at that stage. I was really looking for something to do. Later on I took first aid classes and sewing classes and things like that with the nurses and the wives of the medical boys—see that's the patronage: medical 'boys'. That plus the family certainly gave me something to do. I wasn't as busy in many respects as I would have been had I been back in Sydney . . .

Pat Andersen comments that this necessity to find jobs to fill her days disappeared 'once the family came'.

Glenda Riley argues that gender was the prime determinant of a woman's responsibilities.[12] Whether on the frontier of the American prairie or the plains and whatever the occupation of her husband, she was responsible for the household. In Papua New Guinea this involved at least two key tasks: relations with servants and managing the home, particularly in terms of ordering food and preparing or designing meals. It was not only married women who were expected to keep house. A single woman could also be required to stand in for a wife where none was available:

There were 5 roomy flats with verandahs back and front for the staff. These were close to the beach and looked out to sea. The first one was occupied by Groves, and the new male teacher, as well as Rev. Bishop who was the minister of the Anglican church in Rabaul and a close friend of Groves. I occupied the next one, and at that time 3 and 4 were occupied by 2 Government servants from Rabaul and their wives, and in the last one was domiciled the other senior school teacher and his wife. I took over the housekeeping for Flat No 1 and myself with the help of a native cook and 2 houseboys.[13]

Once established in a place a wife might grow to love it; but she was often required to leave a posting she had made into a home and follow her husband's job yet again. Pin and Claude Champion were ordered to move at such short notice that Pin had to pack her wet washing; she also complains that she had just got the fowls laying.[14] Halis (Namatanai) was Isabel Platten's only real home in Papua New Guinea, an 'island paradise'. She left it unwillingly when Gil Platten was promoted to George Brown College near Rabaul. Grace Young, whose husband succeeded Gil Platten to the Namatanai posting, also left Halis reluctantly. However she accepted the commitment to do 'God's work' by opening up the Highlands at Mendi. Grace Young recounts the episode, which reveals how a wife's feelings and needs are secondary to the minister's. Mr Gribble, the General Secretary, came to Halis in 1950 and while Grace Young was preparing dinner in the kitchen suggested the move to her husband:

> When they came in to the meal they talked to me about it and I said, 'Of course you know perfectly well I wasn't accepted on health grounds to come here in the first place'. 'Oh' he said 'That won't make any difference'. So, it was a bit of a bombshell, we were very happy in Namatanai. And I thought, well . . . I suppose if I was all right, I could stand what had been already, then maybe I could do that, and if that was God's will then that was it . . . We really did get attached to those people and I really didn't want to leave but—that's another thing.

White women as mothers

One of Callaway's respondents describes touring with her husband as her 'greatest joy'[15], while many women who went to India said that the tours were among their favourite memories.[16] Similarly Marjorie Murphy's fondest memories are of patrolling with her husband in the early years of their marriage. Elsie Champion greatly regretted that her husband would not allow her to accompany him on patrol.[17] Time and again, women report that pregnancy and motherhood deprived them of the pleasures of touring.[18] Pin and Claude Champion had no children, so she accompanied him on patrols, on one occasion being left entirely alone.[19] Motherhood meant no more patrols for Marjorie Murphy:

> We flew to Wewak where John was Acting District Officer till Reg Rigby arrived. I was a mother then and it was a full-time job

although you could get quite good assistance from the native women . . . I must admit I was envious of John flying around the district visiting the outstations, Maprik, Angoram and Aitape while I had to stay home with Kerry and the hermit crabs which clattered across the concrete floors. Despite my lack of experience with babies, I was thrilled at having one at long last . . .

It was while her children were in Australia that Isabel Platten was able to share in her husband's adventures. In 1937 Gil had taken a group of students to the Baining escarpment to study its fossils, and demonstrate to the students that the Bainings had once been on the seabed:

It had been an exciting trip. So exciting that Gil promised the villagers where they broke camp that they would return next term break and that he would bring me. The college term break came and off we went to the Baining mountains. The narrow slippery tracks were difficult. Somewhere along the track we made camp overnight but very early we were on our way. I remember using our hands as much as our feet, grasping vines etc. to move onward. One vivid memory was clambering around a large tree with very little space between it and nothingness . . . We were . . . very hungry but there was no time to start unpacking food. Along came some village women with piping hot taro, crusty and floury. We did find our butter and what a feast it was! For me that remains the most memorable and delicious food I have ever tasted.

When Isabel Platten returned to Halis after the war, again without her children, she sometimes accompanied Gil in his work:

Now I was free to go with Gil as he visited around the many villages and to meet the people who greeted me with much warmth. To the children I seemed particularly attractive. They wanted to touch me—sometimes hug me.

Pat Murray, too, notes the lost opportunities of motherhood:

Before we left Luburua, Anne had turned five and I had to start on the correspondence teaching racket. In 1960 Evelyn was born, and so what with two littlies and two older children with correspondence lessons, I was pretty much housebound. I used to still do the plantation books and write letters and do the medicines. I missed out on a certain amount. Peter used to go to town more often than I did because it was a lot of business going to town with small children and too expensive to stay overnight in the Club.

But one of the main concerns was that if we went in we went on a working day which meant that a day of school work was lost. And quite often the day after was lost, because there were things to be done and the children were tired and I was tired. You can't do that very often and maintain a decent standard of schooling. I was very particular about my kids' schooling . . . As a result I missed out on quite a few things I would have liked to go to. The D.C. might send out an invitation that 'the German ambassador (or some other interesting visitor) was visiting Kavieng and requests the pleasure of your company over lunch'. I rarely, if ever, went . . . So Peter went to these things and I only went to, I suppose, about one in every half dozen.

For some women, motherhood was an unadulterated blessing. Isabel Platten describes motherhood as a 'a completely different journey of my life'. Following their arrival in the Territory, Eva Butcher and Ann Deland write long letters home, discussing and evaluating political events. With the birth of a child, the letters change dramatically, focussing almost completely on the newborn infant. Letters are shorter and less frequent, silent testimony to the demands of childcare which filled up their hours. Ann Deland writes:

> Vanikoro,
> 3rd November, 1927
>
> Dear All of You:
> It is such a long time since I wrote to you that I scarcely know where to start, but of course I really do know, for the most engrossing topic of the moment is OUR SON, by name one Raymond John Deland, known to some people as 'Rastus' . . .
> I don't think I have ever seen a baby laugh so much for now he laughs aloud—you simply have to laugh to see him, for he is absolutely comical . . .
> [Some paragraphs later] I had better close down on the subject of our son and heir, or you will all be making humorous remarks about people with their first baby!

Isabel Platten used motherhood as a shield against involvement in the work expected of mission wives, a strategy that a number of white mothers adopted according to Jean Mannering: 'Some wives became involved with their families and didn't have much contact with the native people, and so didn't learn much of the language'. Ilias Taba worked for Isabel Platten at Namatanai and recalls her distance from mission life.

She was really worried about her children. When they wanted to go out, she called them back. If they didn't listen after she called a few times, she'd come out and pull them back to the house. They were really bigheaded when they were kids. But they were only bossy towards their mother—their father was always busy doing other things. After the marama shows us what to cook for the day she goes back to her room and reads books. She taught the kids their lessons.[20]

Giving birth in the tropics was not always without its attendant dangers. Pat Murray's sister Di was only saved from death by a Methodist mission nurse who, discovering that the placenta would not come away, went with Di in the back of the utility in a mad dash from Kimidan to Kavieng, the closest place which had the required drug:

They tore into town; they got Di to the hospital. But before they got to the hospital, Marjorie told me afterwards 'She was going. I could see her just going. I had to'—so she went in manually and [removed the placenta]. You get the average nurse out of hospital down here wouldn't be game to do it without the doctor's say so.

Daphney Bridgland lost a child:

One of my worst experiences was losing a son between my first daughter and my second daughter. I was about four and a half months pregnant and I got what they call breakbone fever, the Fijian form of Dengi. It was a dreadful thing. It takes you about six months to get over it. I knew when I was getting the pain that I was going to lose the baby. I had a temp around 105. At half past three in the morning I was walking around as I couldn't lie down. There was a gale blowing. So I waked Leon and said I must get to a doctor. He couldn't drive because there were eighteen lucena trees down across the road between our house and the main road. He had to get a big five ton truck with twenty boys in the back of it. They chopped the trees down and picked me up and off we went. They chopped all the other trees down across the road as we went. We arrived at Tunnel Hill just after daybreak and there was a huge breadfruit tree down, right across the road. We had to crawl over that in the rain. I walked up as far as Con Papas' Freezer on Malakuna Road, before Jack Chipper came along and picked us up and drove us up to Namanula to the hospital. Later that day I lost the infant. That was a grim night. But I was lucky, at least we did have roads even if they did have trees over them, I wasn't like the women who were on outlying plantations.

Of the sixty-five children born during their parents' missionary service in Papua before 1920, fifteen died.[21] Benjamin Butcher mentions concern for his child 'far from help when things went wrong'.[22] Isabel Platten believed the greatest price she could pay for living in New Guinea was the death of a child:

> The one thing I tried not to think about was if the children should have a really serious accident. I tried not to let them do anything dangerous, although we could probably fix a broken leg and suchlike. I remember seeing this little tombstone with "Margaret" on it— I think the greatest catastrophe would have been to lose a child.

None the less, Isabel Platten decided not to go into Rabaul for the birth of her second child, but to have Paquita at home with the help of two nurses:

> August 1931 our daughter arrived. Generally we white women went to Rabaul to be confined. As I did not like staying too long with our always kindly missionaries, believing it to be unfair to them, I gave it a great deal of thought. It could mean quite a spell for Newell and myself staying with one or other of our friends. One lesson I had already learned was that little children did not like being away from their home. Around me babies were being born to our native mothers all the time. I convinced myself that as I had already had a successful confinement which could have been handled by a mid-wife why not repeat the event. And so it was. Sister Daisy Coltheart came from Rabaul and Constance Brereton (a trained nurse) assisted at the birthing. On 12th August our daughter, Paquita Margaret, was born without much ado. We were both very well. Of course there was criticism from many; we accepted that. I did take a chance and I was glad I did.

A night birth in Kavieng in the 1950s was a public event:

> In those days the town power used to go off at ten o'clock. The hospital had a lot of pressure lamps but they had an arrangement that they would ring at any time and there was always a bloke on duty at the power station who could get the power up and start the lights. But Dobbie [the nurse] said 'I won't do that. Nothing's going to happen very much. Nothing that we can't do by pressure lamp for the next couple of hours. If I ring up and get the power on all those silly blighters who left their switches on when the lights went off are all going to wake up and say "Oh, oh, Pat Murray must have gone off" '. So I said 'Don't get the power on

for heaven's sake'. Anne was born about midday the next day, so there was no great panic. [Pat Murray]

For women who enjoyed motherhood, an early painful separation was in store if children were sent to boarding school. In the early days, this separation was unavoidable if children were to receive a secondary education. Even after the war:

> We could have sent them to Port Moresby High School but part of the motivation for me was just that there was a greater range of things they would get in their education here. And also I felt that their future appeared to us to lie in Australia and they had to know what that was all about. In fact, Ian who had had a very happy childhood, thought of Australia as a country where you went on holidays and you saw your relations and you joyfully went home to New Guinea afterwards. In fact as a very young child he wasn't at all shy of New Guinea people and he was pretty shy of white ones. He had to make all those adjustments. [Mary Pulsford]

Callaway describes the almost impossible role of a wife who must be content to be alone yet cheerfully put everything aside when her husband returns; who must know her husband's needs yet appear suitably awed and ignorant as to his work.[23] An advice book to wives concludes with a discussion of separations, putting the topic last. Callaway suggests this accurately reflected colonial cosmology, women were seen as wives but not mothers. In every colony mothers regularly, and sometimes routinely, put the role of wife ahead of that of mother. In pre-Bowlby days women were generally expected to send their children home to school, and think little of it. Yet this wrench was often painful. For over a decade, Isabel Platten was dogged by the conflicting obligations to her husband and her love for her children. She chose first for husband, then for children, then for husband again, balancing the perceived needs of her two children against those of her husband:

> It was time to return to Rabaul. It was at this time that I believe we made our biggest mistake. We would leave our children in Australia—Newell to go to a boarding school, Prince Alfred College, and Quita to stay with Gil's sister and her husband . . . I am not sure now why I accepted Gil's decision. I know only how devastated I was and it wasn't long before I was planning and saving to return to them. It took me about 18 months to do that.

Isabel returned to Australia, saw both her children, and returned to New Guinea with Quita. Correspondence lessons replaced schooling in Australia.

The family was united by the war but afterwards Isabel again confronted the demands of a separated family:

> 1946 went by quickly for Newell, Quita and me. I did not dwell on the reality that one day I would be told a passage had been booked for me to return to New Britain. I was happy to be with my children and dreamed of perhaps asking Gil to return to South Australia. I even dreamed that perhaps the Conference of South Australia would reward Gil and would, in their combined 'goodness of heart' generously appoint him to a circuit which would allow us to keep our family at home while they finished their tertiary education. I even thought that by making a few enquiries of some of the Conference leaders, I could begin to plan a strategy towards that end. How very naive I was. Reasonably I approached the Conference secretary to put before him our needs as a family, and if we returned to the 'Home Work' we would need to be near the university. I had no qualms of conscience, believing that any circuit that got Gil as their minister would be most fortunate. This man turned on me with outrageous accusations concerning my (to me quite innocent) impertinence, audacity etc. in thinking that by such an appeal I could get preferential treatment. Only Conference could make such decisions. Knowing full well about the wheeling and dealing concerning the postings of various ministers—and what I was probably guilty of myself at this time—I left the secretary's office more than a little humiliated, and much more cynical about the whole church scene.

The mission leader made it very clear that family considerations came a long way behind the obligations of a minister to carry out God's (and man's) work.

In many ways then, practising motherhood in a colony was a hard role—dangerous, attenuated, forcing choices between a mother's needs, a child's interests and a husband's job. Women who chose for their children were sometimes seen as deserters, especially if this need took them back to Australia. Women who chose for their husbands received little compassion from an administration that only gradually made it possible for white women to raise their children in comfort and security in the Territory.

God's family in the missions

Between the middle of the last century and the early decades of the present one, a handful of middle-class women escaped the confines of Victorian domesticity and became Spinsters Abroad.[24] Invariably they felt confined by the 'duties' required of a daughter or wife to tend to ailing and demanding male relatives, and the constraints of a male-dominated education system which refused to recognise their training or talents. They were lured by freedom and movement, promised in the tales of their peripatetic male relatives and family friends. This freedom contrasted sharply with their own lives, in which they could not even walk unchaperoned down a public street. Although these women escaped their 'duty' for 'self-fulfillment' abroad, they continued to weave aspects of obligation into their travels. They collected money for philanthropic causes, specimens for scientific endeavours, and excavated sites to expand archaeological knowledge.[25] The siren call of freedom was made more enthralling by the desire to face danger, to go where white civilisation had not yet left its mark. The repressed sexuality of their youth found a late flowering in the sensuous pleasures of new sights and experiences.

At home they remained women; even after their adventures they were only 'lady travellers' with no scientific status.[26] Abroad they were white, and shared in the power of colonial rulers. They adopted the racial superiority which allowed them to command servants, travel unmolested, and draw crowds of interested people to their activities. The indigenous people often addressed them as 'sir' or by an equivalent male title and endowed them with almost superhuman power.[27] Beatrice Grimshaw when travelling in Fiji was addressed as 'Andi' an honorific title used by Fijians to denote royalty.[28] Gertrude Bell, despite her first-class examination results at Oxford, was denied the award of a degree because she was a woman: 'But she could write excitedly to her father from Syria that "in this country—they all think I was a Person" '.[29]

From the 1920s lady travellers began to lose their special status. Their role as powerful representatives of the Empire depended on travelling alone; if in the company of white men they were ignored. Once wives came in sufficient numbers to a colony, a dependent and distinct place for white women was marked out. The lady travellers, whatever their own plans, were confined to this space. Colonial administration became a more bureaucratic affair and lady travellers lost their roles as informal advisors to governors. Science became more professionalised and the findings of their 'field trips' lost status.[30] Beatrice Grimshaw, friend and advisor to Murray, is probably the best-known 'lady traveller' to Papua. Lucy Evelyn Cheeseman (1881–1969), a naturalist from the British Museum, spent more than six years in the interior of New Guinea in the 1930s and made extensive field trips to the highlands of Papua. Her last expedition was in 1954–5, when she was 74 years old. She published twenty-four books, four for children. While she was in the Hebrides, the inland tribes put a '*tabu*' on her, 'signifying that her personage was sacred'.[31]

Independently-minded women also worked as philanthropists and reformers in colonies such as India between the 1860s and the 1930s. Barbara Ramusack's study of five such women reveals that four were single, and none had the responsibilities of motherhood when they came to India.[32] Most were close to their fathers, whose relatively early death left them free to pursue their own projects. All saw India as a location that allowed greater possibilities of social experimentation, professional development or spiritual satisfaction than were available to them in Britain.

Lady travellers required an independent income; they were the elite among single women who ventured over the seas. Other women, like Beatrice Grimshaw, had to work their passage. Sometimes women 'of spirit, independence and "respectability" ' paid for their adventures by working as governesses, for example in India in the 1920s and 1930s.[33] However, the great majority of spinsters abroad chose the missionary route to tropical adventure. The religious revival of the nineteenth century allowed these women to fling open their front doors and escape Victorian domesticity for participation in public life.[34] Having few other opportunities for advancement, personal authority, vocational security, independence and status, single women formed 60 per cent of female missionaries in China in 1890.[35] By the early twentieth century the women's missionary movement was the largest women's movement in North America and was responsible for sending and supporting over two-thirds of the overseas mission force to China between 1900 and 1949.[36] The Society for Promoting Female Education in the East operated from the mid-nineteenth century. The *Female Missionary Intelligencer* in January 1897 called for lady missionaries:

The Committee of the Society for Promoting Female Education in the East are anxious to secure the services of several ladies for Japan, China, India, and the Holy Land . . . Personal piety, love for souls and good health are indispensable. Private means or friends to help advisable in some of the cases.[37]

Professional women's medicine was developed in Canton in the late nineteenth century by American women, outsiders in the medical profession at home. American female doctors founded and headed separate women's medical institutions to train Chinese women as physicians.[38] By the 1920s, the tide of women's overseas missionary work was beginning to turn, and not only because other employment options were opening for women. Women's claims to spiritual equality brought attacks from men in the mission field.[39] The all-female mission societies in the four largest Protestant denominations were closed down by the 1920s.[40] Female missionaries had too often to be reminded of the 'natural and predestined' 'headship of men in ordering the affairs of the Kingdom of God'.[41] With the closure of the female branches, the missions lost their female dues-paying members and could no longer staff their overseas posts.

In 1891 Flora Timms was 'called' to India from Cowra in New South Wales. Margaret McNeill wrote of her in 1899: 'A strong woman, one might say there was a touch of masculinity in her make-up, and in her sense of humour and wit, yet none more tender than she in her profession, especially with little children'.[42] She worked solely with other female missionaries near Madras, until in 1912 an ordained man was put at the head of the mission. After 1923 'there were no single women missionaries in the field, formerly manned by women'.[43]

Father Bachelier MSC comments on the absence of the sisters from mission histories: 'We do speak of them without naming them. Wherever we are, they are there too'.[44] So they were, as Langmore notes. One third of the missionaries to Papua during the forty years before 1914 were women. Of the 327 European missionaries, 115 were women; the Sacred Heart Mission had 65 sisters, the Anglican mission had 28 women among its 74 missionaries; the Methodist Mission had 22 sisters; only the London Missionary Society had none. There were also 29 LMS wives and 18 Methodist wives.[45] The first single female missionary to arrive in the Pacific came in 1845 to Wallis Island. The first missionary women to arrive in Papua were a contingent of Daughters of Our Lady of the Sacred Heart, who came from France in 1887. The first two Methodist sisters sailed in 1892.[46] Initially this was seen as a rash experiment, but soon mission stations were clamouring for women. In 1904 a woman established a new mission in the Solomon Islands.

Both Bishop Navarre and George Brown of the Methodist Mission recognised the need for female missionaries to meet and mould the influence of indigenous women.[47] Benjamin Butcher of the London Missionary Society also noted the influence of indigenous women. One of his female workers, Gotadou, was an accomplished linguist and preacher. Butcher lured her away from a life of ministering 'to the lusts of men' to a life of ministering to God and advocating the values of a Christian marriage and home.[48]

The Catholic and Methodist sisters and the Methodist wives worked exclusively among the women and girls.[49] Education invariably included domestic tasks such as sewing and hygiene. The wives also became involved in 'women's business' particularly childbirths:

The usual set-up young mother in darkened hut sitting on log over hole in ground . . . after an attempt at manual removal [of the placenta] and fearing a haemorrhage and the girl's life I managed to obtain permission to take her to Kavieng.

The truck was prepared with a bed of leaves etc. and we left about 3 am next morning. Result—successful operation.[50]

Dorothea Freund despaired that the women would ever learn to help each other in childbirth:

I found the woman had just given birth to her baby in a sweet potato field, and the baby was lying in the mud. It took quite a lot of talking to have the woman carried into a hut so I could clean her up.[51]

Even Isabel Platten, who firmly eschewed most missionary work, was caught up in saving the life of a discarded twin. She gave the baby to Malagai, the only childless married woman on the station:

> Malagai was one of the apparently dullest in the group . . . I sent for Malagai to come and see me and explained to her about the baby and asked if she would help me. Never have I witnessed such a transfiguration, as I was privileged to be part of that day. As Malagai cradled the tiny baby her face lit up. Gone the dull eyes, the disinterested expression. She came alive. As time went on and Malagai and the infant bonded together Gil and I thought it would be best if Malagai and her husband could lawfully adopt the infant. This was satisfactorily arranged between all parties and Moses (name chosen by Malagai) became her son.

Generally the missionary's wife was expected to be a 'helpmeet' to her husband, to set an example with 'the gracious influence of wise and thoughtful womanhood'.[52] Mission wives were to be passive purveyors of middle-class Christian values[53]; some Mission Boards rebuking them for overstepping this role.[54] When Benjamin Butcher brought his bride Eva to Kikori, he was pleased that she could 'greet them looking clean and presentable'. Later she set an example of 'husband and wife working together in happy companionship'.[55] Despite her youth, Eva Butcher became known as *mamu* or mother, while her husband was *abea* or father. Benjamin Butcher, however, later became *copu-abea* or father of the villages; the equality of their domestic companionship did not extend to comparable public recognition.[56] The wives often complained that the church hierarchy ignored them, one being stung into writing: 'I should like you to know that a wife and mother can also burn with missionary enthusiasm'.[57] Other Anglican wives resisted the stereotype of heroine or martyr: 'Beatrice Abel once said crossly to her husband "I personally have never knowingly risked my life for Christ's sake. Don't say I have" '.[58]

One of the three tasks of the Daughters of Our Lady of the Sacred Heart was to see to the mission's material needs, as cooks, seamstresses, cowhands, cleaners, farmers, gardeners.[59] Bishop Navarre described their work as 'all the things that the numerous occupations of the Missionary do not allow him to do'. Indeed, they were the Catholic mission's housewives. As a result of the death of Sister Joachim, Navarre accepted that the missionary zeal of some young and authoritarian fathers had placed impossible demands on the sisters. He gave them their own Superior and moved them farther away from the priests, although they chose to continue cooking and laundering for the priests.[60] Physical separation did not negate the subordinate status of Catholic sisters. Evelyn Cheeseman reports meeting Sister Rosa of Mount Tafa in New Guinea.[61] The father was a 'remarkably understanding man' allowing the sisters much freedom. None the less when Sister Rosa ordered the stores, the father 'crossed out what he thought unnecessary and the Father didn't like jam' so he eliminated it from Sister Rosa's order.

Daphney Bridgland notes:

> The Catholic mission, look at the wonderful work it's done. Vunapope is the most incredible place. They saved my life twice . . . and the sisters there are such beautiful women. They work so hard. The priests don't; the sisters spoil them, wait on them hand and foot. They have the best of wines and the best cigars and the best food. One day I called in and Sister Mary Bernadette said 'Are you going up to the printers?' and I said 'Yes'. She said 'Would you try and get me some offcuts of paper, so I have something to write notes on'. The sisters even had difficulty getting offcuts of paper. So I went up and they gave me a great stack which I took down to the sister.

Sister Bohdana Voros describes the trying conditions just after the war:

> For almost ten years I didn't have a table, only a bed, and I'd sit on a box. After school I came home exhausted. The priests had no vestments. We had to make their vestments, raincoats and all sorts of things we needed. I came home from Madang one day, and I can remember I was exhausted, after the whole day in that heat. They said 'We can't have our evening tea. The boxes [from the Provincial in the United States] have to be unpacked'. I lay down on the concrete and I waited until I regained a bit of strength. It was very exhausting on the coast . . .

Several years later when a generator for electricity was installed, it was the father's decision when the generator was switched off between half past nine and ten at night: 'We had to go to bed before that and then father switched it off'.

Within the Methodist Mission, the sisters were generally viewed as subordinate, not only to the minister but also his wife. One mission wife, Mrs Bromilow, 'with all the authority of a married woman over single, supervised them like recalcitrant schoolgirls' even to upbraiding the General Secretary for publishing a sister's letter ahead of her own in the Missionary Review.[62] The minister and his wife were the *talatala* (father) and *marama* (mother). Jean Mannering, who first went as a *marama* claims there was no difference in treatment between wives and sisters. However she retained her title of *marama* even when she lost her husband and became a sister. Following the birth of her son Newell, Isabel Platten spent some time with the sisters at Raluana, near Rabaul:

> Living with them gave me an insight into the work they did. Perhaps I should explain about the division of labour. The sisters were unmarried and were using their lives caring for, mostly, women and young children, and at Raluana a large number of mixed parentage girls . . . They also looked after a clinic in the nearby village . . . I was deeply impressed with what my friends were so successfully doing and marvelled at from what depths of character came such love and dedication. Rather sadly I knew I did not possess it. I was only 21 but I was married and so I was accorded a higher status than the sisters. If we were introduced to anybody, I would be introduced before the sisters. That made me angry, when I thought of the work they did. But you couldn't do anything to alter it.

All but two of the *talatalas* had been killed in the war, and were replaced by much younger men. The sisters who returned to New Guinea were thus older and more experienced than most of the new ministers. Dorothy Pederick comments on the resulting ruptures to the hierarchy:

> When Dorothy [Beale] went to Kimidan, there were two older sisters there, and the minister was a young Queenslander, Roland Barnes . . . Yes, and there was a bit of friction there too, a couple of older experienced sisters and a young Australian couple. That's the only time I remember knowing of real friction. Dorothy was a very forthright go-ahead lady. What Dorothy said went. There were two houses being put up there. This is as I remember it . . . She had decided that this would be the sister's house because it was nearer to the hospital and the minister thought that as it was the one where people came into the mission station, it would be his house.

Because anyone approaching the mission station would come to that house, and it would be right for the visitors to come to the talatala's house. And there was a definite tussle there. I think Dorothy won. The visitors always came to Dorothy's house.

The talatala was supposed to have the say, even in the hospital affairs. You had to get around it a bit. Basically you got on well with them. You were good friends and you were Christian people who solved your problems in a Christian way. I remember being a bit angry with Jeff Robinson a few times because he was so high-handed in hospital things. I thought it's not really his job. But then on other occasions I was very glad of his help.

Dorothy Beale was the first triple-certificate nursing sister to join the Methodist Mission in New Guinea. She worked first at the Stewart Hospital in Vunairima and taught hygiene and baby care to the senior girls' classes, until the outbreak of the Second World War. After the war she became well-known as a dedicated but strict nurse. She used her furloughs to fill perceived deficiencies in her education, for example training in medicine dispensing, dental treatment, and complications in childbirth. In 1948 she was put in charge of the new hospital at Kimidan (New Ireland) and retired in 1954.

Ironically, women in the Anglican mission formed neither a separate order as the Catholic sisters did nor a separate branch as in the Methodist mission, yet were recruited as individuals and retained a separate status. Rather than resigning on marriage, they were encouraged to see their vocation as a life service and received the same allowance of twenty pounds a year that men received.[63] They taught the boys as well as the girls, and sometimes took charge of stations, exercising authority over men and boys in the process.[64]

Women as workers: the mission sisters

Doris Groves went to Papua shortly after the First World War:

On the first morning about 500 children assembled on the mission grounds. The senior school marched off to their classes and rather more than half of all the children under 10 were left for me. We then marched into the infant schoolroom . . . During the weekend I had learned several sentences in Motu from Mrs Clark such as stand up (Atoriasi) Sit down (Helai Diho) What is this . . . Oibi Yes, Lasi, No. Come here (Aoma) and one or two others to help me get organised.

I felt deeply grateful that I had been well trained in blackboard drawing with coloured chalks. I drew pictures—such as—the sea, the sun, trees, a house, scenes with boats, birds etc. The children told me what they were in Motu, and I told them in English and wrote the Motu word and English word on the board. We were teaching each other, thus I learned Motu in which I had to pass an exam later, according to mission requirements.

Two senior boys and two senior girls were allotted to help me, and I divided the children into 5 classes according to age—and as in a country school I went from class to class in rotation whilst teaching the 3 Rs. All joined together for stories, singing etc.

The girls were dressed in grass skirts, and the boys in short calico lava lavas, which many of them removed as soon as they left the school door and with them folded under their arm ran back to the village, unclothed.

Some were very clean and bright, and quite a few dirty and unkempt, with very dirty running noses; so we made some rules for hygiene. All the village houses were built over the water on the shore, so all children must have a bathe in the sea, before coming to school; if they came dirty there would be a tub of water, and they would be given a bath in school. Fortunately this only had to happen a few times.

We cured the nose problem by morning handkerchief drill—of course the children did not have handkerchiefs, so I decided to use a roll of toilet paper torn into squares, and after the drill they kept the paper as a handkerchief, and soon there was never a dirty nose. Later the sale of the children's raffia and pandanus work, kept us in paper, and later still enabled us to buy a piano.

After the war Jean Mannering taught with the Methodist Overseas Mission at George Brown College at Vatnabara on the Duke of York Islands, and then at Vunairima on New Britain, when the College was relocated there four years later. She left the mission field in 1953. Jean Mannering produced an English to Kuanua dictionary, and several readers in Kuanua, starting from the shaky foundations provided by two weeks' training at Vunairima: 'they taught us a few phrases that would be useful to us like "Do it this way", "Don't", "Come here", "Go away", "How much is it?". That was very limiting—you couldn't really get very far'. (It is interesting that most of the phrases taught were ordering phrases (do this, do that). Jean Mannering helped prepare lessons for the local teachers, who had no books. She gave lessons in English and mathematics and also gave some lessons to the wives:

> I got a very wide vocabulary when I prepared all these different lessons, so I decided to compile a dictionary: English into Kuanua. It took me about seven years. First of all I turned Mr Linggood's Kuanua book back into English. As I prepared all these lessons, I wrote down new words I found and their meanings. When I thought I had about as much as I could, I sat down with two teachers, one from the Kabakada area and one from the Raluana area, and checked through what I'd written to see if it was right.

Jean married the Rev. Con Mannering in 1956, returning to New Britain in May 1959 where they lived first at Vatnabara and then Vunairima, before leaving at the end of 1965. Con had bought some land at Dromana, on the Mornington Peninsula in Victoria. A friend of both the Mannerings, Saimon Gaius (appointed Bishop of the New Guinea Islands Region in 1968), spent a year in Australia doing translation work on the Bible in 1949. During that time he helped Con Mannering build their house at Dromana; his signature is on one of the rafters in the roof.

Sister Aquilonia Ax was an administrator of the Holy Spirit mission centre after the war:

> Mingendi as a mission station consists of a number of farflung smaller centres, nearly all housing a teacher and a catechist and a place for worship—a church. On the station itself we had a large church built by an Australian businessman from Sydney, single teacher classrooms with three European teachers (one from Melbourne for several years), a hospital for general patients and a maternity clinic, pre- and post-natal care and child welfare. We fed about 200 people daily, all living on the station, and among them 50 boys and 50 girls taken as the best students from outlying stations and living within walking distance of Mingendi. All would attend our school to prepare for secondary school in Kundi, at first for boys only but later co-ed.
>
> My duty was to teach the bigger boys and girls, hire the teachers for the station schools and supervise their work. There were so many aspects of the various groups, the problems the sisters faced to assure a smooth running and satisfactory handling of the situation. The sisters were capable and responsible. Sr Veronica bought all

necessary food supplies from native women and laid out before noon daily the supply for individuals or families or groups. The staple food was the kaukau—a kind of sweet potato that lasted no longer than a week, then it was unfit even for pigs.

Sister Bohdana Voros had considerable autonomy on Manam Island:

> The people on Manam Island are unique. Separated from everybody by sea, they feel masters of their destiny. They are carefree, humorous, developed their own customs, enjoying the nights of the full moon. They can sing beautifully, dance graciously, are slim, good looking, clever, love sport and music.
>
> Manam was fourteen to eighteen hours by boat from Madang, depending on the roughness of the sea. On the whole island one father was here, one father was at another station and we five sisters, that was all. Two nurses, two teachers, one cook. More or less it was on all stations like that.
>
> In Manam we had about 350 pupils. Children were bright, there was no trouble with teaching, rather with the discipline. They were lively and active like the volcano.
>
> On Fridays they cleaned the whole station and grade six girls went to the church to sweep it. Each one has assigned her job, what she has to do on the side and in front of the altar. They have brooms made from the ribs of coconut leaves. They were in the sacristy. In the evening the superior [visiting] from Rome told me 'You should have seen the girls. They took the brooms out of the sacristy, and the first one as she was going held the broom up and was dancing around the altar, and then the second one, all of them dancing, dancing. It was so graceful how they danced'. I said 'You can tell them a hundred times . . .' They do whatever comes to their mind.

Dorothy Pederick grew up on a farm in Wagin, the only daughter in a family of five sons. She went to New Guinea as a nurse with the Methodist Mission in 1947 and worked there until 1967, except for a period in Australia between 1955 and 1957. My first sight of her was a figure pedalling down the road on her bicycle, having just spent the morning working at the Wagin historical village, one of her many community activities. Dorothy describes the routine at the head station of Vatnabara:

> At Vatnabara, when I was first there, it was the site of the George Brown College where people trained as pastor teachers. So at six you got up and went to the hospital just to see how everybody

was in the morning and make sure everybody was doing what was expected. There was a programme to help the trainee missionaries' wives and two of those would be on roster. I think it was week and week about so by early morning they'd be there lighting the coppers and getting some water ready to bath all the babies in the village. It was quite a village of trainee missionaries. They were from mid teenagers to perhaps thirty year olds. We had people like Saimon [Gaius] and Eliuda Laen who'd been in college before the War, back to finish their training and go out. Gaius was a teacher and Eliuda was a student.

So at the hospital while the students' wives were getting the bath routine ready and waiting for the rest of the village to come, there were two Duke of York girls who were Dorothy's [Beale] helpers working as nurses. They'd be getting the people awake and suggesting that they get a wash and anybody who couldn't walk, they'd take them a dish of water. Old army equipment, old tin bowls, they were the babies' baths and the patients' baths, and all the water was carried by buckets from tanks and put into coppers to warm them, and taken out again. So I'd check on everybody. M & B, the sulphidamide drugs, were just being used then. So anybody on M & B for pneumonia and so on had to be given that four hourly round the clock. I don't think there was one night that I wasn't up at 2 a.m. in those six and a half years because I didn't think to let anyone else do it. It was my responsibility; I went and did a round at two o'clock, did a round again at six in the morning, and then went back for breakfast.

Jean [Mannering] would be getting her school regime under way and I'd have done my quick trip to the hospital and we'd have breakfast. And then she'd go off to school, I think they started at half past eight, and I'd be back at hospital then. We did the hospital outpatients first usually and that would be anything from 20 to 30 people, tropical ulcers, injuries. They'd be sleeping at the hospital—but there again each village was encouraged to build their own house at the hospital, so when they came in (plus family, hangers-on, anybody), they'd live in their village house.

After breakfast we did the outpatients work, and there were routine things. Twice a week, maybe Monday and Thursday, it was giving injections for yaws, and penicillin was the answer but we didn't have it then. It was a preparation of arsenic and had to be given intravenously and it was quite dicey. You might have thirty of these intravenous injections, two mornings a week. Well as soon as you got your immediate outpatient work done, you started on that day's special work. Another morning programme was an ante-natal clinic, and often the mums were waiting at the hospital in the last weeks of their pregnancy, perhaps two months. Because if there was a rough sea they wouldn't be able to come in anyway. Besides the village mums, the students' wives would also come across from the College houses nearby for the ante-natal clinic.

Another morning each week, I used to walk through to Ulu, about two miles or perhaps a mile and a half away, to see the indentured labour line there. It was very methodical, very 'army' they'd all line up and I'd walk along and look at them all, and each one would turn around and show the soles of his feet, to see the sores they used to get or injuries to toes. I guess it was a labour ordinance requirement. Some plantations had medical personnel, or if not the boss or assistant boss did it. But because the mission sister was new there and it was a mission plantation, we did it that way.

Later in the morning, by the time I'd got injections over (or whatever the day's work was), the students' wives would have got the baby bathing all done, the floors all swept out with their coconut brooms, the lysol swished around and then it was recess for the college boys and they all came up for their little bits of cough mixture, eye drops. There might be fifty of them in half an hour, and that was sort of busy, and the two nurse girls would be helping; we used to have two students on roster helping too. One would be putting on gentian violet or putting in eye drops and I would be giving mixtures. And then they'd all be back at school, it would be over in half an hour.

So it was fairly regimented. People used to say 'Did you have any time off?'. Well we nearly always had time off straight after lunch. We didn't have days off, Sunday was the same as any other day, but we had time. I used to say to people who asked me that, 'Well, what about a mum with a family, does she ever have time off? No of course she doesn't, but she has time to make a frock or read a book'. We had nice times fitted into our days.

The bell went for the school boys at one o'clock and usually between twelve and one we were definitely on our backs or having a rest. And then at one, schoolboys were allotted to the nursing team to do jobs for us if we wanted. If we wanted the garden cleaned or the grass cut or drains at the hospital cleaned out, we went with the boy to tell him what was wanted. We'd run round and get things organised. Then there'd be a bit of time before afternoon outpatients, about four to five p.m. At one o'clock we'd get the work boys going and I'd be up at the hospital at two o'clock and I'd patrol around to see to medicines there. [Dorothy Pederick]

Besides the patient, other members of the family would come to the hospital, and watch the sister's ministrations:

If Mum was the patient the under twos wouldn't sleep away from Mum, so they'd be on the bed with her, under the bed. Dad would be in and out, Grandma would be there cooking for all of them. If the mother was the patient a lot of the family came in. If it was the father, it was sometimes an older child, who could bring water for him and Mum would come and go with food. She'd be looking after the garden and the family at home. [Dorothy Pederick]

In outlying villages, people were often less secure about coming into the hospital for treatment. Dorothy Pederick came close to kidnapping a baby with a hare-lip:

But they said 'Oh no, we don't want to take it away from home'. I remember the boat boy standing near me, I was arguing with the father, trying to persuade him to let this baby come, and it would need to go over to the doctor at Kavieng, to come to the main hospital and he was saying 'Oh no, he didn't want it to go'. And the boat boy was saying 'Talk to the mother, sister'. He could see that she was a bit more interested. She said 'Oh yes, I'll give it a go'. So in the end we were getting ready to leave, I had the baby in my arms and we'd been talking about it. And I said 'You go and get your things, I'll take the baby to the boat and you come in a minute'. I walked out to the boat, and thought afterwards that was a dreadful thing for anybody to have done. But it worked, they came, and when in a few months it was back, beautifully mended, that made other similar babies more allowed to go. [Dorothy Pederick]

Constance Fairhall suggests a wide range of tasks for the 'medical missionary' including taking Sunday service in a white church:

A medical missionary has all sorts of fun. Amongst other things, she helps make native gardens, lies flat on her back scraping the underneath of canoes to remove barnacles, beautifies graveyards, cleans out hen-houses, drags along sackloads of stones to make roads, hauls up buckets of water to scrub hospital floors, goes out night fishing (and catches nothing), paints the inside of her house, and tries to be a carpenter. Incidentally, please don't believe that a missionary's life is to show the natives how to do things, and then leave them to it. It is only when one does things with them that one finds out how much fun and joy there is in it. I am taking a Sunday service in Port Moresby white church soon. I shall take it on 'The joy of living'.[65]

Treading on a man's territory

Because most colonial administrations started with few women, white male clerks and secretaries worked in offices, indigenous male domestic servants worked in homes, indigenous women were taken as sexual partners, and wives remained at home to perform the only role left to them, reproducing the race.[66] Gradually white women took on some of the other functions. They came to colonies as missionaries and nurses in the first instance; later they came as mothers and wives; still later they became junior administrators.[67]

Each of these intrusions into a male world provoked hostile responses until an accommodation was reached. One junior administrative officer was greeted with 'I do not like women in offices. I think women are alright in Bed and Nowhere Else'.[68] The first three women to win the right to medical instruction at Madras Medical College were told by the male surgeon that 'although he could not prevent them from walking around the wards with him, he was determined not to teach them'.[69] Callaway reports that the only overt antagonism of Nigerian men toward women as colonial administrators occurred when one was asked 'what had become of the great British Empire if all they could send out was women. If there were no men left, then Nigeria could supply them'.[70] She also notes that the Emir in 1930 was unable to accept the services of the first female doctor until he decided to regard her as 'a worker, not a woman'.[71]

Joan Refshauge tells such a story:

> I will begin at Canberra where it all started. When both my husband and I were ultimately discharged from the Army he informed the Department of Territories he would return to Papua New Guinea and as was usual in those days he paid a courtesy call on the Secretary of the Territories in Canberra. While with him, he discussed the possibility of me going with him to the Provisional Administration's Department of Health. I was taken to see the Secretary and he then told me I would be welcome for they were considering starting infant and maternal care and that was the only work I could do— 'Because the Territory was a man's country and men expected men to look after them'. I could never work in a native hospital except

if, as was unlikely, babies or mothers were patients. To attend a male patient would endanger me or other European women . . .

It was not until my retirement that I learned why my appointment had been delayed. At a party the then Director of Health read out from the file a letter from the Acting Director of Health when I had applied. He had informed Canberra that the appointment, a woman medical officer, would lower the standard of medicine in the Territory. But his successor squashed that. There was much mirth when this was read out—but it is an interesting thought that the same sentiments have been recently expressed for many have heard or read it: that the increasing number of women entering the medical profession will reduce its status as it has done for the teaching profession.[72]

The Director of Health, Dr John Gunther, supported Dr Refshauge's appointment. In 1949 the Administrator, J.K. Murray, noted that more female medical practitioners were required so that contact with the 'native women shall be fully welcomed and effective'.[73] Contrariwise, Joan Refshauge envisaged problems in dealing with male Papuan patients:

[At Samarai] I appeared to be accepted by the people without any objection, the native people worried me though for most of the patients were men. However I had a good co-operative EMA [European Medical Assistant] and native orderlies and I never saw a male patient without the EMA and a respected native orderly with me. Also before any native patient was seen by me it was explained to him it was a woman doctor with the same skills as their male doctor who I was relieving. Another thing—if any condition was under the rami [lap lap or length of material worn from waist down] I made the EMA do the examination and report to me. If I felt it necessary for me to then examine the region, it was explained to the patient and my two escorts were present and interpreted what I said . . .

I had to go very steadily, because again I found that men didn't like working with women, and it was no use being a new broom when my sex wasn't accepted . . .

When I returned to Moresby I was appointed M.O. [Medical Officer] Port Moresby . . . It was not long before the objection came. I was quite unaware of the incident at the time. The R.S.L. asked the Director to attend a meeting when they would be discussing health. It all boiled down to discussing the bad policy of appointing a woman doctor. There was the Director and his Assistant Director, both men, and the R.S.L. wanted their men, at least, treated by these men. But the Director told the R.S.L. they had a fully qualified and experienced M.O. at the hospital and if they didn't want her they could go without anyone. I was not told of this until a few weeks later. I must admit I felt hurt, resentful and also thought it funny but I did see their point. It was quite an abnormal community life at that stage and some of the men were worried because their wives were trying to reform them and I presume thought as a woman I would talk.

I also had trouble at the native hospital. I knew if I could keep an EMA for six weeks he'd settle down and work with me. But I was bailed up on more than one occasion and told quite plainly by EMAs 'I will not work under a woman—I have no intention of taking orders from a woman'. Well I'd agree it must be tough on them but as I was responsible I would take the responsibility of my own mistakes but not take on anyone else's and I would suggest they had the choice of trying me out for six weeks or asking for a posting. I also took to dropping in if I had a spare moment and, by discussing interesting patients, teach them.[74]

White men refused to be subordinate to Joan Refshauge, either as EMAs or as patients. She handled these problems with sensitivity and concern for the men's injured pride. Apparently, even white women saw her role as a disruption of their expectations:

There was quite a bit of resentment among the doctors' wives, I found, against a woman doctor. They hadn't had a woman doctor in the Territory until that date, except that Lady Cilento had been in the Territory with her husband when he was in Rabaul for a short time.

[My mother] also had to bear the burden of hearing criticism of me, and gossip. 'You know, my dear, I think you ought to know . . .', 'You know what I think of you and your daughter, but . . .' and these things she would gradually let me know. One of the biggest things that hurt her, was a woman saying that she couldn't go to the hospital and go round and see all the people, because I had insisted on visiting hours. This was because women who had nothing to do would come in, look over screens to see who was there, and then gossip about it down in the town. The hospital was not supposed to give out any information. I insisted that we have the same ethics as in Australia: that what happened in the hospital was not to be discussed outside.[75]

In fact there is some evidence that Joan Refshauge was more comfortable with either single career women (like her Matron, Taffy Jones) or the Papua New Guineans:

> Mother was kept very busy with all the charity organisations. I asked her not to go onto any committees, because committees with women are always a bit troublesome, and there is always a lot of picking.[76]

Single nurses resented Joan Refshauge's appointment because they were looking forward to an 'eligible gentleman'. Callaway's respondents also report resentment by wives, especially of women earning more than their husbands. But each was deprived of what the other had: married women had husband and children, single women autonomy and adventure. Because of the marriage bar a woman could not have both.[77]

Female nurses came early to most colonies for two reasons; it was a female-dominated occupation while cross-sex treatment of patients was often considered undesirable.[78] The government hospitals were staffed almost entirely by men, which meant that white medical assistants turned away indigenous pregnant women.[79] Female nurses and doctors seemed inevitably to concentrate their attention on infant and maternal welfare.[80] It would appear from Joan Refshauge's memoirs that infant and maternal health work was the line of least resistance. Although Joan Refshauge never received any complaints from male Papuan patients, the Papua New Guinean population endorsed gender distinctions in medical work. Local women by-passed government hospitals to attend the mission hospitals, while male patients went more willingly to government hospitals.[81]

Pat Murray's secretarial job in 1939 with the Kavieng administration was a direct result of loss of manpower due to the war. She rewrote the first report the District Officer gave her to type, explaining:

> 'Well sir, I thought you'd like me to take your notes and type it up as best I could in report form. I don't really know much about typing reports. I just hope it's okay'. He looked at me and I think he was wondering whether I was trying to be smart or not, and saw I wasn't. He said 'That's all right'. And do you know what the old bugger used to do after that. He used to send rough notes and I used to have to expand them into letters: 'Write a letter to the D.O. in Madang and tell him we can't possibly do so and so because of this or the other'.

In her violation of status boundaries, Pat Murray's revision of the District Officer's report achieved legendary proportions. The next District Officer accused Pat Murray: 'I understand you're in the habit of tampering with Mr Penglaze's correspondence'.

According to Callaway, women were given administrative positions in Nigeria as a buffer between the rising Nigerian ranks and the departing white male civil servants.[82] Even so, there was considerable resistance from subordinate men to the recruitment of women. A mechanism which is often used to prevent contamination of masculinity in these circumstances is internal differentiation of the workforce. Thus male lawyers monopolise criminal and corporate legal work, leaving family law and conveyancing to the female lawyers; men become financial advisors when women become accountants. In Nigeria men retained a monopoly of the truly male work of touring, while women took up the desk-bound jobs.

Most of the jobs married women did in the Territory were located in the interstices of career jobs. Marjorie Murphy, trained as a secretary, helped out with minute-taking and other secretarial tasks many times in her husband's career. Suzanne, in colonial French Africa, was her husband's secretary, superintendant of supplies for tours, photographer, statistician, and general supernumerary, all tasks done without official reward or recognition.[83] Rather than receiving thanks, such a wife was often attacked: 'She commands the subdivision'.[84]

When the government legislated that the plantation workers were to be paid in wages, plantations established trade stores and Pat Murray took on the job of managing a number of these. Isabel Platten took up piece-work sewing in Sydney to supplement the family's income. The one pound a week she earned added to the five pounds her husband received: 'What was welcomed by me was that I could earn the money without going away from home, and I really enjoyed the work'.

In the 1921 census in Papua, of the 670 white women, 133 were described as breadwinners; of the total of 1408 men, 1123 were described as bread-winners. In Port Moresby in 1928 only 14 per cent of the total female population were described as breadwinners. However women were entre-preneurs, running plantations or businesses: for example Elizabeth Marnie, or Mrs Bowles who ran a sawmill near Rabaul, or Mrs D.G. Irvine who managed the hotel at Madang. Emma Hoepfel, widowed during the outbreak of the First World War, became a trader on the North Coast.[85] 'Queen' Emma owned steamships and plantations, but they were run by men.[86] After the death of her consort and trading partner, Tino Stalio, in 1892, 'Emma needed a husband, and he arrived in the person of Herr Kapitan August Karl Paul Kolbe', an inspector of police with the Neu Guinea Kompagnie.[87]

In her old age, Phebe Parkinson, 'Queen' Emma's sister, in order to earn a living was forced to work as a labour recruiter.[88] Women's workforce participation was often explained in terms of exceptional circumstances. Many such women were widows or single, or their men were absent. Lyng described the women as 'looking after things' but as Judy Davis puts it:

> there were women running plantations on their own account, both in Papua and New Guinea. And several of them were noted for their competence in managing staff, including the 'native' labour lines, and for their business acumen. There were women who were not afraid to be alone in remote places and who, in fact, enjoyed it.[89]

When Pat Murray's father went off to war, her mother ran the plantation. Daphney Bridgland describes two women who wielded considerable power in the plantation community:

> [Mrs Watkins] was like a dowager duchess. She used to come to the planters' meetings with a gold headed walking stick and a hat like a bird's nest. There were two of them; there was old Mrs McLean from Bougainville. Her sons were all District Commissioners or Assistant District Commissioners.

Pat Murray deprecatingly describes her own experience of bringing in a copra crop: 'I had a funny little lease on Libba for a few months and ran it myself'. Pat and her sister Di leased Libba for three months in order to raise money for a holiday at Surfers Paradise. They hired their father's truck, managed the labour line, and brought in a copra crop; all after five o'clock when they could be spared from their father's plantation.

After the Second World War, Pat Murray was the only woman in New Guinea to receive an ex-servicemen's loan, but she stoutly denied that women should run a plantation. She and Peter decided it would be preferable to have the loan in their joint names:

> They were very pressing on the subject of what would I do if Peter were to die and leave me with the property, how I would run it. I simply said that I would find myself a manager. 'Oh, would you? You wouldn't do it yourself?' And I said 'No, I think in these days it's no longer practicable for a woman to run a plantation. It used to be feasible once upon a time but it isn't anymore' . . . The end result was it achieved very little for me, because the Development Bank absolutely insisted that my name be removed from the ownership of the property, and furthermore they made us pay for the transfer from joint names to Peter only.

One of the more famous female entrepreneurs was Ma Stewart, the first female civilian to return after the war, who ran the Hotel Cecil at Lae.

[In 1949] We brought Kerry back as a little baby, on the *Bulolo*
I think. We went to Lae, I'll never forget Lae Hotel. Ma Stewart
had taken over the AAMWAS barracks as a temporary Lae Hotel.
It was quite comfortable, but it was raining all the time and you
had to put your raincoat on to go to the toilet or the showers.
Ma was wonderful. She only had this funny old stove to cook for
the whole hotel. She put native spears up so I could put the nappies
there to dry. Then I'd run out of nappies, used all my Kotex and
then John found a woman who was a seamstress who made up
nappies for me out of mosquito netting because you couldn't buy
much so soon after the war. [Marjorie Murphy]

Marjorie Murphy speaks approvingly of Ma Stewart's managerial capacities,
but she was also described as something other than a woman: she 'dressed
in man's sandals and was burned black by the sun'.[90] A planter's wife echoes
this notion that only a certain kind of woman could do a man's job: 'I
don't think I could have managed unless I had such a tough upbringing.
I didn't have any excuses made for being a girl'.[91] Judy Tudor, a journalist
in the Pacific for over thirty years, 'didn't get much of a reception when
I landed there . . . they thought I was going to be a pain in the neck'.
She reports that some women ran their own gold mines at Wau. On the
whole women kept to their traditional role, and did not go to New Guinea
to 'show men what they could do'; rather, circumstances sometimes demanded
that they take over.[92] Women in other occupations came to Papua New
Guinea: Beatrice Grimshaw the novelist; Margaret Mead, Beatrice Blackwood
and Hortense Powdermaker as anthropologists; Evelyn Cheeseman and Mary
Clemens as naturalists.

Yvonne Mann, the wife of Sir Allen Mann, the Chief Justice in Papua
New Guinea from the mid-1950s, although a lawyer herself, didn't practise
'because it wasn't done, my dear, for a woman to practise up there'. When
there was a shortage of lawyers, she offered to be Sir Allen's associate.
He said it would look too much like he was taking his home comforts
with him on circuit, echoing Callaway's point that a woman is out of place
on tour. Before he arrived there was no law reporting so Yvonne took
down Sir Allen's judgments in shorthand. Others accused her of writing
them, but Yvonne Mann claimed that she was a mere scribe, Sir Allen
complaining 'if I so much as raised an eyebrow over what he wrote'.[93]

There certainly was little incentive for women to work in Papua New
Guinea. As elsewhere, women's wages were lower. In 1935 the salaries
of junior officers in the Second Division ranged from 300 to 400 pounds,
of female officers from 285 to 315 pounds. Married (male) officers received

a supplement to 400 pounds if their salary was below this. The 'various offices are classified with minimum and maximum salaries according to the importance and character of the work performed'. The Lieutenant-Governor and Judge were worth 1800 pounds, a resident magistrate was worth 636 to 732 pounds, a patrol officer 325 to 420 pounds, a plumber and ironworker 370 to 418 pounds, a chief medical officer 828 to 1000 pounds and a typist 156 to 310 pounds. A matron was worth only about half a plumber and ironworker at 216 to 240 pounds, while a nurse was worth slightly more than a typist at 170 to 194 pounds.[94] For all the encouragement single women received to join a mission, they too only received about half the salary of an unmarried man,[95] unless they joined the Anglican mission where they were allowed the same twenty pounds, if they needed it.[96]

No doubt these ratios had changed little some twenty years later when Joan Refshauge wrote to the Director of Public Health, expressing her concern that nursing should become a career service. She noted that it was 'entirely due to the temporary employment of married women that the section can carry on at all'. However one could not rely on married women staying in employment, or being available in smaller centres. She argued that 'One thing is certain, that no longer can we look to the sense of dedication a nurse, or any other professional person, may have in this world with its monetary outlook'. In order to establish an efficient career service, Refshauge recommended good wages to compensate for the lack of amenities, greater increments for each year of service, the opportunity to attend nursing conferences overseas, payment for undertaking postgraduate courses, and the creation of new senior positions to improve the chances of promotion.[97]

While it may not have been a deliberate policy, white women in Papua New Guinea also acted as something of a buffer between the outgoing Australian administration and the incoming Papua New Guinean one. The immediate reasons for the employment of white women were no doubt the rapid expansion of education, health and administration and the lack of qualified men to fill the jobs. In the 1950s and 1960s, married women often filled the gap in both nursing and primary teaching; because of the marriage bar they were appointed only as temporary officers. It was only in the mid-1960s that the removal of the marriage bar allowed such women to become permanent employees. Even Joan Refshauge, a singular woman in terms of the status to which she rose, suffered from this discrimination. While on a temporary appointment, she did not accumulate superannuation. After a long battle she was the first woman to get permanency and ultimately superannuation.

But, and this made me really mad—in fact I fought like a fish wife to no avail—I lost my wage status and was only worth a portion of a man, I've forgotten what portion. So even today I suffer, for my superannuation is still less. I had worked harder than most men and longer hours and so had my staff.[98]

Although women may have been subordinates in the male world of work, they were quick to criticise the pomposities of their superiors:

At Higaturu, when they learned I could do typing and shorthand, the District Officer, O.J. Atkinson put me on and I had a temporary job as his secretary. He was mad about a place called Abau—it must have been his favourite posting. I'd go in to take down a letter and he'd say 'When I was at Abau'—so I'd put the pen down because I'd know we were going to talk for about an hour about Abau. [Marjorie Murphy]

Dorothy Pederick quietly asserted her medical knowledge against the doctor's:

I remember when I first started putting a line in that there was a meningitis case, and an ex-Army doctor came across the return. He said 'Aren't these meningitis really cerebral malaria?' I said 'Well, from my teaching of what is meningitis'—you see we had to diagnose everything ourselves, there were no doctors around—'he had all the symptoms of meningitis, would that have happened with cerebral malaria?' I said 'I've got one in now' and he came over. There was a test for meningitis. You put the patient on his back, and you lifted the knee and tried to straighten the knee out and it was always tight behind the knee. And he came over and had a look. 'Oh well it could be meningitis too'.

Pat Murray is less generous to 'bloody silly Scragg' who so miscalculated her pregnancy that Anne arrived, by his figures, six weeks late. As her punishment, Pat Murray was dosed with castor oil:

Of course it had the obvious result, I spent my whole time absolutely tied to the loo. After three days I staggered up from the Club to the hospital and he said 'Mmm, didn't work eh? Sister' he said 'Give her another dose'. She said 'Over my dead body'. And I said 'Don't worry Dobbie, I'll throw it in his face'. He said 'What do you expect me to do then?' I said 'Nothing, let's let nature take its course'. So it did.

Single women on the loose

Given that single women chose their passage to Papua New Guinea, and, within the constraints of job prospects or mission demands, where to work and when to leave, one might assume they had more freedom of movement than married women. Such conclusions ignore the semiotics of sex and race in colonial society. Super-imposed on the topographical map of Papua New Guinea was a symbolic map with implicit messages on it: 'No unaccompanied white women beyond this point'. By the 1920s, the towns were deemed to be safe and appropriate locations for white women; but the back country was still out of bounds, was still imagined as a dangerous untamed frontier, where single women, weak and delicate creatures that they were, should not venture. Even if they pleaded physical fortitude, single women were deemed to be a temptation to Papua New Guinean men. Single women responded that they would take their chances, and some whites agreed that single women on the loose should 'get what they deserved'. However, as single women posed a danger to all women, even virtuous married ones, they must stay in the towns, or travel under male escort.

Sir Hubert Murray felt that Evelyn Cheeseman 'would not be able to deal with Papuan carriers without the help of a white man'.[99] She travelled up the Kokoda trail without the letter of permission that she required from Port Moresby: it had been filed in the 'too hard' basket. She matter of factly reports:

It seems to be taken for granted that to go alone into wild places like New Guinea and encamp, as I have done, a long distance from any civilized people, requires courage. Actually, it is not so much courage that is called for, but endurance. I should place independence first, and then endurance, neither of which are virtues, but acquired habits.[100]

Miss Waddell was only allowed to travel ten miles through an uncontrolled area in 1936 if accompanied by a European male and 'the necessary number of natives'.[101] Marjorie Murphy flouted the rule that prevented white women from joining patrols into uncontrolled areas; the administration probably turned a blind eye because she went with a suitable protector:

To tell you the truth I wasn't supposed to be on patrol with John at all, but nobody knew so who cared. So I went on patrol. It was uncontrolled area. On a patrol John had done earlier, one of his police boys was shot with an arrow. It was too dangerous for women. Not that I'm brave. I just thought 'Oh well, John's taking me, I've got all these police boys round the place, it can never happen to me'. When you're young nothing can ever happen to you.

When Joyce Walker asked to remain alone in the Baining Highlands, when her partner, the other medical sister, married and left, there was considerable resistance from the Synod:

> There always had to be two sisters in any isolated area. The mission wouldn't allow you to be on your own . . . they told me I had to close down the hospital. All the work I'd done for two years or so and I'd got the confidence of the people only to be abandoned. They had a great need, those poor old Bainings and I had a deep feeling for them. I refused to close down the hospital and go. I'd got the women to come in and have their babies in the hospital and I said 'I'm not going to leave'. Well there was a great old argument at synod and they must have talked about it at length. I was out there working on and praying hard that I'd be allowed to stay and the missionary who used to come out every fortnight and bring our goods and mail came out and said 'They've had their meetings about it and they've decided they'll let you stay until they can get another sister'. So they let me stay and I was there for nearly a year on my own.

Joyce Walker was comforted on her first night 'alone' in the Bainings by the minister:

> The dear old native minister, Aquilla, was a tower of strength to me. The first night I was left on my own I had a case in labour ward and I didn't finish until about ten or eleven o'clock. I made my way back to the sister's house for the first time to be on my own after Shirley had gone. There sitting on the steps was old Aquilla. He'd got the Aladdin lamps, pump-up lamps, and he'd hung two of them, one each side of the house to have it bright. He was sitting on the steps waiting for me and he just wanted to see me in and safely settled. Just that little homely touch that I thought was wonderful. He talked to me about my mother. We'd got friendly before this and I had told him my mother was very old, she was in her late seventies. I remember him pointing up to the moon, it was a lovely tropical moon, and he said 'You're all on your own but my wife and I will look after you. And see that moon up there, your mother's looking at that same moon back in Australia'. I thought that was a wonderful thought and a wonderful feeling, it just did something for me, and forged a link with home.

Joyce Walker shared in the communal evenings of her village in the Bainings: 'I'd sit round the camp fire at night with the women and men and roast peanuts and potatoes in the fire and talk. They were real friends—I was really happy with them.'

Similarly, Joan Refshauge's decision to stay in villages when doing medical work placed her in moral danger:

> In 1948–49 I did a depopulation survey in New Ireland. I had taken from Port Moresby a trained nurse and two native trainees and was given, much against my will, a policeman. I felt that the survey had no right to be forced on people through the presence of a policeman. The proposal was that, as patrol officers did, we would live in the village and work from around and so on. The planters objected. By living in a village it was inviting rape of me or my female staff and if not us then their wives. I did stay at plantations when they were suitably situated for the work—but mostly in villages. One such village was a Catholic one and the luluai asked me where I intended to work. I told him and with great courtesy he asked me could I leave there and work elsewhere as there was a singsing sponsored by the church some distance away. I asked where the nearest non-Catholic villages were and was told. I agreed and the village agreed we should work there [at the non-Catholic villages] and the Catholic villages were free to go to the singsing. He did not and I asked him why. 'There are bad people in every village and I am responsible for your safety and must guard you' he replied. I pointed out the staff already present to guard me but it took a lot of persuading to get him to go to the singsing . . . These native men, and women for that matter, were/are more courteous, considerate and understanding than their white counterparts. Our own men regarded us as women who had no understanding of the dangers.

There were to be no loose women in the Territory. Single women, like Joan Refshauge and Joyce Walker, broke this (man-made) rule; but not without members of the white community taking notice and disapproving. The work of single women undercut male authority in a further way. A number of Australian women, in focussing their attention on Papua New Guinean women, strengthened the voice of the most silent of all the colonial actors, the indigenous women. This, and other threats to the male empire, are explored in Chapter 8.

In the 1920s most women in Papua New Guinea were wives or mission workers, all securely inscribed into a family of one sort or another. Although women often picked up the reins when a husband died or was absent, few women were in the category of Beatrice Grimshaw and Evelyn Cheeseman, unattached women known for their independence. Following the Second World War, more women became nurses in the government hospitals, but Joan Refshauge met considerable resistance as she carved out her singular path as the only female doctor. From the 1950s, more women worked as teachers and clerical workers, although many of them were married to men in the Territory. The 1960s and 1970s saw an increasing number of young and single women come to Papua New Guinea of their own accord. For a decade or so before Independence, a younger more sexually-balanced workforce enjoyed a short moment of adventure in the tropics before taking up their careers back in Australia. This chapter has explored the differential effects of a woman's role in the Territory, depending on whether she came as wife, mother or worker. Another major determinant of her daily experiences was her destination, whether she came to outstation or white town, as the next chapter discusses.

4

In Town and Down the Road

W hile colonial accounts of tensions between mission, plantation and administration abound, there was also a difference between those who lived in the administrative centres and those who lived 'down the road' (as it was called in New Guinea). In town a self-referential white society was possible, at least after a certain stage of settlement. The top echelons of the administration sought to preserve a decorum (like the 'Raj' as Isabel Platten describes it), that was not possible for those living with lesser incomes or amenities. White people living down the road were far more likely to become involved in the life of local villagers, in relationships standing somewhere between feudal and reciprocal exchanges. Pat Murray, Mary Pulsford, and Joyce Walker all lived 'down the road' at some stage during their time in Papua New Guinea. For Mary Pulsford and Joyce Walker, this was a special experience. It allowed them to become acquainted with a life and people very different from their own, and additionally, in Joyce Walker's case, as yet untouched by white customs.

Outwomen

While Evelyn Cheeseman tells the sad tale of Mrs Field who died in a mental home in Australia because she 'lacked the will to become acclimatised to solitude'[1] the story that circulated in Papua New Guinea concerned poor Mr Field and his misfortune in such an unsuitable wife:

Poor Field! He had a ghastly time getting her to the nearest anchorage by canoe. He dared not leave his plantation for long, you know, and it was a mercy they found a

1. A first taste of the tropics, Rabaul c. 1928
Isabel Platten samples coconut juice.

2. A tropical baby's cradle, Rabaul, c. 1928
An Australian women's magazine awarded a prize for this photograph of baby Newell Platten in a clam shell.

1

3. Ann Deland and son Ray, Sanda Kuta, 1928

4. The Deland family, Vanikoro, 1927
The Delands relax with friends on the verandah of their house.

5

5. On the Old Wharf, Rabaul, late 1920s

White residents including Isabel (between 2 and 3) and Gil Platten (2) and the Rev. (4) and Mrs J. H. Margetts (3) eagerly await the arrival of a ship bringing news, friends and relatives from Australia. The wharf labourers sit out of the way in the background.

6. A weekend outing to Vulcan, Rabaul, late 1920s

7. Children's transport, Halis, c. 1932
Paquita and Newell Platten in their 'little house', used to carry them around New Ireland. 'Of course in some ways, having the natives to look after the children was slave-like.' p. 125 [Isabel Platten]

8. Laying out a tennis court, Halis, c. 1932
Many of the wealthier plantations had tennis courts constructed of white ants' nests stamped flat by the local people at a sing-sing: 'an enchanting scenario of natural enjoyment and fair exchange'. p. 117 [Judy Davis]

9. Huris, New Ireland, c. 1934
Paquita and Newell Platten enjoy the lagoon at the family's 'seaside resort'.

10. The Platten house at Halis, c. 1938
The Platten children return from a swim.

11. Isabel Platten with Paquita and Newell, Halis, c. 1938

7

8

9

10

I

12. A well-surfaced road, New Ireland, 1930s
Gil Platten was called 'Masta Rot' (Mister Road) by the New Irelanders because of his obsession with mending the roads as he travelled around the island. (p. 176)

13. Road transport, New Ireland, c. 1940
The purchase of a car relieved Gil Platten from the several weeks it took to walk around his circuit. Paquita Platten is shown on the duckboard, with eager local children looking for a ride.

12

13

4

14. George Brown College, near Rabaul, c. 1937
George Brown College was the headquarters for training Methodist ministers and their wives.

15. After the eruption of Vulcan, Rabaul 1937
Restoration work following the volcano's eruption included scraping pumice from the roofs of buildings. Here the pumice is so thick it must be removed in two stages.

5

16

16. Otibandu Police Post, 1941

(L. to r.) Turutaba, the major domo; Ono; Anton, the cook; Baranoma, the camp boss; and John J. Murphy, the Officer in Charge, seated at front.

17. Marjorie Murphy, near Mingke, Otibandu, south-west of Wau, c. 1941

'Bring-'em-back-dead Murphy' was the caption John Murphy gave to this photograph of his wife standing over a wild boar from the forest.

17

German woman who wanted to get to Sydney. Yes, we're all sorry for that poor bloke, with everything against him and the copra prices fallen again.[2]

Judy Davis' 'outwomen', women living on outstations, dated events in relation to severe illnesses or periods of extreme isolation.[3] While their husbands were on tour, wives could spend months alone and immobilised in a bush station, miles from the nearest doctor for their children. The presence of women in the field was discouraged, no concessions were made for them and conditions were only grudgingly upgraded. Wives were rarely, if ever, mentioned in reports unless killed or 'something dire happens to them'. Wives were told not to speak to the prisoners working around the residency, but to communicate through the constable. Some husbands would not let their wives or children speak Motu, thus further restricting communication. When husbands returned from patrol, they were fussed over and cosseted by a wife and children eager to share the adventures of the trip. In French colonial Africa, by contrast, wives were more likely to be the unofficial administrator while their husbands were on patrol. They often resorted to negotiation or speaking with their husband's authority: ' "If the commander was here, I think he would say this, do that". "You are right, madame, this is what he would say" '.[4]

Even having a few other Australian families nearby may be a mixed blessing:

> Living on an outstation you really have to try and get on with everybody from your own community and sometimes it's very difficult because people can be very different from one another, and really have very little in common except for the fact that they're all Australians. That can be stressful in some situations. On the other hand, whenever a crisis occured people were absolutely wonderful in the way they helped one another. They were really terrific; they really propped each other up and helped each other in all sorts of ways in emergencies. Nobody batted an eyelid about doing it. So that was one of the good things about it. [Mary Pulsford]

The enforced idleness of some women's lives contrasted even more unfavourably with the life these women left behind them. Mary Pulsford and Pat Andersen interrupted their careers to go to Papua New Guinea; Daphney Bridgland gave up all prospects of a career.[5] However, both Mary Pulsford and Pat Andersen describe their relatively short time up country with pleasure. Mary Pulsford's husband went to Papua New Guinea after the war as an agricultural extension officer. Mary, a science graduate from Sydney University, was working in Canberra when she met Bob, down on leave from New Guinea. A year later, in April 1953, they married and went to live on the north coast of New Guinea, at Urip village in the Sepik District. Mary lived there for eighteen months:

> The site of our house had been the site of Simogun Peta's house. He was a very famous coastwatcher during the War and quite an eminent local leader. He was very concerned after the War to have economic development for his people and to that end he wanted an agricultural extension officer. To help all this happen he pulled down his own house and had a beautiful house built for Bob on the site, at one end of Urip village.

Their son Ian was born during this time. Bob was then posted to Manus as the District Agricultural Officer. They had a daughter, Susan, born at Lorengau. In 1958 they moved to Taliligap, a station close to Rabaul and then Rabaul itself, when Bob became the District Agricultural Officer for New Britain. They settled in Port Moresby in 1963 and Mary became a science teacher in 1964, at Port Moresby High School. In 1968, she was appointed as the first botany tutor in the new University of Papua New Guinea, where she taught for six years.

In town, the timber houses followed a Europeanised style of construction. In contrast, many of the houses on outstations were made of bush materials; they were almost always large by local standards. Mary Pulsford describes the conveniences of her house in the remote village of Urip:

> The house was all built of native materials, but was about eight times as big as any other village house. I realise now it really was palatial, in their terms. The living quarters were covered with thatch, and the outer walls the skin of betel nut palms, and the inside walls and ceilings were woven strips from the stalk of the sago leaf. This type of matting which was always woven in beautiful patterns was called plaited panggal. The floor of the house was black palm which was a very strong hard floor but was corrugated. There was a verandah on the seaward side. It was very pleasant to stand on the verandah and look across the forest to the sea and along the coastal hills. There were three bedrooms and a wide hallway between them, a dining room like a large square verandah in the middle of the house, and a big kitchen and storeroom on the back. Off to one side of the dining room was a little walkway leading to a shower recess. The floor of the shower recess was marsden matting and we had a bucket shower. Two gallons of warm water would give one a comfortable and very satisfactory shower. We didn't have to worry about pulling out the plug because the water

just fell through the marsden matting and went down the hillside to the forest.

The toilet was a deep pit latrine, with a little house over it, built outside at one end of the house. Washing water was caught with 44 gallon drums placed at strategic points around the house. We could catch washing water even from the thatched roof. But drinking water was caught only from the galvanised iron roof which was over the kitchen part of the house. It ran into a little square tank which my husband managed to find on one of his forays. There were all sorts of materials left behind by the war in that area, because the last part of the New Guinea campaign was fought there. In that area you could say that shell cartridges were turned into flower vases and bomb caps into village bells. We had brass shell cartridges in our house with bunches of flowers or leaves just to brighten up the house. They were widely used in village churches in that way. A bomb cap hung under our house and was the bell which was rung to summon the village meetings from time to time. One of the reasons we had a galvanised iron roof over the kitchen was so it wouldn't catch fire.

Virtually all the water had to be carried and washing was done in very large galvanised iron tubs just in the open out the back, and the clothes were boiled in a copper, which was just a copper basin sitting inside a 44 gallon drum with a fire under it. Clothes were scrubbed on one of the old wooden ripple boards with the sort of brush that in Australia you'd scrub the floor with. At that stage cotton was the universal clothing for Australians in New Guinea. Not only was it cooler, but it would also put up with the beating it seemed to get at the hands of the person doing the laundry. Ironing was done with a benzine iron, with a little petrol tank on it.

Most white women had little prior experience of living in isolation and sometimes without refrigeration. Mary Pulsford was no exception:

One of the things I had to get used to straight away was how you ordered the food for two people for several months. I'd never housekept on any scale before; I just didn't know how much food two people ate in a week, let alone three months. But anyway my husband was able to steer me through some of these pitfalls. He said 'Well, you know, you buy a sack of sugar'—which I think was 70 pounds—'and a case of flour'—which would have been 100 pounds—'and a case of Sunshine milk powder, and a case of butter and a case of jam' and a case of a whole lot of different things, tinned fruit and tinned meat, and so on.

Mary Pulsford, like many women in the Pacific, ordered her supplies through McIlraith's. She discovered from the price list that she could buy spices by the pound as cheaply as by the two ounces:

> So I got a pound of spice and a pound of cloves and a pound of ginger. In due course it all turned up. Well the cloves lasted me twenty-five years and the ginger and spice I never finished, I had to throw them out before I ever got to the end of it!

Pat Andersen also comments on the problems of large orders:

> When you order things there, because you only get stores every three, four, five or six weeks, you order large quantities. One of the things we ordered was a bag of sugar—I think it was 25 pounds. We had to go into the general committee meeting at Port Moresby. When we came back the sugar, from the humid climate, had just dissolved and it was trickling right across the store, underneath the partition walls, right across the study—and that was the end of our sugar. It was dreadful.

Everyone good-naturedly accepted that flour was sifted several times to remove at least some of the weevils. But the secret of making bread rise without yeast was elusive:

> Making bread—oh my. I'd never been taught to make bread and we had no yeast. Every one of us tried different yeasts. Out at Raluana they did something, the Bainings girls did something with rice, one said 'Use lemons'. Gordon ate the bread, it was more holy than righteous, I think. Eventually when the ship came in, we got 'Dry-Barm' and we were able to make bread. [Grace Young]

The introduction of refrigeration was a significant improvement—a shift from tinned meat to fresh meat was possible, cold water (and beer!) could be kept in the 'fridge, finally even icecream could be kept frozen:

> We had tinned meat, but once a week a native lad went in on a bicycle to Rabaul, in one day and back the next; and brought the mail and a small amount of meat for the Malabonga sisters and for us. But he couldn't bring much on his bicycle. As well as that we didn't have any refrigeration, and it wouldn't keep until the next day. So if the lad arrived back at midnight, we had to get up and cook the meat. [Jean Mannering]

Isabel Platten describes the decision she and Gil made to purchase one of the first refrigerators, the 'Icyball':

> About this time (end of 1938) we were told about a marvellous invention that was changing the way people who lived away from electricity sources could now get what we desired very much, some way to chill and preserve our food. It was named 'Icyball'. I don't know who invented it but nothing was more desirable. We went into serious discussion, Gil and I, as to whether or not we could, or should, indulge ourselves this one luxury. The cost was 30 pounds. Does that sound ludicrously cheap to need to question our buying one? To put it in perspective, it was more than a month's salary. But we splurged and bought one. Until the Japanese occupation our Icyball served us well. The kerosene powered refrigerators superceded the Icyball during the war but were apt to break down, leaving us back in square one, without refrigeration again.

Mary Pulsford reports that her Silent Knight kerosene refrigerator did indeed constantly 'go wrong'. Eventually it was replaced with a more reliable one.

Diet for those on outstations depended a good deal on whether the local villagers or the mission station grew food, and this often depended on the soil and climate, as well as the skills of the gardeners. Gil Platten became a devotee of organic gardening and attempted to convert the local people wherever he went. He even made a vegetable garden on the beach at Tabar. For others, the supply of food depended on local gardening and trading habits:

> There was plenty of fresh fruit and sweet potatoes and other vegetables in that area and we used to buy it with sheets of the *Sydney Morning Herald* which was what people wanted: for smoke paper for home made cigarettes. That had recognised trading value in those days, it was actually worth tuppence if you tried to put a monetary value on it. You always knew when the village mothers were short of smoke paper because a line of children would come up to the house each holding a pawpaw. Although we couldn't possibly eat all the pawpaws that they were prepared to sell to us, we had to give them smoke paper which they so desperately needed. [Mary Pulsford]

On the other hand, Pat Andersen in the impoverished delta country of Papua, had to be more resourceful:

> What you had to do in planning your menus was work out how you could camouflage a tin, because mostly we had tinned food.

> I did have a little garden but it was such a humid climate and
> such a heavy rainfall that I didn't have a great deal of success.
> There were a few things I was able to grow—Chinese cabbage and
> tomatoes, not much else. We had some chooks—which we shared
> with the local pythons! Snakes were something of a problem.

The main fresh food were fish so large that they were cut into steaks,
and crabs which escaped from their twine bindings overnight: '(Y)ou'd go
to the kitchen and see these enormous crabs loose which I must confess
I never tackled. I used to get one of the girls or the cook boy to hold
them down with a stick while they negotiated the enormous nippers'.

Pat Andersen identifies the need for versatility:

> We used all the things which we had in many ways. We used pawpaws
> not only as fruit but as a vegetable when they were green, a bit
> like a marrow at that stage. Pumpkins we got, and the stems of
> the pumpkin you could cut up small and use like a bean.

Jean Mannering (then Poole) notes 'we had tinned butter, tinned peas, tinned
everything you could think of'. Because the Baining people had no use
for money the Pooles traded in salt: 'a handful of salt would buy a couple
of eggs. But you weren't always sure they were fresh'. However:

> We collected quite a few fowls as time went on because whenever
> my husband baptised a baby, they generally made a present of a
> little chicken. There were no fowl runs up there; everybody just
> let their fowls roam loose. They roosted in the trees and the pythons
> ate quite a few, but there were many survivors. If you wanted to
> kill a fowl, you'd just say to the two houseboys 'Go and get a
> fowl for me' and they'd tear off after the fowls, round, under the
> house, everywhere until they grabbed one.

Gil Platten balanced the scales: whenever he caught a snake he cut it up
and fed it to the fowls.

Mary Pulsford describes evenings in her village:

> I very much valued starting life in that country in a New Guinea
> village. The tenor of life was so different from the life of the town.
> The women, and some of the children who went with them, would
> go off to the gardens soon after daylight, and then they would come
> back at about four o'clock in the afternoon. And then village fires
> would be going and people would be sitting around relaxing and
> talking. That was a friendly communal sort of time. In the time
> that I lived there I was able to see quite a lot of the ways in which

they made grass skirts, processed sago, or prepared lime from seashells for eating with betelnut.

My friends were mainly women. I think it was just because I was young and new, and they were very friendly. There were no social problems somehow about me being friendly with teenage girls. The older women were very busy.

The women of Mary Pulsford's village conferred a birthing ritual on her son:

> While we were there we had our first child, he was born in Wewak European Hospital. I went in about ten days before his birth. But it was a lovely place to have a baby because everyone there regarded having a baby as the most normal part of life. When I returned with my baby, two of the old women who were also our special friends came to see him and they did a little dance of joy backwards and forwards in front of him which was a welcome to the baby, which I thought was rather special.

Isabel Platten was invited to view the *beri beri* birth celebrations on Tabar, in which the women engaged in ritualised violence against the men. These birth rituals in some ways parallel the men's death rituals of the *malagan*:

> I was once invited, by the women, to join their menfolk in a very special feast. Gil was not invited and I was curious why I should be. We all—the men and I—sat on mats on the sand and the food was brought to us. So far it was about the same as most village feasts. At the end of the feast the women rushed out from the kitchen wielding switches with which they hit the men. Both the men and women thought it to be a great lark, no one protested, I noticed they took great care to see that I was not lashed.

Isabel Platten commented, sharing perhaps with the women the pleasure of a moment's insubordination: 'I liked that one where they hit the men with sticks. I thought they were having a great time, getting their own back on the men. And the men liked it too.'

Generally white women were merely spectators of the feasts and celebrations performed by their local villagers. However, Mary Pulsford at one point shared in the work of the women of her village:

> I hadn't been at Urip very long when a family who were our neighbours on the hill and who owned land just below the hill on the seaward side, offered us the use of this land to grow some food. The offer was that village people would clear the land and plant the food

garden and we could have some of the food from it. It was always the women's work to clear the undergrowth when making and planting a new garden and the men's work to cut down the trees and do the burning off. On the day when work was to begin a group of women arrived with their bush knives and Bob said to me 'This is your garden and you are a woman so you must go and work with the women in clearing it'. So I donned jeans and boots, a long-sleeved shirt and a hat, grabbed a bush knife and went along with the women. Well we worked away all afternoon cutting vines and clearing undergrowth and all the time everyone was talking and laughing. They worked much faster and more efficiently with their knives than I could manage. I ended up extremely hot and with blisters on most fingers of my right hand and various bugs fell down inside my shirt. I developed a tremendous respect for these village women for their skill and physical stamina in doing this sort of work as a normal part of life in a hot and steamy climate. In due course we had some very nice vegetables from that garden.

However, even such adventurous 'outwomen' as Mary Pulsford, Pat Andersen or Isabel Platten longed occasionally for the comforts of home or someone who shared their cultural orientations and language. The outstations looked back to the towns as the source of civilisation—mail, books, visitors. Down the road the highlight was the arrival of mail:

Anything you wanted you had to get up from south. I used to send down to my family and then in time things would come up. If it was really urgent they would put it on a plane but that was expensive. From Port Moresby we had to get it out to us. There was one occasion when the post office decided that they had to have all the mail bags the same size. So they sent a letter out to people saying no bags would be used unless they were the right size. We didn't get the letter to say they wouldn't use our bags any more because they didn't send the bag. We went for nearly six months without any mail at all. I was nearly berserk, because mail is so important. It wasn't until we eventually went into Port Moresby that we discovered what had happened and we were able to get six months of back mail. Can you imagine six months of *Sydney Morning Heralds*? . . . Even when we had it every three or four weeks, we used to put out all our *Heralds* and go through them. We picked them over but we used to put them down in order so we could follow things through. It meant the local people were pleased because we had all these papers and they liked the *Sydney Morning Herald* for smoking. [Pat Andersen]

Fortunately the Port Moresby library had a very good system for people away from the centres. They sent to us wooden cases of books. Books of great variety and my mind greedily consumed them. I became addicted and am incurable. And I learned that one would never be lonely so long as books, books of all manner of ideas, were available. I remember that I feared I would devour all of the books supplied too quickly so took to rationing myself. [Isabel Platten]

The centre could also make life difficult on an outstation. It was the source not only of civilisation but of power. Ann Deland, Helen McLeod and Lorna Fleetwood point to the central administration's inadequate understanding of local needs.[6] It was asserted that those in the centre were isolated from and unaware of the inconvenience or even impossibility of enforcing their bureaucratic regulations at the local level. McLeod describes her husband's conviction that the obligation of villagers to provide carriers to take goods to a remote station had reached the 'highest pitch of passive resistance',[7] but the administration in Port Moresby would not listen to his evaluation of the situation. Eventually Colonel Murray intervened, toured the area and accepted the need for an airstrip. Ann Deland wrote home:

> Mervyn is awfully fit and is leading a hectic life. The Customs Office in Rabaul has just introduced a rule that all boats going more than 30 miles have to be cleared. So Mervyn runs up and down the hill clearing little tiny schooners. In Rabaul there is someone at the office all day, but here it has to be sandwiched in with other work.[8]

There are subtle hints that a women's culture existed beneath the public world of men and the colonial project. The women interviewed for this book often described the topography of their local landscape in terms of the distance to other white women. Although not unhappy, Mollie Parer notes that she didn't see 'a black or white woman for eight months' while at the Black Cat mine. Doris Booth decided 'after three years on the goldfields—which had been spent without the company of my own sex—it was time to be leaving New Guinea'.[9] Other women report similar feelings:

> I think the main thing for a woman was that most of the visitors were men, and you hardly ever saw another white woman. [Mary Pulsford]
>
> About two weeks after I landed Reg had to go out on patrol so I went with him . . . But we didn't go so very far out: to a

Catholic mission station. The nuns were so thrilled to meet a woman and they were beautiful to me. [Dixie Rigby]

Even though you're not so far from New Ireland, I did get terribly lonely on Tabar. I was the only white woman there. Two years I sat it out, and then we went back for leave. I had to find the resources within myself during that time. [Isabel Platten]

Opening up the Highlands: Mendi

Even after the war there were Highland people who had no contact with white culture, except the sound of aeroplanes flying over during the war. Joyce Walker and Grace Young were among the first white women to be seen by the Mendi people. In 1950 Gordon Young was asked to open up Mendi in the Southern Highlands. Several months later Grace was able to join him, in 1951. She notes the different treatment of indigenous and white women:

I wasn't allowed to go in to Mendi until they had a teleradio but I was able to get the pastors' wives in, Miriam and Doris and Dulce, they went on a plane two or three weeks before I did. That was the funny part about it, no restriction on them going in. This was a government restriction; I was white but they were brown. [Grace Young]

The Youngs left Mendi in 1960, only for leave, they thought, but their son needed medical attention and they stayed in South Australia.

Joyce Walker was among the first Australians to return to New Guinea (in 1946) when hostilities ceased. Her levelheaded pragmatism opened the path to a number of unique experiences. Against the wishes of the Mission synod, she stayed on alone at the Bainings hospital when her colleague left to be married. She was in the first party of white people to make contact with the Highlanders at Mendi, where she continued her nursing work for a number of years. The District Administrator's wife at Mendi, Helen McLeod, describes Joyce Walker as an 'open-hearted person full of love and good fellowship' with an 'exhilarating personality'.[10] Joyce Walker describes how she went to Mendi:

After five years working in New Britain, establishing hospitals, the General Secretary of overseas missions came up from Sydney and asked would I be prepared to go over to the Papuan Highlands. They'd discovered during the War that people were living there, flying over they'd seen signs of habitation . . . The party was Reverend and Mrs Gordon Young from South Australia as the leaders, Reverend Roland Barnes, his wife and child, Elsie Wilson, a teacher, and myself.

The men of the party walked into Mendi, taking ten days to complete what was to become a flight of twenty minutes. Once they arrived, they encouraged the Mendi people to perform *singsings* in exchange for food and thus prepared a landing strip:

> They came in their hundreds and thousands and gave this sing-sing, jumping up and down, singing and gesticulating and they did that for a few days and nights. Then one of the government men, who was capable, went out and tested the ground, and no it wasn't hard enough yet for an aeroplane to land. So more sing-sing, more meat, more stomping up and down, more rice . . .
>
> By this time the native people there had got used to the men, who were like men from Mars would be to us, different creatures altogether suddenly appearing. But when we arrived, we were women, and we were a different cup of tea altogether. They were fascinated. It was really an experience. Nobody knew their language but our men had tried to explain to them—all done by action and gesticulation and so forth—that women were coming in. But I don't know if they got the message right or not. When we arrived they came with their spears and bows and arrows and tomahawks, all stone and wood, they'd never been contacted. They came in wearing their great headgear, they're the only wigged people in the world. They had these huge wigs with everlasting daisies and cassowary plumes all over them. They looked rather ferocious tearing down to the aeroplane in their hundreds, 'woo-haaing' and 'oh-ooing' and going on. They couldn't make out what we were at all. They'd come to feel you and walk around you and touch you and 'um' and 'oh'.
>
> Our school teacher, Elsie Wilson . . . was gifted enough to sit down with them and work out something of the language. But they led her on a lot. They told her a lot of swear words for things that later on she found she was using this horrible language and they were rolling round with laughter . . . They had a good sense of humour, they purposely did this, so we found out later.
>
> It was a very interesting period with this untouched people. We found they were very hesitant to come for treatment. They were people who believed in evil spirits. Everything that happened, like sickness or an accident, was attributed to an evil spirit. They didn't seem to have a concept of a good spirit, like God, or a spirit of

love. If you were sick an evil spirit had done it. You had to kill pigs to appease the evil spirit. There was a lot of broncho-pneumonia up there. It was five and a half thousand feet altitude, and it was cold. You'd wear a jumper and you'd sleep under a couple of blankets, four blankets some of the staff used. The people had little low houses, no windows, with a smoky fire going all the time and the pigs and the women lived together in one long house and the men lived together in another. I suppose they met up somewhere or other. The children too had a lot of broncho-pneumonia and the people suffered a lot that way. Well you could get a patient with a temperature raging and part of appeasing the evil spirit that had taken possession of him would be to kill some pigs and then drag the sick person down to the river and dip them in a few times. They didn't have much of a chance.

The only antibiotic that was used then was tablets and injections of M and B which was the original penicillin. They were very painful injections, you had to give them with a wide bore needle because it was an oily substance and it had to go deeply into the muscle, or it would develop an ulcer, and suppurate. It wasn't a very pleasant treatment. If you got someone to come and let you try to cure his child or baby— or hers—when you produced the long thick needle on the end of a syringe, that was the end of it. They'd pick up their child and run.

I had to give myself injections which took a lot of courage, took me about five attempts to get in, to show them. They walked around me and watched me for about an hour to see I wasn't going to drop dead before they'd let me give the first child an injection. That's how I started—by giving myself an injection.

But it took a long time to get the faith of the people. They especially thought that myself as an unmarried woman and the school teacher without a man, we were there to steal their babies. Their babies are very precious, they are very family oriented people and love their children dearly. We had no children . . . Naturally we would steal their children. They carry their children in a woven bag knotted on the top of the head and hanging down their backs. If we had a gathering and we went over to look in the bag, they'd snatch the bag away and think we were going to steal the child. It was hard with no language in that period to get them to realise we were there to see how healthy the baby was or what it needed in the way of treatment.

Joyce Walker started her work with the motherless babies by kidnapping a baby.

We had to have a permit to move over a mile's radius from the government station . . . I was given permission, being a nursing sister doing medical work, to go further under escort. Whenever I heard of a sick baby or sick people or an epidemic anywhere I had to go down and get an armed escort. So I'd traipse off with two or three armed native police to investigate anything. I heard about a woman who was dying and a couple of sick children a couple of miles up the hill from us. I went down and got an escort and went up. Sure enough the woman was just about dead by then and they were having wailing ceremonies. While I was there I took the oppor- tunity to look round in a few bags to see how the babies were going. I sat down with an old wizened grandma-looking lady in the long grass and she suddenly pulled out of her bag a skeleton of a baby, just skin and bone, and put it onto her long breast, which was just hanging skin, to try and make it suck. I couldn't believe this. I sort of got it out of her that it couldn't be her baby, she was too old. No, it was her daughter's baby, her daughter had died and she was trying to keep it alive. I thought it was dead so I took out my stethoscope and listened but I picked up a faint heartbeat and I realised the baby wasn't dead yet. I tried to get her to come with me down to the hospital and let me do something for it. But no, she put it back in the bag and that was that.

I sat there and I thought and I prayed and I thought 'I've got to get their confidence somehow. I've got to get over to them I can help them'. I didn't know what to do. And I did a terrible thing I suppose because, after a while, I suddenly thought 'I'll snatch the baby'. She'd put the bag beside her and was watching the ceremony for this dying woman and I thought 'I'll grab the bag and I'll go for my life'. I waited until she was distracted doing her wailing ceremonies with the women. I snatched the bag and I ran down the hill through the long kunai grass and she jumped up and she grabbed her digging stick. A digging stick is a very heavy hardwood stick flattened at one end like an oar, and they dig their sweet potato up and do their gardening with it. She grabbed this and she ran after me and I ran and she ran. I ran over a mile to the hospital with her yelling and chasing me and waving the digging stick around. I got to the sister's house where the schoolteacher and I lived and I slammed the door shut and she was outside bashing on the door.

By this time others had followed and there was a whole mob round the house yelling and going on. I got the baby all wrapped up with hot water bags and a blanket and I got some milk formula made. I got an eye dropper and I started to feed the baby, and got little drops down. It began to respond. I took it over to the window and I showed them yelling outside the baby wrapped up and me putting drops down with an eye dropper. But it didn't do much good. They stayed there all afternoon and all night; they were there for a couple of days on and off, coming and going.

Eventually I got the baby suckling on a soft teat and a bottle and I'd take this bottle to the window and show them what I was doing. The old grandmother came up to the window and she was astounded when she saw it suckling and the milk going down and she began to have a bit of confidence. She'd go round telling other people to come and watch, and they'd come and watch. After that day had gone, that night instead of them all stopping round the sister's house they went home to their villages. But grandma stayed and a couple of others and they slept outside on the grass.

They began to realise something helpful was being done, so I was able to open the door by this time and go out among them and take the baby and show them. It was looking better and responding. This went on for a week. Everyone would come and go and watch but no hostility. Grandma had accepted it and I'd give her the baby to nurse and I'd wait round and take her inside and show her the box I'd put it in and so forth. After a week I thought 'This is no good, she's got to have enough confidence in me to leave me the care of the baby completely and tell others about it.' So I took the baby to her one day and I gave her a bottle and I said 'Now I'm going off to the hospital and you can take the baby and go home with it'. I hoped I was doing the right thing. She fed the baby and I came back from the hospital a few hours later and she'd taken the baby and put it in the box inside and she'd gone off to her hamlet. I didn't see her for about a week. I realised then I'd had a breakthrough.

That's how I first started the work amongst the mothers and babies. However I do not recommend this method to others, I just did it in desperation on the spur of the moment.

In the following five years, Joyce Walker reared hundreds of motherless babies, caring for them until the father remarried and reclaimed his child. After becoming very attached to one child she had nurtured for three years in New Britain, Joyce Walker was careful to avoid over-involvement. Once she 'got the confidence of the people' her role expanded into other nursing and dental work. Extracted teeth became prized necklace decorations, 'and the stories of their extraction told over and over again with many embellishments and great hilarity. Eventually I was being asked to extract teeth just for necklace value. I soon put a stop to that as dentistry was not my greatest accomplishment'.

Ill health forced Joyce Walker's return to Australia, where she worked in the nursing profession for twenty-five years. She is now retired and lives in a house on the Sunshine Coast, often visited by her many nieces, nephews and their children. Twenty years after her arrival at Mendi:

> The government said because we had arrived at Mendi and set up as the first people to do this sort of work they would put a cairn up to our arrival on the original mission site. Twenty years afterwards we got an invitation to go back to the ceremony to mark our arrival and the unveiling of this cairn.
>
> The locals came in many many thousands and singsings went on and on. This one little girl that I'd snatched and run away with, they brought her to me and she put her arms around me—of course they told her, she couldn't remember what had happened. She was twenty and she was to be married that week. She put her arms around me and said the words in her language 'My mother, my mother'. She'd heard how I'd saved her life I suppose, and that was very touching and interesting for me.
>
> They re-enacted me stealing the baby and running; that was part of the ceremony. They're great play actors. They dressed up a person in a uniform like I had, they'd got it from the missionaries who were there then. They re-enacted exactly what had happened, me tearing down the hill and the woman chasing. They thought it was a great joke. They re-enacted our arrival, they made a big aeroplane out of materials they got and they brought it in; and had women dressed up like us arriving, and the people 'oh-aahing' and jumping around. They re-enacted me getting out a little collapsible table every morning and sitting out in front of the hospital and trying to get the women to come and bring the babies, and the women hiding in the long grass and 'ooh-aah' 'no-oo ah' and all that went on. A lot of it I didn't know went on. They were showing all the people who came just how hard it was for me to get a start and how they didn't trust us. They re-enacted the whole thing which was really fascinating—especially the men dragging the women off and beating them if they got too friendly.

There was another little girl who I'd got out of the women's and pigs' house very sick with bronchial-pneumonia and treated with injections of M and B and whatever was available. She was cured and went back to the women and the pigs in the longhouses. When we went back for the reunion, we were down at the airstrip and I happened to say to one of the missionaries working there 'What happened to so-and-so?' They said . . . 'she is now working out at Goroka'. That was a couple of hundred miles off. She'd learned to type and was trained as a secretary. They said she'd be coming back this afternoon on the 'plane that was due in soon. So I waited to see her and she stepped off the 'plane in a little mini-skirt with a transistor radio on a strap over her shoulder. She was coming home for the week-end. It was such a transition in twenty years, but the world had moved on.

The 'little bush manor'

Three prevalent scenarios are used to describe the relationship between an isolated plantation house or government outstation and the surrounding indigenous people. For some, the story is one of unalleviated power and exploitation. Thus Rowley's portrait suggests coercion rather than reciprocal relations as the mainstay of plantation organisation:

The tensions between the white manager and the coloured labour force, the first with his family in the house, the second housed in the dreary barracks of the labour lines, have been expressed for far too long in the (long illegal) use of threat of violence as the basic 'incentive'.[11]

A second model constructed the relations as familial, muting the strong if invisible chains of power which bound the colonised to the colonisers. Prudence Frank describes an enchanted life:

European women had plenty of time to care for their complexions, clothes and appearance. Entertainment was conducted in our homes, not the hotels. We had a picture theatre 'Papuan Theatre' where silent films were shown. I was the pianiste. The natives were also happy, my servants would call me 'Mama bilong mi'. My cook boy called his daughter Prudence.[12]

Daphney Bridgland and Pat Murray make similar comments:

It always infuriated me how some government officials and wives took it for granted that if you employed native people, you were

automatically on bad terms with them. It's this us and them attitude
of the blessed labour unions and people. For the most part it was
a friendly relationship. [Pat Murray]

Any property that Leon and I ever went onto you look on them
as your family and they were part of your way of life. There's a
very good and close relationship and a lot of respect there. It
really used to upset me, the talk about slave labour. [Daphney
Bridgland]

In India the ayah 'practically became part of the family'.[13] Those who have
taken the trouble to ask servants for their opinions have often discovered
that servants did not consider themselves 'part of the family'. Jacklyn Cock's
study of servants in the Eastern Cape in South Africa argues that while
the family analogy is the major leitmotif in the literature, 'in no case . . . did
the domestic worker consider herself as one of the family'.[14] Most employers
were ignorant about the central aspects of their servants' lives, for example
their children's ages, the cost of rent or schooling, and the length of the
servant's trip to work. Servants felt bound into a powerless relationship:
'I have to like her to earn a living'.[15] Employers, even when describing
their relations with servants in familial terms, also stressed the need to
remain invulnerable, knowledgeable, to be 'firm but kind'. Of course one
might argue that race relations in contemporary South Africa are far more
fraught than those in colonial Papua New Guinea. But we do not know;
the stories of those who worked on plantations and in white houses have
not yet been freely told. Certainly our New Guinean interviewees did not
reach for family analogies:

I worked in the kitchen and also looked after his [Platten's] two
small children. Sometimes I went to school and sometimes I worked
in the kitchen. Although I came to go to school, I didn't complain
because whatever the talatala wants I have to do it. Sometimes I
ran back home.[16]

Mrs Mason suggests that relations with the Papua New Guineans were based
on a model of the 'little bush manor'.[17] Claudia Knapman echoes this with
her description of good servant-mistress relations as a kind of 'feudalism'.[18]
Judy Davis suggests that many of the wealthier plantations had tennis courts
constructed of white ants' nests stamped flat by the local people at a singsing,
'an enchanting scenario of natural enjoyment and fair exchange'.[19] She suggests
that feudal loyalties developed between plantation owners and household
staff or local villagers, but not with the plantation labour force. This third
model, lying between the other two, constructs a relationship of reciprocal

but different obligations. These obligations denote both the superior power and resources of the white family, but also an accepted obligation to place at least some of those resources at the disposal of surrounding villages and employees in times of need. Just as feudalism had its *noblesse oblige* and rendering of services to the lord, so too were plantation owners expected to care for the welfare of their labour line and even those living farther afield. Black lives were indeed saved by white masters. Pat and her sister treated children in the surrounding villages for a measles epidemic in 1947. Following the war, Pat Murray's father and a number of other plantation owners treated the local people for a dysentery epidemic:

> When Dad got back they'd established a dysentery hospital on the banks of the creek at Bol at the village because it was a good supply of fresh fast flowing water which was vital for cleanliness. And Dad was dishing out this stuff to people and coping as best he could. Then Dad came over to Rabaul to meet my mother and myself when we came home, and while Dad was away there were seven deaths on the plantation. Just before he came over to meet us, he himself got violently ill, and he was dosing himself. But he became incapable of doing anything, and Kessa . . . was nursing him and making him little bits of soup and trying to spoon feed him, changing his linen and bed bathing him and all the rest of it. And after three days of being absolutely out to it he started to come good, he said 'Kessa you look exhausted. Why don't you go and have a rest. Send Suap in to help me'—that was her husband. 'Masta, he's just as bad as you are. I'm looking after him in our own house'. She was nursing these two dysentery cases. She saved his life absolutely.

Thus white lives were also saved by black servants. Several years later Pat's father was able to return the favour, saving Kessa's life by purchasing an expensive drug she needed but could not afford.

Mary Pulsford draws a portrait of the interdependence between her family and Urip villagers:

> We lived in a mutuality with the village people. We were very dependent on them for many things. They provided us with fire wood. If we had a long dry spell and washing water became very short, they would carry water up from the river and fill up our 44 gallon drums. It was mostly the women and teenage girls who did that, carrying buckets of water on their heads with a big leaf over the top of them. I think the way Bob organised it was to

tell the tultul of the village that we needed wood or water, and he would arrange for it to be done.

But they understood very clearly that we couldn't survive without their help and at the same time we provided health care for them which they valued tremendously. So I always felt it was a very good sort of situation, because we both respected and valued each other. Bob was able to help them learn how to run a rural progress society and also learn how to grow rice and peanuts and market these things.

When Mary Pulsford moved to Port Moresby, she had a house with domestic quarters. She was looking for:

a nice reliable married woman who would be motherly to my daughter, just to keep a motherly eye on her if I was late home. It worked out extremely well. Kun, in the end, became like a member of the family. Her fourth child was born while she was working for us.

In fact we've kept in touch with her family ever since: they're all grown up now. I think we were able to encourage the education of her children who were all very young when she came to work for us.

When Mary Pulsford failed to tell Kun she would be home late one night, Kun became extremely agitated. Kun's father-in-law derived much amusement from Mary's lapse:

Her old father-in-law who was staying with her at the time shook his finger at me every time he saw me for the next week for being so naughty as to have upset his dear Kun! I never dared go anywhere without telling her where I was going for the rest of the time that Bob was away.

So you know there was that very nice side. I felt it was in the same way that the village made itself responsible for me when I was first married. The same sort of thing about knowing you were there and knowing you were alone, and knowing somebody cared about it.

Mary Pulsford tells the story of one Australian who had a house built for a servant to provide him with a secure retirement after the family returned to Australia.

Daphney Bridgland reports how a servant, Josef, saved her life by alerting the white community to her condition:

Josef came to us at Rainau. He was a very dignified old fellow. He must have served with the army because he had quite a bearing about him. He came to me and said that he was a good wash and iron man, but what he didn't tell me was he had been someone's magnificent cookboy for about twenty years. I didn't find that out until I became very ill. I had nephritis and nearly died from it. Leon was away, and the children weren't there . . . I hadn't been interested in eating anything that the other two boys had prepared. They didn't worry very much, just stood at the door and said there was food but I was too sick to go and get it. On the third day, Josef knocked on the door. He had a big tray with a beautifully ironed cloth on it, and a flower in a vase; a perfect omelette and a small baked custard and a fresh orange juice. Beautifully presented. He said '*Missus*' (and all this was done looking the other way, he didn't look at me because I was in bed). '*Supos yu no laik kaikai you laik di nau. Mi wokim kaikai, nau yu kaikai pinis olgeta.*' He was saying I had to eat or I'd die. By this time he'd stirred up enough interest going round borrowing a couple of eggs from one wife, and an orange from somewhere else. Then they came and took me to hospital. But he was the one who sounded alarm bells going. He was very faithful.

The final comment—'He was very faithful'—underscores the feudal nature of this relationship, compared with Mary Pulsford's story, which suggests that Kun's father could at least toy with an age-based status in his relations with Mary.

Indeed Daphney Bridgland asserts the need to maintain control:

Once a manager loses control of his labour he's had it. He can just pack up and go. You might find if you had different tribes on the one property, you'll get one bighead in each lot and he'll be a real bush lawyer. He'll try to make trouble and he'll be a real big mouth, a real humbug. Talk about political infighting, my goodness, the natives had that sewn up just so well.

They're very very quick, the natives, to pick people for what they are. Any fellow who lived in the club or pub and didn't attend to his plantation was very quickly dubbed a 'rubbish masta true'. But most Europeans knew they had to look after their folk because if you didn't you didn't get much work out of them.

Sometimes we had dreadful riots. The Sepiks are warriors and no-one dared hit a Sepik. If you hit a Sepik he'd hit you right back. The idea that natives were bashed up a lot isn't right. Natives who had other natives working for them on plantations treated their plantation workers shockingly. No white man would ever treat a native as badly as a native would treat another native. There were instances when European managers have had to fight and have had to knock men down. In one instance one plantation wife shot a native to save her brother who was visiting her. It was always done in self-defence. Leon and most of the men I knew, knew you could control a mob with talking to them. As long as you kept talking to them you could control them.

[At one stage Leon was bailed up by 40 Sepik workers.] Leon would have been killed because there was one man coming who had an axe. Leon had had an axe in his hand, he had been using it for some reason, but he got rid of it. He threw it in the bush, because if they get it away from you they can use it on you. In the early days we always had a shotgun and a shootboy on the property and he would shoot birds or pigs or anything for food for the labour. We got rid of the shotgun because we felt it was safer; it could be used against us.

These women tell stories of reciprocity, friendship and esteem. As long as authority relations were not questioned, there was considerable scope to laugh, play, teach, and learn. However, the joke was not always mutual. Callaway, commenting on the near-invisibility of women in colonial memoirs, attributes this to 'the conventions of the literary genre, a type which gives little attention to the domestic scene, other than comic accounts of failed communication with the cook or grateful remarks about faithful servants'.[20] White women's voices are refracted through the dominant genre, featuring both comic tales and gratitude.

Ann Deland starts a letter home in a businesslike manner, but rapidly moves on to recount those humorous servants' tales which circulated in all colonial societies:

Of course I had to learn pidgin and to manage natives. Now pidgin must be taken seriously if you are going to manage it at all, also one should remember that one's cook is dealing with unfamiliar foods. One lady of my acquaintance told Motoi to cut up the cake and make sandwiches. He sliced up her beautiful rainbow cake and spread bloater paste on every slice. Kirassi was lent to me. He was a very well trained boy who carefully scrubbed his hands before touching food, so on occasions I got him to make sandwiches. The *Anzac* and the *Australia* were paying us a visit and some of their people were coming up to tea so I urged Kirassi to make very nice tomato sandwiches. He spread strawberry jam in with the tomatoes.[21]

Daphney Bridgland describes how servants negotiated favours:

In later years one could get good freezer meat, but in the early days it was only available when freezers had stocks. You mostly lived on tinned stuff. On one occasion we had guests coming for dinner. On Saturday morning Josef came and asked me '*Missus mi gat liklik parti long tonait, yu gat one gutpella leg abus i stap. Mi laik kisim long parti bilong mi*'. Abus is meat—he asked me straight out for my leg of lamb and I just about blew a gasket. He said '*Orait, mi triam yu, tasol*'. If you're silly enough to say 'Josef do take my leg of lamb, I'm sure you'll enjoy it for your party' he'd have it.

Joan Refshauge's servant Idau 'used to cook on a small range (electric, oval shaped) a four course meal with one saucepan on top of the other. I don't know how he did it, but they were always perfect meals'.[22] Isabel Platten's best house boy Marcus 'could make beautiful things. He would get jealous of me if I made the bread, he was a perfectionist'.

Eva Butcher was both frustrated and grateful for her servant's help:

June 17 1915

Annie is a fearfully careless girl. She won't measure anything and she spills everything and of course unlike a white girl you must not send her off. She is fearfully careless at times but nevertheless I am glad to have her for she does our simple little bit of cooking very well when I put everything ready for her and keep an eye on her. It saves me the heat of standing at the fire. So it might be worse.

Washing day brought more pleasure:

27 April

The girls did the washing which really means a day out, down at the creek . . . it is half-play. My 'Tulips' I call them for what they wear while working. A gaudy red petticoat with a big yellow pattern in stripes on it and their shiny brown backs and sturdy arms and legs are bare of course. They do look so nice coming up the hill with a small basket of white clean clothes on their heads. They sail along with such a funny sort of sideways walk rather graceful in its own way, nothing jerky about it.[23]

Pat Murray's Highland plantation workers sought to retrieve her when she married Peter and left her father's plantation. Thirty-five men, in tribal dress, arrived at Pat's and Peter's plantation the following Sunday morning:

It finally transpired that they thought Dad and John were a pretty poor pair of males to allow a perfectly good able-bodied working female to be carried off from under their noses, and they had come to take me back.

The situation is treated with great amusement by both Pat and her New Ireland house staff, and Pat firmly corrects their misapprehension.

It was all I could do not to burst out laughing, and our house staff who were local New Irelanders were in the kitchen listening into this, and they were in convulsions of mirth. I said 'Look, your fashion is that the man marries and joins the wife's clan and so on. Our fashion is the woman marries and she goes with her husband and her father and brothers will not allow her to marry a man if he is such a man rubbish that he cannot provide a home, and a livelihood for her. If he can't do that she won't marry him. This is our fashion and it's quite different from yours. Yours is a good fashion for you and this is a good fashion for us'. Anyway I had to go through this in the usual kanaka style about three times over in different phraseology and finally they got the message.

The 'manor' and its family life were aloof, but not entirely separated, from the work of the mission or plantation. Langmore[24] suggests the missionary's wife did not draw McAuley's 'circle of exclusion around her domain'[25] but was 'in varying degrees' accessible to the hundred or so Papuans who lived within the missionary compound. But there was a barrier, the symbolically charged doorstep.[26] Saimon Gaius notes how he stood on the steps to speak to Gil Platten.[27] Gil Platten could cross the threshold into a clean house and say how nice it was to come home. Dixie Rigby also evokes the significance of the threshold:

> They used to come up to the verandah at night after we'd had our dinner, and sit on moonlit nights. The whole village would come up and sit and talk. We'd be on the top steps and they'd be on the bottom steps . . .
>
> We loved the natives. That didn't mean to say I was going to invite him home to dinner, but in their place we liked them.[28]

Normal spatial boundaries were, however, breached in times of crisis. Local villagers slept inside the house to protect Mary Pulsford while her husband was away. Following an earthquake Daphney Bridgland brought the terrified house girls to sleep in the living room. Jean Mannering speaks of being 'huddled together on the cement path with our native friends' during an earthquake. Doris Groves shared her house with the mission girls while the leaky roof of their house was being fixed:

> Life went on busily and fairly happily in the new home. The rats, mice, and little lizards called geckoes settled in as well, and one day we came home to find a big carpet snake up in the rafters of the roof, having a wonderful time. As we had heard that carpet snakes kept down the rats and mice this one was very welcome, and we christened it 'Clarence'. Fortunately it never left the roof while we were there . . .

One day we experienced a very bad tropical storm, and the roof of the small girls room (pastors' daughters who came to the mission for education at Metoreia) began to leak badly and as it was going to take some time to repair, we brought the girls and their mattresses over into our living room. During the night I heard cries of fear in Motu 'Itiai Gaigai' which means 'look at the snake' or 'I see a snake'. I realised they were terrified of Clarence, and therefore got no sleep. After three days of rain and storm and very little sleep, we felt compelled to ask one of the senior boys to spear Clarence—much to our regret.[29]

Doris Groves also opened her house in Victoria to two New Guinea boys, Salin and Lue.

Childhood was a time when race relations were less rigidly enforced, while children often softened formal adult relationships.[30] Whites who grew up in the Territory had close childhood friendships with local children; but also realised 'they weren't allowed into the house'.[31] Pat Murray and her brother often played with a New Guinea lad who worked in the house:

For quite a few years we had a canoe which was a great joy. Quite against rules and regulations we used to take it way out to sea. As kids we needed three paddlers to handle it well so we were forever grabbing one of the houseboys to go with us, particularly a young houseboy called Yoel who was much the same age as we were.

Mary Pulsford, Pat Andersen and Daphney Bridgland report that their children had indigenous playmates:

That particular time of my life I was so preoccupied with babies, that somehow that rather dominated what I was doing just then. I was very glad there was another little girl on the station. Her father did our washing and ironing. And she was literally the only other child who was anywhere near Ian's age. She was a year older than Ian, and she was an absolute Godsend to him because—I suppose he was to her in a way too—they were playmates as little children. Ian really would have been a very deprived child without that other little girl to play with. They had a lot of fun together. They used to look such a contrast because at that stage he was very blond and white skinned and she was very dark. [Mary Pulsford]

Judy Davis notes that village and plantation children played together, the plantation children often being incorporated ceremonially into the village structure.[32] Mary's son attended a mixed-race school in Rabaul, teaching Chinese, mixed descent, and several Tolai children: 'All these children were there together, and I thought it was a wonderful way for children to start'.

On the other hand, even children appeared to be aware of their 'superior' position over the local people:

> When the time came that I decided my son was being treated as a big personage, instead of as a child, by the natives (he had quite an air of authority, and even the adult natives obeyed him), and I thought Moresby atmosphere was not conducive to a normal life, I decided to send him to boarding school.[33]
>
> I looked after Ian entirely myself . . . I didn't want him to be given so much attention that he would become a little tyrant. [Mary Pulsford]
>
> Of course in some ways, having the natives to look after the children was slave-like. For example they would swing the children on swings. They were carried too in their little house with mosquito netting around it. [Isabel Platten]

Pat Murray and her brother Jim learned how to make water bombs and one Saturday when the labourers were waiting for their rations, the children bombarded them from the branches of a tree:

> We used to try to bomb each boy with a water bomb as he went past. We hardly ever hit them and the boys used to think it was a bit of a joke too and they used to yell out and dodge and everything. But Dad didn't take a very good view of that and told us not to do it any more.

Although the accounts gathered in this book do not tell tales of economic exploitation or physical violence, such exchanges clearly marred much of colonial life. Furthermore, white missionaries, plantation owners or government outstation workers may have reached for the family analogy more often than Papua New Guineans. But there can also be little doubt that, at whatever cost of accommodation and adaptation, there were many instances of humorous, friendly, and reciprocal exchanges between those who lived in and around the little bush manor down the road.

White society in town

Mollie Parer's description of life in Wewak reveals the pleasures and amenities of life in town.

The life in New Guinea, in Wewak, it was a lovely peaceful, beautiful life. I never cared if I came back to Australia. I had six natives to do the work for me. In the morning the natives would bring you a cup of tea. You'd get up and they'd have the table laid and the wood stove ready. We always had a proper breakfast, bacon and eggs. We had swings on the wide verandah and two native girls and one boy would play with the children during the morning. I had baskets of hibiscus right round the bush materials house and every morning they'd take the baskets out and throw the hibiscus away and fill up all the baskets with fresh flowers. We all had plenty of silver, wedding presents and all the rest of it, and used it because the natives did the cleaning. They cleaned the bronze one day and the silver the next. I'd just be reading or doing something pleasant.

I had a garden boy and I'd go out and inspect what he was doing and see what the washing boy was doing. He'd wash the clothes and just throw them over—I've forgotten what they used to call it—it was like a vine that he made into a clothesline. He had a sleep while the clothes were drying under the paw-paw tree. Then I'd shake him and tell him to wake up because the clothes were dry. He'd light the iron with coconut shells and he'd iron and bring all the clothes in. I'd think to myself 'Isn't it a nuisance having to put all these things away'. It was terrible when I think about it. Oh dear, I was spoiled.

After our lunch we'd always have a sweet. At night we'd always have soup with our meal. We'd have a siesta after lunch and the girls would wake you up to say afternoon tea was waiting. They'd always serve the silver, serve it properly. We didn't have to clean it, didn't have to do anything.

Then we'd get dressed to go down to the beach. I used to wear two frocks every day, one in the morning and one to go down to the little town in Wewak every afternoon. No washing to do, no ironing to do, never used a serviette a second time. We'd go to the beach and I'd have a book and the natives would play with the children, making castles, and I'd just sit there reading. Oh, what a lazy life.

I grew very fond of my servants. They had a sense of humour, at least the ones I had. I liked them.

Back in Australia after the evacuation:

All I did was work, all the washing and the ironing and I wasn't used to it because I'd had help. That's all I seemed to do was work, work, work. I was caring for my aged mother too and dad

[Mollie's husband] always had someone staying. I was just like a machine. There was no electricity, no gas. I had to make a fire every morning, I had to chop the wood. It was frightful. I'd look at the table at night and think 'All these dishes belong to me'. For a joke sometimes I'd call out 'One fella boy come rausim all together something belong table—quick time!' I'd stare at all these things.

Lilian Overell notes the indolence induced by the availability of servants, as she and her hostess looked at photos:

I, having of course been well brought up, after looking at a photo, placed it on the little table at my left hand.
  'Oh', begged my hostess, 'please do not give yourself so much trouble! Simply drop them on the floor, the "Maries" are here to pick them up'.
  So I languidly let them fall and tried to make believe that I had always been a princess with slaves to wait on me.[34]

Life in town was punctuated by annual collective events—picnic races, swimming carnivals, cricket competitions between Rabaul and Kavieng (Pat Murray), Christmas parties at government house, Anzac Day celebrations. As Daphney Bridgland notes, important people in or near town were routinely invited to meet visiting dignitaries:

> It was a good life, it was exciting, because when we lived there we met quite a few interesting overseas visitors. When visited by members of the Royal family, you stood a good chance of meeting them. If your husband was number one of anything you were invited to most social occasions. I don't really agree with that. I feel there were other people in the community who were entitled to be given those opportunities too.

Dignitaries visited outstations far less frequently, and their arrival was preceded by anxious preparations. The Administrator, Colonel Murray, and his wife, visited Dixie Rigby's house in 1949. Mrs Murray was apparently afraid of spiders and Dixie Rigby and her houseboys vacuumed every corner of the house. Even so Mrs Murray found a spider in her bedroom. Isabel Platten, while Gil was chairman of George Brown College, agonised over the entertainment of the Governor-General and his wife, Lord and Lady Gowrie. She was told by other members of the Rabaul community that she should not suggest they needed to 'freshen up' or use the toilet. However, the visitors in true Vice-Regal style put Isabel's fears to rest:

> I indicated where the water and basin etc. were; she looked at me most kindly and said, 'My dear, you have thought of everything'.

There was one other necessary item we needed to consider, the all-important 'loo'. We all, of necessity, had outside 'loos' which were located some metres away from our living quarters. Would it be an embarrassment for our guests to be so obviously on the move, so to speak! . . . Lady Gowrie asked for the convenience saying 'I never miss an opportunity'.

Membership of the white race but proximity to the dominated race produced an 'ambiguous position on the margins of social distance' for those who lived down the road.[35] Thus the 'junglies' of India 'knew more about India than perhaps was good for them and, even more oddly, they seemed rather to enjoy their isolation'.[36] The missionary was in a particularly ambiguous position, lacking the material resources and often the inclination to maintain the distance deemed appropriate by more affluent white settlers. Some missionary women in India 'so far forgot themselves as to preach in bazaars, to live in an Indian style, and even to wear Indian dress'.[37] Kenneth Ballhatchet goes on to say that some missionaries, especially those from a working-class background (for example, Salvation Army workers), argued that to enjoy close relations with Indians, missionaries should eschew relations with the white elite.[38] White society often saw such austerity as reflecting badly on them all; no white should 'get too close to India'.[39]

Reed reports the same attitudes in New Guinea:

There is a strong prejudice among the general European population against missionary work itself. Working intimately with natives, missionaries cannot and do not observe all the strict canons of white prestige, the code of caste.[40]

Ostracism was a function of the mission's role and position in white society. Their role was to educate, if only in limited ways; their position in or close to the village exposed them to contamination by propinquity. This is revealed in Pat Murray's discussion of an anthropologist who failed to live up to the standards of white society:

I asked Sally if she would like to stay with us while her husband was away. She said 'I'm not afraid to stay alone in the village. Undoubtedly you'd be afraid to stay by yourself'. I said 'Sally, I wouldn't be the slightest bit afraid to stay and the reason is I'm known as a missus, and I expect and get the respect as a missus. You have chosen not to behave like a missus, you may not get the respect a missus will get'.

The comparison of town and country suggests that those living on plantations, government outposts and mission stations shared a relationship with the indigenous people which contrasted with the more limited interactions between the racial groups in Rabaul or Port Moresby.[41] Some white people in towns only ever spoke to Papua New Guineans who were servants, and only to give orders.[42] To town dwellers, the Papua New Guineans were a hazy collectivity, a combination of picturesque backdrop and vague ever-present menace.[43] Down the road, on the other hand, there was daily contact with local people, either living their customary village life or in a process of transition to white mores.

This claim that contact produced knowledge and better race relations is a reflection of the liberal assumption that prejudice grows out of ignorance, while tolerance comes from knowledge of other races. This belief often forms an unexamined basis of colonial histories. Marian Fowler traces the history of the Raj in India in the nineteenth century through four portraits of First Ladies. Emily Eden, sister to the Viceroy Lord Auckland, in 1838 was shaken out of her passivity, lethargy and racism by a tour up country. The famine of Cawnpore brought home to her the 'suffering India exacts from its own, and from its conquerors'.[44] She was later to claim that Britain's commercial greed in India had 'merchandised it, revenued it, and spoiled it all'. 'No other Lady Sahib would see more clearly than that.'[45] Following the Indian Mutiny, which punctured the life of the next first lady, Charlotte Canning, the position of the Viceroy and his consort gradually became more formalised. Vicereines became more distanced from the suffering of India, and lost any capacity to criticise the British Raj. Charlotte Canning's response to the Mutiny was to wonder why the sepoys weren't grateful for what the Government was trying to do.[46] Edith Lytton arrived when Anglo-British society was organised in the most detailed hierarchy; a new Warrant of Precedence in 1877 ranked everyone from Viceroy down to Inspector of Smoke Nuisances. Cosseted at Simla, she would fail to see the effects of famine.[47] Mary Curzon's time was marked by even more formality of relations and the British Raj's ostentatious display of its riches; both captured in her glorious and famous gown, made of peacock feathers with an emerald sown into each eye. Bt this time a flood of memoirs had cast the British experience in India as one of self-sacrifice and self-pity; Lady Curzon adopted this role.

Two points (which have eluded Fowler) may be drawn from this series of biographies. While it is the contact up country with the 'real India' which opens Lady Eden's eyes, she lives in India at a time when she can view that contact sympathetically. While such contact was less likely once British society reached a certain size, Edith Lytton also passed through famine on her way to Simla. But by now a different ideology prevented her from seeing Indian poverty as in any way connected with British rule. Similarly, the women who lived down the road or went bush were not necessarily less racist than those who lived in town. They certainly had more opportunities for contact with indigenous cultures, born at least in part from the dearth of white contacts. But what they made of these contacts was another matter, as the comparison of lady travellers and mission sisters reveals.

Dea Birkett's Lady Explorers sought to emulate white male explorers who had populated the fantasies of their youth.[48] They called their servants derogatory names like 'monkeys', 'Baboon' or 'Caliban' and infantilised them. They sought out powerful men in the communities they visited, assuming that women had no power. Susan Blake paints a rather different picture of female travellers. Male explorers ridiculed the pretended power of indigenous female sultans but Mary Hall identifies a reciprocity between herself, the 'white Queen' and her host, 'their own Sultan': 'She is accustomed to feeling vulnerable, used to deferring to men' and this crack in her own superiority, which comes from her inferior gender, 'can be widened to shed light on the concept of the Other', the people with whom she comes into contact.[49]

While female missionaries were written into colonial society as improvers of the indigenous women, lady explorers defended the exotic cultures that gave them so much freedom and pleasure.[50] Lady explorers sought to maintain their racial superiority by claiming that changeless customs were appropriate for inferior races. They identified with the power of the indigenous men, while female missionaries sought links with the less visible indigenous women:

It was nearly always with the African or Asian man that the women travellers drew their intimate comparisons, for while they were travelling they both were perceived and saw themselves as masculine. In contrast, women missionaries in the field, employed in the feminine sphere of administering to women and children, portrayed foreign societies with a specially keen eye on and sympathy for women's place within it.[51]

Diane Langmore describes the close contact between mission sisters and the villagers:

The diaries of the Methodist sisters record their walking hand in hand with the women, putting their arms round the girls as they read to them, or dancing a Scottish reel with them . . . The sisters of the Sacred Heart Mission describe women and children clinging to their hands, their robes and their veils, kissing them and rubbing noses with them.[52]

Saimon Gaius, who worked with Isabel Platten in her house in 1938 and 1939, notes the closer relationship of the sisters: 'The sisters had a much better and closer relationship with the people than the wives of ministers. I think that was because the wives of ministers always had to move around'.[53]

Mary Woolnough, who 'reached the hearts of the people more than anyone else'[54] spent most of her life at Raluana:

She was here from 1913, before I was born, and came back after the War and left around 1950. She was very close to the people . . . My father was a pastor teacher working in the church. When he came to Raluana for a meeting, Mary, who was very fond of children, asked him to bring the family in. She gave us lollies and toys . . . Raluana was her place. That's why the vocational school here is called the Woolnough Vocational School. When she died, she left some money for the work of the women in Raluana. They had a big service, and her ashes are under that monument.[55]

The sisters went into the villages as servants of the people—dressing sores, tending wounds, and nurturing children. Mary Woolnough has a College named after her; Sister Gabriel was drummed to her grave with the honours of a great man of the village.[56]

Amirah Inglis suggests another reason for this sharp distinction of attitudes between town people and those who lived down the road.[57] Australian administration was a contradictory business, on the one hand attempting to 'civilise the native' but on the other hand preventing too much civilisation. In the towns Papuans had sufficient knowledge of white ways to emulate them. But such emulation was a threat to the whites' superior position, hence the regulations regarding dress, or the common appelation of a Papua New Guinean with education and self-respect as a 'big-head'. In the villages and on the plantations where pre-contact lifestyles were still pursued to a considerable extent, the distinctiveness of the two cultures remained more marked. Educated Papua New Guineans were likely to migrate to towns where work in the police force, the administration or as house boys was available. There they were likely to find other people of their own persuasion and education. Thus race relations in the towns were often contradictory and explosive. The whites lived a grander lifestyle and they lived it among Papuans and New Guineans who more often wished to emulate it. Down the road, amicable relations were maintained through a more widespread consensus over the pursuit of separate 'fashions', reminiscent of the feudal notion of status differences rather than class divisions.

Chapter 2 explored one of the structural forces shaping the lives of expatriate women in Papua New Guinea: whether their destination was government, mission or plantation. Another factor, explored in Chapter 3, was whether they came on their own or someone else's initiative, whether they travelled as wives or single women. A third factor, as this chapter has argued, was that life on an outstation encouraged more contact with Papua New Guineans than did life in the white society of a township.

But these women's experiences also had a temporal dimension. The few women who arrived as pioneers before the 1920s, or came when Independence was close, are outside the scope of this study. None the less, there were significant differences in the temper of racist practices in the decades on either side of the Second World War, as the next two chapters explore.

5

War, a Watershed in Race Relations?

Anumber of commentators emphasise the pervasiveness of place as a metaphor of racial distinction in colonial societies. Race relations could be harmonious as long as the subordinate group 'stayed in their place'.[1] Another strain of the argument focussed on the need to 'keep' the 'native' in his place, and to immediately correct 'cheeky niggers'.[2] Thus 'In the Manichean world of the coloniser and the colonised, of the master and the slave, distance tends to become absolute and qualitative rather than relative and quantitative'.[3] Not only is a subordinate place identified in terms of spatial arrangements, it is reinforced by rules and laws governing incredibly trivial elements of conduct, dress and language. These rules are underscored by power, the power to shoot or imprison or punish. Conquest and control by law and superior means of force stand scarcely concealed behind the patterns of interaction that develop between the two caste-like groups. Both in ideology and the Territory, Papua New Guineans and white women had a place: a place defined in opposition to that of white men. But because both these groups were defined as different from white men, and yet not the same as each other, there were contradictions in the placement of these subordinate groups, as Chapters 7 and 8 explore. This chapter addresses the substructure of imperialist ideology, the use of force and the regulation of land and labour, particularly in the pre-war period. The Second World War created the conditions for changed race relations, and these are explored in Chapter 6, particularly the expression of changing economic relations in cultural markers of difference during the post-war period.

The racism of imperialism

Accounts of Papua and New Guinea written before the First World War reveal a racism that is painful by today's standards. Repeatedly the indigenous people are described as children[4] or as animals,[5] themes which fitted Darwinian evolutionary theory.[6] The Papuan was like a child in his inability to understand complex matters, lack of self-discipline, fluctuating morals and simple beliefs.[7] Being like a child, he must be disciplined in the same way, with physical punishment.[8] Jens Lyng in 1925 suggests 'These primitive people—one-third children, one-third men, and one-third beasts—lack that sense of honour which in civilized communities makes imprisonment a deterrent to crime'.[9]

Beatrice Grimshaw in 1910, an advocate for the colonisation of Papua, describes the people of the villages close to Port Moresby as having 'swallowed all the civilisation they could digest a good many years ago'.[10] They did not fully understand the value of money and wore European clothes only on ceremonial occasions. Later in her book, Grimshaw describes 'the [male] native':

His life is a tissue of murder, fraud and oppression, and his pleasing wife (one of a large number, regular and irregular) never enjoys a moment's pleasure, amusement, or peace during the whole of her miserable life if he can help it.[11]

Civilisation was evidenced in a knowledge of commercial values and the ability to mimic white customs, including the treatment of women as creatures of leisure and refinement. But civilisation could not be learned without the right physiognomy. Thus one group of cannibals is described as 'an ill-made, ugly-looking set of ruffians, and not at all healthy-looking, which is certainly what one would expect'.[12] Lilian Overell in 1923 suggested that the half-caste population, having some 'white' blood, can be 'raised nearer the white level' with appropriate education and training.[13]

Turn-of-the-century imperialist ideologies were pervasive in two ways. They could be found in writings as diverse as social Darwinism, evolutionary anthropology, medical tracts, psychology, boys' adventure stories and other literary traditions, and in 'muscular' Christianity. A 'deeply ingrained Weltanschauung of racism' produced its own poets, philosophers and statesmen.[14] Furthermore, the 'central unifying assumption behind its diversities in rationale and practice in regard to race, social class and gender was the acceptance, often unstated and unconsciously held, of the "natural" superiority of the English gentleman'.[15] In Australia, too, at least in relation to race and gender, if not class, there was an acceptance of this natural superiority: 'Still we may claim we are an imperial race'.[16] A number of writers suggest that racism reached its peak between the 1880s and the 1920s.[17]

Van den Berghe asserts that racism was not a unique invention of nineteenth-century western Europe (for example, the traditional kingdoms of Rwanda and Burandi of Central Africa claimed superiority on the basis of height over the Bantu majority).[18] The first slaves, according to Mason, were Europeans enslaved by Moors who captured British and other ships.[19] However long-distance migration, which provided the necessary visual underpinnings of racism, only became common with colonial expansion. The exploitation, expropriation and slavery which marked European colonial expansion required a justificatory rationale. In 1850 Herbert Spencer, in *Social Statics*, adapted Malthus' 'struggle for survival' into the 'survival of the fittest'. Charles Darwin's *On the Origin of Species by means of Natural Selection* (published in 1859) was combined with the prophets of progress, such as Adam Smith and David Ricardo, to align civilisation with capitalism and produce the 'Social Darwinism' which characterised the last decades of the nineteenth century. Anthropology in this period contributed tales of cannibalism and despotism to further justify a hierarchy of races, with white men at its apex.

Social Darwinism, with its vision of human progress, displaced any lingering Romantic visions, for example Rousseau's 'Noble Savage' or 'Natural Eden'. Beatrice Grimshaw rejected the idea of the Noble Savage, arguing that no savage matched a white man in pluck or endurance, and few in physique or strength; while all were thieves or demanded a full return for anything they gave.[20] Rather than living in a natural Eden, they worked hard to defend their villages, had little knowledge of the surrounding plants and their medicine was 'sorcery pure and simple'. Other commentators clung to a transformed notion of the Noble Savage, degenerated in the tropical climate. Its religious variant was the Fall of Man.[21]

There were always some who advocated a 'civilising mission', the development of native peoples under appropriate tutelage. Even at the supposed 'high point of imperial enthusiasm' Mary Kingsley in 1897 and 1899 argued that the cultural development of Africans was possible.[22] The most liberal position was thus one which ascribed black inferiority to purely cultural factors, and argued that it could be overcome with education.[23] No-one in this period had the vision of 'cultural relativism' a respect for black cultures, as opposed to black people.[24]

Thomas Arnold, Regius Professor of History at Oxford in 1841, claimed that a series of races made its maximum contribution before 'leaving the heritage of civilisation to a greater successor'; except, happily for Arnold, England's achievement was 'not merely the latest stage in history, it was the last'.[25] Dr Robert Knox's *The Races of Man* in 1850 claimed 'Race is everything: literature, science, art—in a word, civilisation depends on it'.[26]

In 1855 Alfred Wallace, on a small island near the coast of New Guinea, was struck by his reading of Malthus to realise:

it suddenly flashed upon me that this self-acting process would necessarily improve the race . . . the inferior would inevitably be killed off and the superior would remain— that is, the fittest would survive.[27]

Social Darwinism allowed the partial 'bettering' of indigenous peoples through the introduction of some extremely selective 'fruits' of civilisation, and the eradication of 'barbaric' practices like cannibalism, suttee and polygamy. Furthermore, the colonisers confronted with equanimity the decimation of conquered peoples through syphilis, tuberculosis and the common cold, as well as slave-trading and the shotgun. Such events merely proved the inherent superiority of the white race. By 1910 such views were no longer respectable. Beatrice Grimshaw disapproved of genocide, commending instead the 'peaceful call on a hostile tribe' to be followed by work on the plantations and other forms of betterment.[28]

In its colonisation of the globe the English ruling class ranked conquered civilisations in terms of their closeness to savagery—their distance from European culture. Thus Indian and Chinese cultures were superior to African; Polynesian cultures were superior to Melanesian, and both to Australian Aboriginal cultures. In Fiji, the British and Australians believed Indians were better house-servants than Fijians and had a better understanding of capital-labour relations.[29] Rowley suggests that 'Tough and clever Chinese, culturally adapted to the requirements of business in frontier situations, have in the Trust Territory managed to thrust a way into economic power through the gap between the other races'.[30] The Chinese in Kavieng worked as carpenters, fishermen and pastrycooks, as well as businessmen, owning stores and the taxi service. However, Pat Murray suggests 'most of them were in the coolie class, not much higher education than the kanaka'. This obsession with the hierarchy of the races found its expression in a succession of measurements—skull size, brain size, and lastly IQ testing which survives to this day. In all these measurements white middle-class men were found superior to blacks, the working class and white women.[31]

In a colonial setting, racist ideologies harden as the struggle over resources intensifies, and as the subordinate group begins to dispute the natural 'superiority' of the white rulers. At the beginning of the nineteenth century the Africans and the Europeans ate and drank together for several days as they negotiated the trading; it was slavery which marked the emergence of racist attitudes.[32] Margaret MacMillan suggests that with the extension of British rule in India, the curiosity of the British and their social interactions diminished.[33] Similarly, in Australia mutually curious frontier contact escalated into a bloody frontier war, once it became clear that exploitation and not mutual advantage was the coloniser's script.[34]

Most explanations for racism connect it with the economic rationale of imperialism. Other commentators, in offering psychological explanations for racism, perhaps believe it will always be with us. Mannoni suggests that economic rationality would commend 'efficient workers' over 'lazy slaves';[35] it is the desire to be absolute master which explains the preference for the latter. Uncertainty or inability to read other cultures is translated into a notion that subjected people are inherently 'evil'. This is a projection of the 'white man's fear of himself', a projection of his own worst attributes. As Wolfers adds, the colonised become a reflection of the coloniser's 'inner difficulties'.[36] Pierre van den Berghe is critical of psychoanalytic explanations for human behaviour.[37] He accepts that the apparently non-economic basis for racism prompts the search for answers based on repressed fears or self-loathing. But for van den Berghe it is not the beast within which prompts racism. Rather, it is the selfish gene within, seeking its own propagation by resisting reproduction with genes from totally different gene pools.

The black races lacked all that which distinguished the superiority of the white gentleman: a rational intellect, a dedication to hard labour, moral constancy and backbone, Christian values and beliefs, self-control and self-discipline. The mutual reinforcement of racist ideology and the structures of economic, cultural and political subordination make race relations peculiarly enduring. Because the subordinate races were 'inferior' education and material resources were 'wasted' on them; thus perpetuating their 'inferiority'.[38] Or as Amirah Inglis puts it, 'all whites were masters of black servants' and black servants received far lower wages than any masters, adding economic barriers to those of caste and colour in the prevention of a shared social life.[39]

The colonialism of the colonised

Australians, although inventors of the White Australia policy, sometimes describe themselves as more benevolent colonisers than the imperial powers. Other commentators emphasise the implications of the White Australia policy, for example in barring Papua New Guineans and Chinese from the colonial public service[40] or from receiving passports.[41] Sir William MacGregor, the first administrator of British New Guinea, adverting to their treatment of Aborigines, described Australians in 1888 as 'the leading opponents of primitive peoples'. He had earlier refused to employ an ex-Queenslander, stating that a man with a Queensland 'knowledge of blacks' would not be 'a desirable policeman here'.[42]

'MacGregor found the decision to hang people difficult and distasteful'; and wrote that no prisoner was flogged during his time in Papua.[43] Instead MacGregor advocated imprisonment followed by a place in the constabulary as educational experiences for Papuans. After his prison term, the Papuan was offered a place in the police force. He later returned to his village with a little property and self-respect, spreading the coloniser's word.[44] Under the British there were no white policemen in Papua. The 1906 Royal Commission opined that Australians would resent being arrested and guarded by a member of the Armed Native Constabulory and recommended that expatriate policemen should be appointed.[45]

Legally prisoners could be chained in New Guinea in 1918; Sir Hubert Murray believed the practice would be disallowed in a British colony. In 1919 the Australian army's 'field punishment number one' consisted of suspending prisoners by their wrists so that they could barely touch the floor with the tips of their toes. The practice was only banned following a complaint by a Methodist missionary to the then Administrator, Brigadier-General George Johnston.[46] Flogging was widely practised in New Guinea when the Australians took over. Despite protests from planters and local officials, it was outlawed in 1919 at the Australian government's insistence.[47] In 1945 'many men' had been sentenced to whippings; the Australian government banned further whippings or hangings without its approval.[48]

Hank Nelson's detailed, if somewhat gruesomely titled, study of capital punishment, 'The Swinging Index' concludes that under the ten years of MacGregor's administration eleven men were hanged; during Hubert Murray's first decade in Papua seven men were hanged. Between 1918 and 1942 about ninety men were hanged in New Guinea, most of them convicted of killing other New Guineans.[49] In Papua there were only two executions, one for rape of a white girl and one for multiple murder. There was closer control of field staff and hanging was seen as a means of protecting the small white community rather than as a method of securing government control, as in New Guinea. Captain H.B. Ogilvy, the Commanding Officer of Native Affairs in New Guinea, conducted expeditions which commonly involved shooting people, killing pigs, and burning houses. He told his police to open fire if there was any resistance and keep shooting until he blew his whistle.[50] In summary, Nelson draws a distinction not so much between British and Australian administration, as between the two Australian administrations.

Under MacGregor it was possible for a Papuan to become an administration official with the same rights and duties as a European; this provision was removed in 1909 by the Australian administration.[51] The British Civil Service, as a career service, was staffed with graduates and based on a supposedly colour-blind estimation of merit.[52] As Kenneth Ballhatchet has observed for the Indian Civil Service, it meant that suitably qualified Indians did in time meet the entry qualifications, becoming from the 1880s members of the upper echelons of the Civil Service and judges of the misdemeanors of white residents.[53] On the other hand, Janice Brownfoot suggests that the British women in Malaya thought the Australians and Americans were 'too egalitarian' and 'too casual' in their treatment of the Asian population, partly because there was no equivalent of the British Civil Service based on a public school and Oxbridge tradition.[54]

On the Australian mainland 'native administration' was synonymous with police treatment of Aborigines. Recruits to the public service in Papua New Guinea completed secondary school and two years (later one) of specialised academic training. After two years as a cadet, the recruit might become a magistrate or policeman.[55] Rowley claims that the first action of the Australian government when New Guinea became a mandated territory was to expropriate the German plantations; 'native administration' was 'a series of after-thoughts'.[56] Australians did not have a long imperial tradition of colonial service viewed as the obligation of trained men, a latter-day version of *noblesse oblige*.

None the less it is often argued that the colonial rule of Papua New Guinea was a relatively benevolent concern. A government document in 1910 proclaimed that the 'colony-making methods of earlier days', extermination or enslavement, were now displaced: the 'chief effort of the rulers is to preserve the colonial races, civilise them, reform them from their savage ways, and use them as a means of honestly developing the country'. The 'Papuan is by a long way the best treated black in the world'.[57]

In comparison with the German administration, this claim may have contained a germ of truth. The punitive raid was more a feature of German than British rule, forty such raids being mounted in German New Guinea between 1898 and 1912.[58] Brigadier-General Wisdom described the German period thus:

Every employer could and did flog his employees, and it was practically impossible to find a white man, except the Missionaries, who had not his mary, and that in the procuring of the mary her like or dislike was not of the least importance.[59]

Policing of regulations improved under Wisdom; fifteen Europeans were prosecuted for offences in 1922–23, while fifty-three were prosecuted in 1925–26.[60] On the other hand, Nelson's study suggests that the Australians picked up where the Germans left off, an estimation echoed by Wolfers: 'New Guinea legislation tended to be harsher and to separate the races more firmly than its southern counterpart'.[61] On the other hand the Germans generally left the New Guineans alone, and controlled them only for the purposes of providing labour for the plantations. Against this, Australia's 'paternalistic' administration in both Papua and New Guinea involved extensive interference in village life, following the 'MacGregor system'.[62]

The Australian administration's paternalism often confused the people: 'Australian policy in Papua and New Guinea always traversed a narrow path between devotion to the civilising mission, and contempt for those who needed it'.[63] Thus government officers could initiate proceedings as nominal plaintiffs 'on behalf of any native who appears to have a bona fide claim and who is not able to institute and conduct his own litigation'.[64] The government officer, not the intending plaintiff, decided whether the claim was bona fide. Contracts for the sale of boats which were not canoes and for a value of more than five pounds were to be expressed in writing, or they were illegal. 'Certain natives may be exempted by the Commissioner for Native Affairs from the provision of the Ordinance by reason of their ability to understand the nature of commercial engagements.' Money or property of more than fifty pounds in value left to a beneficiary 'known [to] have squandered money received in a lump sum' was to be administered by a court-appointed trustee.[65]

Feminist writers have agonised over similarly protective legislation for women. While such legislation accepts and attempts to redress imbalances of power, its very operation contributes to the definition of women as subordinate, as needing special protection. As with married women last century, Papua New Guineans were limited in the commercial dealings they could make and the disposition of their property, in their case not by giving that power to a husband, but to a white administration.

Sir Paul Hasluck disapproved of 'paternalism' with its underlying notion that a community can reach 'an age of majority'.[66] However, he sidles uneasily between conceptions of superiority and equality: 'When one gives a hand to a lame neighbour, one has to take care not to act as though he is weak in the head as well as wobbly in the legs'.[67] Thus it was not the mind (inherent capacity) of the Papua New Guinean which was wanting, but the body (culture).

Ultimately Wolfers suggests that the more extensive racist legislation under the Australian administration in Papua may have been due to the increased work of exploration and pacification rather 'than any real difference between the racial sensitivities' of Britain and Australia.[68] Australia's colonial rule was further modified by the lateness of the colonial experience, entirely contained within this century, and the influence of the League of Nations and the United Nations on Australian administration of at least New Guinea. Perhaps, too, the long-term effect of Australia's colonial impact is best captured by the term 'benign neglect' which identifies the niggardly resources expended by Australia on the colonial task, and the focussing of those resources on political administration and health care rather than education. As a result, it was many years before Papua New Guineans had a voice which would command the attention of the colonisers, the English-speaking voice of Australians themselves. This issue is taken up in the next chapter.

Paul Rich suggests that the 1914–18 war marked the end of a clear belief in white racial superiority.[69] Home rule and black nationalist movements emerged in Africa from the formation of the African National Congress in 1912. In 1919 E.B. Du Bois called the first Pan-African Congress in Paris. More Britons came to accept the desirability of the multi-racial commonwealth. The League of Nations developed the notion of colonial trusteeship, emphasising the obligations of the 'advanced nations' to undertake their 'sacred trust of civilisation' of those in their 'tutelage'.[70] Australia's trusteeship of New Guinea brought questions from the League of Nations, for example concerning the use of corporal punishment in supposedly economic labour contracts. Australia, itself just two decades earlier a collection of colonies, had neither the diplomatic nor economic resources to fulfill its role on this international stage.[71] Responses to the League oscillated between servility and hostile over-reactions to criticism.[72]

Edmund Piesse was appointed in 1921 to ensure that Australia's obligations under the League of Nations were met. He recommended that all non-European owned land should be vested in New Guineans, urged expenditure on health facilities, education in handicrafts and agriculture, attention to the effects of labour recruiting on local populations and specialised training for civil servants.[73] Most of these suggestions were too radical for Wisdom and the Prime Ministers, Hughes and Bruce, both of whom endorsed the claim that 'The Territory must pay its way'.[74] Australia was protected from intensive scrutiny by the League by the fortuitous silence or silencing of its harshest critics, and the even more blatantly racist policies practised in South Africa.[75]

The fall of Singapore in 1942 and war in the Pacific dealt another blow to white supremacy,[76] only retrieved by the arrival of the apparently rich Americans who routed the Japanese.[77] However, the Americans called the Papuans 'Joes' and treated them in a more egalitarian manner than the Australians had.[78] Internationally, the notion of partnership replaced trusteeship in an attempt to recruit colonial manpower to the war effort.[79]

African and Asian colonies clamoured for independence after the war. The new attitude was captured in the United Nations Charter, with its assertion that the role of trusteeship was to end at the earliest possible date. The basic objectives of trusteeship were laid out in Article 76: to 'further international peace and security' 'to promote the political, economic, social, and educational advancement of the inhabitants of the trust territories, and their progressive development towards self-government or independence as may be appropriate' to their circumstances, and 'to encourage respect for human rights and for fundamental freedoms for all without distinction as to race, sex, language, or religion'.[80] The Australian Mandate of New Guinea was again sensitive to criticism from the United Nations. The Minister for External Territories in 1950 (P.C. Spender) asked officials to prevent New Guineans submitting petitions to the touring United Nations mission.[81] In 1955, following United Nations pressure, curfew hours were reduced, and later abolished.[82]

A number of African colonies became independent in the years following the war, seventeen colonies of the British and French Empires in Africa gained independence in 1960, and even Belgium 'shortened her timetable for the independence of the Congo from thirty years to seven months'.[83] Challenges to race superiority produced contradictory results. 'Old hands' responded to the new uncertainties with a more strident racism, calling for a clearer delineation of the places of ruler and ruled. None the less more members of the colonised race received a Western education, entered the public service, and became the educated elite who successfully demanded independence. This educated elite gained access to another civilisation and lifestyle, and could now make the empty claims of racism clear: 'colour's everything to do with it 'cause nothing else is'.[84]

Rule by force: kiap versus missionary

The patrol officer, or *kiap* was the sharp end of government power and the point at which most villagers had contact with white rule:

> I think the early administrators were trying to do things in a peaceful way, at least the best of them were. But it was an invasion—there's no doubt, just as we invaded Australia. And, as there was in Australia, there was hostility and the people were subdued and 'civilised'.
> [Pat Andersen]

'In practice, the administration had to subdue almost every district by force'.[85] The 'power of life and death' resided in the patrol officer, while few villagers were articulate enough to know their rights or question his actions.[86] Villagers, themselves used to violence in the competition for power, may have understood the force of Australian pacification.[87] Certainly the justification for hangings and floggings was based on setting such examples.[88]

The *kiap* did not patrol alone, but with Papua New Guineans, 'savages in serge' as Sir Hubert Murray once called them.[89] From MacGregor onwards, one objective of the native constabulary was to turn savages, often ex-prisoners, into men who could 'keep open the laneways between civilisation and the Stone Age', who by mixing with men from other tribes and working in many corners of the Territory could understand and spread the idea of a nation to Papua New Guineans.[90] These noble sentiments were not always realised in practice. The indigenous police force were not above using their position against other Papua New Guineans, in rape, assault or extortion.[91] The Native Police in Queensland, often brutalised ex-prisoners, have been described as the most brutal of the 'pacificying' forces in the frontier wars.[92] It appears that the native constables in Papua New Guinea, who had no kin or other affiliations with most of the villagers they met, were also on occasions violent when not properly controlled by their white superiors.

Some patrols produced a tangled web of paybacks and violence. The 'Tinai Valley Patrol' resulted in the death of fourteen people in three incidents, three government carriers amongst them. Following an enquiry, six constables were tried and found guilty of murder or attempted murder (receiving four and three years' imprisonment) but the white Patrol Officer and Constable were acquitted.[93] On another patrol, Tawi (a villager) was stripped naked and he, his wife and his promised wife were bound to crosses in the village. Tawi had refused to obey a constable's order and attempted to prevent the abduction of his promised wife by a native policeman. According to Kituai, prisoners were kept in holes in the ground, where native policemen defecated and urinated on them.[94] He concludes that the 'colonial state was imposed by violence and intimidation'.[95]

In 1931 an Austrian was sentenced to death in Papua following a 'nightmare of shooting and rape' as he and three other white men travelled across the Highlands.[96] By contrast Michael Leahy was not punished for the killing which accompanied his prospecting trips into the Highlands in the early 1930s. Leahy's 'contact' with Papuans consisted of shooting at least thirty-one men (his diaries implied many more). The Anti Slavery and Aborigines Protection League in London pressed the Permanent Mandates Commission of the League of Nations for an enquiry. While it may have been acceptable for government officers to kill indigenous people in the name of exploration, scientific or geographical enlightenment, it was felt that the pursuit of gold by a working-class privateer was quite a different matter. However, the enquiry whitewashed Leahy; the Australian administration being more sympathetic than the Permanent Mandates Commission to Leahy's pursuit of gold.[97]

After 1917, a child who did not attend school could be whipped, and only in 1929 was some notice taken of the parents' desire for children to attend religious festivals.[98] There were many battles between the Mandates Commission and the New Guinea administration over the use of flogging as a punishment for indentured labourers. In 1924, prompted by scandals in the Australian press, A.S. Canning conducted an enquiry into flogging and forced labour. The Methodist mission was sufficiently convinced of Wisdom's good intentions to withhold information from Canning,[99] who suggested that physical punishment was not alien to local culture: 'One trait of native character which was brought out before me is that he will not complain of a blow or punishment if he thinks he has deserved same'.[100]

Villagers often turned to their local minister to protest the intrusions of the *kiap* or the district officer on patrol. Missionaries had several advantages over *kiaps* in their relations with the villagers. Missionaries learned the local dialect, they stayed in the one location longer, their intentions were professedly more benevolent, and they trained a group of local helpers and supporters.[101] In some areas the villagers consulted the mission before obeying the command of an officer.[102] Missionaries accompanied police on patrol as interpreters and to ensure innocent people were not arrested.[103] *Kiaps* often felt that missionaries were intriguing against them,[104] and not without good reason:

> Let us even cover up their faults and failings, as a father does with his children; do not hand them over to the civil authorities unless they are dangerous criminals and even in this case let us first try to correct them ourselves.[105]

Shrewd villagers recognised such conflicts of interest, and played *kiap* and missionary off against each other.[106] Robinson Butbut, a minister with the United Church in New Britain, suggests a widespread use of physical punishment:

> The kiaps of those times were like this. If they wanted goods carried when they went on patrol, we would carry their goods. If you didn't want to carry the goods or didn't understand them, they would beat you. Kiaps' ways were different to that of the missionaries. The plantation owners, too, if they thought the people didn't work properly, they would hit them and be angry with them. The people of the church did not get angry with the local people, so we were not afraid of them. They would sit down with us, show us things and so on.[107]

Ilias Tabar draws a similar distinction:

> It is true that the station bosses used to beat their workers, but the talatala doesn't do things like that. The kiaps also bossed us

about. But we took it because if we tried to be bigheaded something might happen to us. After the War, however, we started looking after ourselves and these practices changed.[108]

Jean Mannering comments on the role of the missions in settling disputes:

A young patrol officer came through the villages in the Baining Mountains from time to time. And he'd just say to his police boys 'Kill that pig. Kill those fowls up there'; and he'd just commandeer one of the native houses for his police boys. People couldn't do anything about it. They'd come to the missionary, for the missionary was their only representative, to stand up for them. They couldn't say anything to the kiap because they were frightened of him. Almost every time after a patrol officer had been through, we had someone up complaining about something. It might be a pig someone was fattening up for a feast, and they just shot it without asking his permission.

Saimon Gaius maintained his childhood suspicion of the government until the late 1960s.[109]

In 1914 a government party killed ten Papuans (including one woman, a boy and two girls) near Kikori, ostensibly because they were about to attack the mission. Eva Butcher is sceptical:

Why did they not fire at us when we came past three or four days before the launch with Police on? They fired at the Police not us and then they were here two days before the fight helping us carry goods up from Sir Arthur.[110]

The enquiry blamed the mission for the outbreak of violence. In 1933, following the killing of Father Mosscheuser, the District Officer of Morobe blamed the missionaries:

[their] forces were small and inadequately protected, carrying as they usually do one or two rifles and three or four shotguns. They do not appear to handle the natives with the necessary firmness.[111]

Ann Deland also comments on such disputes in January 1928, (before the birth of her son directed her attention inwards to the domestic sphere):

I am afraid the quarrel between the Government and the Mission is not helping matters. The Government has done nothing for the natives here. They pay Mervyn 100 pounds for treating Natives in the Group, but as they seldom do their rounds he has no chance of seeing the natives . . . The Mission has done all the charting of the coasts and exploration work that has been done.

On the other hand, the Mission has been opposing the Government where it can. They are afraid to let the control go to the Government, and, worse still, they are in one or two cases, urging the natives not to pay their taxes, as the Government does nothing for them. That, of course, makes for trouble.[112]

While the New Guinea administration was in its infancy, the local Methodist Chairman, W.H. Cox, had the advantage of years of local knowledge. It was said that he and the Administrator ran the Territory:

and there was much in it . . . He knew the laws and regulations and why they were made, he had an amazing grasp of property matters, and he knew the native people, all of these far better than anyone else.

When the Nakanai murders occurred we were at Kabakada (it must have been late 1925). Not sure now whether it was one or two white men speared to death. The culprits were caught and [we] were in Synod when the news came that they had been sentenced to death. Mr Cox adjourned the Synod immediately and hurried to Rabaul to the Administrator. It was his influence that prevented the death sentence from being carried out.[113]

Jean Mannering comments that before the war when ill-treatment occurred in her husband's circuit, the Chairman in Rabaul, Mr MacArthur, was notified. He had a seat on the Legislative Council:

I can remember Mr MacArthur saying that he wouldn't miss that meeting, it didn't matter how sick he felt, because he was the only voice of the people. The other representatives were only representing the whites, the plantation owners, the businessmen and the government. Probably most plantation people felt the missionaries were working against them because they were standing up for the natives all the time. The missionaries taught the native people that they were as good as the white man. It paid the other white people to keep them as servants, and cheap labour, so they didn't like the missionaries preaching that.

However missions also worked with the government. They upheld white law, even though they attempted to negotiate it. They were themselves occasionally guilty of flogging their servants and they were protected by white violence.[114] Monckton, as incoming Magistrate at Samarai, reports a patrol his predecessor (Moreton) recommended: 'Get down and settle the business as soon as you can . . . you may have to burn some powder, but make Fellows [a missionary] safe, for he is a real good chap'. Monckton

apprehended the culprit, but then released him following Fellows' inter-
cession. Monckton later earned a reprimand from Sir William MacGregor:
'Can you not see that, by your action in this case, you have given the
natives the impression that the Mission can summon the Government forces,
have people sent to gaol and then have them released?'[115] Daphney Bridgland
tells of the Catholic priest who, on being told that the District Commissioner
wished to extend the airstrip, convinced the local people at Volopi to accept
a land exchange so the government could achieve its purpose.

The rough justice of the *kiap* was backed by the legal system, administered
in the first instance by the District Officer, and for more serious offences
by judges. Just as missionaries agonised over the correct balance between
local ceremonies and Christian beliefs, so too did judges attempt to negotiate
the dictates of the Criminal Code, designed for white Queenslanders, and
the customary law and understandings of the 'man in the *laplap*'. In the
upshot most judges agreed with J.H.P. Murray, the Administrator: 'it is
our criminal code and not that of the Papuans that is going to survive;
so we punish murder and we punish cannibalism'.[116]

In fact it would appear that the man in the *laplap* had most freedom
to fall short of the man on the Clapham Omnibus in his treatment of
indigenous women. He was forgiven for having relations with a girl below
the age of consent because he had no notion of 'chronology'; he could
not foresee that 'moderate blows' might kill an old woman; or that if he
kicked his mother and she had a ruptured spleen, she might die. In contrast
with Europeans, mere words were enough to provoke him. In one case
a woman responded to a man's coarse hailing with, 'You cannot find a
woman to marry, and if you talk like that to a girl child you will die
still unmarried'. He lost his self-control and killed her. The judge accepted
the defence of provocation: 'it does not necessarily follow that the same
principle should apply in a native community where sophistication does
not approach that of, say, seventeenth-century England'.[117]

Pat Murray tells a different story of government intervention, or non-
intervention:

> In the 1930s we had a District Officer called Melrose. He became
> a big wheel in Port Moresby later on. He was nice personally but
> he was a woeful kiap. In those days they used to do these patrols
> round and hold courts and hear native complainants then and there
> on the spot, in the village. It was the most sensible way to do
> it. It was quite a show. They'd go in with two or three police
> boys, and they'd put up a bamboo pole and flag, or usually the
> village would have a pole up already. They'd run up a flag and

lay the table out under a suitable tree, usually a big tauan, and all the kiap's papers—and the kiap would sit there and examine the village books and talk to the tul-tuls and luluais and doctor boys and all the various village people.

And then they'd say 'Has anybody got any complaints?' And they'd say 'Yes, we've got two courts we want' or whatever. Then they'd wheel out the complainant and defendant and hear the court. The kiap would make his decision on the spot and dish out whatever penalties . . .

Occasionally there'd be more serious things brought up and Melrose used to give the most incredibly stupid penalties for really serious crimes. Well, the one that really brought him down was when he heard a case (in Lamasong village I think it was) of an attempted murder. And it was a definite attempted murder: the culprit sneaked up on another bloke and had a swipe at him with an axe, but he didn't succeed. It was an absolutely clear cut case, the bloke even confessed that he had tried to kill him. And old Melrose sat there with his head in his hand, apparently. Some other European was there and watching this, I think it was the manager of Lamasong. Kanakas were wondering 'What's going to happen now?' And he looked up and said 'Fine: ten shillings'. And the villagers all burst out 'Ha, ha! Ha, ha!' And the bloke went round to his friends and collected ten bob and put it on the table and he was a free man.

And it was after that that the Planters Association put in a petition to get Melrose moved. That was a culminating thing. All sorts of things like that had been happening. I mean, law and order was just beginning to go out the window because they knew they could do anything . . . we had to live in the bush and if you have potential murderers running around, knowing that they would either get away with it or get fined ten bob, well what protection have you got?

Peter Murray, Pat's husband, identified the antagonism between planters and government: 'I used to say the Annual Congress of the Planters Association were Her Majesty's Royal Opposition in New Guinea'. The Murrays felt that administration under the Chifley Labour government after the war was particularly lenient.

Dixie Rigby and her husband tutored the local people in the ways of white administration. Their response reveals a shrewd apprehension of the power relations in colonial society:

They used to come up to the verandah at night after we'd had our dinner, and sit on moonlit nights. The whole village would come up and sit and talk . . . We were often stumped but you had to just be a bit simpler and use your common sense and go on from there. On one occasion we were getting a new administrator. How did we choose? How did we get an administrator? Why was he so different from everyone else, so high above them? And that was rather a poser to explain qualities to more or less ignorant natives. So I explained he had to be a man of high quality mentally, and strong for the truth, and strong for this, that and the other. Not a strong man who could push you over, but strong spiritually. One of them said yes he could see that and it was a very good idea too. 'Yes, he needs to be strong because you know a great many of us don't want the white man here. But I myself don't mind because as far as I can judge, if you kill one white man it's just like the ants, a lot more come to take his body away and stay'.[118]

Land ownership: the fruits of benign neglect?

It is commonly assumed that the Australian administration's protection of indigenous land rights assured post-Independence stability in the villages. Isabel Platten claimed that as long as they kept their land, the people maintained a secure means of livelihood. Because of the inhospitable terrain and the lateness of white contact, even after the Second World War many of the Highlands people were still insulated from white contact. Tribes were 'discovered' as late as the 1970s. Thus some areas of Papua New Guinea remained unaffected by white administration, even up to Independence in 1975. Fortuitously, this benign neglect may be described as 'the greatest benefit conferred on New Guineans. It left so much of the Territory's resources underdeveloped until New Guineans would have a chance to share in that activity'.[119]

In some areas there were extensive expropriations, and all land not occupied by New Guineans was brought under government ownership by the Australian administration. Rowley claims there was no thought of repatriating the expropriated German plantations to the New Guineans, even though it was in these areas that land pressures were the greatest.[120] However, local land rights on expropriated properties were investigated and validated in most adjudicated cases.[121] By 1939 only 1.5 per cent of land was under plantation, but 80 per cent of the plantations were in the Gazelle Peninsula and other parts of New Ireland, where the villagers experienced severe land shortages. New Guineans resented the loss of their land.

> When my husband first came to Fisoa and started to delve into
> its history, he found much bitterness against the white man. He
> was told of how the village land had been acquired in the early
> days, of the inclusion into European plantations, adjacent to the
> village, of certain land sacred to the clan and bound up with its
> material and spiritual welfare; of the alienation of the land of the
> sea front, and the passage in the reef where the best fishing grounds
> were situated . . . The beautiful road around New Ireland, skirting
> the sea-front had brought only bitterness and hatred to the surrounding
> villages. It was built under the supervision of Bulominski in German
> days. Actually it amounted to slave labour, treating the natives as
> beasts of burden. He forced the men and in some cases the women,
> to do all the heavy labour, whipping and beating them when they
> rebelled.[122]

The Land Ordinance of 1935 preventing Papuans from selling or leasing
land to anyone other than the Crown was subject to the provision that
'no purchase or lease of land may be made until by sufficient enquiry he
[the Lieutenant-Governor] has become satisfied that the land is not required
or likely to be required by the owners' and only leaseholds of ninety-nine
years or less were permitted.[123] Rowley suggests that official investigations
were usually hasty formalities.[124] Perhaps this is unsurprising, given the non-
correspondence between landholding peasants and the 'free' labour force
required for capitalist endeavours. As Karl Marx said of the Swan River
settlement, so too did the *Rabaul Times* note despairingly 'every native is
a landed proprietor' and dismissal 'holds no terrors'.[125] Contrariwise, Sir
Paul Hasluck expressed concern over the creation of a 'landless proletariat'.[126]

Labour policies: benign intervention?

The ideological justifications for imperialism often had simple economic
bases. In 1849 Thomas Carlyle in 'The Nigger Question' claimed that it
was man's 'sacred appointment to labour' and if the 'Quashee' refused
to do 'what work the Maker of him intended':

bringing out these sugars, cinnamons and nobler products of the West-Indian Islands
for the benefit of all mankind, then I say neither will the Powers permit Quashee to
continue growing pumpkins there for his own lazy benefit.[127]

The Protestant work ethic justified slavery and commerce as the harbingers
of improvement and civilisation. Beatrice Grimshaw describes a labour

recruiting expedition in which the captain lured 'half-scared, half-excited' men with promises of wages which would later buy the tobacco, calico, fish hooks and wife 'that were to make them so important in their village'.[128] Happily the 'leaven of civilisation works' and the labourer acquires 'a taste for good and regular food and undisturbed sleep' while the 'cannibal' loses his violent ways in the security of legal enforcement of his 'excellent treatment'. Similarly Lilian Overell argued: 'It is a good thing for the young boys to learn to work, and they are far healthier than if left in the unwholesome moral and physical atmosphere of their native village.'[129] Indeed, returning labourers gained skills, cash and prestige derived from knowledge of distant places.[130]

Government involvement in the recruiting process was based on a variable combination of its own labour requirements, the necessity at times to supplement the lure of exotic goods with physical compulsion, and a sense of guardianship over 'fair' labour contracts. Pierre van den Berghe is cynical about the intentions of colonial administrations[131]:

Successful administration of a tropical dependency had to be done with as few Europeans as possible. Europeans were expensive to bring in and to maintain at the princely level to which they quickly became accustomed in their colonies; they were notoriously susceptible to disease and alcoholism, and they were allergic to hard work.[132]

It was suggested that the numbers of offenders held on outstations was tailored to the government's labour needs.[133] To 'maximise the output while minimizing the overhead' colonial administrations utilised local power structures (indirect rule) wherever possible.[134] The indigenous population became labourers through the levying of a head tax, which required them to work to earn it. The Australian administration's schizophrenia is revealed by the 1918 Native Plantations Ordinance which attempted to offset the impact of the native tax by setting up plantations near villages. Here cash could be earned by selling copra, rather than requiring men to enter labour contracts.[135] It was not until the 1950s that the labour force in the Territory was able to contract 'freely' as to terms and conditions. On the other hand, the administration did protect villagers from some excesses and iniquities. According to Heather Radi:

prohibition of forced labour is significant. It was the concrete instance of Australia's confidence in their own progressiveness and of their own assumption that their administration of a subject people would be based on humanitarian principles.[136]

Government supervision of labour contracts was not solely the result of benevolent attitudes. Under the League of Nations mandate Australian administration in New Guinea was expected to 'endeavour to secure and maintain fair and humane conditions of labour for men, women, and children'.[137] Endeavour may at times have been the key word. In 1925 Dr Cilento reported that half the indentured labourers had beri-beri.[138] In one year in the late 1930s more than 700 indentured labourers died.[139] In the decade up to 1910 in Papua, there were twenty-seven deaths per thousand indentured labourers; in the next two decades the rate fell to seventeen. In New Guinea in the same twenty years the rate was nineteen. These figures compare with thirty-five deaths per thousand in Queensland between 1893 and 1906. The death rate fell as resistance to disease increased, as labourers were re-engaged for further contracts, and with better nutrition and housing.[140] Indeed all the blame for death in service cannot be laid at the feet of the planters. Daphney Bridgland comments on Highland recruiting after the Second World War:

> When you recruited in the Territory, to recruit a 'plane load of men cost you $30,000 just for the aircraft. Now you had to walk into the mountains or wherever they lived, you had to get them out. That might take you a week or a fortnight to do that. Then you had to feed them and clothe them until you could transport them. For the first six months they were so full of grillie and yaws and hookworm and tropical ulcers . . . We had labourers come out of the Highlands who had never seen a wheel . . . So when they say they only get two pounds a month or something like that, they might have in the early days but they got much better conditions. Any good plantation knew that if their labour wasn't well fed and well looked after they'd not be getting any work done.

Weber and Marx both saw slave labour as irrational and backward. The purchase of slaves was expensive, there were difficulties in 'recruitment' and slaves were rarely educated in the use of tools or machinery. In comparison, free labour was cheaper and allowed for more complex forms of production.[141] The dull compulsion of the market is sufficient where labourers have no other choice; in colonial societies where labourers control their means of production (land), the state, coercion and the law must step in. Class differences in capitalist societies are sufficiently maintained by economic mechanisms. In colonial societies these are overlaid by racial distinctions enforced by political control. Thus the state becomes involved in the regulation and supply of slave labour, indentured labour, and other forms of unfree labour.[142]

Connolly and Anderson claim that 'The Administration's main activity in these pre-war years was ensuring that village men went to work as labourers for Australian private enterprise'.[143] Thus the government not only ensured that labour contracts were kept, it also returned absconding labourers. Percy Robinson in the pre-war years reports that twenty-four recruits absconded with their axes and blankets, but that seven were captured and returned by a patrol.[144] In 1939 in New Guinea more than 1200 labourers deserted, which perhaps gives some support to Rowley's contention that if there was a way of earning cash without working for the white man the Papua New Guinean chose it.[145]

The government officers were supposedly required to ensure the willing entry of labourers into their labour contracts; that villages were not denuded of able-bodied men; the correct distribution of rations to the labourers; and their general health.[146] In 1933, to facilitate the employment of labourers in the mining industry, the limit on employment within a hundred miles of the labourer's village was removed. In 1934 the Mining Ordinance removed restrictions to allow employment for twelve months without a written contract of service and, under certain conditions, with no limit as to duration.[147] Rowley describes this as 'a balance of justice with expediency',[148] Jean Martin as 'enlightened self-interest'.[149] The system attempted to ensure conditions that would not deter further recruiting, but also would not cripple the nascent plantation economies. Between 1937 and 1939, fifty-eight *mastas* were convicted of assault, but in the latter year 174 labourers were convicted of failing to show reasonable diligence and 115 for failing to obey a reasonable order.[150]

Dixie Rigby's husband did not see his role in terms of 'enlightened self-interest' but as a protector of the labourer's conditions:

> At the plantations you see . . . natives all had to be paraded. All their rations and everything, their cups and their plates and their spoons and their laplaps and everything, if you were doing your job properly they all had to be inspected. And Reg wouldn't let the plantation owners there, which used to annoy them. I said to him once 'What does it matter?' He said 'They won't speak to me freely in front of him'. That didn't necessarily mean he was a bad man, but they knew there was a difference. We never stayed at plantations—that's one of the reasons I didn't meet many people in New Guinea. Because Reg said 'If I go and accept his hospitality, if it's a verdict against him, I can't honestly do it'. So that was that. But once when we were there, it was a manager. And of course the managers were paid terribly badly. We were paid badly, but they were on pittances—twenty pounds a month was the average wage for a New Guinea manager. You really couldn't live on twenty pounds a month in spite of the fact you had a plantation.

However, he'd clear the whole lot of them out and they'd have to parade their things. And I said to him one day 'Why did you do that?' He said 'Didn't you notice anything?' I said 'They all looked as if they had all been issued with new rations, with new laplaps and new cups'. And he said 'Exactly'. 'If I leave it like it is, they'll all go back to the store'. Oh yes, a lot of people made their money that way. You see the manager or owner would take you by the elbow and lead you, 'Come and have a whisky'. My husband doesn't drink, never has. They couldn't take Reg up to have a drink because we didn't drink. So he said 'I'll see their dinner served'. So their rice would be dished up on new plates.[151]

The Australian administration sought to rely on the coercive elements of the relationship much longer than the League of Nations thought desirable or necessary. The League, and later the United Nations, sought to re-define the contract as truly that of wage-labour. In 1928 corporal punishment was still allowed, despite the Permanent Mandates Commission's claim that breach of contract was a civil offence and should not be met with a penal sanction.[152] In 1929 the International Labor Organisation suggested to the Mandates Commission that penal sanctions for breach of labour contracts were inappropriate and that civil sanctions only should apply. Murray asserted that 'the penal sanction must remain as long as the indenture system is retained . . . I would not even contemplate its abolition for many years to come . . . it protects the native as well as the employer'.[153]

The 1929 Rabaul Strike was possibly the most famous instance of labour indiscipline in the colony's history. Although largely peaceful, it shook the white community to its foundations—the businesspeople turning on the administration for its poor handling of the 'natives' and the missions for their apparent participation in the strike. Bill Gammage attributes the strike to a number of factors. He identifies the exceptional position and personality of the leader Sumsuma who had become a boat's captain and had banked seventy pounds of his pay, 'astronomical' by the New Guinea standards of five or six shillings a month.[154] Sumsuma was aware of strikes in Samarai and Australia. In 1929 the 217 native police had unusual responsibility and were supervised by only eight inexperienced European policemen. Sumsuma used *wantoks* (members of the same clan) to spread news and rally support. On the other hand, and perhaps contributing to the rapid collapse of the strike, the Rabaul workforce was divided by tribal hostilities; there was little discontent over wage rates except perhaps among boats' crew who had been mocked by American Negro sailors.

Isabel Platten describes the morning of the strike.

At some time whilst we were in Rabaul there occurred an event that shook the complacency of the European population. The entire native population of Rabaul went on strike. On a Monday morning Gil and I woke up to a servantless house. This event wasn't all that odd because we had experienced the inconvenience of staff taking off—sometimes with a good supply of goodies from our store room. Then I did notice a strange sight. White men returning from 'house-ice' carrying blocks of ice on their shoulders. One man made a sorry sight. He had forgotten the all important hessian bag on which the ice sat. A thin tropical shirt was no barrier to the discomfort of a close encounter with a very large ice block.

Opposite our house was the building of the German Club and the man in charge there was very obese. So much so that he was not able to put his shoes on and was standing in the middle of the road waving his shoes and pleading with all the passersby to help him. I think Gil went across to his aid.

News soon trickled around. The fact that we were without servants had been arranged by the native police force and no one in the European population knew a whisper about it. The native people divided into two groups according to religion, the Roman Catholics and the Protestants, and these two groups quietly marched to the church centres at Malaguna. The Methodist Mission Chairman, Rev. Margetts, was alerted very late at night to a very large group of people wanting to be heard. He was nonplussed as to how to deal with such a touchy administrative matter. But he handled it well. He was well aware how the people loved to sing so he started them singing. And that was how he and the natives passed the night away. Next morning he told them to return to their places of employment and he would go into the matter of grievances with the authorities. About mid-morning three rather sheepish young men returned to us. The Europeans, or some of them, got a bit paranoid about it all and reacted strangely.

The strikers walked to either the Catholic or Methodist mission, depending on their religious affiliation. Rev. Margetts, of the Methodist Mission, believed they should be paid a 'little more' and promised to convey this message to the government, but also encouraged them to disband. Many men from the Catholic Mission went immediately and quickly back to work. None the less, the townspeople reacted with a mixture of rage and fear, saying they could 'finish us up properly', a 'mere handful of people'.[155] The townspeople had their way. The strike leaders were beaten for confessions, and kept below decks in a sweltering hulk with insufficient food and water. They were punished by being made to stand on deck until they collapsed in agony, their 'skins bubbling'.[156] Two hundred police deserters were tried and sentenced to six months' imprisonment, and the strike leaders given the maximum sentence of three years.[157] Many employers took their own illegal retribution: 'If General Wisdom attempts to prosecute residents who thrashed their deserters, he may find that he will have to prosecute them in batches of a hundred at a time'.[158]

Rowley notes that there was no thought of paying a family wage in the Territory; the village bore the cost of keeping the labourer's family.[159] Daphney Bridgland's husband introduced a system which allowed wives and children to live with the labourers:

> Most of the indentured labour couldn't keep their wives with them. My husband was running the plantations for Mick Thomas. Mick Thomas believed indentured labour worked better and were happier if they had their wives and children with them . . . these people were allocated land to build a native materials house for themselves and to have food gardens. That was good for them, because they had the best of both worlds, the wives to work in the garden, school for their children to go to, medical treatment available or if they had anything seriously wrong straight into Vunapope Hospital.

However, another innovation, the payment of a bonus if extra work was done, was suspiciously supervised by the government:

> Mick's idea was they were paid for the work they did. They were given a mark. If they completed that work for the day and they could do more they were paid for the extra, and this encouraged the men to work and not be lazy. The system was magnificent but the Labour Department was always trying to pick faults with it and trying to make it difficult. [Daphney Bridgland]

The war took men away from villages, where some of them earned comparatively large salaries. There was a huge increase in cash in the hands of villagers as a result of war-time employment (130 000 pounds were spent in the Production Control Board Trade Stores in 1944–45).[160] With few consumer goods available, there was increased gambling and higher bride prices. Some of the young men did not wish to return to village life and customs after the war, and remained in the towns. Daphney Bridgland contrasted the 'older type natives' who were 'fair' with the 'rascals' who 'will just take what they want, and they'll kill you, and they'll maim'.

After the war hours were lowered, wages were increased and the term of the labour contract was reduced from three years to one year. Penalties were lowered and some penal provisions were abolished. The administration promised to abolish indenture within five years. These reforms met with protests from the planters, who were short of labour due to the war.[161] As a result, planters were forced further afield, into the recruiting of Highland labour (Daphney Bridgland and Pat Murray). In 1950 the remaining penal provisions were abolished.

Some years after the war it was decided that all labourers must be paid in cash rather than rations: another extension of the free-wage labour principle to employment contracts. Even so, according to Dixie Rigby, exploitation continued across the counters of plantation trade stores. Dixie Rigby accepted that Papua New Guineans were willing participants in this process, but said 'when you knew what rubbish he was getting, it was offensive to me. But then of course we were never involved in trading, trading wasn't our job'.[162] Pat Murray managed several trade stores for some years, supervising the allocation of stores, checking the accounts and hiring and training indigenous store operators.

Although labourers finally became free to enter civil contracts, they were not free to join and create unions. In 1950 the Ordinance punishing an outsider for creating 'disaffection' against employers was extended to Papua.[163] Sir Paul Hasluck felt that the workers had not 'reached the stage' where they could successfully engage in collective bargaining.[164] He argued that political organisation should be based on 'broader questions' and that an industrially organised political party would be divided on racial lines.[165] Instead he recommended an employment advisory board with representatives from the government, employers and employees; and he was able to prevent the Legislative Council ceding excessive power to the planters on this board.[166]

In the early days, Papua New Guineans worked mainly as policemen, unskilled plantation labour, and house servants. Over time, however, they became carpenters, boat captains, sergeants, medical orderlies, nurses, drivers, mechanics, telephonists, plumbers, printers and overseers. The Second World War saw the number of medical orderlies grow from 297 to 738, and the native police force from 1400 to 24 000.[167] Pat Murray points to the skills that were passed on through employment:

> They kept telling us we were exploiting the country and exploiting the natives and you look at the native communities. You think how many kanakas learned good agricultural practice from planters, how many of them got seed coconuts from us if they wanted them.

And how many were taught things—driving trucks and cars and doing mechanics' jobs, carpentry and plumbing.

When describing their relations with Australians, disgruntled Papua New Guineans used two images: 'We are your dogs, your pigs'[168] or we are the 'pick, shovel' of the white man.[169] In the Solomon Islands, Malaita men said 'We have been used as beasts of burden or engines for work'.[170] These terms capture two notions: that black men were treated as white men's property, and that they were merely useful tools in white men's work. Nevertheless, an expanded role in the colonial workforce was one mechanism by which Papua New Guineans pressured race relations into a new form; a far more significant mechanism was the post-war expansion of education. As time went by, particularly after the Second World War, Papua New Guineans would feel they were deliberately deprived of education as well as economic rewards, as will be explored in the next chapter.

The 'Fuzzy Wuzzy Angels'

Once collective racial ideals become established, they mould personalities and channel inter-racial communication.[171] However, an open social system must have mechanisms for socialising its newcomers and controlling its visitors. Newcomers were encouraged to learn from the old hands if they did not wish to expose themselves to ridicule and ostracism.[172] Transient visitors to colonies were a continuing problem; they did not necessarily share the same racist ideologies and certainly did not have the same vested interest in reinforcing them. In Rabaul in 1929, visitors indulged in the 'disgusting' behaviour of singing, dancing and playing football with the 'kanakas' who are thus 'apt to grow insolent'.[173] During the Second World War, visitors, in the form of soldiers, ignored the old social structures. Imperialist pretensions were sorely tried by retreat in the face of Japanese attack and reliance on Papuan bearers.

The new image of the Papua New Guinean, captured by the term 'fuzzy wuzzy angel', was forged in the absence of white women, evacuated ahead of the Japanese invasion of New Guinea, as was discussed in Chapter 1. The New Guineans were left behind after the white men also 'ran away':

> We had to follow the orders of the Japanese, no talking back, no refusing. We didn't know the Japanese cut throats but he [Gil Platten] told the pastors to tell us to be careful with the Japanese.[174]

> I came out to do the work of the villages when the Japs came.

I continued for a bit but it was very hard for us, for we were in the Bainings area. This is why we worked for the Japanese for four long years.[175]

A number of personal accounts treat the war as a watershed in the 'democratisation of relations' between the two races. However, there are other darker tales of the experiences of war. The propaganda surrounding the 'fuzzy wuzzy angels', the Papuan bearers who saved the lives of many Australian soldiers on the Kokoda Trail, neglects to mention that many were never rewarded for their service.[176] The term 'fuzzy wuzzy angel' derives from a poem written by Bert Beros, a coal-miner, on the Owen-Stanley track in October 1942. He claimed that Australian mothers could send a prayer for 'those impromptu angels with their fuzzy wuzzy hair'. This was printed in the *Courier-Mail* and then in the largest Australian circulating magazine, the *Women's Weekly*. Children in government primary schools learned the poem, and an Australian mother wrote a poem in reply.[177]

In 1965 Osmar White sardonically noted that the bloodthirsty cannibal with a bone through his nose had been transformed into a 'dusky-skinned, mop-headed, sexless Florence Nightingale';[178] perhaps out of a necessity to quieten the fears of Australian mothers, reliant for their sons' safety on such recent savages. Towards the end of the war, the masculinity of the angels was asserted by a medical officer: 'They are not gods—they are not even angels—they are men, and splendid men'.[179]

Although it was not a partnership of equals along the Kokoda Trail, white men's lives depended on the skill and dedication of the bearers. The soldiers treated the Papuans in a far more egalitarian manner than the B4s, and also performed manual labour.[180] Instead of being called 'boys' or 'niggers', the Papuans were called 'Joe' (by the Americans) or 'Sport' (by the Australians). Sir John Guise describes the white soldiers as 'a different type of white people who were friendly'. When 'coloured American soldiers came along we said "Well, we didn't know that a black man could be a captain" '.[181] The Papuans distinguished between the 'English' the pre-war settlers, and the 'Australians' who had come with the war: 'The English would not let us go near them. They said we were dogs not men'.[182] The Australians, however, would share a trench with a Papua New Guinean during a bombing raid.

The 'English' resisted these threats to racial segregation, publishing a booklet, *You and the Native*. This contained advice such as: 'Joke with him . . . But while you play the fool don't forget that you have to maintain that pose of superiority . . . Don't deliberately descend to his level'.[183] If you meet a 'bad egg' 'There is only one thing to do in these circumstances, crack him'.[184] But Australian defence personnel also published racist advice: 'it is impossible to regard the natives as being generally more intelligent than white children at about the age of 8 or 9'.[185] Similarly Chatterton reports an ANGAU (Australian and New Guinea Administration Unit) official as saying 'These Papuans will get along alright so long as they remember that they're kanakas'.[186]

War: a watershed?

The Second World War is often seen as a watershed in the history of Papua and New Guinea. Before the war there were two administrations; afterwards they were combined. Before the war only a 'good class' of whites came to the Territory; the end of the war brought transients and others who did not know how to 'handle natives'. Before the war most education was mission-controlled; after the War the government gradually extended its provision of primary education, and introduced secondary education. Those who went there before the Second World War are called 'B4s' and were described by those who came after as racist, paternalistic, and unsympathetic to the project of propelling Papua New Guinea into the twentieth century. Sir Paul Hasluck, as Minister for the post-war Territory, found 'an unacceptable colonialism among many officials of the Administration'.[187] For their part, the B4s felt themselves to be the true pioneers: 'You might be fortunate enough to be descended from B4s' or marry one.[188] The war, in its disruption of traditional lifestyles and authority relations, encouraged alternative visions of the future.

Lorna Hosking, a B4, describes the pre-war situation: 'Men were men, women were women, children obeyed their parents and the natives knew their place'—akin to 'state wards'.[189] Some turn-of-the-century missionaries sounded as racist as any white in the colony: 'one has to be savage with savages' or 'Never touch a native, except to shake hands or thrash him', 'Rarely agree with a native, and then only when he is alone'.[190] The war brought an end to such certainties. Australian B4s 'ran away' in defeat, to be replaced by more egalitarian visitors, the American and Australian soldiers. After the war, returning B4s attempted to restore the old order, but by the 1950s it was clear that the pre-war days had gone forever. There were too many new arrivals; the Australian government developed a clearer notion of trusteeship; international attitudes to racism changed as colony after colony achieved independence and joined the United Nations.

All of the interviewees who had been in Papua or New Guinea before the Second World War commented on the difference in race relations when they returned. Jean Mannering points out that before the Second World War, the local pastor teachers always sat at the back of the Synod, 'always took a back seat' and only spoke when asked a question. Sister Aquilonia after the war adopted a maternalistic mode, rather than an overtly authoritarian approach: 'natives can do everything themselves provided you . . . supervise', although she adds that 'you mustn't make them feel you are superior. You are one of them and they must be able to come to you with all their troubles, family everything. I had to be a mother to them'.

Saimon Gaius notes:

> We helped in the house and we went inside to clean things and so on, but we didn't sit with them, we have to sit outside. When the local ministers and local tutors came to see them, they had to sit on the floor, they didn't sit on the chairs. Or Gil or the headmaster would stand at the door, and they stood outside and talked. I can say this freely because the change between 1950 and 1960 made me much closer to the Europeans. I remember one day I called a European minister 'John' and the other minister said, 'You shouldn't call him John; you should call him Mister "his name" '. But in the seventies I worked with a man by the name of Don Marshall who came from New South Wales. I was very close to him and called him Don.[191]

A similar point is made by Sios Tabunamagin:

> In those days the Europeans didn't want to be our friends, to sit down and talk freely with us or eat together. They organised it so that we would be separated from them and eat like pigs and dogs. Both the church and the government were alike in these practices. We just accepted it but in those days none of us were arrogant/self-confident [*bik het*] enough to say anything directly to them.[192]

Isabel Platten also notes these changes, but evaluates them differently:

> After the War things changed completely, straight away. Only Gil and Rodger Brown were left, of the old staff. Even most of the sisters had been imprisoned. So all these new young people came, with more democratic ideas. The government was worse than everybody else. They really changed the natives. It must have been a tremendous puzzle to the natives to be suddenly transported.
>
> We thought it would go on and on, just as it was in the pre-war years. We would be sending missionaries up there forever. We

didn't imagine the impact of wars and suchlike. I've often wondered about whether our impact was the best. But there would have been an impact of some sort. Ours was perhaps the kindest one.

Jean Mannering suggests that all the Methodist Chairmen before the War, although benevolent, were autocratic; none were autocratic afterwards. Dixie Rigby suggests: 'After the war the attitude was altered, it was altered on both sides—both acceptance of the European and the European's feeling towards the native'.[193]

Prudence Frank comments:

> After the war ended in 1945, a different type of European arrived in the Territory, some with the interests of the native people at heart, but there were some that introduced bad habits to the Natives. Unfortunately the native people strove to be like the Europeans in their dress, stealing started. Some Europeans introduced them to drink, then when it was legal for them to drink, and a number of the 'old' residents of Papua decided it was time to leave, the writing was on the wall. Doors had to be closed and locked at night, thieving was prevalent, there was no more singing by families and friends under the coconut trees. I used to tell the students that I considered they were better off living in their villages with their pigs, fowls and dogs than trying to be like Europeans, striving to get this and that which was beyond their means. It made me sad.[194]

Generally those who commented on the racism of Australians also denied it in themselves. A common justification was the allusion to a common humanity: 'I treated the children as I would Europeans' or 'some of the half-caste people would come up from Hanuabada to see me—but mostly Mother—and have afternoon tea and bring their children. They were entertained just the same as Europeans. They were people'.[195] 'All men are equal in the sight of God. It makes me very annoyed when I hear people speaking the way they do about other races'. [Jean Mannering]

Mary Pulsford comments:

> There were individual Australians who were absolutely magnificent in the way they interacted with other people. There were some Australians who were absolutely dreadful. I was totally ashamed of them. They were so rude and so obnoxious. They were just absolutely dreadful, and apallingly arrogant . . . The people who often had wonderful relationships were people who could handle that business of recognising other people as people. To me that was one of the great plusses of living in that cross-cultural situation.

When I say all that I realise the tremendous difference in their framework and their ways of looking at things from mine. Also I was aware of when people were trying to take advantage of me, and I wasn't ready to be taken advantage of. But then people do that in any community, they do that when they belong to the same culture.

Both Mary Pulsford and Jean Mannering comment on the bridges built through humour: 'One of the things about pidgin as a language is that it's a wonderful language to have a joke in. It seems that people can get along together if they can laugh together'. [Mary Pulsford] 'The native people had a great sense of humour. They'll turn anything into a joke . . . They'd laugh at my jokes'. [Jean Mannering]

Before the war there could be no attempt at racial equality. Few whites in Papua New Guinea possessed a worldview which comprehended such a possibility, few Papua New Guineans possessed the white cultural capital which could demand it. Even following the war, authoritarianism really only gave way to paternalism, not to egalitarianism. What was at issue was the distance that separated the whites from the local populace, whether this distance should be gradually or quickly closed, and in what manner.

6

The Civilising Mission

Staying in line: cultural markers in colonial society

A series of laws and economic structures from the profound to the most trivial separated the lifestyles, occupations and places of residence of the two races. Only gradually during the post-war years were these laws abandoned and attempts at a semblance of equality gradually gained momentum. At first there were racially mixed uncomfortable social gatherings; followed by non-racist legislation and an expansion of opportunities in education and employment; and finally self-government.

Once the relations of domination and subordination are clearly established, every black person is a servant of some sort and every white person a master or mistress at some level.[1] As the Royal Commission into Papua in 1906 put it:

No matter how little a particular white man may deserve the respect of the native, it is still necessary in the interests of all white men that the native should not be in a position where respect for the ruling race will be jeopardised.[2]

So entrenched is the white/superior and black/inferior bifurcation that a *bosboi* of a labour *line* identified the anomalies of his slightly superior situation by calling out 'You think I'm a black man. No I'm a black white man'.[3] A Papuan wrote to the *Post Courier* in 1972 'People are so impressed with my ability to speak English and maintain an intelligent conversation, they say that I am not a black man but a white man'.[4] The mutual reinforcement of unequal structures and racist ideologies finally broke down in the face of the anomaly of educated black men (and even women).

In colonial New Guinea the pidgin word *line* referred to a group of indigenous workers assembled or employed for certain tasks. Plantation owners referred to their field workers as the 'labour *line*'. These men were required to assemble in line for the allocation of daily tasks, the distribution of provisions, for government regulated medical checks and so on. The government officer also assumed the right to *line* the villagers, for instructions, inspections, taxation, to select carriers and workers. This was both inconvenient and coercive, and reminded returned indentured workers of plantation *lines*.[5]

Today the usage of the term survives, although generally only unmarried men and women work in village *lines*, thus minimising the inconvenience to garden work. While Deane Fergie and I were at Tatau on Tabar there was a 'Wednesday *line*', a day dedicated to the building of the new medical aid post. Young men and women unloaded and transported long planks of wood to a truck waiting at the end of the wharf. There was much laughter and sexual *frisson* as male and female teams joked and competed over the number of planks they could carry on their heads. A word from the days of colonial rule and indentured labour has survived, and while still applying to work, describes labour of a voluntary community-oriented kind.

Once, however, the Papua New Guinean was required to stay in line, not only on the plantations, but also when in town and in the white man's house. In a country where the subordinate race were also labourers, servants, and members of the flock, spatial markers were sometimes incredibly trivial. An accentuation of symbolic spatial separation became a counterpoint to the daily propinquity of the two races. The colonised people were 'marked as powerless through a variety of means, including naming, clothing, hairstyles, language and body marks'.[6] One aspect of this was distinct dress standards; for example, servants were forbidden to wear perfume.[7] The Scottish salesman on the Port Moresby drapery counter told Chatterton that the white women would only buy a dress length from him on condition he sold none of the material to Papuan customers.[8] An English nudist colony in Bombay was frowned upon, as 'imperialists without clothes might lose their authority'.[9]

Isabel Platten comments: 'They still wear those loose blouses, the "Mary" blouses. Some of our people hated them, but they're beautiful. Why I didn't have the sense to wear one myself, I'll never know. Really, they were so comfortable and cool'. But, of course, in the context of colonial dress standards, Isabel Platten could not wear the same dress as the indigenous people. Danish female missionaries to India argued that it was not appropriate to copy Indian dress. However one missionary, Miss Neilsen, occasionally donned a sari to give the schoolgirls and teachers 'some fun'. This 'fun' was not a denigration of the Indians, but a self-mocking act which both bridged and maintained the categorical distinctions between the races.[10] Miss Neilsen did not describe her more common refusal to wear a sari in terms of superiority, but in terms of self-respect, of being true to 'what you are' which rejected 'condescending imitation' and 'superficial identification'.[11] Nevertheless, whatever her personal reasons, Miss Nielsen was abiding by and reinforcing the public meaning of the dress codes which distinguished coloniser and colonised.

The ordinances that most rankled with the Papua New Guineans were those preventing them from wearing European clothing on the upper parts of their bodies, and the ban on drinking alcohol. Both of these were justified in paternalistic terms. If Papua New Guineans wore shirts in the rain they were likely to catch pneumonia; while it was widely believed that they did not know how to drink alcohol in moderation.

The first regulation passed in Australian Papua required a Papuan to wear a loincloth in public.[12] When a Papuan came to Moresby he or she was required to be half-clothed, or half-civilised. A Papuan was not to emulate the European form of dress, which was often described as making the Papuan look 'silly'.[13] The Ordinance was fussed over in the years between 1920 and 1924, largely to grant the status of European clothes to workers who were servants, police, or government and mission personnel. The rule remained in force until 1941.[14] The penalty for the first offence was a fine of ten shillings or one month in gaol, doubled for subsequent offences. An anomaly of the rule, in terms of white codes of decency, was that it applied also to Papuan women, requiring them to expose their breasts. Its application to women was studiously avoided, according to Percy Chatterton.[15]

When Doris Groves first went to the London Missionary Society school near Port Moresby in 1921 she identified the gradations of clothing among the Papuan members of the church:

> All sat on the floor (except the white mission staff who sat on chairs). Men on one side of the church and women on the other, and the sawn wooden floor had a high dark polish, due to the emanation of coconut oil from the bodies of the worshippers over many years.
>
> The children sat on the floor up in the front, near a huge window, and if they chattered or became restless a big stick, wielded by a deacon stationed outside came through the window, and with a tap on the head order was restored. Most of the men wore only a G-string, a few clean white lavalavas—these included the half dozen native lads who lived for a time at the mission, and were

being prepared to become pastors, and men who were employed in jobs in the town. The women too were mostly in bare tops and grass skirts—except the mission girls and the wives of the student chaps living at the mission. They wore calico dresses which were known as Mother Hubbards.[16]

The white rulers imposed on themselves exaggerated standards of civilisation, often long after these costumes or customs (for example, dressing for dinner) had been abandoned elsewhere[17]: 'Everyone dressed for dinner in long frocks for women, starched Saigon linen suits for men. Even the drunks were clean and clothed in well-ironed suits'. [Marjorie Murphy of pre-war Rabaul]

Isabel Platten was warned not to entertain the Governor-General in a hatless state:

It became known I had no hat to wear, mine being totally destroyed by the volcano [eruption of Vulcan]. One person told me, most dogmatically, that I would be committing a most unforgiveable indiscretion against the King by lunching without a hat in the presence of his representative. I did wonder for a while whether I would be arrested . . . After greeting our guests, I led Lady Gowrie to the guest room. The first thing she did was to take off her hat and throw it on the bed, saying 'How glad I am to get that off'.

Gloves and hats remained required wear for garden parties and other social occasions after the war, according to Daphney Bridgland. In the 1960s dress codes were relaxed, even if somewhat surreptitiously:

The only time I wore a hat and gloves was when I went to Government House or when I accompanied the Administrator's wife around the district, so when we were approaching Merauke [to meet a delegation from Dutch New Guinea] we stationed our husbands on the top deck to see if the women in the welcoming party were wearing hats! They weren't so Gloria and I felt comfortable to arrive *sans* hats. Later, one of the wives who spoke English said they were doing the same thing—ready to whip a hat on at the last moment but found a sunshade or umbrella more comfortable in the humid climate. [Marjorie Murphy]

Leonore Davidoff and Catherine Hall suggest that the 'importance of odour in maintaining social hierarchy, which remained until the mid-twentieth century, derives from the way smells represent the object in a particularly powerful way'.[18] In the Territory also, Papua New Guineans were often described as dirty and smelly. Irene Robinson approved of a 'useful' servant who was 'so nice and clean looking'.[19] In 1913 Eva Butcher distinguished the mission staff from the less civilised 'raw dirty ones'.[20] Dixie Rigby responds to inquisitive New Guineans: 'I didn't like them quite so near because they did smell'. Daphney Bridgland describes a strategy to inculcate hygienic standards in her nursemaid:

> To keep her clean and so that I'd know she was clean, I made her some very nice white mumu blouses. I put some broderie anglaise on hers to trim it and she'd wear a white laplap and she'd stroll down through the plantation with the baby in the pusher and she really looked something. So she started a fashion with the other meris who wanted white lace trimmed mumus. That was while we were on Rainau Plantation.

Ann Deland notes a reciprocal revulsion from the indigenous people:

> Bougainville natives are much prized as house servants, very quiet and docile, and, above all other advantages, they do not smell— unless of course they are very unwashed. Natives from the mainland, even the cleanest of them, have a penetrating odour which makes them very unsuitable as table boys. One man who knew his boys well enough to discuss such matters without rancour, was told that the white man also smells, so I suppose it is that we are used to ourselves.[21]

Gavey Akomo of the Highlands also commented 'They smelt so differently, these strange people. We thought it would kill us, so we covered our noses with the leaves from a special bush'.[22] Their solution was produced from relative powerlessness: they could not make the white men wash or go away.

The gradations of the colour-caste system are clear in relation to drinking alcohol. In 1960 whites could drink, mixed-race people required a permit and Papua New Guineans could not drink at all.[23] This ordinance must have seemed particularly hypocritical when most whites in the Territory were devoted to the bottle, a point noted by Mary Pulsford and Dixie Rigby.[24] Indeed, when Chatterton served on a commission of enquiry in the 1960s, many Papua New Guineans argued that if drinking was so bad, the ban should be total. Some educated Papua New Guineans, however, argued for a permit system to selectively allow them into the club of drinkers, a strategy which would have rewarded them for their closeness to white lifestyles.[25] Indeed, according to Sir Paul Hasluck, this demand was seen as a claim for 'equality'.[26] As early as 1938 Father (later Bishop) Louis Vangeke returned from Madagascar, where he had been ordained and lawfully imbibed alcohol, to a country where he was required to say mass stripped to the waist and could not use communion wine.[27]

Race relations are supported by almost unbelievably trivial signs of superiority and inferiority. Before the war, Papua New Guineans were not allowed to enter white stores except on errands for their masters. Even then they always used a side entrance.[28] Some time after the war, Sir Albert Maori Kiki, a foundation member of the Pangu Pati, reports: 'in the Burns Philp Supermarket they had a counter where they served soft drinks, but whereas Europeans were served from glasses Papuans were served from blue plastic mugs'. Kiki complained to the manager who said 'Well it's like that in Moresby'.[29]

Papuans were not allowed to be in Moresby after curfew, unless they had a Magistrate's or Inspector's permission, or unless they were servants.[30] The exception for servants reveals the accommodations made for convenience, so that house boys could serve the evening meal. After 1923 all noise, shouting and drum-beating was to stop at 9 pm in New Guinea. Wolfers claims that the curfew laws in 1959 had a parallel only in South Africa. In 1934 New Guineans were forbidden to ride bicycles in Rabaul.[31] Papuans always stood up for Joan Refshauge's mother on the bus:

> Normally going in the bus, they would stand up to give her room. Normally it was the women with babies and heavy loads who stood up for her; so she would take the baby and the heavy load and hang onto them while the girl stood. Even the men would stand for Mother.[32]

Many of the Ordinances related specifically to spatial segregation. In 1922 New Guineans were required to build their houses fifty yards from European houses and one hundred yards from any road or street.[33] In 1918 in Rabaul and 1919 in Kavieng, 'natives' were forbidden to use public seats and conveniences, because they might soil them; this rule was extended in 1929 to other townships.[34] Natives and dogs were not allowed in the Moresby swimming baths. Papuans were to enter and leave and sit separately from the white population in places of entertainment.[35] Port Moresby had its whites only beach, Ela Beach, patrolled by Papuan police who were 'cursed' by local people forced off the beach.[36] In the 1920s a church minister refused to let Papuans use his church for a service at a separate time from the European service, as it would defile the building.[37] In 1930 Sir Hubert Murray agreed to a fence proposed by the expatriates between the town and the labourers' quarters.[38]

Following the war, the Administrator J. K. Murray worked to displace some of these spatial markers. He was called 'Kanaka Jack' and boycotted by the B4s for a time, after he invited Papuan ex-servicemen to lunch.[39] One plantation owner in 1951 nicely captured the fearful economic consequences of such actions:

I went along to the Anzac Day luncheon . . . to find a couple of Papuan ex-servicemen preparing to sit down at table with us. I naturally thought the two would be admitted after we had eaten . . . I never thought I'd see the day when I'd sit down with two natives complete with ramis and sandals eating our food and sharing our beer. Soon they will be claiming equality with Europeans and the prompt return of all land and plantations kicking us all out of the land we developed and civilized.[40]

The Administrator's wife imposed similar lessons on Port Moresby's women-folk. Vera Foldi, a nurse before the war, found she was sharing morning tea with Papuan women: 'we all had the same tea service'. 'My lips actually burned when they touched that cup.'[41] Such visceral responses ('sharing our beer', 'my lips actually burned') reveal how deeply imbedded in the psyche racist distinctions can become. In daily practices of difference, roles and attitudes are written onto bodies, and become difficult to shift, even by rational analysis. The body holds sway over the mind.

In the mid-1960s, despite passage of anti-discrimination bills from 1958,[42] the administration in Konedobu (Port Moresby) had at least one segregated toilet; the doors identified 'women' and '*hahine*'.[43] In 1947 the use of 'boy' and in 1954 the use of 'native' as a noun in official documents was outlawed.[44] In the 1960s when the administration began to desegregate hospitals, the President of the RSL in Port Moresby threatened to 'horsewhip' the Director of Public Health if he moved one Asian or Papua New Guinean into the European Hospital.[45]

White residents were expected to maintain a racial distance by never 'losing face' in front of a native—never showing fear, or humiliation, never losing control.[46] Marjorie Murphy tells the story behind a photograph of her in long trousers, holding a rifle, with her foot on a dead pig, as though she had been big-game hunting:

We arrived in this village and the rest houses are all on stilts. John was out the front buying the food and I walked up the ladder of just thin logs and then the floor was limbom floor. (Limbom is a tall slender hardwood palm split for floors.) There was a hole that I didn't see and my leg went right through. John could see the house with my leg hanging down. So John came up 'What next?' First of all I'd forgotten the salt, then I'd done quite a few dreadful things using the wrong Pidgin which meant awful things. Then I go and my leg falls through. John said 'All right, now you recover a little bit of face. See that pig down there, I've bought that. We have to kill it. It's for the carriers. Now you shoot it'. He had been teaching me to shoot and I was getting bullseyes but I'd been used to putting my elbows on the verandah rail. So I thought 'Piece of cake, I'll shoot the pig'. Well I shot it all right but I got it where his tail is stuck on. It looked around at me and John of course immediately shot it . . .

Losing face, it was no good for me to whimper and cry about how I was tired or anything like that. You wouldn't do that in front of natives. And you were always in command of whatever was going on, you were supposed to be anyway.

Whites were not to allow the 'natives' to escape unchecked with familiarity or cheekiness: 'the white man's disrespect for himself' would only encourage disrespect from the Papuans.[47]

Dixie Rigby reports:

One of the pieces of advice my husband first gave me was 'Never give an order you can't enforce. Be very careful before you give any orders'. My mother brought us up that we must not give orders to anyone, we must ask, request. So you see I didn't have to worry about that one. I would ask them to do things, and they were so happy to do it. When I tried to start a garden they loved coming up and doing the gardening, and the meris did too.[48]

The significance of these anecdotes, when compared with Beatrice Grimshaw's heroes, is that Marjorie Murphy humourously recounts that she did lose face; Dixie Rigby claims that she never had to rely on authority relations. As Susan Blake suggests, women in colonial settings parodied themselves, looked on with amusement at their own failed attempts to shoulder the white man's burden.[49] White women's treatment of Papua New Guineans did not always mirror official ideology, as Chapter 8 discusses.

Many whites saw civilisation as a series of outward manifestations, like dressing for dinner[50] or 'clothes, diet, hygiene, and technical competence'.[51] It was not the saving of souls, or civilisation of the people, but 'roads constructed, bridges built and forests cleared' which measured colonial advancement.[52] Thus Kipling's characters work at 'keeping up appearances' to protect them from an anarchic universe.[53] Joseph Conrad's characters inhabit an earlier moment of colonial contact, and 'Without the security of that familiar hierarchical social structure there was an inevitable blurring between right and wrong, servant and master, order and chaos'.[54] Conrad's protagonists are forced back onto their inward sources, which are almost always found wanting.[55] James McAuley, Sir Paul Hasluck, Evelyn Cheeseman,

Jens Lyng and C.D. Rowley, in different ways, contrast the superficial form, 'keeping up appearances', with the real content of civilisation: a 'personal and communal life',[56] cultural resources and interest in the country,[57] 'the inward source'.[58] Lyng distinguishes the inhumanity, materialism and sensuality of the 'Kanaka' from the refinement, culture and selfless dedication which particularly characterised missionaries.[59] McAuley's condemnation is trenchant: 'The shapeless cannot give shape, nor the formless form, nor the unbelieving belief, nor the disordered order, nor the meaningless meaning'.[60]

These writers are describing a cultural capital which comes with education, and belongs peculiarly to the middle class. Lower-class whites mistook the outward signs for the inward training. Papua New Guineans also valued this cultural capital, but often invoked it in the register of cargo-cultism. When the expected resources and powers did not come with increased education they suspected Australians of withholding their true 'knowledge, ideas, language'.[61] Educated Papua New Guineans in the towns understood the denial of education as an attempt to maintain colour and class differences. As more of them acquired the passport of Western knowledge and culture, they demanded entry into the privileged club of whites.

Manual and mental labour

In some respects a subjugated race (or gender) has double the knowledge of the subjugating race. A subordinate position requires attention to the values and behaviour of the dominant group, a knowledge of the other, which the dominant group feels no need to reciprocate. Ignorance reflects both the desire and ability to ignore others.[62] As the British community in India became wealthier with more opportunities to enjoy its own society, most whites lost all but an amused superficial understanding of the local culture.[63] From the middle of the nineteenth century memsahibs' novels contained only caricatures of the Indians.[64]

Bill Groves, Director of Education after the war, was a keen anthropologist. Doris Groves certainly understood white ignorance as an active assertion of superiority:

> Before the Second World War very few white residents knew much about native village life. They were too busy exploiting his capacity for labour, and to go near him in his home life and spare time, would lower the white man's Prestige, whatever that really is.[65]

There were 'endless matters of their daily life on which we show colossal ignorance'.[66] Evelyn Cheeseman doubted that Papuans accepted the superiority of white civilisation. None the less 'the faculties of analysis, comparison and criticism I believe are not possessed by a primitive mentality'.[67] Jean Mannering suggests that whites who did not trust their indigenous skippers often ended up on reefs:

> They never contradicted; they generally did what you told them. As they learned to do things we gave them more and more control . . . When we went on a boat we had confidence in the native captain. We didn't give orders, we just relied on his judgement. If we went patrolling through the bush, they knew the bush better than we did. We let them decide just what we should do. You've got to respect their judgement on things they know well.

Pat Andersen, Joan Refshauge and Dorothy Pederick all saw advantages in local medical cures. As Dorothy Pederick notes:

> Before we ever got there they had treatments that worked. And you came to letting them convert you—in some ways. You felt 'Well if that works, fine'.
>
> I remember a Catholic priest down Nakanai way, saying you come to respect them after a while. He'd learned that himself. He said 'The first five years I was doing fine, converting people. The second five years I wasn't so sure, and the third five years they were converting me.'

Joan Refshauge suggested that acceptance of local remedies increased the co-operation from patients, while sensible nurses adapted their nutrition programs to local food supplies.[68] Gil Platten used 'scientific reasoning' to prove that local cures often had the same effects as white ones. He demonstrated that the temperature of a broody hen, used to ease pneumonia, was the same as that produced by the heated paste the sisters applied to the patient's chest: 'The natives thought the disease went into the chicken but that hardly matters. Most white people are terribly superstitious, but you don't send them away from membership of a church'. [Isabel Platten]

In order to maintain a position founded on ignorance, the white race treats its own knowledge as superior. The mind-body split which paralleled the soul-flesh split of Puritan Christianity attributed the virtues of reason and self-denial (repression) to the 'white hero' and the sins of the flesh—lust, manual labour, lack of self-control—to the 'black beast'.[69] This mind-body and reason-passion dichotomy explains why speaking the master's tongue was the sign of reason, a sign that the speaker was a man.[70]

Cheeseman distinguishes between Papuans' knowledge of the natural world and a lack of access to the higher realm of reason. Dixie Rigby described her husband's and the indigenous people's shared interest in 'everything that creeps and crawls': 'Of course that really was entering into their life'. Dixie Rigby is not the only commentator to note the ease with which Papua New Guineans learned pidgin, but her explanation applauds her own lesser ability:

> They were highly intelligent but of course I discovered afterwards, their minds weren't cluttered up like our minds are, they had nothing to discard. They learned pidgin English from the police boys with incredible rapidity. They could learn pidgin English quicker than I could, my mind was too cluttered up.[71]

Clearly there were differences in knowledge between the two races, but Mary Pulsford adopts a cultural relativist position, seeing them as mere differences of culture:

> There were a lot of things I knew about and were a part of my life and which I couldn't share very easily with my Urip friends because their framework was so different . . . There were times when I felt culturally terribly isolated.

Pat Andersen comments that on her return to Papua New Guinea after Independence it was much easier to communicate with local people. When she was there after the war:

> It was very early days. I can remember we had a teacher and his wife, Papuans, for the benefit of any of the local people who wanted to come to school but also for the children of the staff. Miria was such a lovely person but he and his wife didn't really feel comfortable in our home. That was something that was on ahead. We were there at an earlier stage. I can remember in 1975 I went back there . . . and I met university students who were alert, politically aware, vocal, articulate, and it was exciting. It was a different scene. I think we were paternalistic in our attitudes but it was very hard to relate on a level which would make paternalism seem entirely inappropriate.

Or as one of Callaway's respondents says 'There is no doubt that we regarded the colonial period as an educative period . . . I can remember using the analogy of children growing up—you know, which now makes me sort of shudder'.[72]

Knapman focusses on the externalisation and objectification of the body in the form of manual labour, a more debased form of labour than intellectual labour.[73] Thus white society in New Guinea developed a code against manual

.etha

labour, work 'fit only for blacks'. Judy Davis reports two cases of white women who would not marry men they loved because they worked with their hands; a nurse refused to marry a marine engineer, and a Rabaul woman would only marry a policeman when he was promoted to patrol officer.[74] The Official Government *Handbook* of the Territory of New Guinea in 1937 stated that the white man must not labour with his hands; instead three to five servants were to be employed.[75] People who broke that code, like Gil and Isabel Platten, were both chastised by the white community and commended by New Guineans:

> Charcoal irons were the style of the times, the charcoal coming from coconut shells. It was efficient but the problem was the vast quantity of soiled clothes to be reckoned with while all of the men's soiled garments had to be starched. More often than not I was left with the ironing and this led to a clanger I was to make. I had been invited to an afternoon tea party. I was late and apologised to the hostess and guilelessly explained my reason—I had to iron my husband's trousers. Not feeling at all embarrassed I spoke out loud and clear. A hush fell upon the company. I think it was my hostess who gently—but quite clearly—rebuked me saying 'Mrs Platten! Women in Rabaul do not iron their husband's clothes'. I was embarrassed but not abashed because I could see no sense in that at all and continued to iron my husband's and my own clothes whenever the need arose.
>
> This attitude towards manual labour was accepted by most and we gave offence if we did not abide by it. A hedge of hibiscus separated our land from that of our neighbour and one day Gil was giving it a bit of a trim. One of the church members passed by; he was a senior government official. He told Gil to refrain from doing such work as it let the white man down. That the native members of the community might also get an idea that to work with one's hands, to clean away unwanted debris, would be demeaning, was not an idea we wanted to be responsible for. [Isabel Platten of Rabaul in 1928]

When Isabel Platten first arrived at Namatanai she discovered that the previous missionary's wife had been carried by bearers:

> The news of our arrival had gone ahead and towards late afternoon the students caught up with us. To my surprise it seemed they also expected to carry me. A cane lounge on bamboo poles, carried by four strong young men, was offered to me. It was not accepted then or ever.

Gil Platten was so committed to building sturdy roads that he was nicknamed 'masta rot' by the local people.[76] It was significant that Platten worked with the mission students and stayed with them for lunch.[77] Gil's working-class background no doubt convinced him of the value of manual labour.[78]

The Mission schools, but not the government schools, required their students to grow their own gardens. Jean Mannering justifies this practice:

> It's good soil and things grow quickly. My late husband used to say they only needed to work half a day a week in their gardens to grow all the food they could eat in New Britain. Pupils grew their own food and cooked their own meals, washed their own clothes.

Daphney Bridgland and Mary Pulsford assert that showing employees one's own capacity was essential to a successful relationship:

> The other thing was I found talking to other Australian women who had lived there a long time was terrifically helpful. They would give you all kinds of tips. One of the things one of them told me very early in the piece was that if you want to get the best out of your domestic help, when they're new work with them. Show them that you can do anything that you ask them to do and do it properly, and then they will know that you can do it and are not making demands on them that you can't meet yourself. But that's how I always operated. [Mary Pulsford]
>
> And you need to be able to do what you say, you had to be able to do it. And that was one thing my husband always did, he never asked a man to do a job he couldn't do himself. Because that is all they understand, if you can do what you're talking about and expecting them to do, they'll respect you. [Daphney Bridgland]

On the plantations and missions then, white people more often worked alongside their employees. In town, although demonstrations might occasionally be necessary, no white person should admit to routinely performing manual labour.

Paths of righteousness

The planter and the civil servant shared an interest in the material capacities of the villagers. The missionary, in contrast, opposed 'agnostic materialism'.[79] To Bishop Navarre 'Religion is for them, as for all peoples, the most sacred deep-seated reality',[80] a view shared by other commentators.[81] Many

missionaries agonised over the correct combination of their spiritual perspectives with that of the indigenous peoples. Of necessity, the missions
sought to disrupt local social relations and customs:

The raison d'etre of mission work is the undermining of a traditional way of life. In
this the missionary represents the most extreme, thoroughgoing and self-conscious
protagonist of cultural innovation and change. How the C.M.S. [Church Missionary
Society] resolved this role as destroyer with a desire to preserve an idyllic, rural
community is a tangled story. The missionary, at least in part, was unashamedly
ethnocentric, though he saw the struggle to impose his values as loving and
altruistic .. . . this ethnocentrism and proselytization represented a blend of exclusion
and inclusion, domination and brotherhood, exploitation and sacrifice.[82]

This dilemma is most acutely evoked in Grace Young's attempts to describe
how mission work was brought to the people of Mendi. She was aware
that her very purpose was to change these people's beliefs, yet she said
'But what we didn't want to do was to change their way of life'. But
of course, as she quickly realises, the mission did wish to change their
way of life, so she said 'we infiltrated a few ideas':

We wanted them to be themselves. What we planned to do was
not to take out anything from their culture that was good but if
something was bad that wasn't part of their lives, if it was really
bad, then we would try. Perhaps it was something we could replace
with something good. We didn't want to change things, that was
up to them to want to change, not for us to introduce.
   We didn't build a church for ages; we always had the open air
church, because we wanted them to build the church. It was to
be theirs, and they wanted it, even if we infiltrated a few ideas
of how they should do it. We had no instructions about how to
go about it. I don't feel now that at any stage we should try to
force anything onto other people.

On the other hand, Grace Young manifests a clear ethnocentrism when
she discusses the conversion of a woman so untutored as to invade Grace
Young's privacy and status:

A young woman was squatting there with her digging stick. She
was lifting up my skirt to see what was underneath. Everyone was
laughing. Years later when we went back in 1970 for the twentieth
anniversary celebrations, this lass who had lifted up my skirt was
there; and she became a Christian, and came into the first service
we had for the World Day of Prayer and she prayed. Fantastic,
isn't it?

Diane Langmore notes the connection between the growing tolerance of turn-of-the-century missionaries and anthropological knowledge.[83] The Methodist sisters:

> did Anthropology I and II at Sydney University. The Methodist missionaries did that before they went to the mission field. They learned to respect the customs of other people. We were told we were not going there to turn the people into black Europeans. We had to respect their culture. Any changes that took place in their culture were to come from them, not from Europeans. [Jean Mannering]

Some missionaries and some missions attempted to combine traditional practices (where not judged abhorrent) with the Christian teachings. Gil Platten's interest in the local customs was appreciated by the New Guineans: 'when he was here no-one would stand apart . . . He really liked the customs of our ancestors. He didn't try to change them at all, or to stop them'.[84]

Torogen Rontui uses the spatial metaphor—people did not 'stand apart'— to describe both Platten's interaction with the villagers and his enthusiasm for the local customs. Gil Platten in 1932 reported to an unresponsive Synod his concerns that mission education was replacing important customary understandings with irrelevant knowledge. [Isabel Platten] The more common view was that of a contemporary of Platten's who reported the 'lapses in Tabar islands', particularly 'night dancing which is largely sexual in content'.[85] The Catholic mission was unable to stamp out the *malagan* ceremonies on Tabar.[86] Mary Pulsford's Catholic villagers were forbidden Saturday night singsings (because they followed confession on Saturday afternoon). Periodically, like boarding school students, the villagers broke the rule and were excommunicated for several weeks. The Methodist mission's attitude is captured in a program of entertainment performed by the local people for a missionary cruise in 1939. The passengers were entertained with 'heathen customs' but the program culminated with 'Christian customs', including a 'speech of rejoicing because of the difference Christianity has made'.[87]

Papua New Guineans were often more accepting of different customs than their white rulers. They have a saying, if one asks 'Why do people do that?': '*pasin bilong wetskin narapela kain*' 'That is the habit of whites'. Both Percy Chatterton and Father Kirschbaum noted this courteous tolerance.[88] Sister Aquilonia Ax also 'found on the whole the people in New Guinea are quite adaptable, not resenting white people's customs and ways like our Aborigines do'. Doris Groves, despite her commitment to preserving the local customs, breached a rule concerning women's access to the *lemese*. The Orokolo men did not actually bar her path into the men's house: 'The natives looked shocked. There were many angry looks and much muttering, but nobody stopped me so we went through.'[89] Similarly, a young white girl who exuberantly and innocently ran into the men's house, was 'gently' pulled out, the man saying that it was too dark in there to see: 'an example of native tact'.[90]

The increased self-assertion that mission education brought was noted by many, but was evaluated negatively or positively, depending on the community to which the commentator belonged. Plantation owners often saw the mission-educated New Guinean as a 'shrewd and untrustworthy individual'.[91] A government officer's wife described them as 'spoiled' and 'just cunning enough' to maximise their own gain.[92] This was rendered in the colloquial expression 'bighead'.[93] Other terms were 'comic half-educated natives' and 'morally and socially mad'.[94] In Australia a 'cheeky nigger' was condemned. He was a man who showed 'initiative or independence or self-assertion', for example the temerity to look a white man straight in the eye.[95] As late as the 1940s the novelist Jean Devanny reports a hostess in the Gulf country of Queensland as saying 'You've got to keep them down . . . otherwise they become as cheeky as they are stupid'.[96]

On the other hand, Sir Hubert Murray asserted 'backward races' would abandon their old customs and beliefs sooner or later, and would be lost unless compensated with religious teaching.[97] Reed argues that mission educated New Guineans were less subservient, and more questioning and knowledgeable of white ways.[98] Dame Rachel Cleland suggests that the Methodist mission 'developed self reliant people able to run their own affairs'.[99] Mission education sometimes led to political involvement. Cult leaders incorporated elements of Christianity,[100] while an indigenous political movement in Malaita (the Solomon Islands) in the 1960s drew heavily on Christian precepts.[101]

Educating an elite

Despite Sir Hubert Murray's statement: 'The ability of the Papuan to learn is limited only by our ability to teach', almost all teaching was done by the missions before the Second World War.[102] Standards of teaching were lower than those established in British colonies like Fiji or in Africa. Aisoli Salin compares the education of Fijians under British rule with that of his own people:

In 1951 I went to a conference in Fiji. We found that we were about seventy years behind Fiji in our education. Most of the Fijian delegates were products of Oxford University or Cambridge in England . . . in my time it was more or less like giving out rations. We worked most of our time cutting grass and cleaning up around the school.[103]

Swarna Jayaweera disputes the superiority of British education, at least in Sri Lanka.[104] Towards the end of the nineteenth century the government virtually withdrew from education, leaving the field to missions and private enterprise. Only the most prestigious institution, the Colombo Academy for the education of boys, was retained in state hands. Terence Ranger discusses the way the Anglican mission in Uganda not only accepted that some Africans could become members of the governing class but established King's College for these children, at which habits of discipline, team spirit and local patriotism were instilled.[105] King's College was thus a replica of private schools in England.

There was much debate concerning an appropriate education for indigenous people. Even in the 1850s there were those who argued it was not natural inferiority but lack of education that made the African different.[106] But education had its dangers. Educated colonial people were described as being exposed to 'harmful influences from the west' which encouraged them to overthrow white rule.[107] British public opinion was divided on the question of the emancipation of the American negro, especially after the revolts in Jamaica in 1865 and 1866.[108] In such a climate the 'primitivism' of the 'noble savage' gained a new appeal.[109]

Ruth First suggests that colonial education was not a preparation for independence, it was a training in the authoritarian command of white rule.[110] While benign neglect was one way to hold an indigenous people down, education in Western mores allowed the incorporation of a few colonised men into Western rule. In learning the coloniser's language, the indigenous people of necessity learn also the coloniser's values, the Manichean world-view which identifies black as evil. The borderlands between two cultures can produce in this educated elite a rejection of themselves;[111] they may become 'mimic men', in V.S. Naipaul's phrase.[112] On the other hand, they gain access to the means whereby they can evaluate the white rulers in their own terms. All colonial administrations resisted free elections, political campaigning and other practices of democracy, arguing that this would only produce localised ethnic differences and not the nationhood for which they were 'training' the people.

The neglect of education until after the Second World War in Papua New Guinea had considerable (if possibly unintended) effects in minimising attacks on white domination. As Dixie Rigby said of the natives 'They had to come up to my standard, I couldn't go down to theirs'. Indigenous people were confronted with the apparent superiority of white culture; after all, it had been the means of subjugating them:

Every colonized people—in other words, every people in whose soul an inferiority complex has been created by the death and burial of its local cultural originality—finds itself face to face with the language of the civilizing nation.[113]

Indigenous culture is defined as inferior; only access to the language and culture of the white rulers will grant the local people a measure of 'civilisation'.[114] Thus language became a marker of difference: 'language use signifies the difference between cultures and their possession of power, spelling out the distance between subordinate and superordinate'.[115] Both Frantz Fanon and Claudia Knapman point to the use of pidgin to keep the indigenous people in their place.[116] Robin Radford reports that several men arrested in the Highlands were sent to Wau 'to be taught to speak': so ingrained was the notion that only English was a proper language, that other languages were totally discounted.[117] Similarly, Hasluck felt that Papua New Guineans must 'become literate in a modern language' for advancement; he thus endorsed the teaching of English.[118]

Daphney Bridgland asserts that Tumeeun, a New Guinean of 'the old school' who spoke 'excellent English', 'preferred to speak Pidgin'. Similarly they preferred to wear native dress, especially after Independence: 'they did not want European ways'. Conversely, Isabel Platten reports that whites always spoke to Aisoli Salin in pidgin, despite his excellent English. Whites called him a 'big-head' partly because he felt that command of English and other white skills should have been his passport to white society. To Aisoli Salin the justifications for racism had no application to him.

The Australian administration was often accused of spending too little money on education in favour of health and other welfare. Certainly between 1920–21 and 1939–40 the average annual expenditure on education declined, while that spent on agriculture increased by 100 per cent; that on public health increased by 70 per cent and that on public works increased by 120 per cent.[119] In 1944 Camilla Wedgwood recommended the establishment of village, intermediate and high schools to avoid producing an educated elite and ignoring the needs of the masses. She believed that every child should be able to attend a government school.[120]

In 1945 the Papua Central School at Sogeri was taken over from ANGAU. Gil Platten worked there for several years when he resigned from the Methodist Mission. Later, central schools were established at Kerevat and Dregerhafen to train teachers, medical orderlies, and artisans for the government.[121] Wedgwood's suggestion for a complete complement of government schools was almost totally ignored. In 1953 there were 126 000 students in mission schools and about 5000 in administration schools.[122]

By this time government and the missions were debating the relative merits of teaching in English, pidgin or a local dialect. For the lower grades, missions favoured a local dialect, although not always the one known by their students.[123] They argued that lessons would be more readily comprehended (Jean Mannering, who notes the return to pidgin in the lower grades after Independence); and that local people would not become detribalised and 'increasingly remote from their villages' (Isabel Platten commenting on Gil's attitudes). But government-appointed teachers, who came from Australia for a short tour of duty, could not be expected to learn a local dialect. Pidgin was recommended by some, although there were fears that it would become a vehicle of nationalism.

The rising educated elite called for English, the language of the coloniser and of power.[124] Sir Hubert Murray drew the Australian government's attention to a book on teaching in English as opposed to the vernacular, reproducing the following comment:

This kind of educational policy [teaching in the vernacular] is a great disadvantage to both ruling and subject races. It encourages the privileged class to think that all opportunities of development in the country should be assigned to it, while the unprivileged class is driven to the position of begging for what it was once entitled to. It also makes the ruling class feel that the Government is its own, while the subject race is compelled to think of the Government as alien.[125]

In the 1930s, Reed wondered 'why no plan has been prepared for a system of native schooling designed to assist the kanaka in adjusting to his new, partly Europeanized, partly de-tribalized situation'.[126]

Sios Tabunamagin, after initial hesitation, agreed that the refusal to teach English was based on maintaining the barriers between whites and Papua New Guineans:

We realised they [the missions] didn't really give us a good education. As things stand today, they deprived us of knowledge. I think some of them thought that if we got a good education then we'd get on top.[127]

The missionary education was also oriented towards training for the ministry, and was by the government's post-war standards inadequate. After the Second World War, the government became far more involved in education and William C. Groves was appointed as the Director of Education. Much controversy surrounds his management of this task. However, one of the difficulties which Groves possibly did understand better than most was the delicate balance between government and mission involvement in education, as Doris Groves notes in a letter to her husband's biographer:

> In 1946 my husband accepted the position of First Director of Education in the post war period, he suggested to Mr E. Ward, the Minister for Territories, that co-operation with the Missions would be of assistance and a gracious government gesture, seeing that they had undertaken most of the Education (certainly in Papua) pre-War. Mr Ward heartily agreed and called a Conference in Sydney about the middle of 1946 . . . and at regular intervals a Missions and Education Conference was held during my time in New Guinea . . .
>
> I can assure you that the Missions warmly welcomed the Administration in Education, and also were most grateful for the "Grants in Aid" inaugurated by my husband . . .[128]

Sir Paul Hasluck blames the slow development of education on W.C. Groves as Director, a man of vision and dedication to charity work, but unable or unwilling to formulate concrete plans for the establishment of schools.[129] Hasluck decided to focus on primary schools with a scholarship system to Australia for all who were qualified to enter secondary school. Hasluck's educational vision was instruction in hygiene, law and order, the growth of better food, the improvement of houses, overcoming social customs which held the people in a primitive condition, and literacy in English. The Public Service Commission Head and the Acting Administrator, Cleland, criticised Groves and his Department in 1952. Hasluck also claims that Groves hampered co-operation between the mission and government schools, although this seems unlikely given his and his wife's longstanding relations with the missions. In 1958 when Groves retired, his successor G.T. Roscoe gave Hasluck his 'first substantial, constructive and practical proposal I had received in eight years'.[130]

Jean Mannering discusses the way in which the government gradually asserted control over educational standards, paying the mission a small amount for each pastor teacher in the villages and gradually raising the minimum standards required. Sister Aquilonia Ax reports a good working relationship with the government, obtaining all the supplies she needed for her schools, much to the chagrin of the government teacher at Kundiawa. Her strategy was not to berate the government officials, but rather to evince understanding for their difficult job:

> If the laws are made like that, they can't change it. Some of these men did not have a lot of education either. But they were good

people. The Supply Department did its best, but for all that it was a long way from Australia to New Guinea.

Aisoli Salin was one of the first New Guineans to receive a Western education. He boarded with the Groves family in Melbourne in 1929:

> [Salin and Lue] soon settled into school life, and made many friends. Their mates invited them home to meals and the parents made them welcome. They joined the Scouts, Football and Swimming Clubs, learned Boxing and at the end of their 2 year term attained the Qualifying Certificate! Our children loved them and we all missed them very much when they went home.[131]

His problems began almost as soon as he returned from Australia:

> We local teachers had to write our programme and show it to the European teacher, what we planned to teach the next day.
>
> There was a lot of red tape between Papua New Guineans and Europeans in those days. I wrote an article in the *Post Courier* and the District Commissioner read it. I had gone to get a taxi and was told 'You are not allowed to use these taxis, they're for Europeans only.' The District Commissioner said 'What do you mean by writing that?' This was in 1958. When I was in Australia I was mixed up with the Europeans and we shared the same food, shared the same bedroom. When I came back here it was different which didn't please me.
>
> A lot of Europeans didn't like it that we got our education in Australia because they felt we went against them in a lot of ways.[132]

Aisoli Salin was one of the first three Papua New Guineans to be appointed to the Legislative Council. It was assumed in a newspaper article that the opening address, given in English, had been 'prepared for him and well rehearsed', perhaps 'to help the boy through an extremely difficult ordeal'.[133] Salin's experience there was so frustrating that he resigned because 'they used me as a talking machine'. He felt he achieved nothing in three years.[134]

'Big-headed' was the term used to describe Papua New Guineans who expected some sort of equal treatment from the whites. As Isabel Platten suggests, this term may have derived from an insecurity on the part of the whites; some 'Europeans were as big-headed as you could get' but 'they couldn't stand it in a native person'. According to Isabel Platten, Aisoli Salin was a 'big person'; he was later awarded an MBE:

> But Aisoli was a member of the Legislative Council, he could speak beautiful English. When the Legislative Councillors were flying back

to Hagen from Moresby, they'd give everyone a drink but Aisoli. They talked pidgin to him, wouldn't talk English. [Isabel Platten]

Bill Groves researched local customs in Aisoli's home village of Tatau on the Tabar Islands (off New Ireland) in 1933. Doris Groves describes in her diary how Bill relied on Salin to make contact with the local villagers, and obtain help in building a house.[135] According to Isabel Platten 'Groves had been on Tabar when we were at Namatanai. Groves had liked Gil's 1932 Synod address when he criticised the mission's methods for native education' and this may have prompted Groves to choose Platten for the 'Tabar Project'. In 1951 the lives of Groves, Platten and Salin became intertwined over the Tabar project:

> Soon after we returned to Port Moresby we were told we were to go to Tabar Island for another S.P.C. [South Pacific Council] experiment . . . It seemed these people were dying out and the S.P.C. wanted to know why and maybe Gil would be able to find the reason. The S.P.C. intended to put a lot of money into the experiment, and quite a bag full of goodies were to come to help the dream succeed. I remember my disappointment that I would not be living at Sogeri . . .
>   And so we came to Sos. Living was a bit uncomfortable at first because there was no house or shelter we could even sleep in. So we put up the bed on the beach. That was fine until some ants found us as a prime source of protein. The house was built around me and much native material was used. It was a very pleasant house built almost on the high water line . . .
>   So we settled in and waited for the materials we were told to expect. Nothing arrived. Then along came a letter from our Director to tell us the change of Government in Australia meant the scrapping of the Tabar experiment . . . Our Director told us to stay on Tabar and to do whatever we could.

The Tabar experiment caused much friction between Gil Platten and Aisoli Salin:

> Gil was sent there to teach the people gardening and hygiene, that sort of thing. Aisoli Salin, who came from Sos, was in charge of the school. Aisoli had a rotten time. We were put over him which was not easy for Aisoli to handle. Gil was a bit insensitive to that, he thought Aisoli was being a big head. Gil treated him as a colleague, but a junior colleague.

A government enquiry ensued. Isabel Platten comments 'It was instinctive for us to build a fence around our garden, to keep the pigs out. There was no trouble doing things like that in the mission'. However Gil was rebuked by the administration for fencing off his garden on Tabar: 'Whilst aware of the need for protection from marauding pigs and fowls we feel that the fences and gates represent something more than a tangible barrier'.[136] In this respect the report was no doubt right. Chatterton reports an incident in the 1940s when his trainee pastors queried the existence of a fence dividing the mission from their quarters.[137] In pidgin the word for fence is '*banis*' intriguingly close to the English word 'banish'.

Aisoli Salin chafed against his subordination to another teacher. Prudence Frank reports how the acquisition of equivalent skills but the denial of equal pay produced disaffection amongst the local people. Shortly after the Second World War, on J.K. Murray's suggestion, and with the approval of her new Director, W.C. Groves, Prudence Frank taught typing after hours:

> One native from each Department would come to the Education Department carrying a typewriter. A messenger with the Department, Sinaka Goava, and one of my pupils, Rurua Rurua, became ministers with the government later. Students consisted of men as well as girls. Some of the students became very good typists because of their typing to the music of the records which they loved. Classes were later transferred to Hanuabada Girls School where I had 24 typewriters that had been sent to me from the Reconstruction Training Scheme in Canberra.
>
> I was Mr Groves' Secretary from 1946 to 1955 when Mr Butler, the Public Service Inspector, advised me that I had been appointed officer-in-charge of the Typing and Copying Office, that I had been allotted a room in the Public Service Institute under Mr Glastonbury and would be conducting the training full time and after hours. I was issued with desks, cupboards, typewriters, uniforms for the six male typists who would form the typing pool, iron, washing soap, gramophone etc. Anything I asked for was issued to me. As well as the copying typists, students from various Departments were sent to me as well as from the Army. After Mr Glastonbury retired to Australia Mr Chenowith was appointed. My six typists doing copying work were Eafere Semese, Oika Gabu, Sinaka Goava, Laka Kila, Morea Vai, Vana Udu. They would take it in turns to pick up files from the various Departments, signing for them and obtaining signatures on their return.
>
> When I received the uniforms which consisted of white linen laplaps, shirt with green 'T' on it for typist and 'HT' for head

typist, sandals, I instructed them to wash them when they were dirty. The first time they returned them dirty but ironed, so I then asked them to wash them in the office and iron them. They were later sent to various outstations as typists.

My next appointment was Instructress, Public Service Institute. All applicants for a typing position were sent to me for testing. The standard was 45 words per minute for touch typing. I now taught teenage European girls, married women, Army clerks, Chinese, mixed bloods, clerks and telegraphists in training. When the students reached the standard required they were placed in departments as copying typists, taking their place with the Europeans. There was distress over the lower wage received, £ 1.10.0 a month and rations, to £ 14.0.0 a week for teenage Europeans. I was asked was it because they were black that they didn't get as much as Europeans, even though they were doing the same work. I said no, that was how the wages were in Canberra. This caused me a lot of distress.[138]

Prudence Frank's typing pool was a microcosm of the process whereby an indigenous elite learned a set of skills, usually associated with women in white society, but which became a pathway not only to power in the independent country, but to a questioning of the racial distinctions which divided otherwise equally qualified workers.

Albert Moari Kiki was interviewed by Albert Speer for a job in 1947: 'He was the first white man who ever asked me to sit down in his presence. I was afraid to accept, but he finally made me do it'.[139] With Speer's prompting, Kiki attended Sogeri school between 1948 and 1951 and, in company with Michael Somare and other future leaders of the independent country, formed the Bully Beef Club in 1964. Out of this grew the Pangu Pati in 1967.[140]

Among Kiki's concerns, as for many others, was the discriminatory wage structure, added to which some of the Papua New Guineans' wages were paid in rations of rice and bully beef, whether they liked these foodstuffs or not.[141] The wage determination of 1964, in which it was decided that Papua New Guineans were not to receive the same pay for the same work, made even Dame Rachel Cleland 'deeply ashamed'.[142]

After 1962 there was a rapid expansion in secondary education, and the demand for jobs by standard six graduates outstripped the supply. Sisters Aquilonia and Bohdana comment on the difficulties educated New Guineans had in finding a place in society, although Sister Aquilonia is more sanguine:

> Later [in Manam] there were so many completing standard six that they had no work, no jobs. They were not satisfied in the village.

We had P and C meetings and they said 'What will the children do when they finish grade six?' And I said 'What did you do before?' 'Before we worked in the garden but they don't want to now.' There was quite a lot of trouble. Some parents told me that when they scolded their children that they should work in the garden they went to the garden and pulled out the plants. [Sister Bohdana Voros]

Educational provision remained very uneven; of the first students to the university none came from the 30 per cent of the population living in the Highlands. Ultimately an elite was formed and leadership was 'almost synonymous with being educated'.[143]

From the beginning, some local people chose to work with the white colonists. Whole villages sought to befriend the white patrol officers and turn their guns against traditional enemies.[144] Within villages, the *luluai* and *tultul* mediated white rule, often for very little power in return. The local converts to Christianity who became pastors were dressed in some 'brief authority'. Police boys were in a position to exercise physical power over their own race, and described the villagers as 'primitives' still engaged in sorcery and cannibalism.[145]

Some Papua New Guineans chose to seek status by becoming 'mimic men' and emulating the white culture's prescripts. They condemned 'bush kanakas', those innocent of white ways.[146] One of Irene Robinson's servants could not control his mirth when a 'bush boy' fainted on first seeing the store items.[147] Pat Murray's domestic help laughed at the 'unsophisticated' Highlanders who came to take her back to her father's plantation the day after her wedding. The 'beach people very definitely felt they were much superior to inland people and had very little to do with them'.[148]

In Randolph Stowe's novel *Visitants*, Osana, who works for the white administration, describes an unsophisticated tribe as 'idiots always' who 'scratch around together, trying to grow tobacco and steal it from one another as soon as a leaf shows above ground'.[149] A non-fictional 'bitter neurotic educated' Papuan woman tells McAuley that 'Papua is the worst place in the world, I think', the people are slow, stupid, dance too much and sleep instead of working.[150] McAuley, confronted with this racial disloyalty, and in a woman, is clearly uncomfortable; and yet his culture has produced the condemnation of her former world.

In many colonial countries it took some time to realise that conquest was indeed happening; the first signs of traders and missionaries did not tell of the things to come. The tendency of the coastal people to accept the 'fashions' of others as merely other ways, not something they must be converted or beaten into, hardly prepared them for racist attitudes. It is easy to impose our knowledge, born of hindsight and the template of masculine imperialism, on the actions of colonised people. The white dominant culture may consider it almost a reflex action to fight to the death rather than be conquered; but it is a 'reflex action' produced by an expectation that one will be the victor and not the vanquished. By the time some kind of realistic assessment was possible, alliances of one sort or another had complicated race relations. The possibility of a clear division between black and white was further undermined by tribal rivalries. There was no Papua New Guinea nation before Australian intervention; the administration did not seek to forge a nationalism opposed to colonial domination. Indeed the administration only reluctantly and belatedly accepted the need for an educated elite, a common language, and some preparation for self-government.

7

Matters of Sex

The previous two chapters focussed on the racial divisions by which the Papua New Guineans were kept 'in line' or 'in their place'. In frontier societies, it was often felt there was *no* place for a white woman. White women spelled only trouble; they contaminated the masculine frontier and put the purity of the race at risk (in a way that men's broadcasting of their seed never seemed to). It was better that white women stayed at home, with the children. In time, colonial life became more settled, and some at least thought the presence of white women could add to its charm and amenities. But their potential for contamination persisted, and so a place was carved out for them.

India 'was a man's world' and memsahibs were required to fit themselves in and not appear too clever.[1] Helen Callaway reports one of the 'kindest' hosts in West Africa confessing that he considered 'women out of place in West Africa', while the theme of 'no place for a white woman' forms the subject of two women's memoirs.[2] Africa was 'a man's country' where a 'man's job' had to be done.[3] It was peopled, if sparsely, by conquering soldiers, visionary empire-builders and intrepid explorers. Life there was the stuff of boys' adventure stories. Callaway suggests that men's memoirs celebrate a 'lost masculine world' similar to the frontier experience in Australia, New Zealand and America; a world that is or should be devoid of women.[4] New Guinea is similarly described as Australia's frontier.[5] When Dr Joan Refshauge applied to go to Papua New Guinea she was told it was 'a man's territory'.[6] Until the 1920s the London Missionary Society Board felt that Papua was 'not a suitable place for a single white woman'.[7] Doris Booth concludes her memoirs: 'I shall never forget those big-hearted men of New Guinea—comrades all, white men in the best sense of the word, good winners and better losers. They were men'.[8]

White women brought the prospect of both pollution and danger, powerful symbols of disorder according to Mary Douglas.[9] A boat owner, to prevent the pollution of his vessel, refused to take a sick woman from Samarai to Port Moresby: 'I'm not having nappies hanging over the back of the boat'.[10] Pollution and danger were intertwined when white men considered the threats of miscegenation posed by the presence of white women. Proximity to black men put white women in danger, especially if unchaperoned by white men. Some white women refused to behave appropriately and were thus a danger to the whole white community. Danger brought pollution, pollution of the race and pollution of white women. The intricate and complex interconnections between race and gender are the subject of this chapter.

Constructing the feminine: Darwinism and Western dualism

In Chapter 5 it was suggested that black and white was a characteristic ideological dichotomy of the imperialist world-view. A far more pervasive and unquestioned dualism is that of female and male. Both work to align valued attributes—rationality, culture, self-control, mastery of the world (Descartes' 'I think, therefore I am')—with the intellectual white male. His objects of study are found in the natural world. They include (besides animals and plants), women, blacks, and the lower classes, who are variously defined as passive, natural, lacking in self-control, beastly, emotional or passionate. Women and black people were conceptualised as 'mindless creatures' to be dealt with in society in the same way as the body was to be dealt with internally by the (white male middle-class) self—'to be put under stringent control and kept at a distance'.[11]

This appropriation of subordinated races as the object of science was no metaphysical affair. Not only platypuses, but also Aboriginal heads and bodies were sent back to England for analysis. Stephen Gould tells the story of two 'Hottentot' Venuses, African tribeswomen taken to Europe and displayed in cages.[12] Western scientists were fascinated by both the racial difference of the Hottentot, describing her as the missing link between monkey and humanity, and by her sexual difference, her accentuated buttocks and 'Hottentot apron', a flap of skin over the genitalia.

Because of the combination of three scales against the one apex, the contrast of race, gender and class against the white upper-class male, there are also distinctions and contradictions in the placement of the subordinate groupings. On the one hand, subordinate groups are collapsed together as the 'other':

[women] are closer to children and savages than to an adult, civilized man. They excel in fickleness, inconstancy, absence of thought and logic, and incapacity to reason. Without doubt there exist some distinguished women, very superior to the average man, but they are as exceptional as the birth of any monstrosity, as, for example, of a gorilla with two heads.[13]

Not only women were aligned with 'savages' but also the lower classes: 'a beggar by hereditary instinct, and a debilitated wreck of manhood through the transmitted blood of weakness and disease'.[14] It was believed that Papuans were unable to learn English or skilled trades because they had the wit of a 'Sussex yokel' or a 'costermonger'.[15] The English mob was seen as little different from black Jamaicans in revolt.[16]

On the other hand, some groups—working-class and black women—are doubly subordinated, while white women, white working-class men and black men are only once differentiated. Thus while the chief attribute of working-class white women and black women was their sexuality/bestiality, white middle-class women were differently placed. White middle-class women had neither brains nor genitalia, but only wombs and moral sensibilities. While they lacked intelligence and reason, white women also lacked sexualised bodies; their emotionalism, intuition or even spiritualism distinguished them both from white middle-class men and from other women. The empire of women is divided against itself by these classifications.[17] White middle-class women became the 'Angel in the House'—weak, passive, worshipped and on a pedestal. Black women and lower-class white women were seen as sexual, strong, and capable of hard work: no housebound existence for them, but rather the freedom, danger and labour of the streets and factories. Thus Sir Hubert Murray could justify the White Women's Protection Ordinance which did not punish the rape of 'native' women because 'ordinary native women' put no value on their chastity while 'a respectable white woman' did. In a sense, respectable women did not enjoy sex, and for all of them sex was rape.[18]

Brian Easlea notes that negro males were reputedly endowed with large penises and negro women with 'the sexuality of beasts'.[19] In the 1920s a book on India was called *The Land of the Sex-Mad Millions*; the supposed sensuousness and sexuality of Indians preoccupied the British.[20] When their wives went to the hill stations in India, the men remained to take their pleasure with Eurasians and poor whites 'absolutely riddled with sex and very beautiful' who 'were comparatively fair game'.[21] One of the stereotypes of the Papua New Guinean man was an 'ambition . . . to possess a white woman'.[22] The Papuan was 'like most savage races . . . a sensual man' in whom all passions were excessive.[23]

It may seem strange to some readers that black men, but not white men, should be endowed with sexual prowess. Just as there are modes of femininity, so too are there variants of masculinity. In Victorian days (but to a much lesser extent today), an aspect of middle-class masculinity was the capacity for self-control: control of both the body's physical capacities and of sexual urges. Thus boys were trained in sports, trained to regulate and master their bodies, which were then deployed under the direction of their minds. Working-class masculinity, not having the advantage of a public school education, was more disordered and unregulated (for example, finding its expression in brute strength). Only the middle-class gentleman could assert the superiority of the mind over the body. Of course this superiority was not seen in terms of training, but rather in terms of the superior genetic qualities of the upper classes.[24] The self-disciplined body, prepared on the playing fields of Eton to win imperial wars, was aligned with a self-disciplined mind and a respect for hierarchical relations. Callaway suggests that the public school represented adult life in microcosm.[25] In the colonies under indirect rule, the District Officers were the masters, the chiefs were the prefects and the tribesmen were the boys.

Edward Said, describing Orientalism, or the study of the Orient by the European, identifies a sexualised relationship between the subject (the scholar) and the object (the Orient). The Oriental, like the female, is silenced by the practice of Orientalism, in which male European scholars construct and speak for the denizens of the Orient. The 'Orient was routinely described as feminine, its riches as fertile, its main symbols the sensual woman, the harem, and the despotic—but curiously attractive—ruler'.[26] Sir Alfred Lyell could say 'Accuracy is abhorrent to the oriental mind' but 'the European is a close reasoner', a natural logician.[27] A Queensland newspaper in 1876 described the sexuality of South Sea Islanders and the Chinese in feminine terms: the 'soft, pulpy, childish but passionate kanaka' was compared with the 'lithe, yellow-skinned mummy of the Celestian Empire'.[28]

Said argues that the fascination with the Orient, especially in Victorian times, was a reflection of the repression of sexuality in England; fantasies abroad were the displaced reflection of their denial at home.[29] Intellectual mastery hardly compensated for white men's sexual inadequacy; repression and insecurity marked their attitudes to black sexuality. As Said further notes, 'that very sexuality must never be taken seriously' because to do so would attribute power to the conquered races.[30] Instead, Orientalists refused to speak of Arab sexuality, or identified it as merely an 'undifferentiated sexual drive' or associated efforts at colonial liberation with 'a bad kind of sexuality' no more 'noble than a camel's rising up'.[31] Similarly the emerging Indian nationalists were disparaged as 'effeminate'.[32] Beneath all these analyses is the myth of the greater potency and desirability of the non-white male, the fear that cannot be spoken. The fear of black sexuality found its expression in hysteria concerning miscegenation and harsh penal provisions.

None the less, 'connection' of black men with working-class women, even if white, was not seen by some as undesirable. In 1772 an English judge argued that white lower-class women in England were 'remarkably fond of the blacks' and would 'connect themselves with horses and asses, if the laws permitted them'; he opposed the introduction of black servants as the resultant miscegenation would rapidly spread from the lower classes to the upper reaches of society.[33] General Booth (of the Salvation Army) argued in 1890 for the settlement of 100 000 poor women in Africa to introduce civilisation through marriage with Africans.[34] In the 1800s several petitions for clemency for negroes convicted of rape pointed out that the women were of 'low character'.[35] Prostitutes and poor women from New York and Europe were imported by white men to the Witwatersrand to serve a black African clientele in the early years of this century. While the administration, settlers and charities sought to halt the trade, the local brothel owners resisted.[36]

The prevalence of comparisons of lower races and sexes with children derives from the popularity of recapitulation theory in late-nineteenth-century science. This theory proposed that as the child grows up, he climbs his family tree, climbs through the stages from ape to man. Inferior groups, non-white races, women, the lower orders were like children; they failed to grow up.[37] Thus Rudyard Kipling, in his poem 'Take up the White Man's Burden', commands:

> *Send forth the best ye breed*
> *Go, bind your sons to exile*
> *to serve the captive's need:*
> *to wait, in heavy harness,*
> *On fluttered folk and wild—*
> *Your new-caught sullen peoples,*
> *Half devil and half child.*

The *sons* of Europe are sent forth to civilise the children of the colonies. Stephen Gould himself favours neotony, or a theory that the juvenile stages of ancestors become the adult features of descendants.[38] In this theory the attributes of the child—curiosity, play, flexibility of behaviour—are the hallmark of the successful adult. This is an appealing inversion for women, blacks, and the 'lower orders' condemned in earlier times by likening them to children. It is an inversion writers like Gould can only now entertain because women's movements, indigenous people's liberation struggles and environmentalism have challenged the truisms of Western philosophy.

Clearly the racism that led to the White Women's Protection Ordinance in 1926 was not the same as the racism which frowned upon the first marriage of a white woman to a Papuan in 1961. This chapter explores the shifting perceptions of miscegenation in Papua New Guinea between the 1920s and 1950s.

Keeping up to the mark: white men

Of logical necessity, if there *is* a place for white women and indigenous people in a caste-like colonial society, it is defined in opposition to the place of white males. As their place had the cachet of status and income, it is better described as a position. Because it was a position, transgression was possible—the extent of permissible deviation being related to the power of the deviant. Thus Lord Lytton, Viceroy to India in the 1870s, was described as 'The Great Ornamental' for his scent, rings, outrageous clothing, flirtations, frivolities; he even '*lolled* like a sultan on his divan'.[39] Although gossip could be deployed against the most powerful man in the British Raj, lesser men who transgressed, who failed to live up to their position, were ostracised as surely as white women who breached their spatial boundaries.

Brantlinger notes that every traveller must to some extent 'go native', adopt the customs of the country, eat its food, learn at least some of its language.[40] For all who took any interest in the local society, there was the ever-present danger of 'going native'. Randolph Stowe captures this dilemma in his novel *Visitants*. The government official Cawdor speaks the local language and is a skilled communicator. After his wife leaves him he resorts to drink, and finally becomes caught up in the cargo cultism of a Papuan village. Before he commits suicide he says 'I am mad now, Naibusi, and I will not be better. It is like something inside me, like a visitor'.[41] Overtaken by native nightmares, the only honourable escape is death. Nevertheless, the native skipper comments on Cawdor's corpse, covered with dried blood, 'Now he is a black man true'.[42] Meanwhile the inexperienced and ingenuous Dalwood, ignorant of the local language and Cawdor's dilemmas, approaches the local culture through an affair with a Papuan woman. This is not a sign of defilement or loss of white status, and Dalwood succeeds to Cawdor's job.

While suicide may protect the purity of the white community in novels, the Australian administration adopted a more pragmatic solution. New arrivals deposited a bond sufficient to pay their passage home. The bond was refunded after five years, if the new settler did not receive a 'blue ticket', a deportation order:

> But pre-War there was a community in New Guinea in those days, the mean average was a lot higher standard than it is nowadays. They were much more selective about who they let in. People who behaved badly got a 'blue ticket'. [Pat Murray]

Section 10A of the Immigration Restriction Ordinance (1925) in Papua allowed deportation of an immigrant white within five years of arrival who endangered the 'peace, order or good government of the Territory' or 'repeatedly acts in a manner which is inimical to the best interests of natives'. N. Ditton was three times convicted of assault and acquitted of a charge of attempted murder of a 'native' on the grounds that the evidence was 'unsatisfactory'. He was debarred from employing Papuans and applied to the government for sustenance. His board at one of the hotels was paid and he was given a free passage back to Australia, but refused to go aboard. Instead he stormed into the Resident Magistrate's Office, broke a pane of glass, and was again imprisoned. He went on a hunger strike, and was eventually persuaded to leave the Territory. The Lieutenant-Governor said of him that he would: 'very probably be an advancing citizen in Australia but is hopeless with an inferior race'.[43]

Once unable by government order to earn his living in the Territory, it was essential for Ditton to be deported, not merely to protect the local population but also to protect the status of white men. 'An Australian who spent too much time with, rather than over, New Guineans was thought to imperil the entire structure of territory society'.[44] In 1938 an Ordinance decreed that any white person 'found lodging or wandering in company with any of the natives of the Territory' was to be penalised, unless that person could demonstrate that he or she had a lawful fixed place of residence and was only wandering or lodging temporarily and legally.[45] While the law sought to prevent exploitation of New Guineans by loafers and beachcombers, it also sought to maintain the caste distinctions between the two racial groups:

> A man couldn't just decide he wasn't going to work and he was going to squat in a native village and go kanaka or something. There were odd ones who did . . . I remember this fellow called Norris who used to tramp around Tabar, Lihir, round there and he had a little cutter. He put into Bolagila one day when we were only children, I was only ten I suppose. We ran down onto the beach

to see who it was and Dad came down and he said 'Go back into the house'. We said 'Why? We want to see who it is'. He said 'I know who it is and he's not staying here'. His hair was scraggy and his clothes were scraggy and he had great big open ulcers without bandages on his legs and no shoes on, and just nobody got around like that. We said 'Who is he, who is he, Mummy? He's a white man and he looks terrible'. She said 'He's a man named Norris'. We said 'What does he do?' 'He doesn't do anything, he just lives with the kanakas.' We were horrified. We thought it was the lowest of the low that a white man could do that. It wasn't as you might think—snooty—'I wouldn't live with kanakas.' We thought it was very low that a white man would bot off kanakas. He ought to be able to look after himself better than kanakas. [Pat Murray]

Men who 'bot off kanakas' thus become nothing, and the children are sent away from this awful sight. While 'going native' was reprehensible, 'exploiting' the natives—requiring them to support one, plant one's gardens, pay taxes—was seen by some members of the white community in a similar light. Thus some missions: 'live off these people who don't have enough protein for their children to grow up with an intelligent brain. People who are lacking in protein and who are so unbelievably poor'. [Daphney Bridgland] Lilian Overell reports a discussion in which all agree that men who 'deteriorate' with drink or, even worse, rob 'the *kanakas* of their wretched pay' should be deported.[46]

Dixie Rigby commends the Anglican church as the only denomination that did not collect taxes from its parishioners. Ann Deland criticises the government that 'has done nothing for the natives' and collects a tax to boot. Dixie Rigby stoutly asserts the value of the village tax: 'First of all, it's unwise to be continually doing anything for nothing'; the valuable 'anything' Dixie Rigby attributes to the administration was pacification, which allowed the local people to travel without fear.[47]

The belief that white men had an appropriate economic position was no doubt strongest amongst the plantation community; they were the only group that neither collected taxes nor expected gifts from Papua New Guineans. Any lack of reciprocity in their relationship was hidden beneath the surface equality of the cash or rations payment for services rendered. But even this relationship was rendered in terms of a gift *to* the labourers. Daphney Bridgland and Pat Murray assert that they improved their health, clothed and housed them, trained and educated them.

In matters of sex the obligation to stay up to the mark did not fall equally on all white men. While all white men must have the economic resources with which to live apart from the local people, some—those of the 'lower orders'—were permitted to have sexual relations with indigenous women. Generally higher-status white men were expected to maintain their class superiority by exercising self-control. However, the rules about sexual profligacy were never as clear-cut as those concerning economic failure. Sexuality in a man was both a good and a bad thing; it must always be there to express, but its highest expression was under the control of its master. Thus a man was still a man if he had sexual encounters with indigenous women; a man was nothing if he became too much like a 'native' as the respective fates of Cawdor and Dalwood in *Visitants* reveal.

Sexual relations imply an intimate contamination of the master race that no other liaison does. Sociobiologists like Pierre van den Berghe argue that the 'selfish gene' seeks to propagate itself through human carriers.[48] According to this theory, racial characteristics represent, however approximately, different gene pools; thus all human groups develop racist attitudes. However, reproductive strategies for men and women are necessarily different. Ova are big, few and costly, while sperm are abundant, cheap and small. Females seek to select the best partners for their fewer investments while men are naturally promiscuous. In terms of inter-ethnic relations, men seek to protect and seclude their own women while attempting to capture or otherwise inseminate the women from other ethnic groups. Once a hierarchy of races is established, the women and men of the subordinate groups have conflicting interests. The women seek to mate up into the higher caste group, but the men seek to stop this capture of 'their' women.[49] Thus the inevitable promiscuity of men requires fierce policing of racial boundaries to prevent their disintegration:

Interbreeding . . . took place *despite* intolerance. It shows that even the strongest social barriers between human groups cannot block a species-wide sexual attraction. The biology of reproduction triumphs in the end over the artificial barriers of social prejudice.[50]

For van den Berghe then, the key to race relations is not economic exploitation or political domination or cultural annihilation, it is the loss of biological fitness; the loss of women:

Perhaps the soundest reason why foreign conquest and domination are so deeply resented is that they almost invariably represent a direct threat to the biological fitness of the conquered. The very reproductive success and, hence, biological survival of the conquered group is at stake. It is no accident that military conquest is so often accompanied by the killing, enslavement and castration of males, and the raping and capturing of females for purposes of enhancing the fitness of the conquerors . . . It is not accidental that the most explosive aspect of inter-ethnic relations is sexual contact across ethnic (or racial) lines.[51]

Some commentators are sceptical of this analysis, describing it as a convenient justification for male promiscuity. Within its own terms, sociobiology can be criticised to the extent that subordinate women *ever* choose not to mate with the reproductively fitter superior males. Van den Berghe suggests that while individual women may benefit from hypergamy, upward mating, women as a group do not because their men (who share more of their genes) lose fitness (lose female mates to the dominant group).[52] This certainly sounds like obfuscation; moreover, it means that the sociobiological explanation is not falsifiable. Whether women mate upwards into the superior racial group, or within their own racial group, they are serving the selfish gene. Furthermore, Marie de Lepervanche notes that female slaves and other women of conquered races actually have very little room to be choosy.[53] Even where they display no resistance, it is difficult to know whether choice has been exercised by women who mate with slavemasters or conquering soldiers.

For sociobiologists, mating is always a contradictory affair, whether within or across racial boundaries. As genes are driven to propagate themselves, one would expect incest to be rife. However, a hedge against future environmental changes is necessary and this is achieved with exogamy. As a result, every mating is a battle of the sexes, a meeting of two different gene pools. In this at least, the sociobiologists and many feminists would agree. Feminists, however, explain the battle of the sexes in terms of power and domination, psychological or social constructions of masculinity which do not flow inevitably from the fact that a man can produce millions of sperm. Feminists, and not sociobiologists, can thus explain why men ever choose to mate with women who are outside their reproductive years, or masturbate, or view pornography, or engage in countless other activities which do not enhance reproductive fitness. Feminists, and not sociobiologists, can explain why so many societies are constructed to maximise the reproductive fitness of male genes, but not female genes, for example in polygamy, adultery, concubinage and so on. A society which maximised females' genetic reproduction would consist of monogamous, faithful couples with a comparatively few well cared for and well loved children. The fact that in most societies it is the male's reproductive strategy that determines the dominant sexual relations, rather than the female's, requires an explanation which is not available within sociobiology. Indeed, the answer lies in power, not biology, as feminists have always suspected.

Susan Brownmiller argues that rape as a routine part of war concerns power and not reproduction.[54] It is a message written on women's bodies, but directed to the vanquished men, telling them that they have lost their manhood. Sexual relations with the women of the dominated group was 'a form of insulting inferiors and demonstrating prowess', 'a legitimate form of aggression and an expression of superiority'.[55] In the light of these arguments, one would expect that colonial rule condoned sexual relations between dominant men and subordinate women and fiercely punished sexual relations between dominated men and women of the dominant group. The latter was certainly the case; but three distinctions operated to complicate the former issue: the assumed opposition between black unregulated sexuality and white self-controlled sexuality; the distinction between white male working-class and white male middle-class sexuality; and a further distinction between verbal or legislative exhortations and accepted practices.

Rape was the practice of the inferior black man, for example as seen in the constantly circulating tales about the Indian Mutiny.[56] As was argued above, upper- and middle-class white men are identified with reason, as opposed to the passions/emotions of the body. A proper gentleman had control of his body, just as his good government controlled and regulated the activities of women and blacks. It was the mark of the Indian soldier rather than the officer that he was unable to control his sexual urges. While a captain might marry, a subaltern did not. Marriage allowances were only paid to men over 30, and often only 12 per cent of the regiment were allowed to marry. In this situation, prostitution for the lower ranks, serviced by Indian women, was encouraged.[57] Until the mid-nineteenth century in India it was assumed that the chronic shortage of women meant that men 'through necessity as much as choice' took Indian mistresses and wives.[58]

A writer in 1897 decried the likes of a renegade missionary who took an African wife and became a gun-runner: 'members of the white race as are not of the best class, can throw over the restraints of civilisation and develop into savages of unbridled lust and abominable cruelty'.[59] In the 'Heads of a Plan' for the founding of the colony at Botany Bay, it was suggested that the First Fleet should return to sea and collect women from New Caledonia and other nearby islands from where 'they may be procured without difficulty'. Without sufficient women 'it is well-known that it would be impossible to preserve the settlement from gross irregularities'.[60] Working-class men may be pacified with a cargo of women; women fit for middle-class men would not be part of an undifferentiated group. A true middle-class gentleman can avoid 'gross irregularities' without the balm of black women. None the less, there was constant 'fear of backsliding [which] had a powerful sexual dimension'.[61] Ray Evans also notes this difficulty:

Sexually, white males reacted to the black man with a compound of fear and envy and, in the case of the black woman, a compound of desire and guilt . . . Calling the women 'animals' gave them licence to treat them as animals—and the self-loathing they experienced about themselves mating with such defined 'animals' was projected outwards in aggression against blacks in general and, in the realm of sexuality, upon black women in particular.[62]

In the nineteenth century, many planters exercised a *droit de seigneur* over their female workers, but from the turn of the century both indigenous men and some white commentators condemned this practice, the former by striking and the latter by ostracism and where possible economic punishment.[63] Until the early 1800s the British and French fur-trading companies encouraged marriages between fur trappers and Indian women to cement alliances in colonial Canada. Indeed in 1686 the Hudson's Bay Company managers had passed a resolution forbidding wives from joining their husbands posted in Canada. Only by mid-century were the contributions of white women, the 'delicate flowers of civilization', being praised.[64]

In the early days of most colonies, sexual relations between local women and isolated traders, planters, miners and other lower-class men were tolerated; indeed, there was little prospect of their regulation by an infant administration. Thus 'Empire provided ample opportunities for sexual indulgence throughout the nineteenth century, though this was more obvious in frontier situations and the fighting services than in settled expatriate communities'.[65] Between 1892 and 1924 there were thirty-seven marriages of Europeans and Papuans, all of European men and Papuan women. There were none from 1924 to 1940, some argue because the influence of white women in Papua negated the easy-going relations among the races. Inglis suggests that the real reason was the departure of the miners, traders and seamen who had made these mixed marriages—no government official did.[66]

In the early days of a colony only top administrators and missionaries were expected to refrain from sexual relations. All the missions stressed celibacy, but their lay workers were sorely tempted, and Langmore identifies two casual sexual encounters with Papuan women, two liaisons among the lay brothers, three suspected cases, and one substantiated case against a Protestant missionary.[67] All were required to resign from their respective missions. Early London Missionary Society missionaries in Tahiti slept with Tahitian women, some defecting from the mission. In 1929 the Assistant Bishop of Northern Melanesia was forced to resign because of allegations of misconduct; two years later the Bishop himself, F.M. Molyneux, resigned because of whispered homosexual accusations.[68] In many colonial societies it was illegal for administrators to cohabit with indigenous women.[69] In one such directive, given by the Governor-General of Nigeria in 1914, miscegenation was equated with bestiality.[70]

Ronald Hyam argues that 'Pax Britannica was also a "pox Britannica" '.[71]

Victorian Britons lived in an uneasy and often guilty relationship between the 'official prudery' that forbade prostitution, masturbation, homosexuality, sexual pleasure and yet which nurtured more brothels in London at mid-century than schools and charities put together;[72] which condoned the sexual exploitation of servants by their masters and masters' sons; and which provided the perfect environment for homosexual encounters in boys' (and girls') public schools. In the colonies this mass self-deception often allowed sexual transgressions as long as they were not publicly discovered or publicly acknowledged. It was accepted that sexual relations with the indigenous women might occasionally be necessary, but they should never be discovered or socially recognised. In some colonies cohabitation was considered acceptable but marriage not.[73]

As a colony matured, the weight of middle-class notions of appropriate sexual practice gained momentum, and competed with conceptions of indigenous women as merely lustful beasts, or white men as justified in taking their sexual pleasure at will. A sharper distinction developed between a 'true' gentleman who controlled his passions and an inferior man who did not. Many colonial administrations outlawed miscegenation or sought in limited ways to protect indigenous women. This conferred on them at least some shreds of the cloak of passionlessness which characterised Victorian middle-class female sexuality, and was some protection against unwanted sexual encounters. In Papua white men were required to marry indigenous women they removed from their villages. A number of whites believed this rule was excessive: they should merely be required to return the Papuan women, after use, like soiled goods.[74] Joan Refshauge believed that 'there was a rule in Papua that anyone married to a native woman could not divorce her. I think that rule was subsequently rescinded'.[75] John Butcher reports for Malaya that companies from the 1920s disapproved of their planters taking local mistresses.[76] Daphney Bridgland explains the lack of female servants: 'Native women were never allowed in a house where there was only a bachelor'. From 1897 in South Africa Zulu houseboys became nursemaids; female servants in the colonies were even more susceptible to sexual exploitation than their white working-class sisters in England.[77]

From the 1920s, but not really becoming a widely-held view until the 1960s, the conception of female sexuality shifted from the pure unsexed mother of the race, to a belief that women also had sexual desire. Taken to its libertarian conclusion, the notion that male and female sexuality was similar meant that cross-race sexual alliances should be evaluated in the same way, no matter what the respective colours of the partners. In fact the first white woman married a black man in Port Moresby in 1961.[78] None of these positions was uncontested, relying as they did on a complex interplay of class, sexual belief, and sexual possibilities. Thus the response to openly-acknowledged mixed-race sexual relations, particularly in the post-war period, reveals that some Territory members saw them as acceptable while many did not. Peter Murray suggests that a *kiap* was put on indefinite leave without pay because he took a Chinese girl to the pictures and a Burns Philp manager was sacked when he married a Chinese girl. Jackson notes several instances of white men losing their jobs as a result of marrying Papuan women.[79]

Literary representations of inter-racial sexual liaisons also reveal these changing attitudes over the years. Beatrice Grimshaw's novels, written in the first decades of this century, distinguish between true gentlemen, who resist the lure of Papuan women, and those who betray their race. Jens Lyng's 1925 supposedly factual story 'Love in the Pacific' offers some arguments concerning the benefits indigenous women gain from their relations with white men.[80] Robert, a school-teacher from Guam, enlists the help of a neighbour, Captain Jones, when he brings his two sisters to Rabaul. Robert tells Captain Jones that one sister, Susan, has been the German governor's concubine. Robert admits that 'our girls' 'do not remain innocent long unless under close supervision of the missionaries'. 'Fraulein', another of Captain Jones' neighbours, suggests the advantages which accrue to Susan: 'the pet of the mightiest man in the Possession' with 'all her modest desires attended to' and a marriage to one of her own countrymen when the Governor's wife arrives.[81] Fraulein comments:

A white man may be immoral before he comes to the Islands, but in the majority of cases he treats the weaker sex with kindness and consideration. He may sacrifice to his lust the virtue of a woman but he does not ill-treat her. The native does both—that is the great difference between civilized and primitive man.[82]

To this justification for miscegenation, Robert adds another. If Captain Jones does not employ Susan she will fall into greater degradation; as other white men have already expressed an interest in sexual access to her. Lyng believes that the tropics undermine a white man's morality.[83] There he finds a people who think of little else but 'sustaining life and propagating their species' while the 'great dearth of well-bred women and the sensuous climate' increase the likelihood of degradation. Captain Jones now confronts his degradation, taking refuge in a doctor's advice that men who abstain, particularly in the tropics, threaten their mental balance.[84] Susan arrives, and Captain Jones, seeing the child in the fallen woman, sends her to Fraulein. Eventually Robert and his sisters return to Guam. Captain Jones concludes that 'women of their race are . . . born for the pleasure of men'.[85]

In the late 1950s Errol Flynn describes his conquest of the yielding Papua

New Guinean women in *My Wicked Wicked Ways*; but he transgresses the canons of polite sexual manners by also conquering white women (who, however, are more than just bodies for his pleasure). As one of Tim Bowden's interviewees said of Flynn 'He'd steal anybody's wife or dog'.[86] Flynn's father accepted Grimshaw's worldview, writing to his son that 'a man who has anything to do with a native woman stinks in the nostrils of a *decent* white man'.[87] Flynn's attitude was: 'The conventions of mid-England could not easily hold for a vigorous young white man surrounded by feminine and attractive Melanesian girls'.[88] Thus Flynn chose to assert his masculinity through sexual expression and not self-control. In the late 1970s, Randolph Stowe attempts to describe a sexual liaison from both a Papuan woman's and a white man's perspective: 'And I thought yes, yes, she will care, I will be a man to her'.[89] It is through Saliba's words that the two are equalised in sexual encounter: 'then I thought that he too was afraid, this Dimdim, he was afraid that I might hurt him. And when I knew that, there was no difference and no strangeness any more'. Although more palatable than Flynn's conquest of cardboard dusky maidens, this narrative also represses any possibility of racial domination and sexual inequality.

Although there is a general consensus that black women were more sensuous than white women,[90] the attraction of black women to white men is explained not in sexual but economic terms.[91] 'Papuan women are attracted by the wealth and status of Europeans'.[92] Isabel Platten noted that although indigenous women had their own birth-control measures, they chose not to use them in sexual liaisons with white men: 'As always, men used indigenous women for their pleasures, regardless of what would happen to the offspring of such unions. A group of these girls were living with the sisters'.

Certainly indigenous women received far less legal protection than did white women. It was believed that Papua New Guinean women ripened earlier than white women; for many years a belief that a woman had reached puberty, was an absolute rebuttal to averment of her age in a sexual offence.[93] Only with the anti-discrimination legislation in the 1950s were New Guinea girls given protection from certain forms of sexual abuse until the age of 17, in line with the protection afforded expatriate girls under the Criminal Code.[94] The Native Women's Protection Ordinance of 1951 prevented a 'female native' from being on premises other than those normally occupied by her husband unless she was accompanied by her husband or had the prior written consent of the District Commissioner. Thus the law restricted the movement of unaccompanied indigenous women, not white men. During the debate to repeal the law in 1962, John Guise pointed out that Papuan men still risked harassment for friendship with white girls while Europeans molesting Papuan girls were not necessarily convicted.[95]

The unspeakable—white woman and black man

Miscegenation was described in biological terms, although MacMillan warns that earlier generations used the term race when we would use culture or ethnic characteristics.[96] There was a coupling of unnatural behaviour with notions of race disloyalty around the biological act of miscegenation. A white woman violated 'her own nature in marrying a man of coloured race'.[97] In 1926 a newspaper editor commented: 'We regard the creation of the people neither European nor African as the supreme racial disloyalty'.[98] In Fiji such women had a 'debased state of mind'.[99] 'The hybrid and mongrel mixtures of mankind are as unsatisfactory as those of the lower animals'.[100] Rebecca Scott suggests that the anxiety over sexuality is linked to Darwin's construction of the family of man.[101] The discovery that white men were related to black men placed the seed of the black beast in every white man. Suddenly the distance between superior and inferior races was narrowed and bridgeable. To keep the distance and the difference, social injunctions against racial contamination became strident.

Knapman confirms that race relations do not operate in the same way for both sexes, but explains this in terms of miscegenation.[102] Social Darwinism, with its emphasis on biological determinism, encouraged the development of racial purity and eugenics movements at the turn of the century. Women as mothers were crucial to this process, the home being identified as the 'cradle of the race'.[103] 'Women were the souls of the race, children its future. They stood for innocence and purity; they were also dangerously vulnerable'.[104] It was thus necessary to control the movement of women in colonised society, in case they should become the vessels, willing or otherwise, of the contamination of the white race.

But the widespread ideology of social Darwinism cannot be invoked to explain the great horror of a white woman with a black man, if miscegenation was allowed to proceed apace between white men and black women. Why was a woman 'defiled' by such sexual relations while a man was merely 'demeaned'; why was a woman afraid but a man only repelled, to use Inglis' distinctions?[105] This is much more a story of sexual power relations than of biological determinism. Wives were legally the property of their husbands until the 1880s. The legal impossibility of rape in marriage, which survived for another hundred years, perpetuated the notion of a man's ownership of his wife's body. It was the loss of white men's property to subordinate men which provoked racist hysteria in colonial societies. Thus between 1934 and 1958 it was an indictable offence for a white woman in New Guinea to 'voluntarily permit' a native, unless she was married to him, to have carnal knowledge of her.[106] There was no distinction between forced and voluntary liaisons by white women; both were 'injurious to the colonial social order'.[107] One might wish to insinuate that the injury was to the male colonial order.

Both pollution and danger provoked the moral panics, with their invariable sexual imagery, which inevitably punctuated life in colonial society.[108] The danger arises from a widespread white male preoccupation with the superior sexual potency, prowess, desirability and desire of the black man. Negroes were described as promiscuous;[109] and having 'superior physical equipment'.[110] In Africa nudity was related to 'a lack of self-respect'.[111] Indians, and especially Indian princes, were seen as sensuous and lascivious.[112] Papuan men were thought to be more potent and desirable because they were sexually unrestrained.[113] White men everywhere were profoundly jealous of white women,[114] even African missionaries were suspicious of their daughters and wives.[115] Brantlinger notes that the 'Victorians found strong temptations in Africa, as their frequent references to the allegedly promiscuous sexual customs of Africans show'.[116] Last century in Queensland, white men 'sexually repressed by the mores of Victorian convention, deeply feared the supposedly superior virility of the black man'.[117] The myth persisted after Victorian times as a warning in 1958 attests: 'Missionaries must beware of becoming too friendly with the opposite sex. The native has very strong sexual drives which he often is unable to control'.[118]

The prospects of pollution were all the greater because of the 'desirability' (not only the 'desire') of black men. White male ideology had painted itself into a corner: perhaps our women prefer these men. In India there were added inducements when Maharajahs presented bouquets containing diamond ornaments.[119] Thus women became more than the helpless victims of miscegenation. Just as white women are often accused of 'asking for it' when they are raped by white men, so too were they sometimes blamed for improper behaviour in colonial society. Women who developed relations with black men were ostracised far more completely than white men who fell from grace. In India respectable hotels did not want such women as guests and no Europeans visited white women who married Indians, even a Maharajah.[120] In Malaya it was felt that European prostitutes damaged the status of the rulers in the eyes of Malays.[121]

In order to avoid the label 'damned whore', a white woman contaminated by relations with a black man must react with appropriate horror or resistance. Even this may not be enough:

She is perceived as villain rather than victim, a frequent characteristic of moral panics: coupled with cries for more segregation of blacks are scarcely veiled injunctions to white women to *keep in their place*.[122]

Keeping to her place put considerable strains on white women in colonial society, especially given their daily interaction with servants. As James Sinclair, a patrol officer after the Second World War, puts it:

A common offence . . . was, in the quaint legal language of the ordinance, 'being in the curtilage of a dwelling-house with intent to annoy the female within'—in other words, trespass generally for the purpose of peeping . . . I think we often abused this particular section.[123]

Sinclair suggests that 'some of the white women never did appear to recognise that their native servants were men; moreover men without women'.[124] In 1926 Murray warned careless women 'who do not seem to realise that a native is a man with a man's passions, and commonly very little self-control'.[125] On the other hand, Hank Nelson comments that the 'largely unwritten laws about avoiding sexual excitement and how best to deal with servants stopped many white women from ever knowing Papua New Guineans as ordinary people'.[126] This latter suggestion comes closer to capturing the possibility that both Papua New Guinean men and white women were trapped, albeit in different ways, in a legal net made by white men, a point Brownmiller also makes for the ante-bellum South.[127]

The issue is explored in Amirah Inglis' analysis of the hysteria surrounding the supposed imminent and extensive sexual assault of white women by Papuan men in the mid 1920s. In 1921 in Port Moresby there were 203 non-Papuan men for every 100 non-Papuan women. The ratio was higher in the 25 to 35 age group.[128] In Moresby, as opposed to Rabaul, there was no 'buffer' of the Chinese 'to divert black resentment, to provide a complication to whites' notions of their superiority'.[129] The white community was more self-contained: all men being members of the Chamber of Commerce and Residents' Association and all white children attending the Government House Christmas party.[130] It was perfectly acceptable to discipline servants by a cuff and a kick provided blows were administered with the open hand. In April 1930 a servant who complained when a mistress slapped him during an argument was told that he must not be insolent and cheeky to white women.[131]

In the late 1920s a large number of women arrived, contributing to a sense that newcomers did not know how to keep the Papuans in their place, and that women provoked sexual attacks.[132] More Papuans congregated in Port Moresby and were increasingly influenced by white ways. Other factors contributing to the hysteria were an economic depression and widespread resentment of Lieutenant Governor Murray, who was 'essentially a dictator at heart'.[133] Before the 1920s it was generally agreed that for a white woman to be the subject of sexual impropriety from a Papuan man was for her 'a frightening experience' while for men it was an 'infamy' against white womanhood and an 'outrage' against the prestige of the white race.[134] There was a sense that in bygone days, before Papuans were spoiled by contact with the civilisation of Moresby: 'the European woman stood on a plane so infinitely superior to the native that for him even to think of her carnally was an impiety terrifying to the imagination.'[135]

The key to maintaining this sense of awe was rigid and detailed policing of the colour line, for example censorship of films which showed white women in close contact with 'natives' even where there was no sexual suggestion.[136] Inglis suggests that while men's sexual self-doubts were translated into rage, women responded to the supposed sexual threat with fear.[137] Hortense Powdermaker described her boat trips: 'Much of the time I had to escape from the women's never-ending tales about the dangers of being raped by native men.[138] However, other accounts suggest more complex responses. For Lilian Overell the New Guinean male was too cowardly to be a real sexual threat, to be a *real* man.[139] One white woman, a victim of sexual assault, still guiltily wonders whether a dance she performed with a 'little bit of bare midriff' provoked the attack. That night she woke up to a black hand running up her thigh and 'screamed and screamed'.[140]

In 1926 the White Women's Protection Ordinance was passed, at the suggestion of Hubert Murray, the Lieutenant-Governor, despite his conviction six months earlier that offences of this nature were very rare. The Ordinance was extremely harsh, carrying the death penalty both for rape and attempted rape, the life sentence for indecent assault, and flogging 'two or three times' (of fifty lashes each time) for a number of offences. Murray in 1930 and again in 1939 defended capital punishment for rape (or attempted rape) and for the murder of a European: 'the lives of this small garrison and the honour of the women must be protected. A failure to afford an adequate protection would jeopardise the cause of civilisation.'[141]

Ultimately the 'besieged' Port petitioned Murray for flogging and 'emasculation' of offenders.[142] Murray was at odds with the Australian government which intervened to prevent the first execution proposed under the Ordinance. In 1930, however, a police constable Stephen was convicted and hanged for the indecent assault of a 5-year-old European girl. In 1934 the punishments under the Ordinance were brought into line with the Queensland Criminal Code, although the Ordinance continued to apply only to crimes against 'a European woman'. The Ordinance was repealed in 1958.[143] The expatriate community believed that white women would no longer be safe and provided their wives with 'gas guns' for protection.[144]

Similar hysteria was experienced in New Guinea in the late 1930s when 'boy-proof' sleeping rooms, enclosed by heavy chicken wire, were installed at government expense in all houses where white women resided.[145] Daphney Bridgland describes Mrs Lauden's house, a 'perfect hacienda' with internal garden and barred windows.

The evidence suggests that attacks by Papua New Guinean men were rare, especially when compared with the behaviour of white men, no doubt in part because of the heavy penalties involved. In 1920, although his guilt was uncertain, a New Guinean in Rabaul was given twenty lashes for assaulting a white woman. A story circulated that a German woman had propositioned her house 'boy' who was so terrified he committed suicide before her husband returned.[146] Amirah Inglis reports that in 1963 Papuan men would leave the footpath to avoid physical contact,[147] while in Rabaul before the Second World War New Guineans stepped off the pavement if a white person passed. [Marjorie Murphy].

Callaway suggests the only account of fear from a sexual source she discovered was of a drunken white man trying to force his way into a white female doctor's carriage.[148] Marjorie Murphy was harassed by Australian soldiers in Rabaul. Pat Murray also notes that in 1941, while the First Independent Company was stationed in Kavieng, 'as the only single European female under the age of about forty' she had to be very careful, to avoid a bad reputation. However, there 'were in the vicinity of 300 or over and I never once suffered any remarks or approaches or anything unpleasant'.

It was popularly believed among the male European community that inexperienced recently-arrived women provoked assaults by indigenous men: 'The government knew, the protesting men knew, and the white women knew, that the cause of the phase was carelessness on the part of the women.'[149]

The records suggest, where evidence is available, that the women who were attacked were either walking in the street, sleeping, or standing on their verandahs.[150] This hardly accords with the widely told 'lady with the towel' story, concerning a mistress who, on completing her shower asked her servant to bring her a towel. He did so, only to find her naked.[151]

Nevertheless women in all colonial societies were enjoined periodically to 'dress sensibly and avoid rape'. 'Immodest dressing is a temptation to our natives and has frequently led to the abuse of white women in the Territory'.[152] 'It was always white *men* who told the white women what was "too sexy" for "the natives" to bear'. Elsie Champion noted that 'we women believed it was against the law' to wear shorts, while the District Officer or Resident Magistrate summoned women to his office when their dress was unsuitable. One Resident Magistrate 'ruled' that divided skirts were shorts, and therefore 'illegal'.[153] The Administration distributed a booklet reminding white women not to wear shorts or flimsy night dresses when having morning tea. Daphney Bridgland echoes this point: 'When

I went to New Guinea no-one would dream of wearing shorts because the thigh excites the native men. You would always get a sneaky one on his own who might attack a European woman'. Jean Mannering emphasises the cultural significance: 'to show your thigh was shocking . . . We warned Australian girls who came on holiday to us'. Another woman said the 'veneer of civilisation was very thin with those people' and 'I do think if you got around in a bikini—no different from our white men'.[154] James Boutilier reports similar attitudes from the Solomon Islands.[155] One of his respondents thought white women who wore 'too few clothes' constituted a menace to other expatriate women. She herself bathed and dressed in the dark and would not allow her female acquaintances to pull the toilet chain when Islanders were in her home.[156] In the 1970s women were still blamed for causing sexual assaults. A white woman living with a black man in 1969 was raped by another black man; it was suggested that her de facto relationship signalled her availability to all Papuan men.[157]

Thus Inglis suggests that before the 1920s Papuan men did not even consider white women as sexual beings. From the late 1920s, a few Papuans, educated in white ways and noticing and re-evaluating the sexual practices of white men, reconsidered the supposed unavailability of white women. It is unlikely that many white women consciously considered Papua New Guinean men as desirable sexual partners until after the Second World War. Increasingly from this time, the more liberal attitudes of younger arrivals to the Territory conflicted with the mores propagated by planters and missionaries. In the more volatile atmosphere produced by a large population of immigrants, both from the villages of Papua New Guinea and the cities of Australia, a wider range of sexual practices became possible in towns like Port Moresby or Rabaul.

On the outstations, women retained a sense of sexual security throughout the period under investigation. Diane Langmore's study of missionary women in Papua up to 1920 revealed no 'hint of that fear of sexual assault which was to obsess the white women of Papua 30 or 40 years later' despite the long weeks that husbands were on circuit.[159] Jean Mannering commented that white women in New Guinea who thought they were followed by local men 'imagined it' or 'if they didn't like you, they might do it for a prank'. She claims 'I never had an unpleasant experience involving the native people, at any time of my life in New Guinea. I can remember one time I spent a whole week in Molot village by myself'. Other women echoed this sense of security. Isabel Platten comments:

> Gil's circuit was very large. We calculated he covered 300 miles, mostly walking, each time he visited the teachers' schools and

churches; he usually did this three times a year. During these journeys
Newell and I were in our house alone. Perhaps it was naive of
me to be so unafraid—so trusting of the people around me. But
my confidence was never challenged.

Dixie Rigby recalls:

> [I] never had a guard dog, and I never had a gun, and not until
> after the war, did I ever have a door or window. But I made up
> my mind and I formed the impression that was one thing which
> I believed I must stand up for. They must come up to my standards,
> I couldn't go back down to theirs. Reg would be away for three
> months on end.[159]

Being alone (that is without a white man's protection) is always the time
of testing in these accounts. Only Dixie Rigby even hints that Papua New
Guinean men may have entertained sexual desires, but she was convinced
that her race-based authority would dissuade them.

On the other hand, Mary Pulsford reports a concern for her daughter,
at a later date (the 1960s) and in Port Moresby:

> I think one of the things that all white women faced if they had
> daughters was really how to keep an eye on their daughters, how
> to protect their daughters. I don't know why we were always more
> worried about our daughters than our sons. But I know that I was.
> There were just one or two little instances that happened to Susan.
> She came to no harm at all, but I'm sorry they happened, that's
> all. She was going to school one day and somebody she passed by
> opened their laplap. But I suppose that could happen here.

'A man with a man's passions'

'I suppose that could happen here'; 'no different from our white men'.
These comments express the conviction of some white women that colour
does not a different sexuality make. Both black and white men are potential
beasts, unleashed by the naked thigh or breast, the inappropriate comment,
and the thousand other ways in which a woman can get herself into strife.
As Inglis notes, white men and Papuan men may have feared and hated
each other but 'they had in common the myth of the white lady with
the towel', a myth concerning female sexuality.[160] One should be hesitant
to impose the template of patriarchal relations on a foreign culture. None
the less, occasional reports by white women in colonial society, and events

in Papua New Guinea since Independence, certainly suggest that even if the indigenous societies were not patriarchal before exposure to white ways, such attitudes are now prevalent.

Following Independence many Papua New Guinean men opposed the Westernisation of women, and its apparent freedoms. A play written in 1977 by Nora-Vagi Brash portrays a social-climbing, snobbish, wife of a government minister, who derides another woman as 'hardly more than a village woman', refuses to eat traditional food, and encourages her husband to refuse his kin obligations. Her husband's father notes sadly '*meri bilong yu, bosim yu*' (You allow your wife to boss you) while her servant says this *kanaka meri* (bush woman) behaves exactly like a white woman.[161] In 1977 a new law on adultery allowed local magistrates to gaol offending women (men were not to be gaoled).[162] Paliwala suggests that the village court system is deployed to regulate women's behaviour.[163] According to Rowley the system of 'talking out' disputes has always reinforced the power of the 'big man'.[164] Nelson Paulius, as secretary for the Department of Culture and Tourism, reported: 'The tourism industry in this country is still a virgin. It needs to be raped'.[165] Domestic violence is widespread and widely accepted as a punishment by men for wives' failure to fulfill marital obligations; it appears to have increased with the breakdown of family and ritual-based regulation.[166]

In most societies in Papua New Guinea women are exchanged for a bride price. Many Western commentators have been horrified by this, as they were by polygamy, seeing both as the degradation of women. Such horror can be read as an expression of the superiority of white culture, as a manifestation of imperialism, rather than any concern for indigenous women *per se*.[167] Indigenous writers, perhaps not unexpectedly, reacted with a spirited defence of their customs. Francis Bugotu asserts that the bride price signifies women's worth, not that she is a commodity.[168] He also asserts that society (not the man) tells 'the man to protect and command the woman, the woman to obey, contribute and build society'.[169] But one can hardly read the subsequent claim in a non-sexist register: the woman's 'so-called freedom [through fashion] has weakened the man to subjection in a world created and controlled by the woman'.[170] There would thus appear to be a happy coincidence in the assessment of indigenous women's place in society for both the white colonisers and the indigenous men.

When Michael Leahy took his expedition into the Highlands he left behind a half-caste son. Wenta, the mother, describes the payment in goods she received for sleeping with Leahy. Her husband took these from her but: 'I didn't mind going. I was attracted myself to all the different things he had'.[171] To Mokei Kubal Nori, the practice was understandable: 'He didn't have any women of his own with him'.[172] Some husbands exchanged their wives' sexual favours for gifts; some forbade the exchange, beating wives who disobeyed.[173] Sex was so significant a male function to Papuans that Pastor Vicedom of the Ogelbeng Lutheran Mission was once asked whether the Ogelbeng Lutherans actually had sexual organs.[174] One of Joyce Walker's patients offered to save her from the single state the Highlanders of Mendi found so deplorable, but she tartly refused: 'I was not amused and the mission went pigless' (the offered bride price).

While the trading of indigenous women may have suited men on both sides, neither subordinated nor dominated men accepted 'their' women freely choosing sexual relations across the race divide.[175] Papuan men explained attacks on white women as 'a sort of payback' for white men continually taking 'their' women. Interestingly this reason struck no responsive chord with the male administrators; they preferred to attribute the attacks to unrestrained passions. This was an illogical argument as Inglis wryly notes, since unrestrained passions could much more readily and safely be slaked on Papuan women.[176]

In Lyng's 'Love in the Pacific' the position of the Samoan Robert is represented sympathetically: 'we natives have a greater right to our womenfolk than you Europeans have'.[177] Robert continues:

And the most humiliating part of all is that many of the women feel flattered—they will rather be the play-toy of a white man than the legally wedded wife of one of their own kith and kin.

Captain Jones, as a 'British Officer and gentleman', accepts Robert's right 'to continue their race'.[178] White men sometimes sympathised with the position of Papua New Guinean men, emasculated by the ill-treatment of their women, their loss of fierce independence, their confinement to tasks undertaken by women in white society, or their subordination to white women. White men sometimes evinced a masculine mateship across the race divide: 'Malaita men have the right idea, [they] let the women do the work'.[179]

In Doris Lessing's *The Grass is Singing*, the inability (perhaps inappropriateness) of women to supervise servants is mentioned three times.[180] On the first occasion, a kind of link is forged between white and black men: 'Needs a man to deal with niggers,' said Charlie. 'Niggers don't understand women giving them orders. They keep their own women in their right place'.

There was a concern that no man should be reduced in status by a woman. Sir Arthur Gordon thought it quite inappropriate that future parsons should carry the missionary's wife in her chair.[181] In 1902 Charles Abel of the

LMS lamented that a Papuan reduced to gardening and fishing (no longer engaged in tribal fighting) could never be 'a strong man'.[182] The Royal Commission of 1907 restated this theme, which was to echo down the years of Australia's administration. The elimination of tribal fighting rendered the Papuan man 'more effeminate, and correspondingly indolent and wanting in proper manly self-respect'.[183] Wolfers, speaking from his sensitivity to *racial* discrimination, says of the German administration: 'men were men, and generally left alone; they were not treated as dependents'.[184] In 1946 Colonel J.K. Murray deplored the use of the word 'native' with the connotation that it 'meant less than a man'.[185] A Papua New Guinean parliamentarian suggested that handouts had emasculated the local people: 'at one time they were everything that was terrible and horrible to the civilised world but at least they were men'.[186]

Osana, in Stowe's *Visitants*, disparages indigenous men who cower before white men: 'The old headman crouched among the rest, and looked up at Mister Cawdor as if he hoped to become his wife'.[187] Osana is also disparaging of Saliba's excessive devotion to his master Cawdor, which he attributes to the physical deformity which deprived Saliba of a wife. Monckton reduces the people of the Trobriand Islands to the pervasive triplet of child, animal, nature, in describing the islands as famous for 'the cowardice of the men, the immorality—or rather I should put it the total unmorality—of the women, and the quality of its yams'.[188] Papua New Guinean men, like white men, equated femininity with inferiority. During the 1929 Rabaul strike on two occasions the leaders exhorted the men to be brave and participate: 'If you are men, you can do this thing. If you are women you cannot'.[189]

It was not only male commentators who noted the emasculation of Papua New Guinean men, usually as a result of white administration. Not all European women, in the manner of Hortense Powdermaker's travelling companions, frightened each other with stories of potential rape. Some spoke instead of the failure of indigenous masculinity. Grimshaw suggests that the reasons for tribal murders 'were so inexpressibly humorous' that even white women felt little fear.[190] Ann Deland paints an amused picture of the 'hen-pecked' husband:

> Hippua, in hospital with the usual tropical ulcer on her foot, was an exception to the rules for both size and temperament. A strapping wench, nearly six foot high and with a beam to match, she strolled into my husband's office. "Me like make marriage long Piva" she announced. The doctor, thinking the youth should have some say in the matter, shouted for him. Piva appeared and drooped sulkily

just inside the door. "Me no like" he said flatly. Then as he caught a glance from the lady, he sighed resignedly "Me like".[191]

Irene Robinson tells of a servant reduced by illness, 'huge and handsome and commanding—it was piteous to see him laid low and obeying his wife whom he usually rather hectors'.[192]

White missus *and black* boi

The contradictory intersection of the hierarchies of sex and race produced tensions in the mistress-servant relationship. These tensions were heightened in a relationship of close propinquity. As Deborah Kirkwood notes, 'Families occupied the identical overall space of their houses and gardens with their servants', the only exception being that whites never entered the servants' quarters.[193] Physical proximity required strict codes of behaviour to maintain a sense of separation. Knapman suggests that the problems of propinquity were handled with rules of etiquette, 'ritualised interaction' and truncated expression.[194] On the other hand Boutilier argues that 'living as they did in almost complete isolation, plantation wives turned quite naturally to their cook-boys for companionship and support'.[195]

Almost all white women in Papua New Guinea had male assistance with household tasks; this was true of government, mission and plantation workers. Why men were recruited to perform tasks normally done by women has puzzled commentators, although it passed unnoticed among the women interviewed.[196] Indigenous men were more mobile, free to leave their own villages; female servants were often assumed to be concubines (a legacy from the pioneer days); and women were viewed as less intelligent or otherwise inferior as servants.[197] Hansen argues that the central, but unexpressed, reason for the exclusion of Zambian women from the white woman's household was fear of her sexuality, the disruptive effects of her presumed moral laxity.[198] White women protected the household domain from the undermining influence of a different sexual presence.

This explanation was not usually offered by the interviewees in my study, although Mary Pulsford suggests the rule was for the protection of the local women. The work was sought after by indigenous men (Dorothy Pederick, Jean Mannering), and it was deemed necessary to keep a watchful eye on young unmarried girls. Margaret Spencer suggests women 'cannot be spared from the gardens and the pigs', concluding unwittingly 'Theirs is a man's world'.[199] While the status of houseboy was high, men gained in prestige from such work. From the 1960s women were increasingly employed as domestic workers, and Papua New Guinean male attitudes caught up with the white man's evaluation of domestic labour: 'In those days being a houseboy was a prestige job. Nowadays of course they think it's the pits'. [Pat Murray]

Few of these women's accounts identify any sexual difficulties with servants, although Mary Pulsford notes one instance:

> With one person we had much later I realised I had to be very careful how I behaved so the messages were quite clear, there was no encouragement given at all. I think you've got to be very aware of how different people operate, and there are just little things in your own behaviour that give very clear messages. I made it very clear to him without ever saying anything that he was not to come into the bedroom section of the house if I was having a rest and that sort of thing.

Usually male servants adopted appropriate behaviour. Daphney Bridgland notes that her servant Josef spoke to her with his eyes averted when he brought a life-saving meal to her sickbed.

It was not the fear of sexual licence but the possibility of disobedience that characterised mistress-servant relations. In Fiji the directions of the mistress of the house were frequently ignored.[200] Ann Deland points out that male servants often became difficult at about the age of 16, because they would no longer take orders from a woman, even a white woman:

> Bui came to us as a small boy from the bush and when we left Kieta he went with us to Wewak where he became the cook. Always bright and intelligent he made a very good cook, but when he was about 16 he became "difficult". I have seen it happen often. It goes against the grain for a man to take orders from a woman and so they become difficult to manage. Having by now five children I did not feel able to cope with a cook who was "playing up". So I sent him home before we had any real trouble—no hard feelings on either side.[201]

Daphney Bridgland had difficulty with Kombi boys and her husband gave them orders before he went away:

> In the early days native staff would obey. They mightn't like it but native staff took pride in looking after masta's family and they'd guard you. But later on we had Kombi boys and they were the last men we had working in the house. If Leon was away I would be safe as houses because they'd fight to protect me until they died. But they didn't like taking orders from a woman. We never

ever got the work done while Leon was away that I could achieve
with those same boys when Leon was there. It was beneath their
dignity to take orders from a woman. So Leon would tell them
what jobs they had to do before he went.

Perhaps Daphney Bridgland experienced difficulties because in indigenous
society, 'to punish a young adolescent male was a duty for the boy's father
or some close male relative' and thus was more acceptable coming from
the master of the house.[202]

Margaret Mead suggests that house staff played off master against mistress
and 'found having older boys about the place too complicating'.[203] Billy
Burke says 'Certainly Papua New Guineans didn't like working for women'
although in the 1930s there were over 5000 men working for white women.[204]
Valerie Bock, a sister in a hospital, reports 'the male patients find it hard
to take orders from mere female sisters—they just won't take any notice
of what we say'.[205] Another Methodist Mission sister reported that the men
' "try it on" . . . as we are women, to see how far they can go'.[206] Other
missionary women were well aware of the difficulty of getting the local
men to obey a woman.[207] Although an unusual situation, during the Rabaul
strike of 1929 a striker 'swaggering' back to work struck a matron who
reprimanded him, splitting her mouth and blacking her eye.[208]

Sister Bohdana Voros describes the need to 'talk strong' at least to her
younger male pupils:

> Once I told them, (when they were disobedient) 'In the recess you
> will weed'—in the front of the school there were lawns—and I
> would watch them. The children went out and two boys sat in
> the last bench. I was sitting at the table. One of them said to
> the other 'She didn't mean it, she didn't talk strong to us'. I said
> 'I'll help you. What did I say, will you go straight away?' I talked
> strong to them and right away they went. They expect the discipline
> they had under Germans there before. Later when they went to
> high school you could treat them as equals.

There are a number of other accounts which suggest that women expected
and received obedience through assuming it. Doris Booth 'had found that
high-handed action had carried the day with the aid of bluff' and the use
of 'lawyer cane'.[209] She ran the labour line on the Bulolo fields in her
husband's absence; as punishment she stopped tobacco or meat rations.[210]
Mrs Parkinson ordered her disobedient labourers to present themselves for
a flogging, and was 'much disturbed' when one of them ran away instead:
'I never heard of such a thing in my life!'[211] Judy Davis suggests that

women in charge of plantations 'seem to have behaved no differently from any other "masta" and were probably perceived as just that'.[212] Evelyn Cheeseman reports that she achieved obedience because bushmen were curious concerning her strange doings and gained prestige from the stories they could tell in their villages.[213]

None the less, most white men expected obedience almost unconsciously; women more often report the constant possibility that an order or request may go ignored. A planter's wife notes that until she knew they would follow her order: 'I felt my back prickle with apprehension'.[214] Another planter's wife comments: 'I've never kicked before. You being with me must have given me the courage'.[215] Some women lived in real fear: 'I found in myself a fear of black men I didn't know existed'.[216] Irene Robinson's letter in the 1920s tells the following tale:

> You can see from this instance what a fierce watch you have to keep over blacks—you *can't* be kind to them if they are his sort or else they just think they own the earth [an ironic euphemism for an interloper to use].[217]

Irene Robinson also reports spontaneously slapping a Papuan policeman's face when he refused to leave the store. She 'then felt rather alarmed because with no Man in the House I didn't want to start anything . . . Nothing of this showed on my face of course (at least I hope not)'. However Robinson won the day, the policeman later returning to beg for some kerosene, which she gave and 'he bade me farewell with tears in his eyes'.[218] Irene's daughter took after her, and was able to engage 'the boys' in rounding up some cattle, reporting: 'I used all the language Father does when he wants anything done quickly'.[219]

Daphney Bridgland had a fearful episode with a servant who was later discovered to have a brain tumour:

> He should never have been sent to me as a houseboy. I don't know whether he'd been drinking or what, but he came in to the kitchen. I said to him 'You're late, and there's a meal to get ready'. I had meat out and when I gave him instructions he said '*Mi no laik*' and glared at me, and he looked from me to the knife and back to me and me to the knife. So I just started walking slowly towards him talking all the time until I got between him and the knife. Then I said '*Yu raus*'—*raus* is the word for get lost. I was a lot bigger than he was and he didn't have the knife so he took to his heels. Finally they took him to the hospital and found he was crazy with a tumour.

Daphney Bridgland notes that she 'was a lot bigger' than the houseboy.

This sense of physical superiority recurs in a number of accounts, for example white women on the American frontier.[220] Kettle reports a nurse who made a request to a New Guinean orderly.[221] He refused, threatening to take off his belt and thrash her. She, being a tall woman, threatened to thrash him in turn; and they 'got on famously after that'. W.E. Bromilow once weighed a European mission sister against the largest Massim man who could be found near the station. Even though she weighed only sixty kilograms, she 'easily tipped the scales'.[222] David Wetherell describes Nellie Hullett:

known as 'the largest missionary on the smallest island in the world' . . . a humorous, intelligent woman without the graces and airs of some missionary wives. Of iron will and mammoth physical proportions—she weighed nearly 140 kilograms—she used her powers freely to restrain her unruly parishioners on the island of Naniu near Tufi.[223]

White men's criticisms of white women's treatment of servants may well be evidence of repressed male anxieties that women were in a position to give orders to men, albeit black men. As Knapman points out, physical intimidation was rarely used, especially in comparison with white men's treatment of their field labour.[224] In Fiji, while field labour was indentured, servants were not, and so were free to leave. Furthermore they had the care of small children, a relationship that required trust not fear. Ann Deland notes that it was illegal to strike servants in New Guinea, although she was sorely tempted to give one of her 'boys' a whack:

[Tokana] had Ray on his knees and was kissing him. Now Tokana doesn't wash as often as he might, and his teeth are black with betel nut, which usually means pyorrhea and infection. You can imagine what I felt like. One can't help feeling that one box on the ears would do more than lecturing them. However, you can be fined five pounds for striking a boy. Of course, one sees the reason for the rule, but sometimes, as with small boys at home, one whack is better than all the scolding in the world.[225]

Similarly, Alice Keelan, a Resident Magistrate's wife at Samarai noted 'there were many times when my hands ached to give Toia the shaking he so richly deserved'.[226] She had to request her husband's intervention before obedience was restored. As early as 1918 she employed two Papuan women whom she preferred to any of her male servants as 'gentler, more considerate, more grateful, and far more thorough'. Naturally they were not missionised and were 'unspoiled by contact with whites'.[227]

It would appear from these expatriate women's accounts that many resolved the race-gender contradiction by treating their servants in a patronising manner, treating them as 'boys'. They 'learn amazingly quickly' and sometimes 'as with small boys at home' need a good whack;[228] Dame Rachel Cleland had a 'dear little elderly Hanuabada woman called Keke' who was actually 'a woman of some consequence' in her own community.[229] Marjorie Murphy notes 'You don't give good tea-towels to native servants; they are likely to wipe the floor with them'.

Comments concerning the physical characteristics of servants were also common: 'He had the biggest feet I've ever seen in my life and hands like hams' or 'a funny little bloke with an enormous grin and big ears and big eyes and skinny nobby legs and elbows'. [Daphney Bridgland] 'Nawi, he was a little shortie. The Highland people are fairly stockily built. He's a dear old thing, we've seen him every time we've been back. He's got himself married, we thought he'd never marry'. [Grace Young]

For every tale of a white woman's fear of black sexuality there is a jocular or dismissive story; for every episode of a white woman unable to command a servant's obedience, there are tales of white women effectively deploying their racial superiority. For every instance of concern over the emasculation of the indigenous men, there is a counter statement suggesting their inherent effeminacy. These contradictory responses reveal the complexities of a society where hierarchies are volcanic rather than sedimentary. Race and sex and class are not separable structures deployed with the symmetrical precision of a layer cake. Moreover, structures provide only the potentialities for domination or the probabilities of subordination. They represent the hand one is dealt, not how it is played. These structures are embodied in particular individuals who chafe against each other's personalities, making their best of a schizophrenic and highly charged environment.

Little has been said in this chapter about the most invisible members of colonial society—indigenous women. According to the hierarchies of domination, it was the Papua New Guinean women who had the fewest resources for autonomy. The next chapter introduces their story.

18. After the war, New Ireland, c. 1946
Artillery and rusting aeroplane fusilages on beaches are among the traces of the Second World War still to be seen in Papua New Guinea.

19. The Platten house, Halis, late 1940s
After 1945 the Platten house was rebuilt using scrap materials salvaged from the debris of war.

18

19

20. Missionary sisters, Baining Mountains, 1951
Joyce Walker says goodbye to sisters Shirley and Chris before leaving for Mendi in the Highlands.

21. The mobile Hanagabe clinic, Highlands, mid-1950s
Joyce Walker weighs babies and dispenses medicines.

22. Joyce Walker, Mendi, c. 1953
Joyce Walker (far left) is pictured 'teaching bush people how to feed their children'. [Joyce Walker]

23. Joyce Walker, Mendi, c. 1952
With one of her motherless babies and a Papuan girl from the coast who helped her in the house.

20

21

22

23

24. Father and child, Mendi, c. 1952
Hunja Poonk was the first of the motherless babies Joyce Walker saved. This photograph shows the first time her father fed her.

25. 'Departure of Number One Child', Mendi, 1953
Joyce Walker had left Mendi when Hunja Poonk's father was able to reclaim her. He had remarried, so now had a woman to care for the child.

24

25

26. Nurse Silo, Dale and Marjorie Murphy, Daru, 1957
Nurse Silo cared for the Murphy children.

27. The Platten house near Sos on Tabar, c. 1952
'The house was built around me and much native material was used. It was a very pleasant house built almost on the high water line.' p. 185 [Isabel Platten]

26

27

28

29

30

31

28. Garaina, c. 1955
The rundown teacher's house that Isabel Platten believed was only held up by its prolific covering of passionfruit vines.

29. An outing for the white missus, near Sos on Tabar, c. 1951
Isabel Platten enjoys a canoe ride.

30. Isabel Platten landing at Kainantu, c. 1955

31. Saimon Gaius at Raluana, near Rabaul, 1986
Saimon Gaius was appointed Bishop of New Guinea Islands in 1986.

32. Aisoli Salin, MBE, Tatau, Tabar, 1986
Aisoli Salin was one of the first three Papua New Guinean members of the Legislative Assembly in 1951.

33. At Pakinsela Village, New Ireland, 1986
In front of the men's house, Deane Fergie interviews Sios Tabunamagin (to her left), pastor and tutor in the Methodist Mission during Gil Platten's time at Halis.

32

33

8

Making a Space for Women

In this last chapter the role of women in the colonial project will be explored. Until the 1970s it was generally assumed in colonial histories that white women were more racist than white men. In the 1970s, and more particularly the 1980s, feminist historians have re-read the colonial record to claim that the peculiarly racist white woman was a projection of male historians and colonists. The mechanisms for measuring non-racist relations, for example sexual relations across the race divide, are inappropriate to discussions concerning white women's race relations. Not only did women less often participate in such relations, but white men's participation in fact rarely evidenced a lack of racism. On the other hand, recent attempts to redeem the white woman abroad have come under criticism, particularly from Third-world women. These more recent readings of history re-assert the privilege of race that white women had over both indigenous men and women. This chapter explores the relations between white women and indigenous women in colonial settings and the debate concerning white women's role in the 'ruin of empire'.

Women in the colonial project

'Colonisation is essentially a masculine act: to conquer, to penetrate, to possess, to inseminate'.[1] Of the three imperialist aims—economic expansion, affirmation of national power and the civilising mission—only the third readily incorporated women.[2] The impact of economic 'development' in which colonial rulers perpetuated their patriarchal values, widened the already existing gap between men and women in conquered societies. Colonial administrations ignored women's authority and leadership roles; they delivered new technologies to men even where women traditionally performed the associated tasks; they educated men for productive labour and women if at all for domestic work; they confined women to subsistence production in the villages while incorporating men into the colonial project of mission, town or plantation; they ignored women's communal claims over land or produce.[3]

On the other hand—and often the other hand was extended by the colonisers' wives—some women were given an education; some traditional practices which can hardly be described as beneficial for women (like suttee and infibulation) were outlawed; and some women were made nurses, teachers and church members, and went on to have a significant role in the independent nation. Some white women presented the softer face of colonisation in their relations with indigenous women, a relationship as yet barely examined in this book.

This contact was not as extensive as that between white men and indigenous men, partly because of the additional hurdles in its path. Indigenous women were not employed or educated in the same numbers as their brothers and husbands. Sir Hubert Murray in the early 1920s claimed that women should not be indentured as it would threaten the society of the village in a way that the absence of men would not.[4] In 1938 when 41 850 New Guineans worked for Europeans, only 350 of them were women.[5] As late as 1963 only 90 300 girls compared with 140 000 boys were receiving a primary education.[6]

There were language barriers separating white women from the indigenous population. Both Butcher for Malaya in 1931 and Oram for Papua New Guinea note the lower percentage of white women (in comparison with white men) who spoke an indigenous language.[7] This was more often a barrier for white women in towns, but it also applied to women 'down the road' as Pat Andersen notes: 'I never learned Koriki well enough to do more than conduct basic things like "How are your children?" "How are you?" and that kind of thing'. Jean Mannering and Mary Pulsford stress the importance of learning the lingua franca.

Although some white women extended the work of colonisation to indigenous women, care must be taken in claiming that this necessarily undermined the colonial project, or patriarchal relations for that matter. More often than not, white women sought to make indigenous women in their own image: as good wives and mothers. In the process, indigenous women, as women, often disappeared from the colonial calculus. Their education or betterment was seen as a means to improved nutrition, family life, or village stability. While Langmore's missionaries report the desire to improve the status of women from that of 'slave' or 'drudge', their ambition was to make the Papuan woman into a suitable Christian wife.[8] For many years missionary education for girls focussed on appearance, hygiene and sewing;[9] Dorothea Freund, a Lutheran missionary's wife, taught housekeeping skills and a 'bit of reading and writing'.[10] Plantation women, too, taught sewing to the local village women, perhaps allowing them to use the plantation sewing-machine.[11] Mary Slessor, a missionary in Calabar (Africa) in the nineteenth century, was known to the Africans as 'the good white woman who lived alone'. Her biographer comments that to Africans (men presumably) women were merely chattels, but Mary Slessor gave them 'a new conception of womanhood'.[12] Even though unable to set an example of wifely dedication, Mary Slessor successfully stopped women drinking in roving bands, approvingly noting they were 'at home where husbands can keep them in check'.[13]

In the early days, the New Guinea mission did not choose to educate particular girls because they themselves showed promise, but rather because they were or would become pastors' wives (Jean Mannering, Dorothy Pederick). In their role as a pastor's wife, these women would provide 'leadership' in the villages, but this was limited to the domestic domains of hygiene, weaving and sewing. Additionally:

> If you trained a pastor teacher and didn't train his wife, married him to a girl from the bush who had no education, no training in hygiene and cleanliness, he felt ashamed of her. It was likely because he was ashamed of her, he might be angry with her, and she'd run back to her village. So it was to the advantage of all to have a wife who could live up to his standard of cleanliness.
> [Jean Mannering]

In the Holy Spirit Mission after the war, Sister Aquilonia advocated education for the girls to 'improve the lot and raise the status of women' but really it was their status as wives and mothers that was at issue: 'Since boys in New Guinea did gradually receive secondary schooling and teachers' training or held otherwise good positions we felt it was necessary to train girls as teachers as well to become acceptable wives and better mothers and housekeepers'.

Papua New Guinean men also resisted the education of the girls, whether because they could not easily be spared from family chores (Jean Mannering), or the necessity to supervise their morals and thus maintain their bride-price (Dorothy Pederick) or to retain their filial obedience.[14] Sister Aquilonia suggests that once an educated girl fetched a higher bride-price, resistance to education of girls diminished. But even today education of girls is viewed as a waste of time and money which encourages girls to adopt 'unacceptable attitudes' and Western behaviour.[15] While Joan Refshauge suggested that educated girls chose their own husbands,[16] Vera Whittington notes that 'men are choosing their own partners'.[17] The right of selection had shifted from family to husband.

Sios Tabunamagin suggests that the local culture endorsed the prevalent view that girls should not be educated: 'In these days now that the government runs the schools, the girls can get an education just like the boys. Then we thought the women weren't capable of getting an education'.[18]

Sister Bohdana Voros overcame the Manam Islanders' reluctance to educate girls by talking to the 'big man' of the village. Once she convinced him to let his daughter, Maria, go to Standard 5, the other parents followed suit. Sister Bohdana reports that the male students hit the girls the first day they came to school to start in Standard 5, 'But the girls were not afraid any more'. Sister Bohdana showed no compunction in favouring her female students, with a reward of real ink (not made from powder) because the girls were 'tidy'. The boys in retaliation set the mission's dog onto the girls who, running away, spilled their precious ink.

Clearly life at the mission provided a certain freedom and excitement for the girls, even if they were supervised by the sisters:

> They'd come to school and the girls' dormitory was up near the sister's house. Almost weekly there'd be screams 'Oooh! . . . Man!' I think they rather enjoyed the thrill of it—and we'd be tearing up there at night with torches finding out who this man was. One dormitory building was on a raised floor with narrow slats of split black palm . . . The boys had great fun getting under the room, poking sticks up, frightening the girls out of their wits. I remember Nancy Anderson, one of the teachers there, we had visitors for tea . . . and there was this screaming going on and she said 'Oh it's just the girls, it's all right it'll only be a man or a snake'. [Jean Mannering]

Susan Gardner's scathing attack on Sir Paul Hasluck's memoirs concerning his time as Minister for External Territories notes that he devotes only four pages 'to' women and he uses no material by them. He focusses on women's role in 'general' advancement rather than women's specific needs, such as bodily autonomy (control over their fertility, freedom from rape and domestic violence), equal access to education and the professions, or the removal of customary discriminations.[19] While these criticisms are not unfounded, they neglect the fact that the public rhetoric of the mid-1950s gave little attention to such reforms. Hasluck himself, perhaps for the 'wrong' reasons, attempted to increase the numbers of girls in schools.[20] However, despite a 'vigorous' campaign, there was little change, a fact which Sir Paul blamed on his sexist and slothful department. Callaway suggests that female education officers in Nigeria also faced bureaucratic inertia to their strong commitment to the educational advancement of Nigerian women.[21]

Donald Denoon is a trenchant critic, not only of Australia's colonial health policy in general, but also of Joan Refshauge's Maternal and Child Health Division. Its very title suggests that women were only mothers (Maternal), a means to Child Health. Denoon cites Refshauge's comment 'natives . . . are now asking for their wives to be admitted to hospitals' as evidence that Refshauge denied women (even as mothers) any agency at all.[22] Elsewhere Joan Refshauge noted that husbands were unwilling to let their wives attend hygiene education classes because they were not spending enough time in the home.[23] Denoon asserts that the:

medical authorities never managed to focus on women for more than the time required to write a single despatch. There was an unconscious but resonant harmony between Australian thinking and the frame of reference of the black men with whom Australian officers most commonly interacted . . . The virtues of the health services were partly vitiated by the large blind spots of medical planning—and in these blind spots Melanesian women lived and died.[24]

Denoon concedes that 'it is just possible' that the introduction of even a limited maternal health service had a short-term effect on the sex ratio of the population during the 1960s. However, a combination of the indigenous culture's preferential treatment for men and boys and the administration's neglect of women soon reasserted itself. Melanesian society describes women as 'bouncing coconuts' who do not confer any benefit on their own village, but marry into another one.[26] As a result the masculinity ratio is 111.7:100, 'the most masculine country on the face of the earth'.[27] Boys are brought to clinics at twice the rate of girls, maternal mortality rates are high, women age more swiftly than men. The colonial administration may have successfully outlawed infanticide, but it made almost no impact on the neglected health of indigenous women.

In 1953 the Department of Health had only one Papua New Guinean female on staff, an assistant midwife.[28] Dorothy Beale in 1952 recommended a curriculum of training for local women as nurses, commenting that a keen interest would provide sufficient recruits. It was five years before a school of nursing was established, at Port Moresby.[29]

Donald Denoon also criticises Joan Refshauge's identification of the 'well-known tendency towards conservatism in the native communities' as a hindrance to nurse training.[30] Denoon asserts that Papua New Guinean women seized every opportunity for training. The following speech by Joan Refshauge places village 'conservatism' in a context which also sympathetically notes the difficulties for girls who undertake nurse training:

> To select the right type of girl for a village centre well away from the parent training centre is not easy. She must be able to accept responsibility among her own people, to meet an emergency without the support of a European and have the capabilities necessary in a good nurse . . . The girls are not generally amenable to discipline, they find that the drag of village tradition is hard to overcome; there is the loss through marriage and there is the difficulty of finding girls with any sense of responsibility. However, with patience, there are always some who have these necessary qualities and others who develop them in their training.
>
> It has been my experience that marriage is delayed among the girls completing their training. She becomes more independent and not infrequently refuses to marry the man chosen by her parents and in many cases marries the man she chooses. This is inevitable in a socio-economic change but how far reaching the effects will be remain to be seen. These will be further influenced by the increasing opportunities for girls. There are scholarships for girls to train at Suva . . . There are scholarships for which girls can compete with boys for education in Australia . . . No doubt this higher education for women will bring about social upheavals but provided we are aware that this may happen we should be able to protect the individual from harm in such a change, but education of women raises the standard of living of home life and assures the satisfactory education of her children. It may bring loneliness—in this we may help by placing her in employment where she will meet others of the same abilities.[31]

There are both sexist and racist elements in this statement. Joan Refshauge connects the 'education of women' with 'home life' and the 'education of her children'; she does not applaud women choosing their own husbands but describes it as 'inevitable'. However there is an alternative reading. Refshauge identifies the 'opportunities for girls' with education and she notes the possibility of loneliness for educated girls. To accuse her simply of seeing nurse training as a means to better community health, as Denoon does, is to do less than full justice to her position.

It is also to read her anachronistically. Few around Refshauge understood indigenous nurse training in any other terms than the welfare it would bring to others. Hasluck advocated training indigenous women as nurses to improve the nutrition of children and family life, and to reduce the strains of social change.[32] He does not identify any benefit to the trained nurses themselves. Indigenous nurses filled a gap that white women, 'unless of the Missionary type',[33] were unwilling to fill—work in the villages. A European nurse commended the 'gentleness and efficiency' with which a Papuan-trained Infant Health and Maternity nurse delivered a baby on board a boat, but concluded:

I felt I must write and tell you and strongly congratulate you on the training you give these women—and also the conception or idea of giving them this training. It is really wonderful and must be of untold benefit to the vast outback of the Territory.[34]

The close association between 'equality' for women and the wife/mother role is revealed in the following letter, commending Joan Refshauge's work in 1963:

. . . the turnout of Papuan and New Guinean women trained in better housekeeping and therefore more likely to make suitable wives for the growing number of educated indigenous males. By "suitable" I mean that they will be able to take their place on an equal footing—a rather radical idea, I will admit, amongst Melanesian men but one that has not even found 100% acceptance in the Western world, either.[35]

Dr Refshauge was appointed by the Administrator as a member of the Advisory Committee on the Education and Advancement of Women in 1957. The insights she learned on this committee she brought to her work as Acting Director of the Queen Elizabeth II Infant Child and Maternal Health Service and later the Directorship of Maternal and Child Health. She claimed in a public address: 'May I suggest here that the standard for this work [maternity work] should be that which any Australian woman would expect? Some of you will no doubt think that this is idealistic and impossible, that it would not be accepted. This is not so'.[36] She laid the foundation for a unique training scheme of orderlies and fully qualified nurses to gradually replace the expatriate nurses. Dr Refshauge did not take a narrow medical interest in public health, but presented papers on a wide range of issues ranging from child abuse, to the need for childminding services for women who were required to participate in their husbands' careers, to the necessity for learning pidgin.[37]

Joan Refshauge, it appears, made a clear commitment to work for the Papua New Guineans despite hostility from the white community who described her as 'that woman who prefers to eat with the natives than us'. One diary entry notes: 'I went to Hanuana gaol today—this p.m. and was welcomed. Sgt Major Daura said "We prouds of you Dr. Your our Dr Refshauge. You prouds of us native people too" '.[38]

It is clear that Joan Refshauge was more comfortable in a man's world, and perhaps in the company of men; her mother providing that nurturance and support in the domestic sphere which normally falls to a wife. She met with considerable hostility from white wives; she saw them as interfering and indolent. However she formed strong friendships with her female nursing staff, particularly Taffy Jones. It would be hasty to conclude from the preserved fragments of her thoughts that she did not also respect the professional Melanesian nurses whose training she administered. She was perhaps dismissive of mothers who were nothing else; but she could not be said to be dismissive of all women.

Denoon dedicates his book to Dr John Gunther; it is clear from Joan Refshauge's diaries that she had constant battles with Gunther, and felt betrayed and isolated by him. In taking Gunther's perspective, it is possible that Denoon has been less sympathetic to that of Refshauge. In reading Refshauge's actions through a lens fashioned by feminist interpretations, I have sought to explain and perhaps excuse the limitations of her perspective.

There can be little doubt that most white women felt and expressed the superiority of their culture in their diverse plans for colonised women. However, the very act of educating these women must have eroded imperialist patriarchal relations, if only gradually. It gave indigenous women new choices, it gave them the English-speaking voice to which colonial society (and increasingly their educated menfolk) would listen, it offered them different perspectives on the world, even if they chose to reject them. Both Sister Aquilonia Ax and Joan Refshauge identify such outcomes from training indigenous women:

> Much changed in the station of woman; though slow yet it was persistent. Women became aware more and more of their dignity as persons, especially as a result of the influence of the Christian Churches and the women's participation in church groups, the equal opportunity in the field of education, nursing and other specific positions. Polygamy was slowly but surely reduced and there was also a government that recognised and upheld and when needed defended the rights of . . . women. [Sister Aquilonia Ax]

One should not lose sight of the ideological remoulding that mission and charity work involved. Its objective was to fashion indigenous women in the image of white mothers and wives, thus making them acceptable to their husbands as partners in the development process. An example of this was the *foyer* movement in colonial Belgium which in 1957 was instructing 15 per cent of the African women living in Usumbara on the domestic duties of cooking, mending, washing and weaning children.[39] The movement emphasised that women should give up any income-earning activities and focus on appropriate child-rearing: 'To instruct a boy is . . . to form a man; to instruct a girl is to form a family'.[40] The movement focussed on *evolués*, the new urban elite of Africans, and attempted to instil in a wife 'devotion, unselfishness and discreet and intelligent collaboration in the profession of the husband'.[41] However the movement also exhorted husbands to view their wives as partners rather than only as their property.[42] House visits were used to police hygiene and cleanliness among the participating African women.

Thus, it may be anachronistic to interpret white women's activities as simply the female aspect of male-dominated colonialism. Although convinced of the superiority of their own civilisation, many female missionaries invoked a concept of 'women's work for women', the title of the Woman's Foreign Mission Society (American Presbyterian Church) magazine founded in 1870.[43] They sought indigenous women's improvement, not only in the emulation of good housewifery and a companionate marriage, but also in training in medicine and as teachers. By focussing on the role of domesticity, missionary women sought to 'embody traditional notions of nurturance, gentility and affection which distinguished them from men'.[44] Women's work was more intimate, personal, and direct than the men's.[45] Jane Hunter argues that women's mission work was not only a mechanism of cultural imperialism, but also resulted in 'diversifying the weaponry available to indigenous groups'.[46]

The work of Joan Refshauge and others extended the role of indigenous women beyond the confines of home and hearth, to include paid jobs. French feminists, who spoke of their 'Muslim sisters' in colonial Africa as early as 1900, spent three decades debating how best to develop their sisters' potential. Some endorsed the need for Muslim women to become citizens, members of the public world. Others saw women's improvement in motherhood, served by an expansion of medical and other services.[47] There were similar debates in English-speaking feminism at this time, essentially characterised as the 'difference' versus 'sameness' debate.[48] Some feminists argued for women's equality with men in the world of work and politics. Others argued that the difference of women, primarily in their role as mothers, meant that entry into the public world must be with a different voice, for women-centred goals and actions.

I have not discovered any representation of these debates in terms of attitudes towards Papua New Guinean women. However their expression is evident in Janaki Nair's discussion of Western women's attitude to the zenana, literally the women's quarters in rich north Indian households, but a term which came to symbolise women's separate domain and ideas. Initially the zenana was interpreted as the site of primitive tradition, for example polygamy and the 'unscientific' practices of midwives. By 1880 the zenana was seen by some British women as conferring a 'prestige and dignity' Western women lacked.[49] This discourse competed with another interpretation, emerging in 1900, which saw the zenana as the 'unreasonable, illogical space that resisted colonization and, thus, civilization'.[50] On the other hand, some Western feminists exhorted Indian women to express the needs of the 'mother-half' of humanity in the struggle for independence.[51] In Sri Lanka (then Ceylon) too, female European educators disapproved of the intrusion of the local environment into the schools and taught the practices (needlework and book-keeping) and values (dependent wife and domesticity) of the Victorian patriarchal family between the 1890s and the 1920s. Although such an education 'denationalised' Sri Lankan women, and was resisted by the Buddhist and Hindu Revival as 'thoughtless imitation of unsuitable European habits and customs', it gave women access to extra-domestic roles, whether intended by their English educators or not.[52]

Down among the women

Even the expatriate women's accounts collected for this book barely mention interactions and relations with indigenous women. Women talking about women's business—domestic life, family health, the interests of women— are treated as unimportant or peripheral by both men and women:

> Chilla, you once asked me how I and other white people felt about the native women. I have given this a great deal of thought and believe I felt towards them exactly as I felt towards all women. I liked them very much. I felt comfortable with them. I hoped a better standard of living could be attainable but in those extremely difficult days there could be little prospect of that. One knew that by world standards they could be deemed well provided for. They had ample land to grow a good variety of excellent food, a good climate and an abundance of fish in the nearby sea. Perhaps I should have delved more deeply into their lives but, having an innate reluctance to do that to anyone, it was impossible for me to pry into their minds or behaviour. [Isabel Platten]

But white women and indigenous women did interact, and in a number of areas. It was often white women who taught the indigenous women a Western education, including preparation for nursing or teaching. It was not the administrator but his wife who realised that respect must be conferred upon local women if they were to participate in the development process. White wives and mothers used their children and household chores as a bridge of communication with Papua New Guinean women.

White women without paid employment often developed relations with indigenous women through voluntary and charity work. Mary Ann Lind's study of *Compassionate Memsahibs* identifies a group of fifteen women who were neither missionaries nor always paid workers, and who went to India not because husbands took them there, but to practise medicine, education or some other form of welfare. These women spoke the local language and often had parents who had spent time in India. However, with three exceptions, they were 'supportive of the Raj and believed that India was better off as a result of British influence'.[53] Most of these memsahibs worked with women: administering medicine, establishing girls' schools, setting up funds to train women as doctors, nurses and midwives, speaking out against polygamy. They often met with resistance from the Indian community, who thought a literate girl would soon be widowed, or that education would destroy virtuous behaviour.[54]

Compassionate memsahibs were unconventional women, always a dangerous role in the colonial world. As Margaret MacMillan ironically notes, women could have 'enthusiasms' like butterfly collecting, and could be 'mildly intellectual'.[55] Only senior memsahibs did not attract the label of 'going *jungli*' if they sought to improve the position of Indian women, or socialised with them 'in a womanly sort of way'.[56] Annie Besant advocated 'one controversial cause after another, from radical socialism to the rights of women and of workers, to birth control'[57] and finally the Indian National Congress. Barbara Ramusack suggests that the 1910s was the only moment which was neither 'too late nor too early' for alliances between Indian and British feminists.[58] Before this time few Indian women were sufficiently educated or sophisticated in Western political practices to take up women's causes; by the 1930s 'Indian women now demanded the right to formulate their own objectives'.

Janice Brownfoot suggests that white women exerted 'power and influence through traditionally feminine domestic, maternal and charitable duties' forging alliances with Asian women in Malaya in the process.[59] Certainly women were often involved in philanthropic work, starting infant welfare clinics, and assisting in other ways.[60] Callaway argues that women in Nigeria in their professional and volunteer work helped build a 'reservoir of mutual understanding'.[61] This harmonious vision was not universally endorsed by indigenous women. In 1952 Alice Wedega MBE, a long-term activist for Papua New Guinean women, resigned from the girl's training school in soil cultivation she had established. The white woman she worked with 'considered herself in charge and thought that because she was white we should all obey her'.[62]

Nevertheless, as time went by, some of the church-based women's groups emerged as significant political bases for women's action, not only in the church but outside it.[63] For example, Alice Wedega worked with the missions and Girl Guides and was appointed to the Legislative Council in 1961. By Independence she was claiming an equal education for women.[64] In 1981 she argued for the censorship of violent films and the training of girls in cooking and housekeeping; she opposed high liquor consumption which created divorce and hunger in the home.[65] Women have campaigned against the effects of liquor consumption on household budgets and domestic harmony since a march of Tolai women in 1963. In 1974 legislation was passed allowing the wages of an alcoholic husband to be garnisheed and paid to his dependants.[66] Today there is a vigorous debate in Papua New Guinea concerning the effects on women of polygamy and domestic violence, while rural women's clubs and the *wok meri* groups seek to improve the status of village women.[67] The National Council of Women, formed in 1975, is consulted by the national government and campaigns around issues such as large-scale development projects, prostitution, imported handicrafts flooding the local market, and alcohol-related problems.[68]

Many married women in Papua New Guinea participated in charity work, among them Joan Refshauge's mother (who also took on that other female task of caring for Joan's son). Daphney Bridgland helped start the first CWA (Country Women's Association) in Papua New Guinea, at Sogeri with a function: 'of course the men played polo. We had musical chairs with jeeps, we cooked and we had a whole beast we barbequed, and it was terrific'. Daphney Bridgland participated in founding another group in New Britain although she reports 'a lot of trouble getting the native women's interest'. They gave scholarships to European and Papua New Guinean children to study in Australia, and to indigenous women to study nursing in Sydney and Suva.

Doris Groves' diary in 1955 reveals her involvement in a variety of charities on an almost daily basis. In a single fortnight in August she was involved in the following: Scout meeting, Guide campfire, canvassing committee, LMS guild meetings, fete, Children's Fancy Dress Ball, 'Visit by car to Red Cross camp at Sogeri (official) morning'. In the afternoon 'Bill inspects new buildings—I spend afternoon tea with Joan Fell', although she manages to squeeze in one 'Laze on Ela Beach'.[69]

First ladies also forged links with indigenous women. Lady Violet Bourdillon, the wife of the Governor of Nigeria from 1935 to 1943, entertained Lagos market women and danced with them in the gardens (not indoors) of Government House. Joan Sharwood Smith, the Lieutenant Governor's wife, escorted the queen to visit the Emir's wives at Kano.[70] When she arrived in Papua, Dame Rachel Cleland realised how much her husband 'loved it' so 'here I must fit myself in somehow'.[71] Not only did she run the home, both as a retreat for Don and to receive official guests, discussing these latter matters daily with the Official Secretary, she was also involved in the Red Cross and the Girl Guides, and 'seeing people on requests for this and that'.[72] Dame Rachel was instrumental in establishing a Council of Social Services made up of voluntary organisation leaders, when she realised her husband was too distant from local community concerns.[73] She was aware of the low status of Papuan women, both in the white community and among the Papuan men who were aspiring to entry into European culture. One of her proud achievements was to win the approval for wives to attend the reception of the Duke of Edinburgh, realising that 'if we did not recognise them socially their husbands never would'.[74] Cleland instigated Women's Clubs and encouraged government officers' wives throughout the Territory to teach the Papua New Guinean women how to sew, and how to cook, serve and eat European-style food. Marjorie Murphy participated in this work:

> I was very fond of Dame Rachel Cleland (as she now is). She was a staunch supporter of Girl Guides, Pre-Schools and Women's Clubs when the education of native women came about, and the wives of the field staff in the various districts followed suit. Joan Wearne and I used to visit the local villages regularly—Joan taught sewing and I showed the women how to cook the food they bought at the Store. We gave them support and encouragement.

Pat Murray reports a teacher who educated her female students in Western table manners.

As Janet Finch has noted, many women are 'married to the job': there are many occupations where the support of wives is crucial to job performance.[75] None the less white wives in colonial society could be both a support and a slightly displaced voice. Dame Rachel was able to use her position as 'a mere wife' to put disgreeable views to Canberra officials, views her husband often shared but felt he could not voice because of his position.[76] Beryl Smedley, wife of a British Ambassador notes that she was her husband's 'eyes and ears' at public functions, privy to information he was not told.[77] In dealing with women's business, many mission and government wives no doubt gained a slightly different perspective on life in the Territory.

White women shared interests with the colonised women in household (and even husband) management which provided a basis for communication, especially in relation to children. Knapman notes 'women found in their domestic role avenues for humane everyday contact, dispensing medicine, bartering for food, showing concern for women and children'.[78] Daphney Bridgland tells the story of her first nursemaid, Anna, who was crippled. She empathises with Anna's position:

> She was abused by the men in the village, and used. Then she was married off to a really horrible old man who treated her very badly. One day we were driving along and she was holding the baby and she told me how she got rid of him. Apparently, one of the species of taro is poisonous. They pound them up and make fritters out of them. If you eat this poisonous one your throat swells shut and stops you breathing. Then some hours later the swelling goes down and there's no sign of what's killed you. So that's how she eliminated her husband.

Mary Cover Lawry went with her husband to Samoa in the 1820s. She compares her easygoing communications with the local people, often using her child as a bridge of shared interest, with her husband Walter's strategy. He stayed at home despairingly studying the language and worrying about the lack of conversions.[79] Glenda Riley suggests that white men approached the American frontier and its indigenous inhabitants in order to control and subdue it.[80] The outward push to the frontier usually came when white women hoped to establish a home and have children. Women pursued this task on the frontier, and Indians became guides, assistants, purveyors of provisions, nursemaids. They 'exchanged bits of female knowledge, lore, and folk medicine'.[81] Significantly the men traded in arms, ammunitions and animals, while the women traded in foodstuffs, moccasins and handicrafts. Riley emphasises that the shared 'elements of female culture drew these women of different races into a close and easy bond'.[82]

Lorna Fleetwood notes a moment of delighted communication between the District Officer's wife and a local woman when they discovered the same knitting stitch was used in a jumper and a string bag.[83] Marjorie Murphy, when she went on patrol with her husband, used her knitting as a means of communication with the village women:

> I took some knitting and I'd sit and knit with the women. Because we couldn't talk to each other. They couldn't speak Pidgin, not that I was much good at Pidgin . . . I'd knit and they'd go and get something that they had made, and we'd sit round and that's how we would communicate in those days.

Isabel Platten reports a similar experience during her trip to the Bainings: 'They made me feel a most honoured guest and as we chatted next day (no-one knowing what the other said, that didn't matter) we became friends'.

Judy Davis describes the 'universal sign language' used on such occasions: 'the children are well' 'Boys will be boys' 'I don't know when the men will be back'.[84] Cheeseman comments that Papuan 'women seemed astonished and delighted that I could trek in the mountains just as they did themselves'.[85] Jean Mannering shared with one woman her agony as she watched one child after another die during the war.

These tenuous relations were carved out in momentary and ephemeral all-women spaces:

Trading finished, we often sat down together. Sometimes I watch them knotting their string-work, or play with the children . . . once the men start coming I always go inside. They have a way of crowding in, and the women draw back.[86]

Both Ann Deland and Rachel Cleland discuss the shy village girls, or the shy wives of their servants:

The women are scarcely ever used in the house, in fact they are seldom seen. In their own villages they sometimes have their own roads to their gardens "*tambu*" to their menfolk. Only once did I see a native woman in Town who was not required to be there by either police or medical authorities.[87]

> Bui's mother, when he first worked for me, used to bring him in supplies of native foods for which I gave her rice. Beyond smiling at each other, she very shyly, we got no further in conversation— she knew no pidgin and I couldn't manage her "talk".[88]

Irene Robinson reports that the new boys brought their wives up to show her but the women became 'so frightened that they hardly look human'.[89]

Outwomen or white women living close to the villages became more acquainted with the lives of Papua New Guinean women. Doris Groves describes life in Hanuabada village in 1921, the dances and ceremonies of the Hiri ritual in which the men set off in their claw sail canoes to trade merchandise. While the men were away the women worked in their gardens, perhaps pausing on the way to watch the children in school and join in the songs they knew. 'When the garden was reached, the Kiapa with the baby asleep inside, was hung on the branch of a tree—gently rocked by the breeze—and the woman went ahead with her work'.[90]

Mary Pulsford had friends among the Urip village women; Joyce Walker shared the campfire with the Baining villagers at night; Isabel Platten was privileged to participate in the beri beri women's ritual on Tabar. However, not all women responded so readily to foreign cultures. For those who lost children in alien lands, indigenous women could become part of a culture which had snatched their babies' lives. Beneath the surface of sisterly unity 'festered a sense of unbreachable differences beyond colonial inequities'.[91]

There was considerable debate among white observers about whether indigenous women were downtrodden in their role as the economic backbone of village life. Women carried huge burdens.[92]

> On our journey up the mountain many of these tiny, wiry women passed us along the track carrying in their woven bush material bags an enormous burden of food, firewood, a child, sometimes a dog. That was the burden on their backs, while many carried a baby in a bag in front. Were they returning from the sea they would be carrying several bottles of salt water. There was much goitre amongst these people, perhaps it was natural for them to seek out the sea for the salt so badly needed, which they sipped or splashed a little on their cooked food. Their only clothing was a tuft of leaves shielding their bottoms. [Isabel Platten of the Bainings women]

Commentators argued that when tribes warred against each other it was necessary for the women to carry the burdens as the men had to be ready with their spears.[93] But Helen McLeod notes that even with the cessation of tribal warfare, women continued to carry the burdens.[94] Sister Aquilonia Ax also saw the issue in terms of male dominance:

> At my arrival I found the woman the carrier of everything—loads I could not understand small-bodied, often pregnant, women were able to carry. Men apparently considered it below their dignity to carry anything except bow and arrows and bushknife. I have often remonstrated with teachers, catechists and others, but with no success.

White women—the ruin of male empire?

The 'real work' of colonisation in New Guinea was no doubt done by the men, in the opinion of almost everyone in the Territory. Thus Hasluck offers sixty-five biographical notes of European males, two of Papua New Guinean men and one of a European woman, even though women like Alice Wedega sat on the Legislative Council.[95] While many white women lived in the private domain routinely excluded from official colonial histories, indigenous women did not. As workers and potential citizens of the

Independent nation, they should have been given an equal place with their menfolk as objects of colonial endeavour. Their absence from colonial memoirs and policies reflects the expectation that they would join 'civilisation' as shadows of white women, as good wives and mothers.

The hidden work, of being a *marama* or even a sister, was as difficult to discover in the accounts of Papua New Guineans whom we interviewed as it has been in the official detritus of colonial rule. The sex segregation of occupations in Papua New Guinea, as elsewhere in the world, confined women to particular roles. They worked among the women rather than the men; they were the nurses rather than the *kiaps*; they became involved in entrepreneurial work only occasionally and usually as a result of exceptional circumstances, the absence of an able-bodied man. Their role in the work of colonial society, in keeping with women's supposed nurturing functions, was more likely to be the soft face of colonial rule rather than its hard edge. Recent feminist histories of colonialism deploy these facts to argue that white women were the ruin not just of empire, but of a *male* empire.

Until recently, colonial historians accepted that the arcadian easy going relations of early culture contact were suddenly ruptured by the arrival of the white woman. Some historians have represented her as the more or less innocent marker of the emergence of a segregated and self-consciously racist white colonial society. She limited the movement of her husband among the villages and established alternative European entertainments for the colonial community. Just as often, she was depicted as peculiarly racist, particularly in the matter of sexual jealousy, or peculiarly ignorant, afraid and moralistic.[96] She was ignorant because she had no interaction with the local people beyond commanding her servants; she was afraid for her own safety and that of her children; she was moralistic as the prudish missionary 'all whipped up in whalebone' condemning the nakedness of the Samoans.[97] She compensated for own inferiority by domination of racial inferiors. In her sexual jealousy she created a rivalry of woman with woman (for the attentions of white men). As late as 1985 Sir David Lean said 'It's a well-known saying that the women lost us the Empire. It's true'.[98]

This view of white women as peculiarly racist is shared by writers on the other side of the colonial divide. Albert Memmi suggests 'a woman is less concerned about humanity in an abstract sense, the colonized mean nothing to her and she only feels at home among Europeans'.[99] Both Mannoni on white women in Madagascar and Freire on white women in Brazil assert that women are more racist.[100] One of Jackie Huggins' Aboriginal interviewees claims that white women in outback Australia were more racist than white men, as manifested in their mistress-servant relations and because of sexual jealousy.[101]

Perhaps the memsahib, celebrated in anti-heroic proportions by Kipling's writings, is the best-known image of the racist white expatriate. Charles Miller in 1977 described the British memsahib as 'the most noxious figure in the annals of British imperialism'.[102] Charles Allen in the same year attributes India's 'petty intolerances', 'cold-hearted arrogance' and prejudices to these women.[103] Margaret MacMillan admits that when such women were interviewed between 1978 and 1983, they endorsed the most conservative views expressed by the men.[104] One of the most obnoxious comments was made by a memsahib in 1873: 'Let us sit on the verandah to get out of the natives'. She is attending a function at the Governor's palace, the implication being that other guests were willing to mix with the 'natives'.[105]

C.D. Rowley, despite his trenchant criticism of the racist aspects of Australia's administration in Papua New Guinea, declares 'the arrival of the wives forms a turning point; the club becomes the centre of interaction for the tiny group of "whites"; and here they tend to retire from the "natives" '.[106] The wives engage in gossip which determines promotions. Their moral policing discourages patrol officers from sympathetically implementing the policies which lessen discrimination. Marital infidelity leads to disruption of administration through repostings, while sexual hostility prevents relations with the New Guinean women:

Free and easy relationships of the officer with the villagers, especially the village women, become difficult. As 'European' women will tend to be conservative in race relations, feminine influence and concern for children emphasises the colour bar (while making full use of 'native' servants).

Hypocritical, racist, all-powerful, sexually jealous, Rowley's portrait is of an Antipodean memsahib. James Boutilier endorses this perspective:

European women were not well disposed toward island mistresses and the arrival of European women promoted and focussed hostility on the part of European males toward indigenous men. Where European women were seen as civilizers who would raise the tone, they also contributed substantially to the racial cleavage. However, many of them, particularly in the planter/trader community brought with them racialist inclinations that hardened as they absorbed the popular wisdom of Europeans already living in the group.[107]

Wetherell, in relation to the missionary's wife, is kinder, suggesting only that she often 'unconsciously ... created a racial barrier' because now the missionary, instead of living in a bush dwelling, built a more substantial house.[108] Langmore also suggests that the centre of a missionary's attention often shifted with the arrival of his wife—from circuit to home, from parishioners to family, from village life to household, from the work of conversion to providing for a family.[109]

It is interesting to ponder how women, so often constructed as absent from the stage of history, could suddenly emerge as unsupported and central actors in the one issue of racism. James McAuley, very often 'invaded by a feeling of the *sterility* of our contact with New Guinea' wonders why 'nothing flowers', why all the good work of pacifiers, administrators, welfare workers has not taken deep root:

And then sometimes I wonder whether the explanation is not really much simpler than I had thought. The great enterprise of European colonialism . . . bred rejection in the hearts of its subjects, in spite of so much of incomparable value that it brought. Why? Perhaps the simple answer is: the white woman . . . European men . . . entered into a different sort of relationship, socially and sexually, with the people. When the white wife came out all was inevitably different. It is not the woman's fault if her urge to create and defend a home, and bring up children by the standards of her own community, made her wish to draw a circle of exclusion round her domain. People indulge in a lot of shoddy moral indignation about the 'settler mentality'. Let them face in practice the decisions involved, and then talk . . . No, the white woman is perhaps the real ruin of empires.[110]

This extract comes from McAuley's 'My New Guinea', a retrospect in which McAuley assesses the Territory's future. He has harsh words for the educated elite and its antipathy towards the indigenous culture. He yearns for a true civilising mission by Australians, one built on the conception of the 'person' as a 'structure of intellect and free will and moral responsibility'.[111] He wishes such intellectual conceptions could combine with a colourful flowering in 'art and rite and celebration'.[112] McAuley condemns 'disintegrated liberalism' for the soullessness of Australia's administration. He cites with approval Elspeth Huxley's argument that colonial administration is a very one-sided affair, focussing on material and not spiritual advancement.

Then suddenly he changes register, admits to being 'invaded' by a 'feeling' of the sterility of our contact. And with this shift from intellect to emotion he introduces women to cover his disquiet. His analysis requires no additional element to bear the burden of colonial failure, which he has just attributed to 'disintegrated liberalism'. Ultimately he shrinks from accepting his own conclusions, his partially-spoken doubts concerning the 'incomparable value' of colonialism. Furthermore, in finding this new unannounced culprit, he also shifts the goal of colonialism. No longer bemoaning the full flowering of art and intellect, he now bemoans cold-heartedness and hypocrisy. The colony that women's presence has denied is a colourful mulatto slatternly society with only the minor vices of concubinage and sloth.

McAuley concludes that the 'archaic bird-reptile' (New Guinea) refuses the message of the 'white cockatoo' (the Australian administration).[113] Knapman criticises analyses such as McAuley's because they blame a global phenomenon, the decline of empire, on minutiae, like women's handling of servants.[114] But she actually misreads the relationship between the elements in McAuley's text. The Australian administration has already lost before women enter the scene; it is but a shrieking cockatoo in the face of New Guinea's brooding primeval bulk. There can be no taming of this frontier. Women merely represent an even more degraded aspect of civilisation than the Australian administration's 'disintegrated liberalism'. Women represent 'cold-hearted hypocrisy'.

If McAuley has no need to blame women for Australian failure in New Guinea, why then does he? Callaway suggests that women's 'otherness' operates not only in an opposition to male virtues, but also as the solution of unsolved problems.[115] The enterprise of Empire was unsuccessful because of its many inherent contradictions; there is no proof at all of its 'incomparable value'. But once 'incomparable value' is asserted, women serve to explain the inexplicable. Instead of questioning the true worth of the colonial project, the ruin of Empire remains an unsolved issue, but one which can be put down to the mystery of women, themselves an incessant problem.

Female commentators have disrupted this fifty-year-old myth in several ways. Some have constructed women as mere pawns in other games, as only fulfilling expected roles.[116] Beverley Gartrell additionally characterises colonial wives as victims of stressful living conditions, constant moves and the restrictions of the colonial social structure.[117] Elizabeth West asserts an active place in history for white women as exacerbators of racial tensions.[118] A more common argument is that women arrived at the same time as colonial society solidified into a racist segregation.[119] This was not an accidental coincidence, but resulted from the belief that society at this point became safe and appropriate for white women. Now that women's colonial experiences have found their way into narratives shaped by feminist understandings, a new story is being told; one which places the white woman as an actor within historical constraints—the 'inherent limitations' in the colonial roles available to her.[120]

Knapman, following the lead provided by Inglis, makes it clear that claims concerning white women's greater racism are myths and not scientific facts.[121] She notes that key terms are not defined, claims are ahistorical and untested, the evidence that is offered is ambiguous, contradictory, irrelevant, or insufficient. Furthermore, that evidence is often the voice of one or two males attributing racist attitudes to women.

One pervasive assumption of this myth is that interracial sexual relations are proof of non-racist attitudes. However, given the violence and degradation that often attends intra-race sexual relations (at least in Western societies), this is an astonishing assumption. The evidence certainly does not support it, although sexism, as much as racism, may contribute to the poor treatment of indigenous women. The first blow against the myth of the 'racist memsahib' was struck by Amirah Inglis in 1974: 'so far from showing evidence of happy harmonious relations before the arrival of white women put an end to them, many of the liaisons are exactly the opposite'.[122] Inglis cites the example of a Boundary commission official who escaped a rape charge, although it was alleged that one woman was held down by the villagers.

The 'Indian mistress was used merely as a convenience';[123] the Malayan 'keep' (mistress) 'was rejected, often simply told to go, but sometimes pensioned off'.[124] In some African countries 'bitter anger and resentment resulted from white men using their privileged position to take African women'.[125] Isabel Platten comments that white men in New Guinea did not care what happened to the offspring from their inter-racial liaisons. Fijian mistresses were abducted, beaten and mutilated by their 'non-racist' masters; one such man had 'marked her by cutting off her toes, and branding her private parts and arms'.[126] Against this, Diane Langmore argues that the arrival of white women facilitated cross-sex interaction.[127] Male missionaries could only develop social relationships with Papuan women once white women entered the community, precisely because of the requirement to avoid sexual liaisons. Of course, not all mixed-race sexual liaisons were marked by violence, but it is perhaps a little far-fetched to argue, as John Young does, that in Fiji there was 'social tolerance between the races during the 1860s, whatever individuals did to each other'.[128] Surely the doing is more significant than the voiced beliefs, while it is the accumulation of individual actions which constitute the 'social'.

Without doubt, and for good economic reasons given the lack of occupational alternatives, white women were jealous of local mistresses. However, women did not emigrate to the colonies against the volition of men. Indeed the decision to send them was often made by colonial administrations that expected the presence of white women to keep all white men 'up to the mark' and stop them 'going native'.[129] Thus 'it was not women as active agents who *caused* the rift in race relations, but the new structural alignments of the society brought about by official decisions not of their making'.[130] Inglis argues that the arrival of white women in the 1920s was due to the growth of towns and the more settled nature of colonial society; more men held jobs where it was inappropriate for them to have Papuan mistresses.[131] Similarly in French colonial Africa, it was initially assumed that colonies were not fit places for women, and that their presence provoked sexual jealousies among the men. However the objective of populating the race at home and abroad led to the formation of a society for the emigration of women to the colonies in 1897. Marriage in the colonies was now thought to increase the decency and dignity of colonial life.[132]

Women were expected to set the tone in a more mature colonial society, although this was often resented by some of the male population. Thus Peter Murray, present at an interview with Pat Murray, reports how the *grande dame* of Kavieng attempted to control the excessive drinking habits of the men at the Kavieng Club: 'I'd like the incoming committee to make a rule effective as of now that no member of this club over the age of five be allowed to drink directly out of a bottle'. Apparently she was unsuccessful. At the 'Blood House' where the miners stayed while in Wewak 'men were men, and no women by request'.[133]

Dea Birkett summarises these changes:

In the early development of an exiled and in particular a colonial community, there was rarely a well-defined female place, the largely male population resisting the intrusion of white women into the masculine domain of imperial and frontier expansion. At first shunned for appearing to bring the parlours and polite society of Britain with them to the far posts of Empire, women were gradually drawn into the colonial enterprise . . . social distance was employed as a tool of control and division between the colonial and the colonized. Wives and sisters were, often reluctantly at first, incorporated into the elaborate and rigid forms of social organization and ceremony through which this distance was expressed. They became embodiments of fossilized Victorian middle-class values abroad, their place within the colonial hierarchies of race and sex as fixed as that of the colonial subjects.[134]

At a certain stage in colonial development, it was decided to encourage wives, and possibly other white women, to emigrate. This stage was marked by easier travel, a larger European community, and the emergence of amenities like clubs. White women often arrived at a time when the critical mass of colonial 'civilisation' allowed increased segregation of the two races. At this moment colonial administrators and husbands thought that it was appropriate for white women to enter the colonial society; they would lend the social graces that would further demarcate its segregation. This is not to say that white women were mere passive subjects of this process; it is to suggest that few white women arrived in any colony without the blessing of male administrator, mission board or husband.

Once in the colony, a white woman was accorded a power and prestige she did not have at home. She suddenly acquired the status of race. But this status depended to a large extent on her willingness to adopt the expected role, a good wife and mother setting an example for others, including indigenous women. Some commentators see this as a freely-chosen option. In Fiji, white women took it upon themselves to correct moral behaviour: 'it was not that men *thought* that women were offended by nudity, naughty boys and selfish men; they said they were'.[135] But as Claudia Knapman and Caroline Ralston note, such an analysis assumes that women were equal and active participants in history:[136] 'It is unfashionable to blame black people for being exploited because white men *thought* they were stupid. Yet white women have been blamed for racial intolerance because white men *thought* they were weak and so pure that contact with black people was morally and physically repugnant'.[137] White society then acted on these imposed constructions to prevent white women from interacting with local communities, to 'protect' white women from contamination by black men. Thus many British men had 'an insuperable objection' to the women in their families mixing with Indians. The British men were 'getting the wives they wanted—and deserved'.[138]

It cannot be denied that many women actively chose to police the sexual boundaries between the races and carved out the expected role for themselves. But it must also be accepted that a decision to question that predefined role was far more risky than adopting the role of moral policewoman. Yet Callaway found so many exceptions that she was forced to question the underlying assumptions of the 'norm'.[139] While Dea Birkett's spinsters revelled in the freedom of their race-based status, other white women sought in various ways to improve the lot of indigenous women.

Barbara Ramusack's term 'maternal imperialism' captures British women's treatment of Indian women as daughters or at least younger sisters between the 1870s and 1930s. All the British women accepted the imperial political context and lobbied British officials, 'who did not have reforms for Indian women as a major goal'. The British officials 'tended to regard these female reformers as busybodies who did not understand the broader political imperatives of maintaining imperial power or local law and order'.[140] The term 'maternal imperialism' thus captures the ambiguities of white women's position: superior certainly to Indian women and in some ways Indian men in both their own estimation and that of British officials. But their projects were treated as insignificant in the grand scheme of colonial endeavours, and in truth, if they stepped outside their ordained role as mothers of the race, they became well-nigh powerless 'busybodies'.

Some white women were thus 'disloyal' to colonisation, to adapt Virginia Woolf's term.[141] Disloyalty to colonisation brought attendant costs. It often deprived a white woman of the pleasurable (although limited) powers of the memsahib, which many expatriate women must have compared favourably with the nineteenth-century chattel status of the British wife at home. Annie Besant, as a reformer who wished to improve both the 'economic side' and the spiritual life of society, found no ready-made political movement which embraced all her dreams for women. In becoming a theosophist, she was required to give up public speaking, political work and her advocacy of birth control. In becoming the President of the Indian National Congress, she was publicly forced to reject suffrage for Indian women. Her contemporary, Flora Annie Steel, who chose the life of the memsahib, nevertheless advocated a limited franchise for Indian women. Nancy Paxton's comparison of the lives of these two women, born in the same year, shows they had only two choices: they could be either loyal or disloyal to colonisation.[142] They were unable to think a world or speak a politics that stood outside the dictates of racism and sexism, that neither defined itself against imperialism nor confined itself within imperialism.

British feminism in the nineteenth century sought to strengthen white women's political position by deploying imperialist rhetorics: claiming the sacred trust of white women as mothers of the race whose bodies should not be defiled by unwanted sexual contact; and advocating sisterhood with Indian women, which meant 'raising' them to white women's station but did not respect their cultural specificity.[143] None the less, British feminists came closest to escaping the world view of imperialism when they decried sexual exploitation. Josephine Butler sought the repeal of the Contagious Diseases Act, which allowed compulsory detention, painful medical examination and supposed treatment of suspected prostitutes, first in England and then in India. She claimed:

We feel deeply for the ill-guided and corrupted young soldiers but we feel as deeply for the Indian women. Their cause is our cause, their griefs are our griefs . . . We, as women, desire to protest in the strongest and most solemn manner possible against the wrong done to our sisters and fellow subjects in India.[144]

Butler went on to warn of the disaffection such treatment would cause among Indian male subjects and thus the dangers to the Empire. Even so, these quotations reveal an empathy that can flow from sharing the same female body. Whether white or brown, a woman will suffer the same pain from the doctor's knife on her genitals.

Out of this empathy, and women's different structural location in colonial society, grew white women's displaced role in the imperial project. Callaway accepts that women were treated as the 'ruin of empires' partly because they were scapegoated, the muted voice in a dominant world view.[145] But she also suggests that in a sense white women *were* the ruin of empires. The imperial dream was of a masculine empire and frontier. The presence of women spelled the demise of that myth, its contamination and finally its loss. Callaway neatly twists the claim that white women were the ruin of empire, by implying 'and a good thing too'.[146] The masculine mode of hierarchy, authority, control and empire was replaced with more attention to sympathetic understanding, flexibility and diplomacy, the family of nations and the commonwealth. Callaway concludes by suggesting that the study of women in colonial Nigeria has yielded 'another meaning' of the notion 'ruin of empire'; a meaning hidden from view until women's colonial histories were written.[147]

It may be that women's non-identification with empire grew out of their particular structural location. Women had a subordinate place in the project of colonisation, presenting its softer face as nurses, mission sisters and philanthropists, rather than *kiaps*, district officers and judges:

It was not through a more enlightened attitude that the relationship of the women to the people was different from that of the men, but simply through the opportunity for more physical contact and a more profound involvement in the mundane and personal aspects of their lives.[148]

It is possible that the presence of white women signified this softer face to both the indigenous people and the white administration. Ann Deland's flight to spend a Christmas in Maprik in the Highlands was subsidised by the government because 'The people organizing the whole thing were very anxious that some women and children should be there, as it would be a guarantee of our peaceful intentions towards the villagers'.[149]

When Pat Murray describes the Australian government's expropriation of German properties in New Guinea after the First World War, it is from a particularly female perspective:

> The Australian government got that money, the poor bloody Germans got a really rough trot. They took everything from those German settlers. Fair enough, they lost the War and they had to leave the properties. But the Australian government took their personal silver and their personal lace table cloths and their wedding presents— everything—they took the bloody lot. There were women who had to leave their jewellery, every damn thing.

Similarly, the women in Rabaul supported a wife gaoled for killing her violent husband:

> There was a poor woman in gaol in Rabaul when I went there, Mrs Chambers. She'd shot her husband. He was a drunk and she'd shot him to defend herself. The conditions were very grim because the gaols weren't made to cope with a European woman. But some of the women in Rabaul were very good, and very quietly used to go down to keep her company, and read to her, take her cosmetics and things. [Daphney Bridgland][150]

Women accepted the Independence of Papua New Guinea as inevitable and fair; men saw it as a defeat:

The consensus among the women of this group was that they could see long before the men that it was time for them to go. 'We'd had our go, it was only right that it was their turn.' 'Women sense these things more. The men seemed to think of it as a defeat.' 'It was their country and they wanted to run it themselves.' 'Somehow the men couldn't see it really happening. All the women knew.' 'The men took it somehow personally.' 'It really wasn't our country.'[151]

The women 'cried their eyes out' but the men 'felt bitter'. In the years before Independence white nurses began to treat indigenous nurses as colleagues, offering classes on the newly-emerging race relations. Plantation women asked their houseboys to join their white children's classes; Heather Searle suggesting this was never done before the war.[152]

According to Jane Haggis, feminist colonial histories are apologist, claiming that 'colonialism is men's business; women do the best they can with it'.[153] For Haggis, this benign view of white women's role fails to counterweight white women's recollections with the memories of indigenous men or women. Haggis, however, has her own agenda: 'the singular vision of white women also confines and distorts the use of gender in both these studies, precisely through its eclipsing of colonialism, class and race'.[154] Thus colonialism, class and race are more important, and tales which only introduce indigenous women as the reflection of white male sexual aggression or the product of white women's 'reforming and uplifting hands' neglect these latter more significant dimensions.[155] Janaki Nair also questions recent accounts which refuse to 'engage with the intersecting discourses of race, class, and gender', always overdetermined by race and class.[156] In fact, none of these narratives could have been written without taking account of class, race, and colonialism. But *it* is a different account; an account seen from white women's perspective and often, if not always, through their eyes. Like all stories of the world, it is partial. One can ask, as Yvonne Kniebiehler and Régine Goutalier do,[157] 'Are we maternalistic for writing a book' which discusses white women's attitudes to colonial women without adequately representing the voices of colonised women? Is this just a mimicking of the white male's appropriation of his object of study, in which indigenous women remain the voiceless objects?[158] Or does white women's story, however partial, also have a place in recorded history?

Given the evidence in this book, it hardly needs to be said that white women displayed racist views as well as actions. But even in the social sphere, the racially and sexually exclusive club was invented long before the white woman came;[159] while the camaraderie of shared sporting endeavours has been questioned: 'contacts made on the basis of sporting activities are rarely maintained beyond the playing field'.[160] Amirah Inglis discovered little evidence that white women participated in the passage of the *White Women's Protection Ordinance* in 1926, although in 1930 eighty-six European women signed a petition requesting more government protection, including flogging and hanging.[161] On the other hand, Margaret MacMillan notes that in 1883 when the administration tidied up the 'anomaly' that allowed Europeans in the provinces to be tried by a European rather than an Indian judge, there was a storm of protest, connecting the amendment with increased rape of white women.[162] 'The ladies were not slow to take up their own defence' and forsaking 'their usual reticence' wrote to the papers, held public meetings and drew up petitions.

Yet so ingrained are the contours of colonial history writing that John Young can assert that female missionaries had greater racial tolerance because they were missionaries and not because they were women.[163] But they were both, and as this book suggests, being a female missionary produced more intimate physical contact with indigenous people. Similarly Young asserts that Knapman's 'thematic organisation also obscures some issues';[164] but he fails to understand that this organisation follows from a 'feminist social science' in which women's colonial experiences determine the contours of the narrative.[165] Indisputably however, in taking up a feminist position, a writer represses certain perspectives:

White women are simultaneously seen as positive contributors both to the white experience of colonialism: through their support of male endeavours, and through their spread of European enlightenment and civilisation; and to the black experience: through their 'good works' and more sympathetic attitudes to black people, and especially black women.[166]

Thus it is certainly not argued that *no* white women were racist. It is also likely that a greater percentage of white men had thought-out evaluations of the colonial project, which were critical or oppositional. This, I would suggest, is because the colonial project was not the women's project. A very few white women were disloyal to colonisation in an explicit way, endorsing independence movements and questioning the outrages and pomposities of male rule. More were disloyal to a men-only colonial enterprise, seeking to write in a role for women in the general advancement. But the majority of women were indifferent to colonisation, neither loyal nor disloyal, experiencing it in terms which men thought utterly inappropriate.

Both anti-colonialist and pro-colonialist narratives have largely ignored women whose lives have been confined to the private domain.[167] A white woman's main task in the colony was often the same task she had at home, that of supportive wife and successful mother. In India this could create both close relations with servants and complaints about India and Indians in general, as MacMillan notes.[168] MacMillan suggests that most memsahibs did not have strong views on India, they simply ignored it whenever they could. They were often young and unformed by any adult life in England; they sought to learn the ropes from the old hands as quickly as possible and so echoed the prevailing prejudices. Many no doubt aped the views of their husbands; living in 'fiefdom' undermined the potential for autonomous action and female solidarity (for both white and indigenous women).[169]

Women's common concerns for family provided the possibility of contact with other women across the racial divide, and white women's colonial histories reveal this contact. But women's dedication to family meant they also measured the male colonial project in terms of its impediments to family life. Wives wanted their husbands at home and not on tour or patrol; wives wanted financial security for themselves and their children, and not endless adventure in the colonial wilds; wives often called a halt to their husband's colonial service because of family ill-health or separation.[170] Their commitment to family may have manifested itself as intolerance of a country which made being a mother so difficult. Thus Mary Cover Lawry, while identifying the possibility of communication with Samoan women allowed by motherhood, also sees it as a protective insulation:

I think it may be easier for a woman to be a missionary than for a man. Why?
I am able to come to Tonga and bring my work, the shape of my days, with me almost unaltered. The bundle may have been rearranged; a little lumpy in places, but the same elements are still there—wife, mother, housewife . . . a protective shell around me and mine . . . In this tiny area, it is all right to be ourselves.[171]

Indian memsahibs 'lived in a difficult country with bravery and competence' and 'tried to be ladies in all circumstances' but 'Most of all, they simply got on with living'.[172] Knapman echoes MacMillan when she says:

I hope to have restored in some measure the integrity of white women who crossed the seas, loved and endured living with their husbands, bore and wept for their babies, worked, relaxed, laughed, suffered and died—ordinary women.[173]

The interviews of expatriate women whose experiences form the basis of this book point, possibly, to both the greater pragmatism of communication on the part of women and the greater acceptance of different lifestyles. But as Mary Lawry points out, her job was not conversion. Neither was it the job of the District Officer's wife to maintain order. In other words, women were not the explicit purveyors of colonial domination that their husbands were:

British menfolk provided the iron of rigid rule and railroad. Their wives and sisters supplied the irony: the double view granted only to those who stood always slightly to one side, able to picture themselves inside the regime and outside it. It was the British women in India who humanized the Raj, who *civilized* it.[174]

White women provided another view of the impact of the 'white man's burden', the view of an onlooker. As outsiders, their story complements official histories with another perspective. But it is also a different story, a story that cannot be written into the grand sweeps and measured paces of the colonial project. These women should not only be asked whether they were racist or not, whether they sought Independence rapidly or slowly, and what they desired for the Papua New Guinean nation. These were questions produced by male colonisers; the particular experiences of white women in Papua New Guinea have produced different questions—and answers.

Biographical Notes

Pat Andersen

Interviewed by Chilla Bulbeck in July 1987

Pat Andersen studied social work in the early 1940s. In 1948 her husband Neville, a doctor, decided to work with the London Missionary Society in Papua New Guinea. The Andersens went to the delta region in Papua where they established a hospital. Pat Andersen had two children in Papua New Guinea before the family returned to Australia in 1953. Pat Andersen had a third child in Australia, returning to social work on a part-time basis. She and her husband live in Sydney.

Sister Aquilonia Ax

Written by Sr Aquilonia from the transcript of a conversation with Chilla Bulbeck on 22 November 1988

'I was born in a small German village. In answer to God's call and of the needy of the world I left a loving home and beautiful country and entered the International Congregation of the Missionary Sisters of the Holy Spirit at the Motherhouse in Sleyl, Holland. I soon found myself in the United States where I taught for a number of years and also obtained my postgraduate qualifications. In 1948 I was appointed Provincial Superior of the war-ravaged mission of New Guinea, once a flourishing mission, with headquarters at Alexishaven. My chief responsibility was the Sisters and their work from Lae to Aitape and some stations in the Highlands. All mission work had come to a standstill during the war, but new life began to return with the arrival of missionaries from overseas, Priests, Brothers and Sisters, lay missionaries from Australia, Europe and Canada. I arrived in New Guinea in February 1949—the delay caused mainly by difficulties in air travel, not as common as now'. Today Sister Aquilonia lives in Brisbane, where she participates actively in the life of the retirement centre that is her home.

Dorothy Beale
Letter from Sr Dorothy Beale, File: Ex-missionaries' Correspondence, History Room, United Church, Rabaul

Dorothy Beale was the first triple-certificate nursing sister to join the Methodist Mission in New Guinea, working at the Stewart Hospital in Vunairima, until the outbreak of the Second World War. Dorothy Beale was captured, along with many other sisters, and was a prisoner of war in Japan. After the war, Dorothy Beale worked at Watnabara in the Duke of York Islands, before moving to Kimidan (New Ireland) where a new hospital was established with her at the helm in 1948. She became well-known in Mission circles as a dedicated but strict nurse. She retired in 1954.

Dorothy Beale wrote a record of her work in New Ireland. Her letter reveals her commitment to becoming an efficient and effective matron, so much so that she used her furloughs to fill perceived deficiencies in her education, for example learning about dispensing medicines, dental treatment, and complications in childbirth.

Daphney Bridgland
Interviews with Chilla Bulbeck in November 1988

Daphney Bridgland was born in Brisbane where she attended Clayfield College and the Commercial High School. She did clerical and secretarial work during the war and afterwards in her father's office. During this time Daphney was also a Miss Australia candidate. However, her first love was singing and in 1946 she was auditioned by Marjorie Lawrence, who suggested she should study in Italy. This was beyond the family's financial resources and instead Daphney spent three years at the Melbourne Conservatorium of Music. She had two opera seasons with the Victorian National Opera Company before Leon, the brother of a Brisbane friend, and a former sweetheart, came to Melbourne:

> We met again after all this time and he asked me to marry him.
> So I decided this was what I wanted to do. It would have taken
> a great deal more money than we had for me to go and do what
> I needed to do to become a professional singer.

Leon had a degree in agricultural science and worked with the then Department of Agriculture, Stock and Fisheries in Papua New Guinea. In September

1950 Daphney arrived at Sogeri near Port Moresby where Leon was lecturing agricultural graduates. In 1952 the couple moved to Keravat, near Rabaul, where Leon supervised the Lowlands Agricultural Experimental Station. Daphne spent the rest of her time in New Guinea in the Rabaul area. Leon joined Theo Thomas and Company to run an agricultural advisory service in 1959. Several years later he also became manager of three of Theo Thomas's coconut and copra plantations, including the one at Rainau where the Bridglands lived. Ten years later the couple moved to Nonga, where they remained for two years, and then to Rabarua. Robyn, the Bridglands' first daughter, was born in Port Moresby in 1951. Ann was born in 1953 and Rosemary in 1960. Daphney Bridgland left New Guinea in 1983.

Eva Butcher

MS 1881 BENJAMIN BUTCHER, folder 5, Manuscripts Room, National Library, Canberra

Benjamin Butcher served with the London Missionary Society in New Guinea as a medical missionary from 1905 until his retirement in 1938. His collection of papers include some letters written by his wife, Eva, between 1913 and 1916 from Aird Hill, Kikori, to her parents. As with many letters from women in New Guinea, Eva Butcher discusses the produce from her garden and her cows and other animals, waiting for the mails, and the disappointment and sometimes anxiety when they are late. Letters written after 1915 are almost totally concerned with the problems of winning the people over to Christianity. Eva Butcher was carried around in a rickshaw on poles and the Mission had a launch for transport over greater distances.

Ann Deland

MS 4725 ANN DELAND, Manuscripts Room, National Library, Canberra

Ann Deland was the wife of Dr Charles M. Deland. She lived in Bougainville and Vanikoro in the Solomons group between 1926 and 1931. The photographs of her held at the National Library reveal her as young and full of life. She now lives in South Australia. The materials are letters that she wrote home, a reminiscence and a radio talk she gave after leaving New Guinea.

Prudence Frank

MS 6794 PRUDENCE FRANK, transcript of tape TRC 793, Manuscripts Room, National Library, Canberra

Prudence Frank was born in 1907 in Cooktown, Queensland. Her cousin was 'Ma' (Flora) Stewart of the Hotel Cecil, Lae, in New Guinea, and her mother lived in Papua. In 1922 and 1923 Prudence obtained the Superior Public School Certificate (Commercial Classes). In 1925 she travelled to Port Moresby and later became the confidential secretary to Captain Fitch, the Managing Director of Steamships Trading Company Limited. Prudence also worked for Burns Philp and Company Limited in Port Moresby and Rabaul. During the Second World War she worked in Australia, but afterwards returned to Papua New Guinea. She became an instructor with the Public Service Institute and was responsible for teaching all the typists: European, Papua New Guinean and mixed blood. Between 1957 and 1962 Prudence was the representative of East Ward on the Town Advisory Council, Port Moresby. She was also active in the Arts Council, acting in plays and musicals from 1947 and serving as secretary until 1962. She left Papua New Guinea in 1962.

Doris Groves

From MS 6068 WC GROVES, Folder 27; MS 6068 WC GROVES, Box 30; MS 6068 WC GROVES Folder 30; MS 6068 WC GROVES, Folder 31: Manuscripts Room, National Library, Canberra

Doris Smith, a trained Infant schoolteacher, went to Port Moresby in 1921 to join the London Missionary Society's mission and school at Hanuabada. In 1925 she left the LMS and took up an appointment at a government school at Malaguna near Rabaul, where she was in charge of the Junior School. Bill Groves also taught at this school, and they married in the same year. In 1926 they returned to Victoria: Bill to teach and Doris to raise a family. They had three children. In 1930 two former students from New Guinea stayed with them while they attended school in Victoria. In 1932 the Groves family returned to New Guinea, Bill and Doris to study life in the villages of Fisoa in New Ireland and Tatau on Tabar Islands, the project financed by a Rockefeller Foundation grant. After the Second World War, in 1946, Bill became the first Director of Education in Papua New Guinea. During his time in this post he forged links between the state and mission education systems. Doris became involved in a number of local charities. In the mid-1950s the couple left Papua New Guinea. Her manuscripts include extracts from an autobiography Doris was in the process of writing (possibly written in 1975: 'From G string to Independence—The Passing of the Primitive in Papua New Guinea'), extracts from her diaries, and two letters she wrote in 1969 concerning her husband's career.

Jean Mannering

Interviewed by Chilla Bulbeck in December 1987

Jean Mannering first went to New Guinea in August 1940 as the wife of the Rev. John Poole, living on a small mission station at Kalas in the Baining Mountains. Jean was evacuated with the European women and children from Rabaul in December 1941. Her husband, along with most of the other European men on New Britain, was taken as a prisoner of war by the Japanese. All these men lost their lives when the *Montevideo Maru* was torpedoed by an American ship, off the Philippines, while the Japanese were taking their prisoners to Japan. Jean returned to New Britain towards the end of 1946 on the ship that took the first European women and children back to the Territory. She taught with the Methodist Overseas Mission at George Brown College at Vatnabara on the Duke of York Islands, and then at Vunairima on New Britain, when the College was relocated there about four years later. She left the mission field in 1953. During that period, she produced an English to Kuanua dictionary, and several readers in Kuanua. For the latter she wrote the text and drew some of the illustrations.

Jean married the Rev. Con Mannering in 1956, returning to New Britain in May 1959, where they lived first at Vatnabara and then Vunairima, before leaving at the end of 1965. Con had bought some land at Dromana, on the Mornington Peninsula. A friend of the Mannerings, Rev. Simon Gaius, spent a year in Australia doing translation work on the Bible in 1949. During that time he helped Con Mannering build a house at Dromana; his signature is on one of the rafters in the roof. Jean Mannering has a superb native garden at her house, and is active in local church work.

Marjorie Murphy

Interviewed by Chilla Bulbeck on 9 September 1988, and written reminiscences

Marjorie Murphy went to Rabaul in 1940 to take up a secretarial position. She soon met John, a patrol officer, and they were married. After their first leave in Australia together, John was posted to Otibandu on the Watut River. This was an uncontrolled area, but Marjorie accompanied John on his patrols, which she remembers as one of the highlights of her time in Papua New Guinea. During the war John worked in intelligence and was captured by the Japanese. He and six Americans were the only survivors of the prisoner-of-war camp in Rabaul. Marjorie was officially informed that John was missing; but she discovered that he had been captured when, coming home from her work at the bank one day, she picked up the *Courier Mail*. Across the front page was a headline: 'Japs claim capture of Australian spy'.

After the war, John was posted to Higaturu. While waiting in Samarai to go to Higaturu, John became Acting District Officer. A few years later the apparently extinct volcano, Lamington, erupted and everyone on the station was killed. By this time the Murphys were in Aitape after a posting at Wewak. In 1948 and 1949 they went on leave and their son Kerry was born. They were stationed in Rabaul between 1950 and 1955, John as Acting District Commissioner for a time. Dale, their daughter, was born in 1955. John then spent four years as District Commissioner in Daru, and then nine years in Kerema, before the Murphys retired to Brisbane in 1969.

Pat Murray

Interviews conducted by Deane Fergie, December 1987. The text also includes some comments from Pat's husband, Peter, who was present during some of the interview period.

Pat Murray's mother grew up in India and her father spent a couple of years in early childhood in Africa. They married in 1919, after her father joined the Indian Army. They lived in India for three years, during which time they had their first two children: Jim, who was killed during the war, and Pat, in 1922. Unable to support the two children on their income, they moved to a sheep property—two soldier settlement blocks, in southern Queensland. From there they moved to a plantation, Bolegila, in New Ireland on 13 December 1927. In 1951 Pat married Peter and they ran their own plantation. Apart from her schooling in Australia, and the war years, Pat lived in New Guinea until she and her husband returned to Australia, settling in Newcastle in 1982.

Mollie Parer

Interviewed by Chilla Bulbeck in April 1987

The Parer family has had a long association with New Guinea. Ray Parer went to New Guinea in the 1920s where he pioneered aviation, particularly to the goldfields near Wau. In 1920 he, with John McIntosh, was the first man to fly a single-engine aircraft from England to Australia. The flight was provoked by the race which Keith and Ross Smith won; but Parer and McIntosh started so late and met with so many difficulties that they arrived in Australia well after the race was over. In New Guinea Ray Parer took out a miner's right in the Upper Watut and this financed his various flying concerns, his unwillingness to charge unlucky miners being a major cause of the concerns' financial failure. During the Second World War, he was given the job of engineer on the *Melanesia* which worked round the northern coast of New Guinea. Ray Parer, and his two brothers, Bob and Kevin, lived in Wewak during the 1930s.

Damien Parer was Ray Parer's cousin and his name became associated with capturing the Second World War on film, including the battles along the Kokoda Trail and the work of Papuan bearers in '*The Fuzzy Wuzzy Angels*'.

Marjorie Murphy said 'There seemed to be Parers all over New Guinea. When we were going to Otibandu John said to one of the ADOs (Horrie Nile, now Sir Horace): "Any last minute instructions?" "Yes, get on out there and push back the Kukakukas and make room for the Parers." There were a lot of Parers in the Morobe District.'

Mollie Yates was born in Melbourne and went to New Guinea in 1933 as Bob Parer's bride. She lived with him at the Black Cat gold mine until the late 1930s when her husband started a freezer business in Wewak, chartering food supplies and storing them in a freezer works. In 1939 the *Bulolo* which brought in the food supplies for the freezer business was commandeered by the Allies and Bob went prospecting in Bougainville. Mollie and the children stayed behind in Wewak. Her brother-in-law, Kevin Parer, encouraged her to come and stay with his family in Wau. It was from there that she was evacuated, eventually arriving in Melbourne. Later the family moved to Brisbane (where Mollie was to again lose almost all her possessions, in the Brisbane flood of 1974). She now lives in Kenmore and participates in the varied lives of the thirty-five Parers who make up her family.

Dorothy Pederick

Interviewed by Chilla Bulbeck on 8 February 1988

Dorothy Pederick grew up on a farm in Wagin, the only daughter in a family of five sons. Until her early twenties she helped her parents on the farm. When they retired, she moved to Perth to undertake her nursing training. Dorothy went to New Guinea as a nurse with the Methodist Mission in 1947, returning to Australia between 1955 and 1957, after which she again worked in New Guinea until 1967. She worked for a number of years in Narragin before retiring to Wagin, where she is active in the local community, a member of the church and the local historical group. My first sight of her was a figure pedalling down the street on her bicycle, having just spent the morning working at the Wagin historical village.

Isabel Platten

From an account of her life written in 1988 and 1989 for her grand-daughter, Chilla Bulbeck

Isabel married a Methodist minister, Gil Platten, when she was 21 years old on 17 March 1927. That afternoon they left Adelaide aboard an interstate steamer bound for Melbourne and Sydney, and ultimately New Guinea. Gil was the minister in Rabaul until May 1929 when they went to Halis, near Namatanai (New Ireland), which was to become Isabel's favourite place. Newell was born in 1928 and Paquita in 1931. After two years in Perth between 1935 and 1937, Gil was appointed to George Brown College in Vunairima to train the senior teachers as ordained ministers. The Plattens returned to Halis in 1939; they spent the war years in Woodside (South Australia), Sydney and Stirling (South Australia). Gil returned to Halis in 1946 and Isabel joined him in 1947. In 1949, Gil went to Rabaul as Chairman of the District and Principal of George Brown College. Shortly afterwards, due to financial difficulties, Gil resigned from the Mission. He wrote to Bill Groves, the Director of Education, who appointed him as the vocational teacher at Sogeri High School, near Port Moresby. In 1949 Gil and Isabel moved to Sos on Tabar, as part of a project to enquire into depopulation on the Tabar Islands. This was shelved due to a change of government, and Gil remained as a teacher. He also taught in Garaina and Kainantu before retiring in 1958. Isabel returned to Adelaide, shared and solved many of her grandchildren's growing pains and problems, and saw the birth of three great grand-daughters before her death in March 1991.

Mary Pulsford

Interviewed by Chilla Bulbeck on 21 May 1988

Mary Pulsford was working in Canberra after she graduated with a science degree from Sydney University. She met Bob when he was down on leave from New Guinea. A year later, in April 1953, they married and went to live on the north coast of New Guinea, in the Sepik District. Her husband had been asked after the war to do agricultural extension work in Dagua. Mary joined Bob at Urip village, and lived there for eighteen months. Their son Ian was born during this time. Bob was then posted to Manus Island as the District Agricultural Officer. They had a daughter, Susan, born at Lorengau. In 1958 they moved to Taliligap, a station close to Rabaul, and then Rabaul itself, when Bob became the District Agricultural Officer for New Britain. They settled in Port Moresby in 1963 and Mary became a science teacher in 1964, at Port Moresby High School. In 1968, she was appointed as the first Botany tutor in the new university, where she taught for six years. They returned to Australia in 1973 when Bob retired from his position as a lecturer at the University of Papua New Guinea.

Joan Refshauge

'Speech to Mission Conference 18-11-1954', 'An Address on Discrimination Against Women in the Territory' (apparently given to a women's group some time after Dr Refshauge retired), MS 7026, JOAN REFSHAUGE, Folder 11, Manuscripts Room, National Library, Canberra; 'Extracts from Interview of Dr Joan Refshauge conducted by her brother Sir William Refshauge' transcribed by Donald Denoon July 1982; diary and other personal papers held by Sir William Refshauge, Canberra

Dr Joan Refshauge OBE was not only a medical doctor, but also obtained a Master of Science, a Diploma of Education and a Diploma of Public Health. In 1947, after teaching and medical work in a number of Australian institutions, she was given a temporary appointment with the Department of Public Health in Port Moresby. Following her divorce in 1948, she gained a permanent appointment. She served continuously until her retirement in 1963, as Assistant Director of Infant Child and Maternal Health, the most senior female administrator in Papua New Guinea. During that time Dr Refshauge built a network of Maternal Child Health services throughout the country, produced large numbers of practical and self-reliant nurses, and conducted countless tours of inspection. As an example of the scope of her work, in 1959 there were twelve administration centres, thirteen European clinics, three Asiatic clinics, nine permanent Native clinics and several mobile clinics. A trained New Guinean woman and a trained Papuan woman were each in charge of a clinic. There were also 116 missions doing medical work under subsidy. During that year 18 000 adults, 3000 antenatal cases and 60 000 infants were cared for at the Native clinics. As a result of these clinics, Dr Refshauge argued that the infant mortality rate had dropped from as high as 500 in 1000 in some untouched areas to around 42 in 1000 in Port Moresby, although this was still twice the infant mortality rate for Australia.

Dr Refshauge was appointed by the Administrator as a member of the Advisory Committee on the Education and Advancement of Women in 1957. The insights gained on this committee were later brought to her work as Acting Director of the Queen Elizabeth II Infant Child and Maternal Health Service, and then the Directorship of Maternal and Child Health. She laid the foundation for a unique training scheme of orderlies and fully-qualified nurses to gradually replace the expatriate nurses. Dr Refshauge did not take a narrow medical interest in public health, but rather sought productive interactions with the missions in health-care delivery, and wrote and presented a number of other public addresses, ranging from the question of child abuse, to the need for childminding services for women who were required to participate in their husbands' careers, to the necessity for learning pidgin.

In 1964 Dr Refshauge was awarded the Cilento Medal for the advancement of the local population in the Tropics of Australia. Dr Refshauge was the first woman to win the medal, which had been conferred only six times in the previous thirty years. Raphael Cilento wrote: 'The trustees, of whom I am one, feel that there is no person more fitting upon whom it could be bestowed than yourself, in recognition of your work for fifteen years amongst women and children in Papua and New Guinea'. (Letter to Dr Refshauge, 4 February 1964, in personal papers held by Sir William Refshauge.) Dr Refshauge died in 1979 at the age of 72 years.

Dixie Rigby

Interviewed by Rosa Glastonbury on 19 August 1979: TRC 967/1-2, Oral History, National Library, Canberra

Dixie Rigby was brought up in a small English village and in 1979 lived in Blackburn South, Victoria. When Dixie was 18 the First World War started; she joined the Women's Auxiliary Army Corps in 1916 and was in France in 1917. After the war she joined the Army Pay Corps at the War Office in London. In 1919 she emigrated to Australia, and met her husband Reg in 1923. She went to New Guinea because she wanted to travel the Islands and interested Reg in New Guinea. He went up in 1925 as a patrol officer, just after they married. She became pregnant with her son John and stayed in Australia for three years before joining Reg in Rabaul, after his first leave, because there 'was no room for women in Rabaul' before that time. Reg was 'not in favour of taking children up there' so John went to boarding school in Australia. Reg moved to Aitape, the headquarters of the Sepik District, and Dixie went out with him on his first patrol. Reg was in the Sepik area for twelve years, during which time he became an Assistant District Officer, and then District Commissioner. Michael Somare's father was one of Reg Rigby's sergeants and Julius Chan's father was one of the first Chinese she met in New Guinea. They left New Guinea in 1955, when her husband retired. He was then stationed at Rabaul.

Sister Bohdana Voros

As written by Sister Bohdana based on an interview with Chilla Bulbeck, November 1988

Sister Bohdana was born in Czechoslovakia in 1911. In 1947 she went to Manila for six months to study English before going to New Guinea. She was based in Alexishafen where the Holy Spirit Missionary Sisters' Provincial House is located. For the first five years she taught primary school in

Alexishafen. Following this she taught in Madang (fifteen miles from Alexishafen) for three years; followed by Manam Island for six years, and then in several places on the Sepik for seven years. In 1968 Sister Bohdana went to Rome for the General Chapter, and this provided the only chance she has had to return to Czechoslovakia. After a few months she returned to Alexishafen where she was the head teacher for five years. Subsequently she trained the local Sisters of St Therese in Alexishaven. In 1977 Sister Bohdana came to Australia for a holiday. However her health was too poor for her to return to New Guinea. In Australia she worked as an interpreter for a social worker for some years, as she speaks Hungarian and some Slavonic languages and had taught Russian in Czechoslovakia.

Joyce Walker

Interview with Chilla Bulbeck in March 1987

Joyce Walker is now in her seventies and was born and raised on country properties. Before and during the war she studied nursing with the purpose of going to New Guinea to do mission work after the war. She was among the first white people to return to New Guinea (in 1946) when hostilities ceased. Her good sense and efficiency led to a number of unique experiences. Against the wishes of the Mission synod, she stayed on alone at the Bainings hospital when her colleague left to get married. Joyce felt she could not lose the ground she had won with the people there. She was in the first party of white people to make contact with the Highlanders at Mendi, where she continued her nursing work for a number of years. The wife of the District Administrator at Mendi, Helen McLeod, describes Joyce Walker as an 'open-hearted person full of love and good fellowship' with an 'exhilarating personality'.[1] Ill health forced Joyce's return to Australia, where she worked in the nursing profession for twenty-five years. She is now retired and lives on the Sunshine Coast where she is visited often by her many nieces and nephews, and their children. Many of her younger relatives and friends have spent their honeymoon in her house with its ocean view, a gesture she was happy to make before moving there when she retired.

Grace Young

Interviewed by Deane Fergie and Chilla Bulbeck in December 1987

Grace Young married Gordon in August 1942, while she was in the Australian Women's Army Service. She went to Rabaul in 1946 to join Gordon who had become the Army chaplain there. Included in his duties was conducting services for the Japanese in the War Criminal Compound. When Grace arrived in Rabaul, it was the first time she had set up house for her husband. He joined the Methodist Mission some months later, his Army contacts and experiences helping with the purchase of vehicles and the mission boat, the *Talai*. They were stationed at Ulu in the Duke of York Islands, his job consisting mainly of skippering the *Talai* and managing the mission-owned coconut plantation. In 1948 they returned to Sydney for a short period. They were then stationed at Namatanai from 1949 until 1950, when Gordon went to open up Mendi in the Southern Highlands. Several months later Grace was able to join him, in 1951. They left in 1960, they thought only for leave, but their son needed medical attention and they stayed in South Australia. Gordon worked as a minister in parishes around Adelaide, and at Moonta and Broken Hill. Even after retiring, he took two more postings, to Karoonda and Meningie.

APPENDIX 2

Key Events in Chronological Order

This time line is based on Kettle, although some events have been omitted and others added.[2]

1872 The London Missionary Society started at Hanuabada, Port Moresby, with a staff of South Sea Islanders.

1874 Rev. George Brown and other Methodist missionaries selected the Duke of York Islands near Rabaul as their first mission site.

1881 The first Sacred Heart missionaries arrived in New Britain and established Vunapope mission which became their base.

1883 Queensland, concerned about German activity in the region, annexed Papua for the Queen. It was only formally annexed, by Commander Erskine, for the British in 1884.

1884 The German Government annexed New Guinea, which was administered by the German New Guinea Company.

1886 The Rev. J. Flierl, a German missionary in Australia, went to New Guinea and started a Lutheran mission at Finschhafen.

1891 Reverends Maclaren and King started an Anglican mission at Dogura. The first French nuns arrived at Vunapope. Kwato mission, near Samarai, was started by Rev. Abel. The first two German nurses, Auguste Hertzer and Nurse Hedwig (surname unknown) were appointed to Bogadjim near Madang. The first single female missionaries arrived to work in the Methodist mission. The Methodists started their first mission in Papua, on Dobu Island.

1905 A hospital was built in Port Moresby with a native hospital beside it.

1906 British New Guinea was renamed Papua and brought under Australian administration.

1913 Salvarsan, an arsenical preparation, was first used to treat yaws.

1914 War was declared in Europe and the Australian Army took over Rabaul. Seven years of Army administration in New Guinea followed. German doctors were interned and German-owned plantations expropriated.

1915 Australian nurses replaced German nurses at Rabaul. Army orderlies staffed the other hospitals and from this developed the role of the European Medical Assistant.

1921 The League of Nations declared New Guinea a trust territory of Australia. Sir Hubert Murray, of Papua, recommended joint administration but was unsuccessful.

1922 There were eighteen European Medical Assistants in New Guinea, one of whom was a trained nurse. Medical *tultuls*, forerunners of the aid post orderlies, were being trained in New Guinea.

1926 Salamo Hospital (Methodist) on Fergusson Island was opened and became the first formal training school for Papuan nurses. Gold was discovered at Bulolo and Edie Creek, precipitating a gold rush and the death of 225 local bearers through dysentery in five months. Guinea Airways was established to freight mining equipment into Wau and Bulolo where there were no roads.

1927 The first combined mission conference was held in Rabaul with representatives from Sacred Heart, Divine Word, Methodist, Lutheran and Anglican missions.

1928 Rabaul Strike by house servants and policemen: the ringleaders were arrested and imprisoned.

1934 Divine Word Mission staff penetrated the Highlands to Mount Hagen and Mingendi. One was mortally wounded by arrows. A party of Lutherans reached Mount Hagen, Kerowagi and Bena-Bena. Seventh Day Adventist missions started at Kainantu, Omaura and Bena-Bena.

1936 A hospital was opened at Maprik by a medical assistant. The Methodists commenced a maternal and child health service at Losuia.

1937 A volcanic eruption in Rabaul killed over 300 Tolai people.

Seventy cheap hot-air copra dryers designed by administration were in use in villages, an invention which encouraged villagers to increase copra production.

1939 First use of sulphanilamide and sulphapyridine at Rapinidik Hospital, Rabaul.

1940 Death of Sir Hubert Murray, Lieutenant-Governor of Papua.

1941 The Japanese attacked Pearl Harbour, forcing a hasty evacuation of women and children from Papua New Guinea.

1942 *4 January*: the first Japanese bombs fell on Rabaul.
21 January: Madang, Salamaua and Lae were bombed, nurses and doctors walking to safety. Kavieng was captured.
23 January: the Japanese invaded Rabaul.
4–9 May: the Coral Sea Battle, after which Vunapope became a huge Japanese hospital.
5 June: seventeen nurses (four Methodist, seven civilian and six Army) were taken to Japan by ship as prisoners of war for three years.
22 July: Japanese landed at Gona and set out to reach Port Moresby via Kokoda.

1943 ANGAU (Australian and New Guinea Administration Unit) was established for war-time administration of Papua, still under Australian control. Allied bombers wiped out Vunapope which had become a Japanese arsenal. Most missionaries survived in deep tunnels, spending the next eighteen months in Ramale valley. Sogeri was cleared and a convalescent hospital built.

1945 *15 August*: war ended.
September: Australians moved into Rabaul.
24 June: civil administration resumed in Papua and part of New Guinea.

1946 Civil administration was extended to the whole of New Guinea and two territories administered jointly. The Sogeri convalescent hospital became the country's first government school. Two hundred men educated before the war by the missions were assembled for extra education. Native hospitals were functional at Kundiawa, Mount Hagen, Madang, Malahang (Lae), Ela Beach, Gemo Island, Mapamoiwa, Misima and Samarai. Male nurses and medical assistants trained hospital orderlies. Dr John Gunther was appointed as Director of Health. Three POW nurses resumed with the Methodists on New

Britain. Gaulim health centre replaced pre-war Malabunga centre. Nurse training was started at Vatnabara Mission. Anglicans started training Papuan nurses at Dogura and Eroro. Several training schools were established for medical orderlies and aid-post orderlies; most were illiterate men.

1947 Six indigenous men from Sogeri school went to the Central Medical School in Suva to study medicine. Sister Dorothy Beale started a nurse training school in Kimidan.

1948 The Infant Child and Maternal Health Section (later Maternal and Child Health) of the Department of Health was created with Dr Joan Refshauge in charge. At Gemo Island Dr Maruff introduced streptomycin and sulphatrone for the first time, with dramatic results.

1949 Epidemics of measles and whooping cough took a heavy toll of infants. Dr Neale Andersen and Sister Martin started a hospital at Kapunda Mission.

1950 Fifty-seven refugee doctors from Europe were recruited for Papua New Guinea. The Maternal and Child Health (MCH) Service began training female orderlies. The government started 'opening' the southern Highlands and the first Methodist missionary walked to Mendi.

1951 Sister Joyce Walker started a health service with the Methodists at Mendi. The first Papua New Guinean, Dr Wilfred Moi, graduated from the medical school at Suva.

First Legislative Assembly met, with the indigenous population being represented by three appointed members: one New Guinean, Aisoli Salin, and two Papuans.

1952 A total of 153 indigenous co-operative societies had been formed to sell copra through the copra marketing board.

1953 Papuan women went to the Central School of Nursing, Suva, Mary Guise being one of the first. Sister Taffy Jones started the MCH service in Rabaul. Two patrol officers were murdered in the restricted Telefomin area.

1956 From this year local councils were gradually established, replacing the power of *luluais, tultuls* and village constables, and to some extent limiting powers of unilateral intervention in village affairs by *kiaps*.

1957 Dr John Gunther became Assistant Administrator and Dr Roy Scragg,

Director of Health. Salk vaccine for poliomyelitis was administered, to white children only. Penicillin was used in a nationwide campaign to eradicate yaws.

1958 Port Moresby School of Nursing commenced with fourteen trainees. The administration set up a special committee to review all racially discriminatory legislation, resulting in a flood of amendments and the repealing of ordinances.

1959 Len Barnard mounted a patrol into Karimui and reported cannibalism and widespread leprosy.

1961 Matron J. 'Taffy' Jones was appointed Principal Matron on the retirement of A. Thorburn. Sister Dorothy Pederick opened a health centre at Ranmelek on New Hanover Island.

1964 The first election for the Papua New Guinea House of Assembly was held. A public Ordinance introduced a separate salary scale for Papua New Guineans and expatriates.

1965 The first Combined Mission Medical Conference was held at Dogura with twenty-three participants representing seven organisations. It was thereafter held annually and was vocal concerning nurse training.

1966 The University of Papua New Guinea opened with Dr John Gunther as Vice-Chancellor.

1968 By December the Nursing Council had approved eighteen schools of nursing to train MCH and General Nurses.

1969 The first indigenous nurse completed the Diploma of Nursing Education at NSW College of Nursing.

1974 Matron Raula Tabau (née Vele) took charge of nursing in the country.

1975 Forty-seven national doctors filled all senior posts at headquarters, and many at provincial level.
16 September: Independence Day.

Notes

Introduction

1 Hank Nelson, *Taim Bilong Masta: Australian Involvement with Papua New Guinea*, Australian Broadcasting Commission, Sydney, 1982, pp.101, 106
2 ibid., p.102
3 Helen McLeod, *Cannibals are Human: A District Officer's Wife in New Guinea*, Angus & Robertson, Sydney, 1961, p.v
4 Helen Callaway, *Gender, Culture and Empire: European Women in Colonial Nigeria*, Macmillan in association with St Anthony's College, Oxford, Basingstoke and London, 1987, p.22
5 Paul Hasluck, *A Time for Building: Australian Administration in Papua and New Guinea 1951–1963*, Melbourne University Press, Melbourne, 1976
6 Dame Rachel Cleland, *Pathways to Independence: Official and Family Life 1951-1975*, Artlook Books, Perth, 1983; McLeod, *Cannibals are Human*
7 Lucy Evelyn Cheeseman, *Things Worth While*, Hutchinson, London, 1957; Lucy Evelyn Cheeseman, *Time Well Spent*, Hutchinson, London, 1960; Doris R. Booth, *Mountains, Gold and Cannibals*, Cornstalk, Sydney, 1929
8 Yvonne Kniebiehler and Régine Goutalier, *La Femme au Temps des Colonies*, Stock, Paris, 1985; Claudia Knapman, *White Women in Fiji 1835–1930: The Ruin of Empire?*, Allen & Unwin, Sydney, 1986; Marian Fowler, *Below the Peacock Fan: First Ladies of the Raj*, Viking, Markham, Ontario, 1987; Mary Ann Lind, *The Compassionate Memsahibs: Welfare Activities of British Women in India, 1900–1947*, Greenwood Press, Westport, Connecticut, 1988; Margaret MacMillan, *Women of the Raj*, Thames & Hudson, London, 1988; Helen Callaway, *Gender, Culture and Empire*; Diane Langmore, *Missionary Lives Papua 1874–1919*, University Press of Hawaii, Honolulu, 1989; Pat Barr, *The Dust in the Balance: British Women in India 1905–1945*, Hamish Hamilton, London, 1989
9 Judy Davis, unfinished manuscript prepared for doctoral dissertation and held at the Australian National University, Menzies Library. Draft chapter entitled 'Outside Women', p.11
10 Callaway, *Gender, Culture and Empire*, p.227-44

1: Passages to New Guinea

1 These extracts come from the interview Deane Fergie conducted with Pat Murray. Details of interviews are contained in the biographies at Appendix 1. In the text, where authorship is unclear, the name of the interviewee will appear in square brackets. Otherwise no referencing system will be used

2 Custodian of Expropriated Property, *Sale of Expropriated Properties in the Territories of New Guinea and Papua* volume 2, 'Second Group', Commonwealth Government, Melbourne, 1926, frontispiece

3 Custodian of Expropriated Property, *Sale of Expropriated Properties in the Territory of New Guinea and Papua* volume 1, 'First Group', Commonwealth Government, Melbourne, 1925, pp.12, 168

4 Beatrice Grimshaw in Shirley Fenton Huie, *Tiger Lilies: Women Adventurers in the South Pacific*, Angus & Robertson, Sydney, 1990, p.120

5 Huie, ibid., pp.141–61

6 L. Marnie Bassett, *Letters From New Guinea 1921*, Hawthorn Press, Melbourne, 1969

7 Judy Davis, unfinished manuscript prepared for doctoral dissertation and held at the Australian National University, Menzies Library. Draft chapter entitled 'History: version 4' pp.10–11

8 National Library, Manuscripts Room, MS 6068, WC GROVES, Folder 30, 'From G-String to Independence' the first chapters of an autobiography Doris Groves was writing

9 National Library, Manuscripts Room, MS 6794, PRUDENCE FRANK, transcript of Tape TRC 793, interview with Prudence Frank

10 Doris Groves, 'From G-String to Independence', MS 6068, WC GROVES, Folder 30, Manuscripts Room, National Library, Canberra

11 Helen Callaway, *Gender, Culture and Empire: European Women in Colonial Nigeria*, Macmillan in association with St Anthony's College, Oxford, Basingstoke and London, 1987, p.70

12 Ann Deland, MS 4725, ANN DELAND, National Library, Manuscripts Room, Canberra

13 Dorothy Beale, File: 'Ex-Missionaries' Correspondence', History Room, United Church, Rabaul

14 Dea Birkett, *Spinsters Abroad: Victorian Lady Explorers*, Basil Blackwell, Oxford, 1989, p.43

15 ibid., p.20

16 Evelyn Cheeseman, *Who Stand Alone*, Geoffrey Bles, London, 1965, pp.18, 20

17 Beatrice Grimshaw, *The New New Guinea*, Hutchinson, London, 1910, pp.82–3

18 ibid., p.85 italics mine

19 quoted in Flora A. Timms, *Mary McLean: First Missionary of the WMA. A Memorial*, Robert Dey, Son & Co., Sydney, 1943, p.38

20 Ann Deland, MS 4725, ANN DELAND, National Library, Manuscripts Room, Canberra.

21 MS 6068, Folder 30, WC GROVES, 'From G-String to Independence'

22 Lynn Sunderland, *The Fantastic Invasion: Kipling, Conrad and Lawson*, Melbourne University Press, Melbourne, 1989, p.1

23 *Spectator*, 1895, ibid., p.67; *Academy Review*, 1899, ibid., p.68; ibid., p.111

24 ibid., pp.156–71

25 Eugenie Laracy and Hugh Laracy, 'Beatrice Grimshaw: pride and prejudice in Papua', *Journal of Pacific History*, vol. 12, no. 3, 1977, p.154

26 Susan Gardner, 'For love and money: early writings of Beatrice Grimshaw, colonial Papua's woman of letters', *New Literature Review*, Special Issue: Post-colonial literature, 1977, p.12

27 Ann B. Murphy, 'The borders of ethical, erotic and artistic possibilities in *Little Women*' *Signs*, vol. 15, no. 3, 1990, p.568

28 Rebecca Scott, 'The Dark Continent: Africa as female body in Haggard's adventure fiction', *Feminist Review*, no. 32, 1989, p.70

29 ibid., p.71

30 C. Fenn, *Bunyip Land*, Blackie & Son, London, 1885, p.11

31 ibid., p.148

32 ibid., pp.333–4

33 ibid., p.383

34 ibid., p.205

35 ibid., p.384

36 Errol Flynn, *My Wicked Wicked Ways*, Putnam, New York, 1959, pp.56, 71

37 Beatrice Grimshaw, *Isles of Adventure*, Herbert & Jenkins, London, 1930, p.12

38 ibid., p.19

39 Laracy and Laracy, 'Beatrice Grimshaw: pride and prejudice in Papua', p.159

40 Gardner, 'For love and money', p.15

41 Grimshaw, ibid., p.21

42 Gardner, ibid., p.10

43 Grimshaw, *The New New Guinea*, p.87

44 ibid., p.85

45 ibid., p.86

46 Grimshaw, *Isles of Adventure*, pp.26–8

47 quoted in Gardner, 'For love and money', p.13

48 Beatrice Grimshaw, *My Lady Far-Away*, Cassell & Co., London, 1929, pp.203–4

49 Grimshaw, *Isles of Adventure*, p.29

50 Grimshaw, *The New New Guinea*, p.88

51 Grimshaw, *Isles of Adventure*, p.29

52 ibid., p.134

53 quoted in Laracy and Laracy, 'Beatrice Grimshaw: pride and prejudice in Papua', p.162

54 ibid., pp.164, 171; Huie, *Tiger Lilies*, p.21

55 Gardner, ibid., pp.10, 15

56 Beatrice Grimshaw, *When the Red Gods Call*, Mills & Boon, London, 1911, p.9

57 ibid., p.24

58 ibid., pp.50–1

59 Callaway, *Gender, Culture and Empire*, pp.35–9

60 Laracy and Laracy, 'Beatrice Grimshaw: pride and prejudice in Papua', p.167

61 ibid., p.172

62 ibid., pp.168–9

63 Grimshaw, quoted in Laracy and Laracy, p.169

64 Grimshaw, *My Lady Far-Away*, p.104

65 ibid., p.63

66 ibid., pp.251–2

67 ibid., p.288

68 ibid., p.127

69 ibid., p.134

70 Rebecca Scott, '*The Dark Continent*'

71 quoted in Gardner, *For love and money*', p.16

72 Doris R. Booth, *Mountains, Gold and Cannibals*, Cornstalk, Sydney, 1929, p.198

73 Susan L. Blake, 'A woman's trek: what difference does gender make?', *Women's Studies International Forum*, vol. 13, no. 4, 1990, p.354
74 ibid., p.347

2: *Different destinations*

1 Edward P. Wolfers, *Race Relations and Colonial Rule in Papua New Guinea*, Australian and New Zealand Book Co., Brookvale, 1975, p.29
2 Beatrice Grimshaw, *The New New Guinea*, Hutchinson, London, 1910, p.240
3 Stephen Windsor Reed, *The Making of Modern New Guinea*, American Philosophical Society Press, Philadelphia, 1943 p.217; Judy Davis, unfinished manuscript prepared for doctoral dissertation and held at the Australian National University, Menzies Library, draft chapter entitled 'framework', p.2
4 the title of one of the episodes of the ABC's *Taim Bilong Masta* series, produced by Tim Bowden, Australian Broadcasting Commission, Sydney, 1982
5 Robin Radford, *Highlanders and Foreigners in the Upper Ramu: The Kainantu Area 1919–1942*, Melbourne University Press, Melbourne, 1987, p.130
6 ibid., pp.130–1
7 Reed, *The Making of Modern New Guinea*, p.172; James Sinclair, *Kiap: Australia's Patrol Officers in Papua New Guinea*, Pacific Publishers, Sydney,1981, p.36
8 Wolfers, *Race Relations and Colonial Rule in Papua New Guinea*, pp.135–6
9 Hank Nelson, *Taim Bilong Masta: Australian Involvement with Papua New Guinea*, based on ABC radio series produced by Tim Bowden, Australian Broadcasting Commission, Sydney, 1982, p.38
10 Dame Rachel Cleland, *Pathways to Independence: Official and Family Life 1951–1975*, Artlook Books, Perth, 1983, p.216
11 quoted in Percy Chatterton, *Day That I Have Loved*, Pacific Publications, Sydney, 1974, p.24
12 Reed, *The Making of Modern New Guinea*, p.168
13 Wolfers, *Race Relations and Colonial Rule in Papua New Guinea*, p.19
14 Australian Archives (ACT): Prime Minister's Department, CRS CP 316, series 1, bundle 1, part 1, 'Reserved Ordinances Territory of New Guinea' 7/3/35
15 Dixie Rigby, National Library, Canberra, Oral History, two tapes of interview by Rosa Glastonbury, 19 August 1979, TRC 967/1–2
16 Nelson, *Taim Bilong Masta*, p.106
17 Col. J.K. Murray, 'In Retrospect 1945–1952: Papua New Guinea and the Territory of Papua New Guinea', *The History of Melanesia*, Research School of Pacific Studies, Australian National University and University of Papua New Guinea, Canberra and Port Moresby, 1969, p.189
18 Australian Archives (ACT): Prime Minister's Department, CRS CP 316, series 1, bundle 1, part 2, 'Executive Council Meetings Papua' 22/9/33
19 Donald Denoon with Kathleen Dugin and Leslie Marshall, *Public Health in Papua New Guinea: Medical Possibility and Social Constraint, 1884–1984*, Cambridge University Press, Cambridge, 1989, p.46
20 ibid., p.37
21 Sios Tabunamagin, a pastor and tutor in the Methodist mission, interviewed by Deane Fergie at Pakinsela village, 5 July 1986

22 Aisoli Salin, ex-member of the Papua New Guinea Legislative Assembly, interviewed by Deane Fergie and Chilla Bulbeck at Tatau, 13 July 1986

23 Denoon, *Public Health in Papua New Guinea*, p.71

24 ibid., p.74

25 Chatterton, *Day That I Have Loved*, p.24

26 Denoon, *Public Health in Papua New Guinea*, p.87

27 Joan Refshauge, MS 7026 JOAN REFSHAUGE, National Library, Manuscripts Room, Folder 11

28 ibid., letter from Taffy Jones, Rabaul, 7 June 1953

29 ibid.; Joan Refshauge, personal papers kept by Sir William Refshauge, Canberra

30 Joan Refshauge, 'Speech to Mission Conference 18-11-1954', MS 7026 JOAN REFSHAUGE, Folder 11

31 Letter to Dr Refshauge, 4 February 1964, Joan Refshauge's personal papers, held by Sir William Refshauge

32 Reed, *The Making of Modern New Guinea*, p.219; P. Biskup, B. Jinks, and H. Nelson, *A Short History of New Guinea*, Angus & Robertson, Sydney, 1968, pp.53, 100; Davis, unfinished manuscript, 'Plantations: New Guinea', no page numbers

33 Davis, unfinished manuscript, 'Planters: Women and Work', no page numbers

34 Doris R. Booth, *Mountains, Gold and Cannibals*, Cornstalk, Sydney, 1929, p.30

35 ibid., p.118

36 ibid., p.145

37 Diane Langmore, *Missionary Lives Papua 1874–1919*, University Press of Hawaii, Honolulu, 1989, pp.44–5

38 Jane Hunter, 'The Home and the World: The Missionary Message of U.S. Domesticity' in Leslie A. Flemming (ed.), *Women's Work for Women: Missionaries and Social Change in Asia*, Westview Press, Boulder, 1989, p.159. Patricia Grimshaw provides a detailed study of the motivations and experiences of the eighty United States women who became involved in the American Protestant mission to Hawaii from 1819 to mid-century: Patricia Grimshaw, *Paths of Duty: American Missionary Wives in Nineteenth Century Hawaii*, University of Hawaii Press, Honolulu, 1989

39 Langmore, *Missionary Lives*, pp.256–7

40 ibid., p.177

41 ibid., pp.177, 180

42 Reed, *The Making of Modern New Guinea*, p.235

43 Hugh Laracy, *Marists and Melanesians: A History of Catholic Missions in the Solomon Islands*, University of Hawaii Press, Honolulu, 1976, p.63

44 Andre Navarre, *Handbook for Missionaries of the Sacred Heart Working Among the Natives of Papua New Guinea*, Chevalier Press, Kensington, Sydney, 1987, p.39

45 Australian Archives (ACT) Prime Minister's Department, CRS CP 316, series 1, bundle 1, part 1, 'Territory of Papua Mission Activities' and 'Spheres of Influence' 30/4/35

46 Laracy, *Marists and Melanesians*, pp.78, 82

47 ibid., p.75

48 ibid., p.76

49 Benjamin T. Butcher, *We Lived with Headhunters*, Hodder & Stoughton, London, 1979, p.144

50 ibid., p.145

51 Helen Callaway, *Gender, Culture and Empire: European Women in Colonial Nigeria*, Macmillan in association with St Anthony's College, Oxford, Basingstoke and London, 1987, p.67

52 Mary Ann Lind, *The Compassionate Memsahibs: Welfare Activities of British Women in India, 1900–1947*, Greenwood Press, Westport, Connecticut, 1988, p.21

53 Davis, unpublished manuscript, 'White Colonialism', no page numbers

54 Lind, *The Compassionate Memsahibs*, p.14

55 Myna Trustrum, *Women of the Regiment: Marriage and the Victorian Army*, Cambridge University Press, Cambridge, 1984, p.191

56 Callaway, *Gender, Culture and Empire*, p.68

57 Davis, unpublished manuscript, 'Outwomen', p.4

58 Jens Sorensen Lyng, *Island Films: Reminiscences of 'German New Guinea'*, Cornstalk, Sydney, 1925, pp.140–9

59 Davis, unpublished manuscript, 'Plahnters', no page numbers

60 Oala Oala-Rarua, 'Race Relations' in Peter Hastings (ed.), *Papua New Guinea: Prospero's Other Island*, Angus & Robertson, Sydney, 1971, p.137

61 James McAuley, 'Christian Missions', *South Pacific*, vol. 8, no. 7, 1955, p.138

62 Langmore, *Missionary Lives*, pp.236–7; James Lyng, *Our New Possession*, Melbourne Publishing Company, Melbourne, 1919, p.223; C.A.W. Monckton, *Some Experiences of a New Guinea Resident Magistrate*, John Lane, London, 1921, p.43

63 Davis, unpublished manuscript, 'FR Work: White Sexism', p.5

64 Langmore, *Missionary Lives*, p.237

65 Lyng, *Island Films*, p.235

66 Langmore, *Missionary Lives*, p.239

67 Gann and Duigan quoted in Callaway, *Gender, Culture and Empire*, p.13

68 ibid., p.41

69 Helen McLeod, *Cannibals are Human: A District Officer's Wife in New Guinea*, Angus & Robertson, Sydney, 1961, pp.v, 17

70 Bowden, *Taim Bilong Masta*, 'Masta me like Work'

71 Grimshaw, *The New New Guinea*, 1910, pp.118–9

72 quoted in Bob Connolly and Robin Anderson, *First Contact: New Guinea's Highlanders Encounter the Outside World*, Viking Penguin, New York, 1987, p.283

73 quoted in Nelson, *Taim Bilong Masta*, p.163

74 Ralph M. Wiltgenen, 'Catholic mission plantations in mainland New Guinea: their origin and purpose' in *The History of Melanesia*, Research School of Pacific Studies, Australian National University and University of Papua New Guinea, Canberra and Port Moresby, 1969, p.358

75 Claudia Knapman, *White Women in Fiji 1835–1930: The Ruin of Empire?*, Allen & Unwin, Sydney, 1986, p.122

76 Isabelle Moresby, *New Guinea—The Sentinel*, Tombs, Melbourne, 1943, pp.101–2

77 reported in Lyng, *Island Films*, p.238 and Reed, *The Making of Modern New Guinea*, p.125

78 quoted in Knapman, *White Women in Fiji*, p.111

79 Barbara N. Ramusack, 'Cultural missionaries, maternal imperialists, feminist allies: British women activists in India, 1865–1945, *Women's Studies International Forum*, vol. 13, no. 4, 1990, p.320

80 Patricia Grimshaw, ' "Christian woman, pious wife, faithful mother, devoted missionary": Conflicts in roles of American Missionary Women in Nineteenth Century Hawaii', *Feminist Studies*, vol. 9, no. 3, 1983, p.499. Hawaiian chiefs might also demand bonnets they admired or newborn missionary children to be raised as their own: Patricia Grimshaw, *Paths of Duty*, p.60

81 Margaret MacMillan, *Women of the Raj*, Thames & Hudson, London, 1988, p.207

Notes (Chapter 2)   273

82 Pat Barr, *The Dust in the Balance: British Women in India 1905–1945*, Hamish Hamilton, London, 1989, p.23
83 Nancy L. Paxton, 'Feminism under the Raj: complicity and resistance in the writings of Flora Annie Steel and Annie Besant', *Women's Studies International Forum*, vol. 13, no. 4, 1990, p.7
84 Theresa Bloxham in Nelson, *Taim Bilong Masta*, pp.46–7
85 quoted in James A. Boutilier, 'European women in the Solomon Islands 1900–1942: accommodation and change on the Pacific frontier' in Denise O'Brien and Sharon W. Tiffany (eds), *Rethinking Women's Roles: Perspectives from the Pacific*, University of California Press, Berkeley, 1984, p.189
86 C.D. Rowley, *The New Guinea Villager: A Retrospective from 1964*, Cheshire, Melbourne, 1964, p.13
87 quoted in Amirah Inglis, *Not a White Woman Safe: Sexual Anxiety and Politics in Port Moresby, 1920–1934*, Australian National University Press, Canberra, 1974, p.65

3: White women in Papua New Guinea: relative creatures?

1 Sharon W.Tiffany and Kathleen J. Adams, *The Wild Women: An Enquiry into the Anthropology of an Idea*, Schenman, Cambridge, 1985, p.30
2 ibid., p. 99
3 Claudia Knapman, *White Women in Fiji 1835–1930: The Ruin of Empire?*, Allen & Unwin, Sydney, 1986, p.175
4 quoted in Judy Davis, unfinished manuscript prepared for doctoral dissertation and held at the Australian National University, Menzies Library, draft chapter entitled 'The Phoney Colony' p.10
5 C.A.W. Monckton, *Some Experiences of a New Guinea Resident Magistrate*, John Lane, London, 1921, p.61
6 Helen Callaway, *Gender, Culture and Empire: European Women in Colonial Nigeria*, Macmillan in association with St Anthony's College, Basingstoke and London, 1987, p.19
7 ibid., pp.228, 232
8 ibid., p.39
9 Mary Ann Lind, *The Compassionate Memsahibs: Welfare Activities of British Women in India, 1900–1947*, Greenwood Press, Westport, Connecticut, 1988, p.13
10 Callaway, *Gender, Culture and Empire*, p.222
11 ibid., p.220
12 Glenda Riley, *The Female Frontier: A Comparative View of Women on the Prairie and the Plains*, University of Kansas Press, Kansas, 1988, p.199
13 Doris Groves, 'From G-String to Independence—The Passing of the Primitive in Papua New Guinea' MS 6068, WC GROVES, Folder 27, Manuscripts Room, National Library, Canberra
14 Davis, unpublished manuscript, 'Outwomen', p.12
15 Callaway, *Gender, Culture and Empire*, p.179
16 Lind, *The Compassionate Memsahibs*, p.20
17 Davis, unpublished manuscript, 'Outside Women', p.4
18 Davis, unpublished manuscript, 'Outwomen', pp.13, 15, 18; Yvonne Kniebiehler and Régine Goutalier, *La Femme au Temps des Colonies*, Stock, Paris, 1985, p.140
19 Davis, unpublished manuscript, 'Outwomen', p.14

20 Ilias Taba, pastor in the Methodist Mission, interviewed by Deane Fergie at Resese Village, 8 July 1986

21 Diane Langmore, *Missionary Lives Papua 1874–1919*, University Press of Hawaii, Honolulu, 1989, p.75

22 Benjamin Butcher, *We Lived with Headhunters*, Hodder & Stoughton, London, 1979, p.145

23 Callaway, *Gender, Culture and Empire*, pp.42–5

24 Dea Birkett, *Spinsters Abroad: Victorian Lady Explorers*, Basil Blackwell, Oxford, 1989

25 ibid., pp.27–31, 100, 170

26 ibid., p.183

27 ibid., pp.113–17

28 Shirley Fenton Huie, *Tiger Lilies: Women Adventurers in the South Pacific*, Angus & Robertson, Sydney, 1990, p.113

29 Birkett, *Spinsters Abroad*, p.111

30 ibid., pp.242–3

31 Huie, *Tiger Lilies*, p.188

32 Barbara N. Ramusack, 'Cultural missionaries, maternal imperialists, feminist allies: British women activists in India 1865–1945', *Women's Studies International Forum*, vol. 13, no. 4, 1990, pp.309–22

33 Pat Barr, *The Dust in the Balance: British Women in India 1905–1945*, Hamish Hamilton, London, 1989, p.23

34 Anne M. Boylan, 'Evangelical womanhood in the nineteenth century: the role of women in Sunday schools', *Feminist Studies*, vol. 4, no. 3, 1978, p.71; Leonore Davidoff and Catherine Hall, *Family Fortunes: Men and Women of the English Middle Class 1780–1850*, Hutchinson, London, 1987, p.119

35 Jane Hunter, *The Gospel of Gentility: American Women Missionaries in Turn of the Century China*, Yale University Press, New Haven and London, 1984, pp.xiii, 38

36 Leslie A. Flemming, 'Introduction: studying women missionaries in Asia' in Leslie A. Flemming (ed.), *Women's Work for Women: Missionaries and Social Change in Asia*, Westview Press, Boulder, 1989, p.1

37 *The Female Missionary Intelligencer*, January, 1897, last page, held at Cambridge University Library

38 Sara W. Tucker, 'Opportunities for women: the development of professional women's medicine in Canton, China 1879–1901', *Women's Studies International Forum*, vol. 13, no. 4, pp.357–68

39 Patricia Grimshaw, ' "Christian woman, pious wife, faithful mother, devoted missionary": conflicts in roles of American missionary women in nineteenth century Hawaii', *Feminist Studies*, vol. 9, no. 3, 1983, pp.495, 512

40 Patricia R. Hill, *The World Their Household: The American Women's Foreign Mission Movement and Cultural Transformation, 1870–1920*, University of Michigan Press, Ann Arbor, 1985, pp.6–8

41 American Baptist Missionary Union in 1888 cited in Hunter, *The Gospel of Gentility*, p.14

42 quoted in Flora A. Timms, *Mary McLean: First Missionary of the WMA. A Memorial*, Robert Dey, Son & Co., Sydney, 1943, p.17

43 ibid., p.39

44 quoted in Langmore, *Missionary Lives*, p.163

45 Diane Langmore, 'A neglected force: white women missionaries in Papua 1874–1914', *Journal of Pacific History*, vol. 17, no. 3, p.138

[46] ibid., p.141; Langmore, *Missionary Lives*, p.168

[47] Andre Navarre, *Handbook for Missionaries of the Sacred Heart Working Among the Natives of Papua New Guinea*, Chevalier Press, Kensington, Sydney, 1987, p.98

[48] Butcher, *We Lived with Headhunters*, pp.116, 258–60

[49] Charles W. Forman, ' "Sing to the Lord a New Song": Women in the Churches of Oceania', in Denise O'Brien and Sharon W. Tiffany (eds), *Rethinking Women's Roles: Perspectives from the Pacific*, University of California Press, Berkeley, 1984, pp.158–9; Langmore, 'A Neglected Force', p.142

[50] Notes by Marian Lilian Hearnshaw, (who was married to Rev. William Daniel Oakes, who had the Pinikidu Circuit while the Plattens were at Namatanai), History Room, Methodist Mission, Rabaul

[51] Dorothea Freund, *I Will Uphold You: Memoirs of Dorothea M. Freund*, edited by A.P.H. Freund, Lutheran Publishing House, Payneham, 1985, p.182

[52] Langmore, *Missionary Lives*, p.165

[53] Knapman, *White Women in Fiji*, p.36; Winifred Mathews, *Dauntless Women: Stories of Pioneer Wives*, Edinburgh House Press, London, 1949, pp.5–6; Kumari Jayawardena, *Feminism and Nationalism in the Third World*, Zed, London, 1986, p.20; Tim Bowden, *Taim Bilong Masta*, 'Wife and Missus', Australian Broadcasting Commission, Sydney, 1982

[54] Grimshaw, 'Christian Woman, Pious Wife', p.512

[55] Butcher, *We Lived with Headhunters*, pp.112, 116

[56] ibid., p.114

[57] Langmore, *Missionary Lives*, p.166

[58] David Wetherall, *Reluctant Mission: The Anglican Church in Papua New Guinea 1891–1942*, University of Queensland Press, St Lucia, 1982, p.89

[59] Langmore, *Missionary Lives*, p.168; these tasks the Marist sisters also performed on the Solomon Islands (Hugh Laracy, *Marists and Melanesians: A History of Catholic Missions in the Solomon Islands*, University Press of Hawaii, Honolulu, 1976, p.75)

[60] Langmore, *Missionary Lives*, p.181

[61] Evelyn Cheeseman, *Who Stand Alone*, Geoffrey Bles, London, 1965, pp.223–4

[62] Langmore, *Missionary Lives*, p.179

[63] ibid., pp.141, 171

[64] ibid., p.172

[65] Constance Fairhall, *Where Two Tides Meet*, Livingstone, London, 1946, p.40

[66] Callaway, *Gender, Culture and Empire*, p.8

[67] ibid., p.6

[68] ibid., p.46

[69] Margaret MacMillan, *Women of the Raj*, Thames & Hudson, London, 1988, p.209

[70] Callaway, *Gender, Culture and Empire*, p.155

[71] ibid., p.46

[72] Joan Refshauge, 'An Address on Discrimination Against Women in the Territory', MS 7026, JOAN REFSHAUGE, Folder 11, Manuscripts Room, National Library, Canberra

[73] Donald Denoon with Kathleen Duigan and Leslie Marshall, *Public Health in Papua New Guinea: Medical Possibility and Social Constraint, 1884–1984*, Cambridge University Press, Cambridge, 1989, p.86

[74] Refshauge, 'An Address on Discrimination'

[75] Interview with Joan Refshauge transcribed by Donald Denoon, personal papers of Joan Refshauge, held by Sir William Refshauge, Canberra

76 ibid.
77 Callaway, *Gender, Culture and Empire*, p.47
78 Ellen Kettle, *That They Might Live*, F.P. Leonard, Sydney, 1979, pp.100, 104; James A. Boutilier, 'European Women in the Solomon Islands, 1900–1942: Accommodation and Change on the Pacific Frontier' in Denise O'Brien and Sharon W. Tiffany (eds), *Rethinking Women's Roles: Perspectives from the Pacific*, University of California Press, Berkeley, 1984, p.188
79 thus disguising the high maternal mortality rates: Denoon, *Public Health in Papua New Guinea*, p.50
80 For example, Callaway, *Gender, Culture and Empire*, pp.46, 99 for Nigeria
81 Kettle, *That They Might Live*, p.42
82 Callaway, *Gender, Culture and Empire*, pp.141–5, 242–3
83 Kniebiehler and Goutalier, *La Femme au Temps des Colonies*, pp.144–5
84 Suzanne, ibid., p.143
85 Amirah Inglis, *Not a White Woman Safe: Sexual Anxiety and Politics in Port Moresby*, Australian National University Press, Canberra, 1974, p.30; Bowden, *Taim Bilong Masta*, 'Wife and Missus'; Davis, unpublished manuscript, 'Plantations: New Guinea' no page numbers ; Pacific Manuscripts Bureau, Australian National University, Manuscript no. 19, 'Papers relating to Mrs R.H. Rickard'
86 Margaret Mead, *Blackberry Winter: My Earlier Years*, Angus & Robertson, London, 1981, first published 1973, p.178
87 Huie, *Tiger Lilies*, p.160
88 Mead, *Blackberry Winter*, p.180
89 Judy Davis, unpublished manuscript, 'Plantations: New Guinea', no page numbers
90 Bowden, *Taim Bilong Masta*, 'Moneymakers and Misfits'
91 Boutilier, 'European Women in the Solomon Islands', p.187
92 Judy Tudor, pers. comm., 10 May 1988
93 Yvonne Mann, pers. comm., 10 April 1988
94 Australian Archives (ACT), Prime Minister's Department CRS CP 316, series 1, bundle 1, part 1, 'Territory of Papua Public Service of the Territory', 29/1/35
95 Knapman, *White Women in Fiji*, pp.133–4
96 Langmore, *Missionary Lives*, p.171
97 from attached letter in support from Acting Director of Public Health, written in mid-year 1960: personal papers of Joan Refshauge, kept by Sir William Refshauge, Canberra
98 Joan Refshauge, 'An Address on Discrimination Against Women in the Territory'
99 Lucy Evelyn Cheeseman, *Time Well Spent*, Hutchinson, London, 1960, p.213
100 quoted in Huie, *Tiger Lilies*, p.191
101 Robin Radford, *Highlanders and Foreigners in the Upper Ramu: The Kainantu Area 1919–1942*, Melbourne University Press, Melbourne, 1987, p.158

4: In town and down the road

1 Evelyn Cheeseman, *Who Stand Alone*, Geoffrey Bles, London, 1965, pp.13–23
2 ibid., p.23
3 Judy Davis, unpublished manuscript prepared for doctoral dissertation and held at the Australian National University, Menzies Library, draft chapter entitled 'Outwomen', p.11
4 Yvonne Kniebiehler and Régine Goutalier, *La Femme au Temps des Colonies*, Stock, Paris, 1985, p.144

5 Following a husband to foreign parts at the cost of one's career can cause both personal and marital stress as a sample of expatriate women in Hong Kong in 1979 revealed: Mildred M. McCoy, 'Focus on the expatriate woman' in Marjorie Spotts Litsinger and Alice Flinn (eds), *The Expatriate Experience: A Symposium*, In Touch Foundation, Laguna, Philippines, 1986, pp.43–50

6 Lorna Fleetwood, *A Short History of Wewak*, East Sepik Provincial Government, Wewak, 1984, p.19

7 Helen McLeod, *Cannibals are Human: A District Officer's Wife in New Guinea*, Angus & Robertson, Sydney, p.87

8 Ann Deland, MS 4725, ANN DELAND, Manuscripts Room, National Library, Canberra

9 Doris R. Booth, *Mountains, Gold and Cannibals*, Cornstalk, Sydney, 1929, p.184

10 McLeod, *Cannibals are Human*, p.183

11 C.D. Rowley, *The New Guinea Villager: A Retrospective from 1964*, Cheshire, Melbourne, 1964, p.115

12 Prudence Frank, MS 6794, PRUDENCE FRANK, transcript of tape TRC 793, Manuscripts Room, National Library, Canberra

13 Mary Ann Lind, *The Compassionate Memsahibs: Welfare Activities of British Women in India, 1900–1947*, Greenwood Press, Westport, Connecticut, 1988, p.10

14 Jacklyn Cock, *Maids and Madams: Domestic Workers under Apartheid*, The Women's Press, London, 1989, p.67

15 ibid., p.69

16 Ilias Taba interviewed by Deane Fergie at Resese Village, 8 July 1986; describing his work in the Platten household

17 quoted in Hank Nelson, *Taim Bilong Masta: Australian Involvement with Papua New Guinea*, based on ABC series produced by Tim Bowden, Australian Broadcasting Commission, Sydney, 1982, p.80

18 Claudia Knapman, *White Women in Fiji 1835–1930: The Ruin of Empire?*, Allen & Unwin, Sydney, 1986, p.156

19 Judy Davis, unpublished manuscript, 'Planters' Lifestyle', no page numbers

20 Helen Callaway, *Gender, Culture and Empire: European Women in Colonial Nigeria*, Macmillan in association with St Anthony's College, Basingstoke and London, 1987, p.22

21 Ann Deland, MS 4725, ANN DELAND, Manuscripts Room, National Library, Canberra

22 Joan Refshauge, personal papers held by Sir William Refshauge, Canberra

23 Eva Butcher, MS 1881, BENJAMIN BUTCHER, Folder 5, Manuscripts Room, National Library, Canberra

24 Diane Langmore, *Missionary Lives: Papua 1874–1919*, University Press of Hawaii, Honolulu, 1989, pp.80–1

25 James McAuley, 'My New Guinea', *Quadrant*, vol. 5, no. 3, pp.15–27; discussed fully in Chapter 8

26 Shirley Ardener, 'Ground rules and social maps for women: an introduction' in Shirley Ardener (ed.), *Women and Space*, Croom Helm, London, 1981, p.21

27 Saimon Gaius, ex-Bishop of New Guinea Islands Region, interviewed by Deane Fergie and Chilla Bulbeck at Raluana, 3 July 1986

28 Dixie Rigby, interviewed by Rosa Glastonbury 19 August 1979, TRC 967/1-2, Oral History, National Library, Canberra

29 Doris Groves, MS 6068, WC GROVES, Folder 27, 'From G-String to Independence' Manuscripts Room, National Library, Canberra

30 Knapman, *White Women in Fiji*, p.156

31 Tim Bowden, *Taim Bilong Masta*, Australian Broadcasting Commission, Sydney, 1981, 'Growing Up in Papua New Guinea'

32 Davis, unpublished manuscript, 'Planters: relationships', no page numbers

33 Refshauge, personal papers

34 Lilian Overell, *A Woman's Impressions of German New Guinea*, John Lane and Bodley Head, London, 1923, p.35

35 Kenneth Ballhatchet, *Race, Sex and Class Under the Raj: Imperial Attitudes and Policies and their Critics, 1793–1905*, Weidenfeld & Nicolson, London, 1980, p.111

36 Pat Barr, *The Dust in the Balance: British Women in India 1905–1945*, Hamish Hamilton, London, 1989, p.49

37 Margaret MacMillan, *Women of the Raj*, Thames & Hudson, London, 1988, p.210

38 Ballhatchet, *Race, Sex and Class under the Raj*, p.112

39 MacMillan, *Women of the Raj*, p.212

40 Stephen Windsor Reed, *The Making of Modern New Guinea*, American Philosophical Society Press, Philadelphia, 1943, p.243

41 See Deborah Kirkwood, 'Settler wives in Southern Rhodesia: a case study' in Hilary Callan and Shirley Ardener (eds), *The Incorporated Wife*, Croom Helm, London, p.151 for Rhodesia; and Beverley Gartrell, 'Colonial wives: villains or victims' in Hilary Callan and Shirley Ardener (eds), *The Incorporated Wife*, p.166 for Uganda

42 Percy Chatterton, *Day That I Have Loved*, Pacific Publications, Sydney, 1974, p.10

43 Rowley, *The New Guinea Villager*, p.13

44 Marian Fowler, *Below the Peacock Fan: First Ladies of the Raj*, Viking, Markham, Ontario, 1987, p.60

45 ibid., p.62

46 ibid., p.136

47 ibid., pp.216–7

48 Dea Birkett, *Spinsters Abroad: Victorian Lady Explorers*, Basil Blackwell, Oxford, 1989, pp.126–7

49 Susan L. Blake, 'A woman's trek: what difference does gender make?', *Women's Studies International Forum*, vol. 13, no. 4, pp.353–4

50 Birkett, *Spinsters Abroad*, pp.154–6

51 ibid., p.165

52 Diane Langmore, 'A neglected force: white women missionaries in Papua 1874–1914', *Journal of Pacific History*, vol. 17, no. 3, 1982, p.146

53 Saimon Gaius interviewed by Deane Fergie and Chilla Bulbeck at Raluana, 3 July 1986

54 E. Linggood, *New Britain: Three Missionary Studies*, Young Women's Missionary Movement, Victoria, no date, p.26

55 Saimon Gaius, interviewed at Raluana, 3 July 1986

56 Langmore, 'A neglected farce', p. 148

57 Amirah Inglis, *Not a White Woman Safe: Sexual Anxiety and Politics in Port Moresby, 1920–1934*, Australian National University Press, Canberra, 1974, p.8

5: *War, a watershed in race relations?*

1 Diane Langmore, *Missionary Lives Papua 1874–1919*, University Press of Hawaii, Honolulu, 1989, p.127; see also Tim Bowden, 'You Had to be Firm', *Taim Bilong Masta: Australian Involvement with Papua New Guinea*, Australian Broadcasting Commission, Sydney, 1981; Pierre L. van den Berghe, *Race and Racism: A Comparative Perspective*, John Wiley & Sons, New York and London, 1967, p.27

2 Henry Reynolds, *Frontier: Aborigines, Settlers and Land*, Allen & Unwin, Sydney, 1987, p.69; Jules Harmond in the 1920s, cited in Philip D. Curtin, *The Image of Africa: British Ideas and Action 1780–1850*, Macmillan, London, 1972, p.305; Claudia Knapman, *White Women in Fiji 1835–1930: The Ruin of Empire?*, Allen & Unwin, Sydney, 1986, p.120

3 Abdul R. JanMohamed, 'The economy of Manichean allegory: the function of racial difference in colonialist literature', in Henry Louis Gates (Jr) (ed.), *"Race", Writing and Difference*, University of Chicago Press, Chicago, 1986, p.89.

4 Lilian Overell, *A Woman's Impressions of German New Guinea*, John Lane and Bodley Head, London, 1923, pp.19, 176; Alice Jeannette Keeland, *In the Land of Dohori*, Angus & Robertson, Sydney, 1929, p.22

5 reported in Amirah Inglis, *Not a White Woman Safe: Sexual Anxiety and Politics in Port Moresby, 1920–1934*, Australian National University Press, Canberra, 1974, p.12

6 Langmore, *Missionary Lives*, 1989, p.120

7 H. N. Nelson, 'European attitudes in Papua, 1906–1914', in Research School of Pacific Studies (ed.), *The History of Melanesia*, Australian National University and University of Papua New Guinea, Canberra and Port Moresby, 1969, p.609

8 ibid., p.609

9 Jens Sorensen Lyng, *Island Films: Reminiscences of "German New Guinea"*, Cornstalk, Sydney, 1925, p.192

10 Beatrice Grimshaw, *The New New Guinea*, Hutchinson, London, 1910, pp.34–5

11 ibid., pp.117–8

12 ibid., p.234

13 Lilian Overell, *A Woman's Impressions of German New Guinea*, p.19

14 van den Berghe, *Race and Racism*, p.17

15 Helen Callaway, *Gender, Culture and Empire: European Women in Colonial Nigeria*, Macmillan in association with St Anthony's College, Basingstoke and London, 1987, pp.30–1

16 quoted in Raymond Evans *et al.*, *Race Relations in Colonial Queensland*, University of Queensland Press, St Lucia, 1988, p.10, first published in 1975

17 Philip Mason, *Prospero's Magic: Some Thoughts on Class and Race*, Greenwood, Westport, Connecticut, 1962, p.27; van den Berghe, *Race and Racism*, p.15; Kenneth Ballhatchet, *Race, Sex and Class Under the Raj: Imperial Attitudes and Policies and Their Critics, 1793–1905*, Weidenfeld & Nicolson, London, 1980, p.6; Woodruff D. Smith, *European Imperialism in the Nineteenth and Twentieth Centuries*, Nelson-Hall, Chicago, 1982, p.85

18 van den Berghe, *Race and Racism*, p.12

19 Mason, *Prospero's Magic*, p.76

20 Grimshaw, *The New New Guinea*, pp.116–7

21 Michael W. Young, 'Doctor Bromilow and the Bwaidoka Wars', *Journal of Pacific History*, vol. 12, part 3, 1977, p.146

22 Paul B. Rich, *Race and Empire in British Politics*, Cambridge University Press, Cambridge, 1986, pp.30–1

23 Philip D. Curtin, *The Image of Africa: British Ideas and Action 1780–1850*, Macmillan, London, 1965, p.383

24 Stephen J. Gould, *The Mismeasure of Man*, Penguin, Harmondsworth, 1984, p.32, first published in 1981

25 Curtin, *The Image of Africa*, p.376

26 ibid., p.378

27 Evans *et al.*, *Race Relations in Colonial Queensland*, p.13

28 Grimshaw, *The New New Guinea*, p.242

29 Knapman, *White Women in Fiji*, p.124

30 C.D. Rowley, *The New Guinea Villager: A Retrospective from 1964*, Cheshire, Melbourne, 1964, p.13

31 See Gould, *The Mismeasure of Man*, for discussion of this 'scientific' endeavour

32 Mason, *Prospero's Magic*, p.14; Ernst van den Boogart, 'Colour prejudice and the yardstick of civility: the initial Dutch confrontation with black Africans, 1590–1635' in Robert Ross (ed.), *Racism and Colonialism*, Martinus Nijhoff, 1982, p.54

33 Margaret MacMillan, *Women of the Raj*, Thames & Hudson, London, 1988, pp.56–62

34 Alan Atkinson and Marian Aveling (eds), *Australians 1838*, Fairfax Syme & Weldon Associates, Broadway, NSW, 1987, pp.26–31, 220; Neville Green, *Broken Spears: Aborigines and Europeans in the Southwest of Australia*, Focus Education Books, Perth, 1984, p.130; Bob Reece, 'Inventing Aborigines', *Aboriginal History*, vol. 11, nos 1–2, 1987, pp.17–18

35 O. Mannoni, *Prospero and Caliban: The Psychology of Colonization*, Methuen, London, 1956, pp.198–200, translated by Pamela Powesland

36 Edward P. Wolfers, *Race Relations and Colonial Rule in Papua New Guinea*, Australian and New Zealand Book Co., Brookvale, 1975, p.55

37 Pierre L. van den Berghe, 'Ethnicity and the sociobiology debate' in John Rex and David Mason (eds), *Theories of Race and Ethnic Relations*, Cambridge University Press, Cambridge, 1986, p.260

38 John Rex, 'Ethnicity and race' in Peter Worsley (ed.), *The New Introducing Sociology*, Penguin, Harmondsworth, 1987, p.323

39 Inglis, *Not a White Woman Safe*, pp.21, 56

40 Wolfers, *Race Relations and Colonial Rule*, p.102

41 compared with Hawaiians for example: Rowley, *The New Guinea Villager*, p.24

42 quoted in R.B. Joyce, 'William MacGregor: the role of the individual' in Research School of Pacific Studies (ed.), *The History of Melanesia*, Australian National University and University of Papua New Guinea, Canberra and Port Moresby, 1969, p.36

43 Hank Nelson, 'The swinging index: capital punishment and British and Australian administration in Papua New Guinea, 1888–1945', *Journal of Pacific History*, vol. 13, part 3, 1978, pp.132-3

44 Wolfers, *Race Relations and Colonial Rule*, p.18

45 ibid., p.18

46 Roger C. Thompson, 'Making a mandate: the formation of Australia's New Guinea policies 1919–1925', *Journal of Pacific History*, vol. 25, no. 1, p.77

47 Wolfers, *Race Relations and Colonial Rule*, p.78

48 Nelson, 'The swinging index', p.148

49 ibid., pp.144–5

50 ibid., pp.137, 143, 152

51 Wolfers, *Race Relations and Colonial Rule*, p.18

52 Callaway, *Gender, Culture and Empire*, p.41

53 Ballhatchet, *Race, Sex and Class Under the Raj*, pp.7–8

54 Janice N. Brownfoot, 'Memsahibs in colonial Malaya: a study of European wives in a British colony and protectorate 1900–1940' in Hilary Callan and Shirley Ardener (eds), *The Incorporated Wife*, Croom Helm, London, 1983, p.203

55 Rowley, *The New Guinea Villager*, p.68

56 ibid., p.75

57 quoted in Peter Smith, *Education and Colonial Control in Papua New Guinea: A Documentary History*, Longman Cheshire, Melbourne, 1987, p.45

58 Wolfers, *Race Relations and Colonial Rule*, p.65

59 quoted in Thompson, 'Making a mandate', p.75

60 ibid., p.75

61 Wolfers, *Race Relations and Colonial Rule*, p.98

62 ibid., pp.30–1, 65, 93

63 ibid., p.46

64 Australian Archives (ACT), Prime Minister's Department, CRS CP 316, series 1, bundle 1, part 2, 13/11/1933

65 AA (ACT) CRS CP 316, series 1, bundle 1, part 1, Executive Council Minutes Nos 16–29, 1933; Papua Transactions with Natives Ordinance 1933, 21/11/1935

66 Sir Paul Hasluck, *A Time for Building: Australian Administration in Papua and New Guinea 1951–1963*, Melbourne University Press, Melbourne, 1976, p.196

67 ibid., p.73

68 Wolfers, *Race Relations and Colonial Rule*, p.46

69 Paul B. Rich, *Race and Empire in British Politics*, Cambridge University Press, Cambridge, 1986, pp.37, 45–6; see also Sylvia M. Jacobs, 'African-American women missionaries and European imperialism in southern Africa, 1880–1920', *Women's Studies International Forum*, vol. 13, no. 4, 1990, p.392

70 League of Nations Covenant, Articles 22 and 23 extracted in Philip Curtin (ed.), *Imperialism*, Macmillan, London, 1972, pp.65–6

71 Thompson, 'Making a mandate', p.81

72 W.J. Hudson, 'New Guinea mandate: the view from Geneva' in Research School of Pacific Studies (ed.), *The History of Melanesia*, Australian National University and University of Papua New Guinea, Canberra and Port Moresby, 1969, pp.142–7

73 Thompson, 'Making a mandate', pp.71, 73

74 ibid., p.78

75 ibid., p.84

76 James Boutilier, 'Papua New Guinea's colonial century; reflections on imperialism, accommodation and historical consciousness' in Deborah Gewertz and Edward Schieffelin (eds), *History and Ethno-history in Papua New Guinea*, Oceania Monograph Number 5, University of Sydney, Sydney, 1985, p.18

77 James McAuley, 'My New Guinea', *Quadrant*, vol. 5, no. 3, 1961, p.17

78 K.S. Inglis, 'War, race and loyalty in New Guinea, 1939–1945' in Research School of Pacific Studies (ed.), *The History of Melanesia*, Australian National University and University of Papua New Guinea, Canberra and Port Moresby, 1969, p.515

79 Rich, *Race and Empire*, pp.148–52

80 Mandate of the United Nations, extracted in Philip D. Curtin (ed.), *Imperialism*, p.68

81 Wolfers, *Race Relations and Colonial Rule*, p.126

82 ibid., p.127

83 Ruth First, 'Colonialism and the formation of African states' in David Held *et al.* (eds), *States and Societies*, Martin Robertson, Oxford, 1983, p.210

84 as one interviewee put it in E. Ellis Cashmore, *The Logic of Racism*, Allen & Unwin, London, 1987, p.25

85 Wolfers, *Race Relations and Colonial Rule*, p.19

86 Rowley, *The New Guinea Villager*, p.64

87 ibid., p.184; August Kituai, 'Innovation and intrusion: villagers and policemen in Papua New Guinea', *Journal of Pacific History*, vol. 23, no. 2, 1988, p.159

88 Nelson, 'The swinging index'

89 James Sinclair, *Kiap: Australia's Patrol Officers in Papua New Guinea*, Pacific Publishers, Sydney, 1981, p.45

90 J.G. Hides, *Savages in Serge*, Angus & Robertson, Sydney, 1938, p.229

91 Robin Radford, *Highlanders and Foreigners in the Upper Ramu: The Kainantu Area 1919–1942*, Melbourne University Press, Melbourne, 1987, p.162; Sinclair, *Kiap*, p.45

92 Raymond Evans et al., *Race Relations in Colonial Queensland*, pp.56–60

93 Australian Archives (ACT), Prime Minister's Department, CRS CP 316, series 1, bundle 1, part 2, 13/4/1934

94 Kituai, 'Innovation and intrusion', p.157

95 ibid., p.166

96 Nelson, 'The swinging index', p.146

97 Bob Connolly and Robin Anderson, *First Contact: New Guinea's Highlanders Encounter the Outside World*, Viking Penguin, New York, 1987, p.209

98 Wolfers, *Race Relations and Colonial Rule*, p.32

99 Thompson, 'Making a mandate', p.38

100 Australian Archives (ACT) Department of External Affairs: CRS A981, New Guinea Item 50 'Report of Enquiry into Allegation of Flogging and Forced Labour of Natives' by A.S. Canning, 7/5/24, p.15

101 Dame Rachel Cleland, *Pathways to Independence: Official and Family Life 1951–1975*, Artlook Books, Perth, 1983, p.65; Percy Chatterton, *Day That I Have Loved*, Pacific Publications, Sydney, 1974, pp.29–30

102 Rowley, *The New Guinea Villager*, p.154

103 Hugh Laracy, *Marists and Melanesians: A History of Catholic Missions in the Solomon Islands*, University Press of Hawaii, 1976, p.81

104 James McAuley, 'Christian missions', *South Pacific*, vol. 8, no. 7, p.145

105 Bishop Andre Navarre, *Handbook for Missionaries of the Sacred Heart Working Among the Natives of Papua New Guinea*, Chevalier Press, Kensington, Sydney, 1987, p.18

106 Rowley, *The New Guinea Villager*, p.154

107 Robinson Butbut, Methodist Minister, interviewed by Deane Fergie, Rabaul, 1 July 1986

108 Ilias Taba, pastor in Methodist Mission, interviewed by Deane Fergie at Resese Village, 8 July 1986

109 Saimon Gaius, appointed Bishop of New Guinea Islands Region in 1968, Letter to Rev.Harold Taylor 18 September 1974, History Room, United Church, Rabaul

110 Eva Butcher, letter of 31 July 1914, MS 1881 BENJAMIN BUTCHER, Folder 5, Manuscripts Room, National Library, Canberra

111 Australian Archives (ACT) External Affairs Department, CRS A981, Correspondence files, item 28, 'Letter re death of Father Mosscheuser' 9/1/35

112 Ann Deland, MS 4725, ANN DELAND, Manuscripts Room, National Library, Canberra

113 Letter to Mrs Threlfall from Frank T. Walker, 23/4/75, File: Ex-Missionaries Correspondence, History Room, United Church, Rabaul

114 James Lyng, *Our New Possession*, Melbourne Publishing Company, Melbourne, 1919, p.226; Jens Sorensen Lyng, *Island Films: Reminiscences of 'German New Guinea'*, Cornstalk, Sydney, 1925, p.237

115 C.A.W. Monckton, *Some Experiences of a New Guinea Resident Magistrate*, John Lane, London, 1921, p.43

116 Quoted in David Weisbrot, 'Integration of laws in Papua New Guinea: custom and the criminal law in conflict' in David Weisbrot *et al.* (eds), *Law and Social Change in Papua New Guinea*, Butterworths, Sydney, 1982, p.76

117 Quoted in J.F. Hooley, 'The Clapham Omnibus Man in Papua New Guinea' in B.J. Brown (ed.), *Fashion of Law in New Guinea*, Butterworths, Sydney, 1969, p.126. The 'Clapham Omnibus Man' is a colourful characterisation of the 'reasonable man' developed in English common law

118 Dixie Rigby interviewed by Rosa Glastonbury, 19 August 1979, TRC 967/1-2, Oral History, National Library, Canberra

119 Heather Radi, 'New Guinea under mandate 1921–41' in W.J. Hudson (ed.), *Australia and Papua New Guinea*, Sydney University Press, Sydney, 1971, p.81

120 Rowley, *The New Guinea Villager*, p.117

121 Thompson, 'Making a mandate', p.74

122 Doris Groves, MS 6068, WC GROVES, Folder 30, Manuscripts Room, National Library, Canberra

123 AA, (ACT), CRS CP 316, series 1, bundle 1, part 2 'Summary of Main Particulars Regarding Land Tenure in Papua', no date

124 Rowley, *The New Guinea Villager*, p.117

125 Quoted in Bob Connolly and Robin Anderson, *First Contact*, p.231

126 Hasluck, *A Time for Building*, p.229

127 Extracted in Curtin, (ed.), *Imperialism*, p.158

128 Grimshaw, *The New New Guinea*, pp.132–4, 136–7

129 Overell, *A Woman's Impressions of German New Guinea*, p.176

130 Hank Nelson, 'From Kanaka to Fuzzy Wuzzy Angel' in Ann Curthoys and Andrew Markus (eds), *Who Are Our Enemies? Racism and the Working Class in Australia*, Hale & Iremonger, Sydney, 1978, p.172

131 Pierre L. van den Berghe, *The Ethnic Phenomenon*, Elsevier, New York, 1981, p.194

132 ibid., p.94

133 Judy Davis, unpublished manuscript prepared for doctoral dissertation and held at the Australian National University, Menzies Library. Discussion of Lyng and various informants in draft entitled 'Outwomen', no page numbers

134 van den Berghe, *The Ethnic Phenomenon*, p.98

135 Wolfers, *Race Relations and Colonial Rule*, p.37

136 Radi, 'New Guinea under mandate 1921–41', p.76

137 Article 23, extracted in Curtin (ed.), *Imperialism*, p.66

138 Radi, 'New Guinea under mandate 1921–41', p.89

139 Nelson, 'From Kanaka to Fuzzy Wuzzy Angel', p.184

140 Ralph Shlomowitz, 'Mortality and indentured labour in Papua (1885–1941) and New Guinea (1920–1941)', *Journal of Pacific History*, vol. 23, no. 1, p.78

141 Robert Miles, *Capitalism and Unfree Labour*, Tavistock, London, 1987, p.2

142 Miles, *Capitalism and Unfree Labour*, pp.182–4. See also John Rex, 'The role of class analysis in the study of race relations – a Weberian perspective' in John Rex and David Mason (eds), *Theories of Race and Ethnic Relations*, Cambridge University Press, Cambridge, 1986, pp.72–8, who also argues that race-based oppression occurs outside market relations

143 Connolly and Anderson, *First Contact*, p.231

144 Penelope Hope, *Long Ago is Far Away: Accounts of the Early Exploration and Settlement*

of the Papuan Gulf Area, Australian National University Press, Canberra, 1979, pp.176–7

[145] Rowley, *The New Guinea Villager*, p.21

[146] AA (ACT), CRS A981 'New Guinea' item 50; Lorna Fleetwood, *A Short History of Wewak*, East Sepik Provincial Government, Wewak, 1984, p.23

[147] AA (ACT), Prime Minister's Department, CP 316, series 1, bundle 1, part 1, 'Native Labour Ordinance No 11 of 1933'; 'Mining Ordinance 1934' 21/9/1934

[148] Rowley, *The New Guinea Villager*, p.22

[149] Jean Martin, 'Forms of recognition' in Ann Curthoys and Andrew Markus (eds), *Who Are Our Enemies? Racism and the Working Class in Australia*, Hale & Iremonger, Sydney, 1978, p.179

[150] Nelson, 'From Kanaka to Fuzzy Wuzzy Angel', p.176

[151] Dixie Rigby, TRC 967/1-2, Oral History, National Library, Canberra

[152] AA (ACT), Department of External Affairs: CRS A981, Correspondence files, item 52, letter to Secretary of Prime Minister's Department, 'Proposed Whipping of Natives' 21/1/1928

[153] AA (ACT), CRS A981, item 20 9/7/1929

[154] Bill Gammage, 'The Rabaul Strike, 1929', *Journal of Pacific History*, vol. 10, part 3, p.4

[155] quoted in Bill Gammage, ibid., p.19

[156] ibid., p.24

[157] AA (ACT), Department of External Affairs, CRS A981, item 51 'New Guinea General Strike in Rabaul January 1929' 19/3/29

[158] *Rabaul Times*, quoted in Stephen Windsor Reed, *The Making of Modern New Guinea*, American Philosophical Society Press, Philadelphia, 1943, p.234

[159] Rowley, *The New Guinea Villager*, p.61

[160] Nelson, 'From Kanaka to Fuzzy Wuzzy Angel', p.185

[161] Nelson, 'From Kanaka to Fuzzy Wuzzy Angel', p.187; Wolfers, *Race Relations and Colonial Rule*, p.120

[162] Rigby, TRC 967/1-2, Oral History, National Library, Canberra

[163] ibid., p.121

[164] Hasluck, *A Time for Building*, p.227

[165] ibid., p.235

[166] ibid., p.232

[167] Nelson, 'From Kanaka to Fuzzy Wuzzy Angel', pp.176, 184

[168] McAuley, 'My New Guinea', p.19

[169] Rowley, *The New Guinea Villager*, p.166

[170] Laracy, *Marists and Melanesians*, p.127

[171] Knapman, *White Women in Fiji*, p.115

[172] van den Berghe, *The Ethnic Phenomenon*, pp.222–3

[173] Correspondent to *Rabaul Times*, no. 205, 22 March 1929; Editorial 'Mixed football', *Rabaul Times*, no. 153, 30 March 1929

[174] Ilias Taba, of Resese Village, interviewed 8 July 1986

[175] Saimon Gaius, interviewed by Deane Fergie and Chilla Bulbeck at Raluana, 3 July 1986

[176] Wolfers, *Race Relations and Colonial Rule*, p.115

[177] Inglis, 'War, race and loyalty in New Guinea', p.503; Hank Nelson, 'From Kanaka to Fuzzy Wuzzy Angel', p.187

[178] ibid., p.504

[179] ibid., p.504

180 ibid., p.515
181 Sir John Guise in Hank Nelson, *Taim Bilong Masta: Australian Involvement with Papua New Guinea*, Australian Broadcasting Commission, Sydney, 1982, p.173
182 Maiamuta in Smith, *Education and Colonial Control*, p.156
183 Wolfers, *Race Relations and Colonial Rule*, p.115
184 Inglis, 'War, race and loyalty', p.514
185 ANGAU booklet quoted by Wolfers, *Race Relations and Colonial Rule*, p.114
186 Chatterton, *Day That I Have Loved*, p.64
187 Hasluck, *A Time for Building*, p.70
188 Judy Davis, an interviewee reported in unpublished manuscript, 'Framework', p.7
189 Judy Davis, unpublished manuscript, untitled chapter, no page number
190 Diane Langmore, *Missionary Lives Papua 1874–1919*, University Press of Hawaii, Honolulu, 1989, pp. 128–9
191 Saimon Gaius, interviewed at Raluana, 3 July 1986
192 Sios Tabunamagin, a pastor and tutor in the Methodist Mission, interviewed by Deane Fergie at Pakinsela Village, 5 July 1986
193 Dixie Rigby, TRC 967/1-2, Oral History, National Library, Canberra
194 Prudence Frank, MS 6794, PRUDENCE FRANK, transcript of tape TRC 793, Manuscripts Room, National Library, Canberra
195 Joan Refshauge, private papers held by Sir William Refshauge, Canberra

6: *The civilising mission*

1 Amirah Inglis, *Not a White Woman Safe: Sexual Anxiety and Politics in Port Moresby, 1920–1934*, Australian National University Press, Canberra, 1974, p.21
2 Edward P. Wolfers, *Race Relations and Colonial Rule in Papua New Guinea*, Australian and New Zealand Book Co., Brookvale, p.18
3 Tim Bowden, *Taim Bilong Masta: Australian Involvement with Papua New Guinea*, 'Masta me like Work' Australian Broadcasting Commission, Sydney, 1982
4 Cited in Thelma Jackson, Australians in Papua: The Effect of Changing Government Policies on Attitudes, 1945–1973, Honours thesis submitted to Division of Asian and International Studies, Griffith University, Brisbane, 1988, p.78
5 C.D. Rowley, *The New Guinea Villager: A Retrospective from 1964*, Cheshire, Melbourne, 1964, p.86
6 Carole Pateman, *The Sexual Contract*, Polity Press, London, 1988, p.64
7 Philip Mason, *Prospero's Magic: Some Thoughts on Class and Race*, Greenwood, Westport, Connecticutt, 1962, pp.8–9
8 Percy Chatterton, *Day That I Have Loved*, Pacific Publications, Sydney, 1974, p.12
9 Sheila Rowbotham, 'Edward Carpenter' in Sheila Rowbotham and Jeffrey Weeks, *Socialism and the New Life*, Pluto, London, 1977, p.107
10 Geoffrey Burkhart, 'Danish women missionaries' in Leslie A. Flemming (ed.), *Women's Work for Women: Missionaries and Social Change in Asia*, Westview Press, Boulder, 1989, p.72
11 ibid., pp.70, 72
12 Wolfers, *Race Relations and Colonial Rule*, p.46
13 Inglis, *Not a White Woman Safe*, p.50
14 Wolfers, *Race Relations and Colonial Rule*, p.47

15 Chatterton, *Day That I Have Loved*, p.12
16 Doris Groves, MS 6068 WC GROVES, Folder 27, Box 30, 'From G-String to Independence', Manuscripts Room, National Library, Canberra
17 Helen Callaway, *Gender, Culture and Empire: European Women in Colonial Nigeria*, Macmillan in association with St Anthony's College, Oxford, Basingstoke and London, 1987, p.65
18 Leonore Davidoff and Catherine Hall, *Family Fortunes: Men and Women in the English Middle Class 1780–1850*, Hutchinson, London, 1986, p.385
19 Penelope Hope, *Long Ago is Far Away: Accounts of the Early Exploration and Settlement of the Papuan Gulf Area*, Australian National University Press, Canberra, 1979, p.224
20 Eva Butcher, MS 1881 BENJAMIN BUTCHER, Folder 5, Manuscripts Room, National Library, Canberra
21 Ann Deland, MS 4725, ANN DELAND, Manuscripts Room, National Library, Canberra
22 cited in Bob Connolly and Robin Anderson, *First Contact: New Guinea's Highlanders Encounter the Outside World*, Viking Penguin, New York, 1987, p.41
23 Hank Nelson, *Taim Bilong Masta; Australian Involvement with Papua New Guinea*, Australian Broadcasting Commission, Sydney, 1982, p.170
24 Dixie Rigby interviewed by Rosa Glastonbury, 19 August 1979, TRC 967/1-2, Oral History, National Library, Canberra
25 Chatterton, *Time That I Have Loved*, pp.88–9
26 Paul Hasluck, *A Time for Building: Australian Administration in Papua and New Guinea 1951–1963*, Melbourne University Press, Melbourne, 1976, p.339
27 Wolfers, *Race Relations and Colonial Rule*, pp.58–9
28 Stephen Windsor Reed, *The Making of Modern New Guinea*, American Philosophical Society Press, Philadelphia, 1943, p.246
29 Albert Maori Kiki, *Ten Thousand Years in a Lifetime*, Cheshire, Melbourne, 1968, pp.93–4
30 Inglis, *Not a White Woman Safe*, p.49
31 Wolfers, *Race Relations and Colonial Rule*, pp.45, 97, 98
32 Joan Refshauge, personal papers held by Sir William Refshauge, Canberra
33 Wolfers, *Race Relations and Colonial Rule*, p.97
34 ibid., p.97
35 Inglis, *Not a White Woman Safe*, p.51
36 Helen McLeod, *Cannibals are Human: A District Officer's Wife in New Guinea*, Angus & Robertson, Sydney, 1961, p.7
37 Inglis, *Not a White Woman Safe*, p.23
38 Wolfers, *Race Relations and Colonial Rule*, p.51
39 ibid., p.121
40 cited in Thelma Jackson, 'Australians in Papua', p.25
41 Judy Davis, unfinished manuscript prepared for doctoral dissertation and held at the Australian National University, Menzies Library, draft chapter entitled 'FW Race: version 2' p.10
42 Wolfers, *Race Relations and Colonial Rule*, p.135
43 Marie Reay, 'Women in transitional society: aspects of social, political and economic development' in E.K. Fiske (ed.), *New Guinea on the Threshold*, Longmans and Australian National University Press, London, 1966, p.172
44 Wolfers, *Race Relations and Colonial Rule*, p.129
45 Tim Bowden, *Taim Bilong Masta*, 'A Reason for Being There'

46 as Beatrice Grimshaw notes of her white heroes—see Chapter 1

47 quoted in Amirah Inglis, *Not a White Woman Safe*, p.24

48 Dixie Rigby, TRC 967/1-2, Oral History, National Library

49 Susan L. Blake, 'A woman's trek: what difference does gender make?', *Women's Studies International Forum*, vol. 13, no. 4, 1990, p.354

50 Callaway, *Gender, Culture and Empire*, p.73

51 Hasluck, *A Time for Building*, p.70

52 Lynn Sunderland, *The Fantastic Invasion: Kipling, Conrad and Lawson*, Melbourne University Press, Melbourne, 1989, p.17

53 ibid., p.28

54 ibid., p.13

55 ibid., p.73

56 Hasluck, *A Time for Building*, p.70

57 Rowley, *The New Guinea Villager*, p.12

58 Evelyn Cheeseman, *Who Stand Alone*, Geoffrey Bles, London, 1965, p.12

59 James Lyng, *Our New Possession*, Melbourne Publishing Company, Melbourne, 1919, pp.224–5

60 James McAuley, 'My New Guinea' *Quadrant*, vol. 5, no. 3, p.26

61 Rowley, *The New Guinea Villager*, p.166

62 Marilyn Frye, *The Politics of Reality: Essays in Feminist Theory*, Crossing Press, Trumansburg, New York, 1983, p.119

63 Mary Ann Lind, *The Compassionate Memsahibs: Welfare Activities of British Women in India, 1900–1947*, Greenwood Press, Westport, Connecticut, 1988, p.8

64 Margaret MacMillan, *Women of the Raj*, Thames & Hudson, London, 1988, p.62

65 Doris Groves, MS 6068, WC GROVES, Folder 27, Manuscripts Room, National Library, Canberra

66 Lucy Evelyn Cheeseman, *Time Well Spent*, Hutchinson, London, 1960, p.15

67 ibid., p.13

68 Joan Refshauge, MS 7026, JOAN REFSHAUGE, Folder 11, 'Speech delivered to Mission Conference 18/11/54' Manuscripts Room, National Library, Canberra

69 Paul Hoch, *White Hero Black Beast: Racism, Sexism and the Mask of Masculinity*, Pluto Press, London, 1979, p.161

70 Henry Louis Gates Jr, 'Introduction: writing "race" and the difference it makes' in Henry Louis Gates Jr (ed.), *"Race", Writing and Difference*, University of Chicago Press, Chicago, 1986, p.8

71 Dixie Rigby, TRC 967/1-2, Oral History, National Library, Canberra

72 Callaway, *Gender, Culture and Empire*, pp.222–3

73 Claudia Knapman, *White Women In Fiji 1835–1930: The Ruin of Empire?*, Allen & Unwin, Sydney, 1986, p.114

74 Judy Davis, unpublished manuscript, 'White Colonialism' no page numbers

75 Hank Nelson, 'From Kanaka to Fuzzy Wuzzy Angel' in Ann Curthoys and Andrew Markus (eds), *Who Are Our Enemies? Racism and the Working Class in Australia*, Hale & Iremonger, Sydney, 1978, p.177

76 Sios Tabunamagin, a pastor and tutor in the Methodist Mission, interviewed by Deane Fergie at Pakinsela Village, 5 July 1986

77 Salot Sailas interviewed by Deane Fergie at Resese Village, 8 July 1986

78 As masculine and empowering, in contrast with mental labour which is women's work;

Paul Willis, *Learning to Labour: How Working Class Kids get Working Class Jobs*, Saxon House, Farnborough, 1977

79 James McAuley, 'Christian Missions', *South Pacific*, vol. 8, no. 7, 1955, p.147

80 Andre Navarre, *Handbook of Missionaries of the Sacred Heart Working Among the Natives of Papua New Guinea*, Chevalier Press, Kensington, 1987, p.31

81 For example C.D. Rowley, *The New Guinea Villager*, p.155

82 T.O. Beidelman, *Colonial Evangelism: A Socio-Historical Study of an East African Mission at the Grassroots*, Indiana University Press, Bloomington, 1982, p.212

83 Diane Langmore, *Missionary Lives Papua 1874–1919*, University of Hawaii Press, Honolulu, 1989, p.126

84 Torogen Rontui interviewed by Deane Fergie at Huris, 7 July 1986

85 W.D. Oakes, report to the New Britain Synod, 1940, History Room, Methodist Mission, Rabaul

86 Sr A. Capell, 'Report on Education on Tabar', Papua New Guinea National Archives, Port Moresby, Box 72, 83/1/40, vol. 1, p 11

87 Extract from official diary of 'Cruise to New Guinea Sponsored by the Methodist Missionary Society of Australasia, t.s.s. *Katoomba* May 1939, File: Program of New Britain Mission Cruise 1939, History Room, Methodist Mission, Rabaul.

88 Chatterton, *Day That I Have Loved*, p.11; quoted in Lorna Fleetwood, *A Short History of Wewak*, East Sepik Provincial Government, Wewak, 1984, p.28

89 Doris Groves, MS 6068, WC GROVES, Folder 27, Manuscripts Room, National Library, Canberra

90 Hope, *Long Ago is Far Away*, pp.228–9

91 Reed, *The Making of Modern New Guinea*, pp.242–3

92 Alice Jeannette Keelan, *In the Land of Dohori*, Angus & Robertson, Sydney, 1929, p.143

93 Rowley, *The New Guinea Villager*, p.154

94 Callaway, *Gender, Culture and Empire*, p.37; Jackson, 'Australians in Papua' p.62; Abdul R. JanMohamed, 'The economy of Manichean allegory: the function of racial difference in colonialist literature', in Henry Louis Gates Jr (ed.), *"Race", Writing and Difference*, University of Chicago Press, Chicago, 1986, p.88; Knapman, *White Women in Fiji*, p.121

95 Henry Reynolds, *Frontier: Aborigines, Settlers and Land*, Allen & Unwin, Sydney, 1987, p.69

96 ibid., p.70

97 quoted in Ellen Kettle, *That They Might Live*, F.P. Leonard, Sydney, 1979, p.viii

98 Reed, *The Making of Modern New Guinea*, pp.242–3

99 Rachel Cleland, *Pathways to Independence: Official and Family Life, 1951–1975*, Artlook Books, Perth, 1983, p.171

100 Rowley, *The New Guinea Villager*, p.157

101 Hugh Laracy, *Marists and Melanesians: A History of Catholic Missions in the Solomon Islands*, University Press of Hawaii, Honolulu, 1976, pp.126–7

102 Ellen Kettle, That They Might Live, p.54

103 Aisoli Salin, ex-member of the Legislative Assembly, interviewed by Deane Fergie and Chilla Bulbeck at Tatau, 13 July 1986

104 Swarna Jayaweera, 'European educators under the British colonial administration in Sri Lanka', *Women's Studies International Forum*, vol. 13, no. 4, pp.323–32, 326

105 Terence Ranger, 'The invention of tradition in colonial Africa' in Eric Hobsbawm and Terence Ranger (eds), *The Invention of Tradition*, Cambridge University Press, Cambridge, 1984, pp.220–2

106 Philip D. Curtin, *The Image of Africa: British Ideas and Action 1780–1850*, Macmillan, London, 1965, p.383

107 Paul B. Rich, *Race and Empire in British Politics*, Cambridge University Press, Cambridge, 1986, p.36

108 Christine Bolt, *Victorian Attitudes to Race*, Routledge & Kegan Paul, London, 1971, p.77

109 O. Mannoni, *Prospero and Caliban: The Psychology of Colonization*, Methuen, London, 1956, p.198, translated by Pamela Powesland

110 Ruth First, 'Colonialism and the formation of African states' in David Held *et al.* (eds), *States and Societies*, Martin Robertson, Oxford, 1983, p.208

111 Albert Memmi, *The Colonizer and the Colonized*, Orion Press, New York, 1965, p.128, first published 1957

112 Patrick Brantlinger, 'Victorians and Africans: the genealogy of the myth of the Dark Continent' in Henry Louis Gates Jr (ed.), *"Race", Writing and Difference*, University of Chicago Press, Chicago, 1986, p.217

113 Frantz Fanon, *Black Skins, White Masks*, Macgebhen & Kel, London, 1968, p.18, translated by Charles Lam Markham; see also Memmi, *The Colonizer and the Colonized*, pp.121–8

114 Fanon, ibid., p.19

115 Gates Jr, 'Introduction', p.6

116 Fanon, *Black Skins, White Masks*, p.32; Knapman, *White Women in Fiji*, p.155

117 Robin Radford, *Highlanders and Foreigners in the Upper Ramu: The Kainantu Area 1919–1924*, Melbourne University Press, Melbourne, 1987, p.112

118 Hasluck, *A Time for Building*, p.89

119 Adapted from Peter Smith, *Education and Colonial Control in Papua New Guinea: a Documentary History*, Longman Cheshire, 1987, p.137

120 ibid., p.153

121 ibid., p.159

122 ibid., p.196

123 Dorothea Freund, *I Will Uphold You: Memoirs of Dorothea M. Freund*, edited by A.P.H. Freund, Lutheran Publishing House, Payneham, 1985, p.46

124 Pita Simogun and Merari Dickson in the Legislative Council in 1954: Smith, *Education and Colonial Control*, p.195

125 Australian Archives (ACT), CRS CP 316, series 1, bundle 1, part 1, CGT/IT 913/1/255 21/2/35

126 Reed, *The Making of Modern New Guinea*, p.xviii

127 Sios Tabunamagin, interviewed by Deane Fergie at Pakinsela Village, 5 July 1986

128 Doris Groves, MS 6068, WC GROVES, Folder 30, Manuscripts Room, National Library

129 Hasluck, *A Time for Building*, p.85

130 ibid., pp.91, 96, 225

131 Doris Groves, MS 6068, WC GROVES, Folder 27, Manuscripts Room, National Library, Canberra

132 Aisoli Salin, interviewed at Tatau, 13 July 1986

133 *South Pacific Post*, 30 November 1951, quoted in Wolfers, *Race Relations and Colonial Rule*, p.10

134 Aisoli Salin, interviewed at Tatau, 13 July 1986

135 Doris Groves, MS 6068, WC GROVES, Folder 30, Manuscripts Room, National Library, Canberra

136 Sr A. Capell, 'Report on Education on Tabar', Papua New Guinea National Archives, Port Moresby, Box 72, 83/1/40, vol. 1, p.14

137 Chatterton, *Day That I Have Loved*, pp.43–4

138 Prudence Frank, MS 6794, PRUDENCE FRANK, transcript of tape TRC 793, Manuscripts Room, National Library, Canberra

139 Albert Maori Kiki, *Ten Thousand Years in a Lifetime*, pp.68–9

140 ibid., pp.148–9

141 ibid., p.91

142 Cleland, *Pathways to Independence*, p.322

143 Smith, *Education and Colonial Control*, pp.258, 262

144 August Kituai, 'Innovation and intrusion: villagers and policemen in Papua New Guinea', *Journal of Pacific History*, vol. 23, no. 2, p.165

145 ibid., p.157

146 Helen McLeod, *Cannibals are Human: A District Officer's Wife in New Guinea*, Sydney, Angus & Robertson, 1961, p.122: the term used by her cook from Lae to describe the untouched Mendi people

147 Hope, *Long Ago is Far Away*, p.235

148 Dixie Rigby, TRC 967/1-2, Oral History, National Library, Canberra

149 Randolph Stowe, *Visitants*, Taplinger, New York, 1979, p.52

150 James McAuley, 'My New Guinea', *Quadrant*, vol. 5, no. 3, 1961, p.21

7: *Matters of sex*

1 Mary Ann Lind, *The Compassionate Memsahibs: Welfare Activities of British Women in India, 1900–1947*, Greenwood Press, Westport Connecticut, 1988, p.22

2 Helen Callaway, *Gender, Culture and Empire: European Women in Colonial Nigeria*, Macmillan in association with St Anthony's College, Basingstoke and London, 1987, p.5

3 ibid., p.4

4 ibid., p.15

5 Tim Bowden, *Taim Bilong Masta: The Australian Involvement with Papua New Guinea*, 'Moneymakers and Misfits', Australian Broadcasting Commission, Sydney, 1981

6 Joan Refshauge, MS 7026, JOAN REFSHAUGE, Folder 11, 'An Address on Discrimination Against Women in the Territory', Manuscripts Room, National Library, Canberra

7 Diane Langmore, *Missionary Lives Papua 1874–1919*, University Press of Hawaii, Honolulu, 1989, p.164

8 Doris R. Booth, *Mountains, Gold and Cannibals*, Cornstalk, Sydney, 1929, p.194

9 Callaway, *Gender, Culture and Empire*, p.5

10 Elsie Champion in Bowden, *Taim Bilong Masta*, 'Wife and Missus'

11 Claudia Knapman, *White Women in Fiji 1835–1930: The Ruin of Empire?*, Allen & Unwin, Sydney, 1986, p.114

12 Stephen J. Gould, *The Flamingo's Smile: Reflections in Natural History*, W.W. Norton & Co., New York, 1985, pp.291–300

13 Gustave Le Bon, a founder of social psychology in 1879, quoted in Stephen J. Gould, *The Mismeasure of Man*, Penguin, Harmondsworth, 1984, first published in 1981, p.105

14 Andrew Markus, 'Talk longa mouth' in Ann Curthoys and Andrew Markus (eds), *Who Are Our Enemies? Racism and the Working Class in Australia*, Hale & Iremonger, Sydney, 1979, pp.254–5

15 H.N. Nelson, 'European attitudes in Papua, 1906–1914' in The Research School of Pacific Studies (ed.), *The History of Melanesia*, Australian National University and University of Papua New Guinea, Canberra and Port Moresby, 1969, p.610

16 Knapman, *White Women in Fiji*, p.118

17 Hortense Spillers, 'Interstices: A Small Drama of Words' in Carol S. Vance (ed.), *Pleasure and Danger: Exploring Female Sexuality*, Routledge and Kegan Paul, Boston, 1984, p.79

18 Amirah Inglis, *Not a White Woman Safe: Sexual Anxiety and Politics in Port Moresby, 1920–1934*, Australian National University Press, Canberra, 1974, pp.72–3

19 Brian Easlea, *Patriarchy's Confrontation with Women and Nature*, Weidenfeld & Nicolson, London, 1981, pp.82, 125

20 Margaret MacMillan, *Women of the Raj*, Thames & Hudson, London, 1988, p.104

21 as a British man observed: MacMillan, ibid., p.106

22 C.D. Rowley, *The New Guinea Villager: A Retrospective from 1964*, Cheshire, Melbourne, 1964, p.192

23 quoted in Amirah Inglis, *Not a White Woman Safe*, p.53

24 Callaway, *Gender, Culture and Empire*, p.31

25 ibid., p.41

26 Edward W. Said, 'Orientalism reconsidered', *Cultural Critique*, no. 1, 1985, p.103

27 Edward W. Said, *Orientalism*, Penguin, Harmondsworth, 1985, first published in 1978, p.38

28 Marie de Lepervanche, 'Women, nation and the state in Australia' in Nira Yuval-Davis and Flora Anthias (eds), *Woman-Nation-State*, Macmillan, London, 1989, p.42

29 Said, 'Orientalism reconsidered'

30 Said, *Orientalism*, p.311

31 ibid., pp.311–5

32 MacMillan, *Women of the Raj*, p.220

33 Easlea, *Patriarchy's Confrontation*, p.126

34 Paul B. Rich, *Race and Empire in British Politics*, Cambridge University Press, Cambridge, 1986, p.30

35 Winthrop D. Jordan, *White Over Black: American Attitudes Toward the Negro 1550–1812*, University of North Carolina Press, Williamsburg, Virginia, 1968, p.473

36 Charles van Onselen, *Studies in the Social and Economic History of the Witwatersrand 1880–1914*. vol. 1, New Babylon, Longman, Harlow Essex, 1982, pp.137–147

37 Gould, *The Mismeasure of Man*, p.115

38 ibid., p.333

39 Marian Fowler, *Below the Peacock Fan: First Ladies of the Raj*, Viking, Markham Ontario, 1987, p.212

40 Patrick Brantlinger, 'Victorians and Africans: the genealogy of the myth of the Dark Continent' in Henry Louis Gates Jr (ed.) *"Race", Writing and Difference*, University of Chicago Press, Chicago, 1986, p.212

41 Randolph Stowe, *Visitants*, Taplinger, New York, 1979, p.189

42 ibid., p.187

43 Australian Archives (ACT), Prime Minister's Department, CRS CP 316, series 1, bundle 1, part 2, Executive Council Meeting—Papua 5/12/32; memo, 18/10/33

44 Edward P. Wolfers, *Race Relations and Colonial Rule in Papua New Guinea*, Australian and New Zealand Book Company, Brookvale, 1975, p.102

45 ibid., p.102

46 Lilian Overell, *A Woman's Impressions of German New Guinea*, John Lane and Bodley Head, London, 1923, p.178

47 Dixie Rigby, interviewed by Rosa Glastonbury 19 August 1979, TRC 967/1-2, Oral History, National Library, Canberra; Ann Deland, MS 4725, ANN DELAND, Manuscripts Room, National Library, Canberra

48 Pierre L. van den Berghe, *The Ethnic Phenomenon*, Elsevier, New York, 1981, pp.30–1

49 ibid., pp.26–7

50 ibid., p.109

51 ibid., p.75

52 ibid., p.76

53 Marie de Lepervanche, 'The "naturalness" of inequality' in Gill Bottomley and Marie de Lepervanche (eds), *Ethnicity, Class and Gender in Australia*, Allen & Unwin, Sydney, 1984, p.68

54 Susan Brownmiller, *Against Our Will: Men, Women and Rape*, New York, Simon & Schuster, 1975

55 Heath Dillard, 'Women in Reconquest Castile: the Fueros of Sepulveda and Cuenca' in Susan Mosher Stuard (ed.), *Women in Medieval Society*, University of Pennsylvania Press, Pennsylvania, 1976, p.87

56 MacMillan, *Women of the Raj*, p.103

57 Ronald Hyam, 'Empire and sexual opportunity' *Journal of Imperial and Commonwealth History*, vol. 14, no. 2, 1986, pp.64–6

58 MacMillan, *Women of the Raj*, p.56

59 cited in Patrick Brantlinger, 'Victorians and Africans', p.213

60 Reproduced in Greg Martin (ed.), *The Founding of Australia: The Argument About Australia's Origins*, Hale & Iremonger, Sydney, 1978, p.28

61 Brantlinger, 'Victorians and Africans' p.215

62 Ray Evans, ' "Don't You Remember Black Alice, Sam Holt?", Aboriginal Women in Queensland History' *Hecate*, vol. 8, no. 2, 1982, pp.10–11

63 Hyam, 'Empire and sexual opportunity' p.54

64 Cynthia Enloe, *Bananas, Beaches and Bases: Making Feminist Sense of International Politics*, Pandora, London, 1989, p.95

65 Hyam, 'Empire and sexual opportunity' p.75

66 Inglis, *Not a White Woman Safe*, p.18

67 Diane Langmore, *Missionary Lives Papua 1874–1919*, University Press of Hawaii, Honolulu, 1989, pp.245–6. Patricia Grimshaw reports that only two male missionaries fell from grace in her study of American missionaries in Hawaii; she also notes that the stress on marriage for male missionaries was a recognition of the inevitability of strong male sexual feelings: Patricia Grimshaw, *Paths of Duty: American Missionary Wives in Nineteenth-Century Hawaii*, University of Hawaii Press, Honolulu, 1989, pp.84–5

68 Hyam, 'Empire and sexual opportunity', pp.59–60

69 Amirah Inglis, *Not a White Woman Safe*, p.16 for Papua; Kenneth Ballhatchet, *Race, Sex and Class Under the Raj: Imperial Attitudes and Policies and their Critics, 1793–1905*, Weidenfeld & Nicolson, London, 1980, pp.153–4 for Burma; Beverley Gartrell, 'Colonial wives: villains or victims' in Hilary Callan and Shirley Ardener (eds), *The Incorporated Wife*, Croom Helm, London, 1983, p.169 for Uganda

70 Callaway, *Gender, Culture and Empire*, p.49

71 Hyam, 'Empire and sexual opportunity', p.35

72 ibid., p.44

73 Callaway, *Gender, Culture and Empire*, p.49

74 Inglis, *Not a White Woman Safe*, p.16

75 Joan Refshauge, personal papers held by Sir William Refshauge, Canberra

76 John Butcher, *The British in Malaya 1880–1914: The Social History of a European Community in Colonial South-East Asia*, Oxford University Press, Oxford, 1979, p.211

77 Hyam, 'Empire and sexual opportunity', p.61

78 Inglis, *Not a White Woman Safe*, p.147; a very few white women married Nigerian men in the 1960s although there were a good many mixed marriages of Nigerian men and white women abroad (Callaway, *Gender, Culture and Empire*, p.51). On the other hand white women married American Indians on the frontier from the 1880s (Glenda Riley, *Women and Indians on the Frontier 1825–1915*, University of New Mexico Press, Albequerque, 1984, p.181)

79 Thelma Jackson, Australians in Papua: The Effect of Changing Government Policies on Attitudes, 1945–1973, Honours thesis submitted to the Division of Asian and International Studies, Griffith University, Brisbane, 1988, p.36

80 Jens Sorensen Lyng, *Island Films: Reminiscences of "German New Guinea"*, Cornstalk, Sydney, 1925, pp.46–74

81 ibid., p.59

82 ibid., p.61

83 ibid., p.64

84 ibid., p.67

85 ibid., p.72

86 Bowden, *Taim Bilong Masta*, 'Moneymakers and Misfits'

87 Errol Flynn, *My Wicked Wicked Ways*, Putman, New York, 1959, p.71, my emphasis

88 ibid., p.71

89 Stowe, *Visitants*, pp.55, 73

90 Easlea, *Patriarchy's Confrontation*, p.82 and Sheila Jeffreys, *The Spinster and her Enemies: Feminism and Sexuality 1880–1930*, Pandora, London, 1987, p.178–9

91 Roger Bastide, 'Dusky Venus Black Apollo', *Race*, vol. 3, no. 1, 1961, p.12; Calvin C. Hernton, *Sex and Racism*, Andre Deutsch, London, 1969, p.114; Frantz Fanon, *Black Skins, White Masks*, Macgebhen & Kel, London, 1968, p.55, translated by Charles Lam Markmann

92 N.D. Oram, *Colonial Town to Melanesian City: Port Moresby 1884–1974*, Australian National University Press, Canberra, 1976, p.163; see also Jackson, 'Australians in Papua' pp.49, 63

93 Wolfers, *Race Relations and Colonial Rule*, p.99

94 ibid., p.135

95 Jackson, 'Australians in Papua' pp.48–9

96 MacMillan, *Women of the Raj*, p.64

97 Memoirs of the early 1900s, quoted in Margaret MacMillan, ibid., p.216

98 Callaway, *Gender, Culture and Empire*, p.50

99 Knapman, *White Women in Fiji*, pp.135, 168–9

100 The Science of Man in 1907, quoted in Raymond Evans *et al.*, *Race Relations in Colonial Queensland*, University of Queensland Press, St Lucia, 1988, first published 1975, p.109

101 Rebecca Scott, 'The Dark Continent: Africa as female body in Haggard's adventure fiction', *Feminist Review*, no. 32, pp.69–89

102 Knapman, *White Women in Fiji*, pp.113ff

103 Sidney Webb quoted in Knapman, ibid., p.176

104 MacMillan, *Women of the Raj*, p.97
105 Inglis, *Not a White Woman Safe*, p.23
106 Wolfers, *Race Relations and Colonial Rule*, p.106
107 ibid., p.99
108 Susan Gardner, 'Is racism "sexism extended"?: Feminist criticism, "Moral Panics" and *The Grass is Singing*' Hecate, vol. 11, no. 1, p.76
109 Jordan, *White Over Black*, p.35
110 Christine Bolt, *Victorian Attitudes to Race*, Routledge & Kegan Paul, London, 1971, p.136
111 ibid., p.136
112 Ballhatchet, *Race, Sex and Class Under the Raj*, pp.5, 121
113 Inglis, *Not a White Woman Safe*, p.24
114 Ballhatchet, *Race, Sex and Class Under the Raj*, p.6
115 Bolt, *Victorian Attitudes to Race*, p.140
116 Brantlinger, 'Victorians and Africans' p.213
117 Evans *et al.*, *Race in Colonial Queensland*, p.214
118 Quoted in Wolfers, *Race Relations and Colonial Rule*, p.135
119 MacMillan, *Women of the Raj*, p.105
120 ibid., p.215
121 Knapman, *White Women in Fiji*, p.170
122 Gardner, 'Is racism "sexism extended"?' p.88 (emphasis added)
123 James Sinclair, *Kiap: Australia's Patrol Officers in Papua New Guinea*, Pacific Publications, Sydney, 1981, p.177
124 ibid., p.171
125 Wolfers, *Race Relations and Colonial Rule*, p.57
126 Hank Nelson, *Taim Bilong Masta: Australian Involvement with Papua New Guinea*, Australian Broadcasting Commission, Sydney, 1982, p.104
127 Brownmiller, *Against Our Will*, chapter seven
128 In Rabaul there were 533 unmarried males and 89 unmarried females: Inglis, *Not a White Woman Safe*, p.27
129 ibid., p.31
130 ibid., p.37
131 ibid., p.22
132 ibid., p.66
133 quoted in Inglis, ibid., p.57
134 ibid., p.58
135 quoted in Inglis, *Not a White Woman Safe*, p.24
136 ibid., p.53
137 ibid., p.24
138 Judy Davis, unfinished manuscript prepared for doctoral dissertation and held at the Australian National University, Menzies Library, Draft chapter entitled 'Notes on Hortense Powdermaker' p.1
139 Overell, *A Woman's Impressions of German New Guinea*, pp.39–40
140 Judy Davis, unpublished manuscript, 'White Sexism version 2', p.19
141 Hank Nelson, 'The swinging index: capital punishment and British and Australian administration in Papua and New Guinea 1888–1945', *Journal of Pacific History*, vol. 13, part 3, 1978, p.152
142 Inglis, *Not a White Woman Safe*, p.109

143 Australian Archives (ACT) Prime Minister's Department, CRS CP 316, series 1, bundle 1, part 1, 'White Women's Protection Ordinance 1934–Papua 14/9/34'
144 Jackson, 'Australians in Papua' p.36. Daphney Bridgland was required by the police to have a gas gun
145 Stephen Windsor Reed, *The Making of Modern New Guinea*, American Philosophical Society Press, Philadelphia, 1943, p.251
146 Wolfers, *Race Relations and Colonial Rule*, p.99
147 Bowden, *Taim Bilong Masta*, 'You had to be Firm'
148 Callaway, *Gender, Culture and Empire*, p.236
149 Lett quoted by Inglis, *Not a White Woman Safe*, p.86
150 ibid., pp.107-8
151 ibid., p.54
152 Quoted in Wolfers, *Race Relations and Colonial Rule*, p.135
153 Judy Davis, unpublished manuscript, 'White Sexism version 2', p.21
154 Bowden, *Taim Bilong Masta*, 'Wife and Missus'
155 James A. Boutilier, 'European women in the Solomon Islands, 1900–1942: accommodation and change on the Pacific frontier' in Denise O'Brien and Sharon W. Tiffany (eds), *Rethinking Women's Roles: Perspectives from the Pacific*, University of California Press, Berkeley, 1984, p.197
156 ibid., p.187
157 Inglis, *Not a White Woman Safe*, p.146
158 D. Langmore, 'A neglected force: white women missionaries in Papua 1874–1914', *Journal of Pacific History*, vol. 17, no. 3, 1982, p.149
159 Dixie Rigby, TRC 967/1-2, Oral History, National Library, Canberra
160 Inglis, *Not a White Woman Safe*, p.143
161 Nora-Vagi Brash, 'Which way, Big Man?' in Ulli Beier (ed.), *Voices of Independence: New Black Writing from Papua New Guinea*, University of Queensland Press, St Lucia, 1980, adapted for radio by Peter Trist, pp.63, 149
162 Evelyn Hogan, 'Controlling the bodies of women: reading gender ideologies in Papua New Guinea' in Maev O'Collins *et al.* (eds), *Women and Politics in Papua New Guinea*, Working Paper Number 6, Research School of Pacific Studies, Australian National University, Canberra, 1985; see also Heather McRae, 'Reform of Family Law in Papua New Guinea' in David Weisbrot *et al.* (eds), *Law and Social Change in Papua New Guinea*, Butterworths, Sydney, 1982
163 Abdul Paliwala, 'Law and order in the village: the village courts' in David Weisbrot *et al.* (eds), *Law and Social Change in Papua New Guinea*, Butterworths, Sydney, 1982, p.208
164 Rowley, *The New Guinea Villager*, p.77
165 *Post-Courier*, 22 July 1988, p.5
166 See the collection of studies in Susan Taft (ed.), *Domestic Violence in Papua New Guinea*, Law Reform Commission of Papua New Guinea, Port Moresby, 1985
167 Janaki Nair, 'Uncovering the zenana: visions of Indian womanhood in Englishwomen's writings', *Journal of Women's History*, vol. 2, no .1, 1990, pp.16–17
168 Francis Bugotu, 'The impact of Western culture on Solomon Island society: a Melanesian reaction' in Research School of Pacific Studies (ed.), *The History of Melanesia*, Australian National University and University of Papua New Guinea, Canberra and Port Moresby, 1969, p.552
169 ibid., p.551
170 ibid., p.551

[171] Bob Connolly and Robin Anderson, *First Contact: New Guinea's Highlanders Encounter the Outside World*, Viking Penguin, New York, 1987, p.242

[172] ibid., p.240

[173] Mokei Wamp Wan in Connolly and Anderson, ibid., p.241

[174] ibid., pp.240–1

[175] Knapman, *White Women in Fiji*, p.173 for Fiji; Ann McGrath, *'Born in the Cattle'*, Allen & Unwin, Sydney, 1987, pp.76–83 for Aboriginal Australians

[176] Inglis, *Not a White Woman Safe*, p.114

[177] Lyng, *Island Films*, p.66

[178] ibid., p.68

[179] quoted in Boutilier, 'European women in the Solomon Islands', p.191

[180] Doris Lessing, *The Grass is Singing*, Penguin, Harmondsworth, 1961, pp.24, 116, 185

[181] Knapman, *White Women in Fiji*, p.151

[182] Peter Smith, *Education and Colonial Control in Papua New Guinea: A Documentary History*, Longman Chesire, Melbourne, 1987, p.47

[183] ibid., p.46

[184] Wolfers, *Race Relations and Colonial Rule*, p.65

[185] ibid., p.129

[186] Jackson, 'Australians in Papua' p.55

[187] Stowe, *Visitants*, p.53

[188] C.A.W. Monckton, *Some Experiences of a New Guinea Resident Magistrate*, John Lane, London, 1921, p.42

[189] Bill Gammage, 'The Rabaul Strike, 1929', *Journal of Pacific History*, vol. 10, part 3, 1975, pp.10, 13

[190] Beatrice Grimshaw, *The New New Guinea*, Hutchinson, London, 1910, p.89

[191] Ann Deland, MS 4725, ANN DELAND, Manuscripts Room, National Library, Canberra

[192] Penelope Hope, *Long Ago is Far Away: Accounts of the Early Exploration and Settlement of the Papuan Gulf Area*, Australian National University Press, Canberra, 1979, p.232

[193] Deborah Kirkwood, 'Settler wives in Southern Rhodesia: a case study' in Hilary Callan and Shirley Ardener (eds), *The Incorporated Wife*, Croom Helm, London, 1983, p.157

[194] Knapman, *White Women in Fiji*, p.155

[195] Boutilier, 'European Women in the Solomon Islands' p.187

[196] See Karen Tranberg Hansen, 'Body Politics: Sexuality, Gender and Domestic Service in Zambia', *Journal of Women's History*, vol. 2, no. 1, 1990, p.129, for the Zambian case

[197] ibid., p.125

[198] ibid., p.128

[199] Margaret Spencer, *Doctor's Wife in New Guinea*, Angus & Robertson, Sydney, 1959, p.37

[200] Knapman, *White Women in Fiji*, p.152

[201] Ann Deland, MS 4725, ANN DELAND, Manuscripts Room, National Library, Canberra

[202] Judy Davis, unpublished manuscript, 'Planters: Relationships', no page numbers

[203] Margaret Mead, *Blackberry Winter: My Earlier Years*, Angus & Robertson, London, 1981, first published in 1973, p.172

[204] Bowden, *Taim Bilong Masta*, 'Wife and Missus'

[205] Valerie Bock, *Ge Hama*, The Leprosy Mission, London, 1970, p.27

[206] Langmore, *Missionary Lives*, p.174

[207] Winifred Mathews, *Dauntless Women: Stories of Pioneer Wives*, Edinburgh House Press, London, 1949, p.82

[208] Gammage, 'The Rabaul Strike 1929' p.18

209 Doris R. Booth, *Mountains, Gold and Cannibals*, Cornstalk, Sydney, 1929, p.80

210 ibid., pp.133–4

211 Overell, *A Woman's Impressions of German New Guinea*, pp.71–2

212 Davis, unpublished manuscript, 'Planters: Women and Work', no page numbers

213 Evelyn Cheeseman, *Who Stand Alone*, Geoffrey Bles, London, 1965, p.21

214 Joan Gerstad, *The Jungle Was Our Home*, George Allen & Unwin, London, p.192

215 Boutilier, 'European women in the Solomon Islands', p.191

216 Bowden, *Taim Bilong Masta*, 'You had to be Firm'

217 Hope, *Long Ago is Far Away*, p.221

218 ibid., p.208

219 ibid., p.219

220 Riley, *Women and Indians on the Frontier*, p.170

221 Ellen Kettle, *That They Might Live*, F.P. Leonard, Sydney, 1979, pp.50–1

222 David Wetherall, *Reluctant Mission: The Anglican Church in Papua New Guinea 1891–1942*, University of Queensland Press, St Lucia, 1977, p.90

223 ibid., p.92

224 Knapman, *White Women in Fiji*, p.153

225 Ann Deland, MS 4725, ANN DELAND, Manuscripts Room, National Library, Canberra

226 Alice Jeannette Keelan, *In the Land of Dohori*, Angus & Robertson, Sydney, 1929, p.133

227 ibid, p.24

228 Ann Deland, MS 4725, ANN DELAND, Manuscripts Room, National Library, Canberra

229 Rachel Cleland, *Pathways to Independence: Official and Family Life 1951–1975*, Artlook Books, Perth, 1983, p.63

8: *Making a space for women*

1 Yvonne Kniebiehler and Régine Goutalier, *La Femme au Temps des Colonies*, Stock, Paris, 1985, p.17

2 ibid., p.18

3 Chilla Bulbeck, *One World Women's Movement*, Pluto, London, 1988, pp.101–4

4 Susan Gardner, 'Sir Paul and the Sleeping Beauty, or: some reflections on women, "development", and administration in Hasluck's *A Time For Building*, *Research in Melanesia*, vol. 2, no. 1/2, 1976, p.31

5 Stephen Windsor Reed, *The Making of Modern New Guinea*, American Philosophical Society Press, Philadelphia, 1943, p.102

6 O.H.K. Spate, 'Education and its problems' in E.K. Fiske (ed.), *New Guinea on the Threshold: Aspects of Social, Political and Economic Development*, Longmans and Australian National University Press, London, 1966, p.126

7 John Butcher, *The British in Malaya 1880–1914: The Social History of a European Community in Colonial South-East Asia*, Oxford University Press, Oxford, 1979, p.184; N.D. Oram, *Colonial Town to Melanesian City: Port Moresby 1884–1974*, Australian National University Press, Canberra, 1976, p.159

8 Diane Langmore, *Missionary Lives Papua 1874–1919*, University Press of Hawaii, Honolulu, 1989, p.172

9 1940 Synod, report on Namatanai Circuit by G.J. Platten, p.2; New Britain Synod 1933 Special reports—Education, p.2, History Room, Methodist Mission, Rabaul

[10] Dorothea Freund, *I Will Uphold You: Memoirs of Dorothea M. Freund*, edited by A.P.H. Freund, Lutheran Publishing House, Payneham, 1985, pp.55,182; see also Winifred Mathews, *Dauntless Women: Stories of Pioneer Wives*, Edinburgh House Press, London, 1959, p.6

[11] Judy Davis, unfinished manuscript prepared for doctoral dissertation and held at the Australian National University, Menzies Library, draft chapter entitled 'Planters: Women and Work' no page numbers

[12] W.P. Livingstone, *Mary Slessor of Calabar: Pioneer Missionary*, Hodder & Stoughton, London, date unknown but apparently *circa* 1915, p.344

[13] ibid., p.158

[14] Paul Hasluck, *A Time for Building: Australian Administration in Papua and New Guinea 1951–1963*, Melbourne University Press, Melbourne, 1976, p.92

[15] John Connell, 'Status or subjugation? Women, migration and development in the South Pacific', *International Migration Review*, vol. 18, no. 4, 1984, p.966

[16] Joan Refshauge, 'Speech to Mission Conference 18/11/1954' MS 7026, JOAN REFSHAUGE, Folder 11, Manuscripts Room, National Library, Canberra

[17] Vera Whittington, *Sister on Patrol: From the Missionary Experiences of Sister Dorothy Pederick*, Trinity Press, Rabaul, 1968, p.46

[18] Sios Tabunamagin, a pastor and tutor in the Methodist Mission, interviewed by Deane Fergie at Pakinsala Village, 5 July 1986

[19] Gardner, 'Sir Paul and the Sleeping Beauty', p.26

[20] Hasluck, *A Time for Building*, pp.327–330

[21] Helen Callaway, *Gender, Culture and Empire: European Women in Colonial Nigeria*, Macmillan in association with St Anthony's College Oxford, Basingstoke and London, 1987, p.4

[22] Donald Denoon with Kathleen Dugin and Leslie Marshall, *Public Health in Papua New Guinea: Medical Possibility and Social Constraint, 1884–1984*, Cambridge University Press, Cambridge, 1989, p.88

[23] Joan Refshauge, *Sydney Morning Herald*, 28 February 1959, p.11

[24] Denoon, *Public Health in Papua New Guinea*, p.119

[25] ibid., p.90

[26] ibid., p.112

[27] ibid., p.91

[28] ibid., p.87

[29] Ellen Kettle, *That They Might Live*, F.P. Leonard, Sydney, 1979, p.178

[30] Denoon, *Public Health in Papua New Guinea*, p.95

[31] Joan Refshauge, 'Speech to Mission Conference 18-11-1954' MS 7026, JOAN REFSHAUGE, Folder 11, Manuscripts Room, National Library, Canberra

[32] Hasluck, *A Time for Building*, p.330

[33] Denoon, *Public Health in Papua New Guinea*, p.39

[34] Rita Stacy (?), personal papers of Joan Refshauge, kept by Sir William Refshauge, Canberra

[35] Harry Jackman, letter to Joan Refshauge, Konedobu, 28 June 1963, personal papers of Joan Refshauge kept by Sir William Refshauge

[36] Joan Refshauge, 'Speech to Mission Conference 18-11-1954' MS 7026, Folder 11, Manuscripts Room, National Library

[37] Joan Refshauge, MS 7026, Folder 11, Manuscripts Room, National Library

[38] Joan Refshauge, personal papers kept by Sir William Refshauge

39 Nancy Rose Hunt, 'Domesticity and colonialism in Belgium Africa: Usumbura's *Foyer Social*, 1946–60', *Signs*, vol. 15, no. 3, p.447

40 quoted in ibid., p.451

41 quoted in ibid., p.455

42 ibid., p.466

43 Leslie A. Flemming, 'Introduction: studying women missionaries in Asia' in Leslie A. Flemming (ed.), *Women's Work for Women: Missionaries and Social Change in Asia*, Westview Press, Boulder, 1989, p.1

44 Jane Hunter, 'The home and the world: the missionary message of U.S. Domesticity' in Leslie A. Flemming (ed.), *Women's Work for Women: Missionaries and Social Change in Asia*, Westview Press, Boulder, 1989, p.160

45 ibid., p.162

46 ibid., p.164

47 Kniebiehler and Régine Goutalier, *La Femme au Temps des Colonies*, p.112

48 Carol Lee Bacchi, *Same Difference: Feminism and Sexual Difference*, Allen & Unwin, Sydney, 1990, pp.29–50

49 Janaki Nair, 'Uncovering the zenana: visions of Indian womanhood in Englishwomen's writings', *Journal of Women's History*, vol. 21, no. 1, p.19

50 ibid., p.21

51 ibid., p.23

52 Swarna Jayaweera, 'European women educators under the British colonial administration in Sri Lanka', *Women's Studies International Forum*, vol. 13, no. 4, 1990, pp.327-330.

53 Mary Ann Lind, *The Compassionate Memsahibs: Welfare Activities of British Women in India, 1900–1947*, Greenwood Press, Westport Connecticut, 1988, p.4

54 ibid., pp.30–1

55 Margaret MacMillan, *Women of the Raj*, Thames & Hudson, London, 1988, p.200

56 ibid., p.202

57 ibid., p.228

58 Barbara N. Ramusack, 'Cultural missionaries, maternal imperialists, feminist allies: British women activists in India, 1865–1945', *Women's Studies International Forum*, vol. 13, no. 4, 1990, p.319

59 Janice N. Brownfoot, 'Memsahibs in colonial Malaya: a study of European Wives in a British colony and protectorate 1900–1940', in Hilary Callan and Shirley Ardener (eds), *The Incorporated Wife*, Croom Helm, London, 1983, p.208

60 Callaway, *Gender, Culture and Empire*, p.210; Knapman, *White Women in Fiji 1835–1930: The Ruin of Empire?*, Allen & Unwin, Sydney, 1986, pp.70–71

61 Callaway, ibid., pp.239–40

62 Alice Wedega, *Listen My Country*, Pacific Publications, Sydney, 1981, p.85

63 Charles W. Forman, ' "Sing to the Lord a New Song": women in the churches of Oceania' in Denise O'Brien and Sharon W. Tiffany (eds), *Rethinking Women's Roles: Perspectives from the Pacific*, University of California Press, Berkeley, 1984, pp.163–4

64 Margarete Loko, 'The changing role of women in society', *Administration for Development*, no. 4, 1975, p.5

65 Wedega, *Listen My Country*, pp.87, 107–8

66 Geoff Maskelyne, 'Alcohol problems and women in Papua New Guinea', *Administration for Development*, no. 5, 1975, pp.41–49

67 For example see Marie Reay, 'Politics, development and women in the rural Highlands', *Administration for Development*, no. 5, 1975, pp.4–13

68 Susanne Bonnell, 'Equal participation by women: the role of Women's Councils at national and provincial level in Papua New Guinea', *Administration for Development*, no. 19, 1982, pp.30–1

69 Doris Groves, MS 6068, WC GROVES, Folder 31, Manuscripts Room, National Library, Canberra.

70 Callaway, *Gender, Culture and Empire*, pp.28, 76

71 Rachel Cleland, *Pathways to Independence: Official and Family Life 1951–1975*, Artlook Books, Perth, 1983, p.28

72 ibid., p.88

73 ibid., p.321

74 ibid., p.143

75 Janet Finch, *Married to the Job: Wives' Incorporation in Men's Work*, George Allen & Unwin, London, 1983

76 Cleland, *Pathways to Independence*, p.90

77 Cynthia Enloe, *Bananas, Beaches and Bases: Making Feminist Sense of International Politics*, Pandora, London, 1989, p.97

78 Knapman, *White Women in Fiji*, p.161

79 Margaret Reeson, *Currency Lass*, Albatross, Sutherland, 1985, pp.178–80

80 Glenda Riley, *Women and Indians on the Frontier 1825–1915*, University of New Mexico Press, Albequerque, 1984, pp.168–174

81 ibid., p.177

82 ibid., pp.176–7

83 Lorna Fleetwood, *A Short History of Wewak*, East Sepik Provincial Government, 1984, p.26

84 Judy Davis, unpublished manuscript, 'Outwomen', p.1

85 Lucy Evelyn Cheeseman, *Time Well Spent*, Hutchinson, London, 1960, p.126

86 Margaret Spencer, *Doctor's Wife in New Guinea*, Angus & Robertson, Sydney, 1959, p.36

87 Cleland, *Pathways to Independence*, p.62

88 Ann Deland, MS 4725, ANN DELAND, Manuscripts Room, National Library, Canberra

89 Penelope Hope, *Long Ago is Far Away: Accounts of the Early Exploration and Settlement of the Papua Gulf Area*, Australian National University Press, Canberra, 1979, p.216

90 Doris Groves, 'From G-String to Independence' MS 6068, WC GROVES, Folder 27, Manuscripts Room, National Library, Canberra

91 Marjorie King, 'American women's open door to Chinese women: which way does it open?', *Women's Studies International Forum*, vol. 13, no. 4, 1990, p.374, of American missionaries to China in the late 1890s

92 Whittington, *Sister on Patrol*, p.29; Freund, *I Will Uphold You*, p.146; Ena Somerville, *Our Friends the Papuans*, Australian Board of Missions, Sydney, no date, p.40

93 Dixie Rigby, interviewed by Rosa Glastonbury, 19 August 1979, TRC 967/1-2, Oral History, National Library, Canberra

94 Helen McLeod, *Cannibals are Human: A District Officer's Wife in New Guinea*, Angus & Robertson, Sydney, 1961, p.67

95 Gardner, 'Sir Paul and the Sleeping Beauty' pp.27–8

96 Knapman, *White Women in Fiji*, pp.4–9

97 Geoffrey Dutton in ibid., p.9

98 Callaway, *Gender, Culture and Empire*, p.3

99 Albert Memmi, *The Colonizer and the Colonized*, Orion Press, New York, 1965, first published in 1957, p.22

100 John Young, 'Race and sex in Fiji re-visited', *Journal of Pacific History*, vol. 23, no. 2, 1988, p.214

101 Jackie Huggins, ' "Firing on in the Mind", Aboriginal Women Domestic Servants in the Inter-war Years', *Hecate*, vol. 13, no. 2, 1987/8, pp.15–16

102 Beverley Gartrell, 'Colonial Wives: Villains or Victims' in Hilary Callan and Shirley Ardener (eds), *The Incorporated Wife*, Croom Helm, London, 1983, p.165

103 Callaway, *Gender, Culture and Empire*, p.27

104 MacMillan, *Women of the Raj*, p.16

105 ibid., p.62

106 C.D. Rowley, *The New Guinea Villager: A Retrospective from 1964*, Cheshire, Melbourne, 1964, p.74

107 James A. Boutilier, 'European women in the Solomon Islands, 1900–1942: accommodation and change on the Pacific frontier' in Denise O'Brien and Sharon W. Tiffany (eds), *Rethinking Women's Roles: Perspectives from the Pacific*, University of California Press, Berkeley, 1984, p.198

108 David Wetherall, *Reluctant Mission: The Anglican Church in Papua New Guinea 1891–1942*, University of Queensland Press, St Lucia, 1977, p.90

109 Langmore, *Missionary Lives Papua*, p.80

110 James McAuley, 'My New Guinea', *Quadrant*, vol. 5, no. 3, pp.26–7

111 ibid., p.25

112 ibid., p.25

113 ibid., p.27

114 Knapman, *White Women in Fiji*, p.17

115 Callaway, *Gender, Culture and Empire*, p.228

116 For example Caroline Ralston in 1971: see Knapman, *White Women in Fiji*, p.6

117 Gartrell, 'Colonial Wives: Villains or Victims'

118 Knapman, *White Women in Fiji*, p.11

119 Amirah Inglis, *Not a White Woman Safe: Sexual Anxiety and Politics in Port Moresby, 1920–1934*, Australian National University Press, Canberra, 1974

120 Knapman, *White Women in Fiji*, p.17; Callaway, *Gender, Culture and Empire*, p.234

121 Knapman, ibid., pp.10–12

122 Inglis, *Not a White Woman Safe*, p.16

123 Philip Mason, *Prospero's Magic: Some Thoughts on Class and Race*, Greenwood, Westport Connecticut, 1962, p.13

124 Janice N. Brownfoot, 'Memsahibs in colonial Malaya: a study of European wives in a British colony and protectorate 1900–1940' in Hilary Callan and Shirley Ardener (eds), *The Incorporated Wife*, Croom Helm, London, 1983, p.192

125 Callaway, *Gender, Culture and Empire*, p.235

126 Knapman, *White Women in Fiji*, p.138

127 Langmore, *Missionary Lives Papua*, p.80

128 Young, 'Race and Sex in Fiji Re-visited', p.220

129 Gartrell, 'Colonial Wives', p.182; see also Knapman, *White Women in Fiji*, p.131

130 Callaway, *Gender, Culture and Empire*, p.235

131 Inglis, *Not a White Woman Safe*, p.18

132 Kniebiehler and Goutalier, *La Femme au Temps des Colonies*, pp.87–89

133 Fleetwood, *A Short History of Wewak*, p.25

[134] Dea Birkett, *Spinsters Abroad: Victorian Lady Explorers*, Basil Blackwell, Oxford, 1989, p.77

[135] Young, 'Race and sex in Fiji re-visited', p.221

[136] Claudia Knapman and Caroline Ralston, 'Historical patchwork: a reply to John Young's "Race and sex in Fiji re-visited" ', *Journal of Pacific History*, vol. 24, no. 2, 1989, p.221

[137] Knapman, *White Women in Fiji*, p.136

[138] MacMillan, *Women of the Raj*, p.62

[139] Callaway, *Gender, Culture and Empire*, p.29

[140] Ramusack, 'Cultural missionaries, maternal imperialists, feminist allies', p.316

[141] Virginia Woolf, *Three Guineas*, Penguin, Harmondsworth, 1977, first published 1938, p.125

[142] Nancy L. Paxton, 'Feminism under the Raj: complicity and resistance in the writings of Flora Annie Steel and Annie Besant', *Women's Studies International Forum*, vol. 13, no. 4, pp.333–346

[143] Antoinette M. Burton, 'The white woman's burden: British feminists and the Indian woman, 1865–1915', *Women's Studies International Forum*, vol. 13, no. 4, 1990, p.306

[144] ibid., pp.298-9

[145] Callaway, *Gender, Culture and Empire*, pp.227–9, 232

[146] ibid., p.244

[147] ibid., p.244

[148] Diane Langmore, 'A neglected force: white women missionaries in Papua 1874–1914', *Journal of Pacific History*, vol. 24, no. 2, p.147

[149] Ann Deland, MS 4725, ANN DELAND, Manuscripts Room, National Library, Canberra

[150] Lilian Overell, *A Woman's Impressions of German New Guinea*, John Lane and Bodley Head, London, 1923, p.177 reports a more sympathetic treatment of a white male prisoner, allowed the run of Samarai, because at the time Samarai had only a 'native gaol'

[151] Judy Davis, unpublished manuscript, 'Framework', p.8

[152] ibid.

[153] Jane Haggis, 'Gendering colonialism or colonising gender? recent women's studies approaches to white women and the history of British colonialism', *Women's Studies International Forum*, vol. 13, no. 1/2, p.110

[154] ibid., p.112

[155] ibid., p.113

[156] Janaki Nair, 'Uncovering the zenana' pp.13–14

[157] Kniebiehler and Goutalier, *La Femme au Temps des Colonies*, p.317

[158] Nair, 'Uncovering the zenana', p.25

[159] Knapman, *White Women in Fiji*, p.143

[160] N.D. Oram, *Colonial Town to Melanesian City: Port Moresby 1884–1974*, Australian National University Press, Canberra, 1976, p.162

[161] Inglis, *Not a White Woman Safe*, pp.81, 100

[162] MacMillan, *Women of the Raj*, pp.221-2

[163] Young, 'Race and sex in Fiji re-visited', p.215

[164] ibid., p.215

[165] Knapman and Ralston, 'Historical patchwork', p.223

[166] Haggis, 'Gendering colonialism or colonising gender?', p.109, criticising Claudia Knapman and Helen Callaway

[167] Kniebiehler and Goutalier, *La Femme au Temps des Colonies*, p.17

[168] MacMillan, *Women of the Raj*, pp.64–5

[169] Kniebiehler and Goutalier, *La Femme au Temps des Colonies*, p.146

[170] Langmore, *Missionary Lives Papua*, p.80

[171] Reeson, *Currency Lass*, p.177

[172] MacMillan, *Women of the Raj*, p.236

[173] Knapman, *White Women in Fiji*, p.177

[174] Marian Fowler, *Below the Peacock Fan: First Ladies of the Raj*, Viking, Markham Ontario, 1987, p.309

Appendices

[1] Helen McLeod, *Cannibals are Human: a District Officer's Wife in New Guinea*, Angus & Robertson, Sydney, 1961, p.183

[2] Ellen Kettle, *That They Might Live*, F.P. Leonard, Sydney, 1979, pp.336–345; see also P. Biskup *et al.*, *A Short History of New Guinea*, Angus & Robertson, Sydney, 1968

Bibliography

Ardener, Shirley 'Ground rules and social maps for women: an introduction.' In Shirley Ardener (ed.), *Women and Space*. London, Croom Helm, 1981

Atkinson, Alan and Aveling, Marian (eds). *Australians 1838*. Broadway, NSW, Fairfax Syme & Weldon Associates, 1988

Bacchi, Carol Lee. *Same Difference: Feminism and Sexual Difference*. Sydney, Allen & Unwin, 1990

Ballard, John. 'Race and inequality: a critique: Ethnicity as a mask of confrontation'. In Christine Jennett and Randall G. Stewart (eds), *Three Worlds of Inequality: Race, Class and Gender*. Melbourne, Macmillan, 1987

Ballhatchet, Kenneth. *Race, Sex and Class under the Raj: Imperial Attitudes and Policies and their Critics, 1793–1905*. London, Weidenfeld and Nicolson, 1980

Banton, Michael. 'The concept of racism'. In Sami Zubaida (ed.), *Race and Racialism*. London, Tavistock, 1970

Barr, Pat. *The Dust in the Balance: British Women in India 1905–1945*. London, Hamish Hamilton, 1989

Bassett, L. Marnie. *Letters from New Guinea 1921*. Melbourne, Hawthorn Press, 1969

Bastide, Roger. 'Dusky Venus Black Apollo'. *Race*, vol. 3, no 1 (1961), pp. 10–18

Beidelman, T.O. *Colonial Evangelism: A Socio-Historical Study of an East African Mission at the Grassroots*. Bloomington, Indiana University Press, 1982

Birkett, Dea. *Spinsters Abroad: Victorian Lady Explorers*. Oxford, Basil Blackwell, 1989

Biskup, P., Jinks, B. and Nelson, H. *A Short History of New Guinea*. Sydney, Angus & Robertson, 1968

Blake, Susan L. 'A woman's trek: what difference does gender make?' *Women's Studies International Forum*, vol. 13, no. 4 (1990), pp. 347–56

Bock, Valerie. *Ge Hama*. London, The Leprosy Mission, 1970

Bolt, Christine. *Victorian Attitudes to Race*. London, Routledge & Kegan Paul, 1971

Bonnell, Susanne. 'Equal participation by women: the role of Women's Councils at national and provincial level in Papua New Guinea'. *Administration for Development*, no. 19, July (1982), pp. 23–36

Booth, Doris R. *Mountains, Gold and Cannibals*. Sydney, Cornstalk, 1929

Boutilier, James A. 'European women in the Solomon Islands, 1900–1942: accommodation and change on the Pacific frontier'. In Denise O'Brien and Sharon W. Tiffany (eds), *Rethinking Women's Roles: Perspectives from the Pacific*. Berkeley, University of California Press, 1984

——. Boutilier, James (1985) 'Papua New Guinea's colonial century: reflections on imperialism, accomodation and historical consciousness'. In Deborah Gewertz and Edward Schieffelin (eds), *History and Ethno-history in Papua New Guinea*. Oceania Monograph Number 5, Sydney, University of Sydney, 1985

Bowden, Tim. *Taim Bilong Masta: The Australian Involvement with Papua New Guinea*. Radio series broadcast by the Australian Broadcasting Commission, 1981

Boylan, Anne M. 'Evangelical womanhood in the nineteenth century: the role of women in Sunday Schools'. *Feminist Studies*, vol. 4, no. 3 (1978), pp. 62–80

Brantlinger, Patrick. 'Victorians and Africans: the genealogy of the myth of the Dark Continent'. In Henry Louis Gates Jr (ed.) *"Race", Writing and Difference*. Chicago, University of Chicago Press, 1986

Brash, Nora-Vagi. 'Which way, Big Man?' In Ulli Beier (ed.), *Voices of Independence: New Black Writing from Papua New Guinea*. St Lucia, University of Queensland Press, 1980. Adapted for radio by Peter Trist

Brownfoot, Janice N. 'Memsahibs in colonial Malaya; a study of European wives in a British colony and protectorate 1900–1940'. In Hilary Callan and Shirley Ardener (eds), *The Incorporated Wife*. London, Croom Helm, 1983

Brownmiller, Susan. *Against our Will: Men, Women and Rape*. New York, Simon & Schuster, 1975

Bugotu, Francis. 'The impact of Western culture on Solomon Island society: a Melanesian reaction' In Research School of Pacific Studies (ed.), *The History of Melanesia*. Canberra and Port Moresby, Australian National University and University of Papua New Guinea, 1969

Bulbeck, Chilla. *One World Women's Movement*. London, Pluto, 1988

Burkhart, Geoffrey. 'Danish women missionaries'. In Leslie A. Flemming (ed.), *Women's Work For Women: Missionaries and Social Change in Asia*. Boulder, Westview Press, 1989

Burns, W. Haywood. 'Law and race in America'. In David Kairys (ed.), *The Politics of Law*. New York, Pantheon, 1982

Burton, Antoinette M. 'The white woman's burden: British feminists and the Indian woman, 1865–1915'. *Women's Studies International Forum*, vol. 13, no. 4 (1990), pp. 309–22

Butcher, Benjamin T. *We Lived with Headhunters*. London, Hodder & Stoughton, 1963

Butcher, John. *The British in Malaya 1880–1914: The Social History of a European Community in Colonial South-East Asia*. Oxford, Oxford University Press, 1979

Callaway, Helen. *Gender, Culture and Empire: European Women in Colonial Nigeria*. Basingstoke and London, Macmillan in association with St Anthony's College, Oxford, 1987

Cashmore, E. Ellis. *The Logic of Racism*. London, Allen & Unwin, 1987

Chafe, William H. 'Sex and race: the analogy of social control'. *Massachusetts Review*, vol. 18, Spring (1977), pp. 147–78

Chatterton, Percy. *Day That I Have Loved*. Sydney, Pacific Publications, 1974

Cheeseman, Lucy Evelyn. *Things Worth While*. London, Hutchinson, 1957

——. *Time Well Spent*. London, Hutchinson, 1960

Cheeseman, (Lucy) Evelyn. *Who Stand Alone*. London, Geoffrey Bles, 1965

Cleland, Dame Rachel. *Pathways to Independence: Official and Family Life 1951–1975*. Perth, Artlook Books, 1983

Cock, Jacklyn. *Maids and Madams: Domestic Workers under Apartheid*. London, The Women's Press, 1989

Cohn, Bernard S. 'Representing authority in Victorian India'. In Eric Hobsbawm and Teence Ranger (eds), *The Invention of Tradition*. Cambridge, Cambridge University Press, 1983

Connell, John. 'Status or subjugation? Women, migration and development in the South Pacific'. *International Migration Review*, vol. 18, no. 4 (1984), pp. 964–83

Connolly, Bob and Anderson, Robin. *First Contact: New Guinea's Highlanders Encounter the Outside World*. New York, Viking Penguin, 1987

Curtin, Philip D. *The Image of Africa: British Ideas and Action 1780–1850*. London, Macmillan, 1965

——. (ed.). *Imperialism*. London, Macmillan, 1972

Custodian of Expropriated Property. *Sale of Expropriated Properties in the Territories of New Guinea and Papua*. Vol. 1 'First Group'. Melbourne, Commonwealth Government, 1925

——. *Sale of Expropriated Properties in the Territories of New Guinea and Papua.* Vol. 2 'Second Group'. Melbourne, Commonwealth Government, 1926

—— 1927. *Sale of Expropriated Properties in the Territories of New Guinea and Papua.* Vol. 3 'Third Group'. Melbourne, Commonwealth Government, 1927

Davidoff, Leonore and Hall, Catherine. *Family Fortunes: Men and Women of the English Middle Class 1780–1850.* London, Hutchinson, 1986

Davis, Judy, unpublished manuscript prepared for doctoral dissertation and held at the Australian National University Menzies Library

de Lepervanche, Marie. 'The "naturalness" of inequality'. In Gill Bottomley and Marie de Lepervanche (eds), *Ethnicity, Class and Gender in Australia.* Sydney, Allen & Unwin, 1984

——. 'Women, nation and the state in Australia'. In Nira Yuval-Davis and Flora Anthias (eds), *Woman-Nation-State.* London, Macmillan, 1989

Denoon, Donald with Kathleen Dugin and Leslie Marshall. *Public Health in Papua New Guinea: Medical Possibility and Social Constraint, 1884–1984.* Cambridge, Cambridge University Press, 1989

Dickson, D.J. 'W.C. Groves: Educationist'. In Griffin, James (ed.), *Papua New Guinea Portraits: The Expatriate Experience.* Canberra, Australian National University Press, 1978

Dillard, Heath. 'Women in Reconquest Castile: the Fueros of Sepulveda and Cuenca'. In Susan Mosher Stuard (ed.) *Women in Medieval Society.* Pennsylvania, University of Pennsylvania Press, 1976

Easlea, Brian. *Patriarchy's Confrontation with Women and Nature.* London, Weidenfeld and Nicolson, 1981

Enloe, Cynthia. *Bananas, Beaches and Bases: Making Feminist Sense of International Politics.* London, Pandora, 1989

Evans, Ray. ' "Don't You Remember Black Alice, Sam Holt?" Aboriginal Women in Queensland History'. *Hecate,* vol. 8, no. 2 (1982), pp. 6–21.

Evans, Raymond, Saunders, Kay and Cronin, Kathryn. *Race Relations in Colonial Queensland.* St Lucia, University of Queensland Press, 1988, first published 1975

Fairhall, Constance. *Where Two Tides Meet.* London, Livingstone Press, 1946

Fanon, Frantz. *Black Skins, White Masks.* Translated by Charles Lam Markmann. London, Macgebhen & Kel, 1968

Fels, Marie Hansen. *Good Men and True: The Aboriginal Police of the Port Phillip District 1837–1853.* Melbourne, Melbourne University Press, 1988

Fenn, C. *Bunyip Land.* London, Blackie & Son, 1885

Fleetwood, Lorna. *A Short History of Wewak.* Wewak, East Sepik Provincial Government, 1984

Flemming, Leslie A. 'Introduction: Studying Women Missionaries in Asia'. In Leslie A. Flemming (ed.), *Women's Work For Women: Missionaries and Social Change in Asia*. Boulder, Westview Press, 1989

Finch, Janet. *Married to the Job: Wives' Incorporation in Men's Work*. London, George Allen & Unwin, 1983

First, Ruth. 'Colonialism and the formation of African states'. In David Held *et al.* (eds), *States and Societies*. Oxford, Martin Robertson, 1983

Flynn, Errol. *My Wicked Wicked Ways*. New York, Putman, 1959

Forman, Charles W. ' "Sing to the Lord a New Song": women in the churches of Oceania'. In Denise O'Brien and Sharon W. Tiffany (eds), *Rethinking Women's Roles: Perspectives from the Pacific*. Berkeley, University of California Press, 1984

Fowler, Marian. *Below the Peacock Fan: First Ladies of the Raj*. Markham, Ontario, Viking, 1987

Freund, Dorothea. *I Will Uphold You: Memoirs of Dorothea M. Freund*. Edited by A.P.H. Freund. Payneham, Lutheran Publishing House, 1985

Frye, Marilyn. *The Politics of Reality: Essays in Feminist Theory*. Trumansburg, New York, Crossing Press, 1983

Gammage, Bill. 'The Rabaul Strike, 1929'. *The Journal of Pacific History*, vol. 10, part 3 (1975), pp. 3–29

Gardner, Susan. 'Sir Paul and the Sleeping Beauty, or: some reflections on women, "development" and administration in Hasluck's *A Time for Building*'. *Research in Melanesia*, vol. 2, no. 1/2, June (1976), pp. 22–31

—— 1977. 'For love and money: early writings of Beatrice Grimshaw, colonial Papua's woman of letters'. *New Literature Review* special issue: post-colonial literature (1977), pp. 10–20

——. 'Is racism "sexism extended"?: feminist criticism, "moral panics" and *The Grass is Singing*'. *Hecate*, vol. 11, no. 1 (1985), pp. 75–97

Gartrell, Beverley. 'Colonial wives: villains or victims'. In Hilary Callan and Shirley Ardener (eds), *The Incorporated Wife*. London, Croom Helm, 1983

Gates Jr, Henry Louis. 'Introduction: writing, "Race" and the difference it makes'. In Henry Louis Gates Jr (ed.), *"Race", Writing and Difference*. Chicago, University of Chicago Press, 1986

Gerstad, Joan. *The Jungle was our Home*. London, George Allen & Unwin, 1957

Gilman, Sander L. 'Towards an iconography of female sexuality in late nineteenth century art, medicine and literature'. In Henry Louis Gates Jr (ed.), *"Race", Writing and Difference*. Chicago, University of Chicago Press, 1985

Gould, Stephen J. *The Mismeasure of Man*. Harmondsworth, Penguin, 1984, first published 1981

——. *The Flamingo's Smile: Reflections in Natural History*. New York, W.W. Norton & Co., 1985

Green, Neville. *Broken Spears: Aborigines and Europeans in the Southwest of Australia*. Perth, Focus Education Books, 1984

Grimshaw, Beatrice. *The New New Guinea*. London, Hutchinson. 1910

——. *When the Red Gods Call*. 2nd ed. London, Mills and Boon, 1911

——. *My Lady Far-Away*. London, Cassell & Co., 1929

——. *Isles of Adventure*. London, Herbert & Jenkins, 1930

Grimshaw, Patricia 1983. ' "Christian woman, pious wife, faithful mother, devoted missionary": conflicts in roles of American missionary women in nineteenth century Hawaii'. *Feminist Studies*, vol. 9, no. 3 (1983), pp. 489–518

——. *Paths of Duty: American Missionary Wives in Nineteenth-Century Hawaii*. Honolulu, University of Hawaii Press, 1989

Groves, W.C. 'Report on field work in New Ireland'. *Oceania*, vol. 3, no. 3 (1932–33), pp.325–61

——. 'Tabar today: a study of a Melanesian community in contact with alien non-primitive cultural forces'. *Oceania*, vol. 5, no. 2 (1934–35), pp.224–40; vol. 5, no. 3 (1934–35), pp.346–61

——. 'Tabar today: Part II—present day conditions in Tatau Village'. *Oceania*, vol. 6, no. 2 (1935–36), pp.147–57

Haggis, Jane. 'Gendering colonialism or colonising gender? recent women's studies approaches to white women and the history of British colonialism'. *Women's Studies International Forum*, vol. 13, no. 1/2 (1990), pp.105–15

Hansen, Karen Tranberg. 'Body politics: sexuality, gender, and domestic service in Zambia'. *Journal of Women's History*, vol. 2, no. 1 (1990), pp.120–42

Hasluck, Paul. *A Time For Building: Australian Administration in Papua and New Guinea 1951–1963*. Melbourne, Melbourne University Press, 1976

Hernton, Calvin C. *Sex and Racism*. London, André Deutsch, 1969

Hides, J.G. *Savages in Serge*. Sydney, Angus & Robertson, 1938

Hill, Patricia R. *The World their Household: The American Women's Foreign Mission Movement and Cultural Transformation, 1870–1920*. Ann Arbor, University of Michigan Press, 1985

Hoch, Paul. *White Hero Black Beast: Racism, Sexism and the Mask of Masculinity*. London, Pluto Press, 1979

Hodes, W. Willam. 'Women and the constitution: some legal history and a new approach to the Nineteenth Amendment'. *Rutgers Law Journal*, vol. 25, no. 1 (1970), pp.26–53

Hogan, Evelyn. 'Controlling the bodies of women: reading gender ideologies in Papua New Guinea'. In Maev O'Collins *et al.* (eds), *Women and Politics* in *Papua New Guinea*. Working Paper No. 6. Canberra, Department of Political and Social Change, Research School of Pacific Studies, Australian National University, 1985

Hooley, J.F. 'The Clapham Omnibus Man in Papua New Guinea'. In B.J. Brown (ed.) *Fashion of Law in New Guinea*. Sydney, Butterworths, 1969

Hope, Penelope. *Long Ago is Far Away: Accounts of the Early Exploration and Settlement of the Papuan Gulf Area*. Canberra, Australian National University Press, 1979

Hudson, W.J. 'New Guinea Mandate: the view from Geneva'. In Research School of Pacific Studies (ed.), *The History of Melanesia*. Canberra and Port Moresby. Australian National University and University of Papua New Guinea, 1969

Huggins, Jackie. ' "Firing on in the Mind" Aboriginal women domestic servants in the inter-war years'. *Hecate* vol. 13, no. 2 (1987–88), pp.5–23

Huie, Shirley Fenton. *Tiger Lilies: Women Adventurers in the South Pacific*. Sydney, Angus & Robertson, 1990

Hunt, Nancy Rose. 'Domesticity and colonialism in Belgium Africa: Usumbura's *Foyer Social*, 1946–60'. *Signs*, vol. 15, no. 3 (1990), pp.447–74

Hunter, Jane. *The Gospel of Gentility: American Women Missionaries in Turn of the Century China*. New Haven and London, Yale University Press, 1984

—— (1989). 'The home and the world: the missionary message of U.S. domesticity'. In Leslie A. Flemming (ed.), *Women's Work For Women: Missionaries and Social Change in Asia*. Boulder, Westview Press, 1989

Hyam, Ronald. 'Empire and sexual opportunity'. *Journal of Imperial and Commonwealth History*, vol. 14, no. 2 (1986), pp.34–90

Inglis, Amirah. *Not a White Woman Safe: Sexual Anxiety and Politics in Port Moresby, 1920–1934*. Canberra, Australian National University Press, 1974

Inglis, K.S. 'War, race and loyalty in New Guinea, 1939–1945'. In Research School of Pacific Studies (ed.), *The History of Melanesia*. Canberra and Port Moresby, Australian National University and University of Papua New Guinea, 1969

Jackson, Thelma. 'Australians in Papua: the effect of changing government policies on attitudes, 1945–1973'. Honours thesis submitted to Division of Asian and International Studies, Griffith University, Brisbane, 1988

Jacobs, Sylvia M. 'African-American women missionaries and European imperialism in southern Africa, 1880–1920'. *Women's Studies International Forum*, vol. 13, no. 4 (1990), pp.381–94

JanMohamed, Abdul R. 'The economy of Manichean allegory: the function of racial difference in colonialist literature'. In Henry Louis Gates Jr (ed.), *"Race", Writing and Difference*. Chicago, University of Chicago Press, 1986

Jayawardena, Kumari. *Feminism and Nationalism in the Third World*. London, Zed, 1986

Jayaweera, Swarna. 'European women educators under the British colonial administration in Sri Lanka'. *Women's Studies International Forum*, vol. 13, no. 4 (1990), pp. 323–32

Jeffreys, Sheila. *The Spinster and her Enemies: Feminism and Sexuality 1880–1930*. London, Pandora, 1987

Jinks, B., Biskup, P. and Nelson, H. *Readings in New Guinea History*. Sydney, Angus & Robertson, 1973

Jordan, Winthrop D. *White Over Black: American Attitudes Toward the Negro 1550–1812*. Williamsburg, Virginia, University of North Carolina Press, 1968

Joyce, R.B. 'William MacGregor: The Role of the Individual'. In Research School of Pacific Studies (ed.), *The History of Melanesia*. Canberra and Port Moresby, Australian National University and University of Papua New Guinea, 1969

Keelan, Alice Jeannette. *In the Land of Dohori*. Sydney, Angus & Robertson, 1929

Kettle, Ellen. *That They Might Live*. Sydney, F.P. Leonard, 1979

Kiki, Albert Maori. *Ten Thousand Years in a Life Time*. Melbourne, Cheshire, 1968

King, Marjorie. 'American women's Open Door to Chinese women: which way does it open?' *Women's Studies International Forum*, vol. 13, no. 4 (1990), pp.369–80

Kirkwood, Deborah. 'Settler wives in Southern Rhodesia: a case study'. In Hilary Callan and Shirley Ardener (eds), *The Incorporated Wife*. London, Croom Helm, 1983

Kituai, August. 'Innovation and intrusion: villagers and policemen in Papua New Guinea'. *Journal of Pacific History*, vol. 23, no. 2 (1988), pp.156–66

Knapman, Claudia. *White Women in Fiji 1835-1930: The Ruin of Empire?* Sydney, Allen & Unwin, 1986

Knapman, Claudia and Ralston, Caroline. 'Historical patchwork: a reply to John Young's "Race and sex in Fiji re-visited" '. *Journal of Pacific History*, vol. 24, no. 2 (1989), pp.221–24

Kniebiehler, Yvonne and Goutalier, Régine. *La Femme au Temps des Colonies*. Paris, Stock, 1985

Langmore, D. 'A neglected force: white women missionaries in Papua 1874–1914'. *Journal of Pacific History*, vol. 17, no. 3, July (1982), pp.138–57

—— . *Missionary Lives Papua 1874–1919*. Honolulu, Centre for Pacific Studies, University Press of Hawaii, 1989

Laracy, Eugenie and Hugh. 'Beatrice Grimshaw: pride and prejudice in Papua'. *The Journal of Pacific History*, vol. 12, part 3 (1977), pp.155–75

Laracy, Hugh. *Marists and Melanesians: A History of Catholic Missions in the Solomon Islands*. Honolulu, University Press of Hawaii, 1976

Lessing, Doris. *The Grass is Singing*. Harmondsworth, Penguin, 1961

Lewins, Frank and Ly, Judith. *The Second Wave*. Sydney, Allen & Unwin, 1985

Lind, Mary Ann. *The Compassionate Memsahibs: Welfare Activities of British Women in India, 1900–1947*. Westport, Connecticut, Greenwood Press, 1988

Linge, Hosea. *An Offering Fit For a King*. Translated by Neville Threlfall. Rabaul, Toksave na Buk Dipatmen, United Church, New Guinea Islands Region, 1978

Linggood, Mrs E. *New Britain: Three Missionary Studies*. Victoria, Young Women's Missionary Movement, no date

Livingstone, W.P. *Mary Slessor of Calabar: Pioneer Missionary*. London, Hodder & Stoughton, *circa* 1915

Loko, Margarete. 'The changing role of women in society'. *Administration for Development*, no. 4, March (1975), pp.4–6

Lyng, James. *Our New Possession*. Melbourne, Melbourne Publishing Company, 1919

Lyng, Jens Sorensen. *Island Films: Reminiscences of "German New Guinea"*. Sydney, Cornstalk, 1925

McAuley, James. 'Christian missions'. *South Pacific*, vol. 8, no. 7, August (1955), pp.138–46

——. 'My New Guinea'. *Quadrant*, vol. 5, no. 3 (1961), pp.15–27

McCoy, Mildred M. 'Focus on the expatriate woman'. In Marjorie Spotts Litsinger and Alice Flinn (eds), *The Expatriate Experience: A Symposium*. Laguna, Philipines, In Touch Foundation, 1986

McGrath, Ann. *'Born in the Cattle'*. Sydney, Allen & Unwin, 1987

McLeod Helen. *Cannibals are Human: A District Officer's Wife in New Guinea*. Sydney, Angus & Robertson, 1961

MacMillan, Margaret. *Women of the Raj*. London, Thames & Hudson, 1988

McRae, Heather. 'Reform of family law in Papua New Guinea'. In David Weisbrot *et al.* (eds), *Law and Social Change in Papua New Guinea*. Sydney, Butterworths, 1982

Mannoni, O. *Prospero and Caliban: The Psychology of Colonization*. Translated by Pamela Powesland. London, Methuen, 1956

Markus, Andrew. 'Talk Longa Mouth'. In Ann Curthoys and Andrew Markus (eds), *Who Are Our Enemies? Racism and the Working Class in Australia*. Sydney, Hale and Iremonger, 1978

Martin, Greg (ed.), *The Founding of Australia: The Argument about Australia's Origins*. Sydney, Hale and Iremonger, 1978

Martin, Jean. 'Forms of Recognition'. In Ann Curthoys and Andrew Markus (eds), *Who Are Our Enemies? Racism and the Working Class in Australia*. Sydney, Hale and Iremonger, 1978

Maskalyne, Geoff. 'Alcohol problems and women in Papua New Guinea'. *Administration for Development*, no. 19, July (1982), pp.41–9

Mason, Philip. *Prospero's Magic: Some Thoughts on Class and Race*. Westport, Connecticutt, Greenwood, 1962

Mason, David. 'Introduction: controversies and continuities in race and ethnic relations theory'. In John Rex and David Mason (eds), *Theories of Race and Ethnic Relations*. Cambridge, Cambridge University Press, 1986

Mathews, Winifred. *Dauntless Women: Stories of Pioneer Wives*. London, Edinburgh House Press, 1949

Mead, Margaret. *Blackberry Winter: My Earlier Years*. London, Angus & Robertson, 1981, first published 1973

Memmi, Albert. *The Colonizer and the Colonized*. New York, Orion Press, 1965, first published 1957

Miles, Robert. *Capitalism and Unfree Labour: Anomaly or Necessity?* London, Tavistock, 1987

Mobley, Harris W. *The Ghanian's Image of the Missionary. An Analysis of the Published Critiques of Christian Missionaries by Ghanians 1897–1965*. Leiden, E.J. Brill, 1970

Monckton, C.A.W. *Some Experiences of a New Guinea Resident Magistrate*. London, John Lane, 1921

Moresby, Isabelle. *New Guinea—The Sentinel*. Melbourne, Tombs, 1943

Murphy, Ann B. 'The borders of ethical, erotic and artistic possibilities in *Little Women*'. *Signs*, vol. 15, no. 3 (1990), pp.562–85

Murphy, Lindsay and Livingstone, Jonathan. 'Racism and the limits of radical feminism'. *Race and Class*, vol. 26, no. 4 (1985), pp.61–70

Murray, Col. J.K. 'In retrospect 1945–1952: Papua New Guinea and the Territory of Papua and New Guinea'. In Research School of Pacific Studies (ed.), *The History of Melanesia*. Canberra and Port Moresby, Australian National University and University of Papua New Guinea, 1969

Nair, Janaki. 'Uncovering the zenana: visions of Indian womanhood in Englishwomen's writings'. *Journal of Women's History*, vol. 2, no. 1 (1990), pp.8–34

Navarre, Andre. *Handbook for Missionaries of the Sacred Heart Working Among the Natives of Papua New Guinea*. Kensington, Sydney, Chevalier Press, 1987

Nelson, H.N. 'European attitudes in Papua, 1906–1914'. In Research School of Pacific Studies (ed.), *The History of Melanesia*. Canberra and Port

Moresby, Australian National University and University of Papua New Guinea, 1969

Nelson, Hank. 'From Kanaka to Fuzzy Wuzzy Angel'. In Ann Curthoys and Andrew Markus (eds), *Who Are Our Enemies? Racism and the Working Class in Australia*. Sydney, Hale & Iremonger, 1978

——. 'The swinging index: capital punishment and British and Australian administrations in Papua and New Guinea, 1888–1945'. *Journal of Pacific History*, vol. 13, part 3 (1978), pp.130–52

——. *Taim Bilong Masta: Australian Involvement with Papua New Guinea*. Based on ABC radio series produced by Tim Bowden. Sydney, Australian Broadcasting Commission, 1982

Oala-Rarua, Oala. 'Race relations'. In Peter Hastings (ed.), *Papua New Guinea: Prospero's Other Island*. Sydney, Angus & Robertson, 1971

Oram, N.D. *Colonial Town to Melanesian City: Port Moresby 1884–1974*. Canberra, Australian National University Press, 1976

Overell, Lilian. *A Woman's Impressions of German New Guinea*. London, John Lane and Bodley Head, 1923

Paliwala, Abdul. 'Law and order in the village: the village courts'. In David Weisbrot *et al.* (eds), *Law and Social Change in Papua New Guinea*. Sydney, Butterworths, 1982

Pateman, Carole. *The Sexual Contract*. London, Polity Press, 1988

Paxton, Nancy L. 'Feminism under the Raj: complicity and resistance in the writings of Flora Annie Steel and Annie Besant'. *Women's Studies International Forum*, vol. 13, no. 4, pp.333–46

Radford, Robin. *Highlanders and Foreigners in the Upper Ramu: The Kainantu Area 1919–1942*. Melbourne, Melbourne University Press, 1987

Radi, Heather. 'New Guinea under mandate 1921–41'. In W.J. Hudson (ed.), *Australia and Papua New Guinea*. Sydney, Sydney University Press, 1971

Ramusack, Barbara N. 'Cultural missionaries, maternal imperialists, feminist allies: British women activists in India, 1865–1945'. *Women's Studies International Forum*, vol. 13, no. 4 (1990), pp.309–22

Ranger, Terence. 'The invention of tradition in colonial Africa'. In Eric Hobsbawm and Terence Ranger (eds), *The Invention of Tradition*. Cambridge, Cambridge University Press, 1984

Reay, Marie. 'Women in transitional society: aspects of social, political and economic development'. In E.K. Fiske (ed.), *New Guinea on the Threshold*. London, Longmans and Australian National University Press, 1966

——. 'Politics, development, and women in the rural Highlands'. *Administration for Development*, no. 5, October (1975), pp.4–13

Reece, Bob. 'Inventing Aborigines'. *Aboriginal History*, vol. 11, nos 1–2 (1987), pp.14–23

Reed, Stephen Windsor. *The Making of Modern New Guinea*. Philadelphia, American Philosophical Society Press, 1943

Reeson, Margaret. *Torn Between Two Worlds*. Madang, Kristen Press, 1972

———. *Currency Lass*. Sutherland, Albatross, 1985

Rex, John. 'The role of class analysis in the study of race relations—a Weberian perspective'. In John Rex and David Mason (eds), *Theories of Race and Ethnic Relations*. Cambridge, Cambridge University Press, 1986

Rex, John. 'Ethnicity and race'. In Peter Worsley (ed.), *The New Introducing Sociology*. Harmondsworth, Penguin, 1987

Reynolds, Henry. *Frontier: Aborigines, Settlers and Land*. Sydney, Allen & Unwin, 1987

Rich, Paul B. *Race and Empire in British Politics*. Cambridge, Cambridge University Press, 1986

Rickard, Mrs R.H. Papers of Mrs R.H. Rickard relating to the New Guinea Islands. Manuscript No. 19, (no date). Pacific Manuscripts Bureau, Australian National University

Riley, Glenda. *Women and Indians on the Frontier 1825–1915*. Albequerque, University of New Mexico Press, 1984

———. *The Female Frontier: A Comparative View of Women on the Prairie and the Plains*. Kansas, University of Kansas Press, 1988

Rowbotham, Sheila. 'Edward Carpenter'. in Sheila Rowbotham and Jeffrey Weeks, *Socialism and the New Life*. London, Pluto, 1977

Rowley, C.D. *The New Guinea Villager: A Retrospective from 1964*. Melbourne, Cheshire, 1964

Said, Edward W. *Orientalism*. Harmondsworth, Penguin, 1985, first published 1978

———. 'Orientalism reconsidered'. *Cultural Critique*, no. 1, Fall (1985), pp.98–107

Scott, Rebecca. 'The Dark Continent: Africa as female body in Haggard's adventure fiction'. *Feminist Review*, no. 32, Summer (1989), pp.69–89

Shlomowitz, Ralph. 'Mortality and indentured labour in Papua (1885–1941) and New Guinea (1920–1941)'. *Journal of Pacific History*, vol. 23, no. 1 (1988), pp.70–9

Sinclair, James. *Kiap: Australia's Patrol Officers in Papua New Guinea*. Sydney, Pacific Publishers, 1981

Smith, M.G. 'Pluralism, race and ethnicity in selected African countries'. In John Rex and David Mason (eds), *Theories of Race and Ethnic Relations*. Cambridge, Cambridge University Press, 1986

Smith, Peter. *Education and Colonial Control in Papua New Guinea: A Documentary History*. Melbourne, Longman Cheshire, 1987

Smith, Woodruff D. *European Imperialism in the Nineteenth and Twentieth Centuries*. Chicago, Nelson-Hall, 1982

Somerville, Ena. *Our Friends the Papuans*. Sydney, Australian Board of Missions, no date

———. *Papuan Secrets*. Sydney, Australian Board of Missions, no date

Spate, O.H.K. 'Education and its problems'. In E.K. Fiske (ed.), *New Guinea on the Threshold: Aspects of Social, Political and Economic Development*. London, Longmans and Australian National University Press, 1966

Spencer, Margaret. *Doctor's Wife in New Guinea*. Sydney, Angus and Robertson, 1959

Spillers, Hortense. 'Interstices: a small drama of words'. In Carol S. Vance (ed.), *Pleasure and Danger: Exploring Female Sexuality*. Boston, Routledge & Kegan Paul, 1984

Stember, Charles Hubert. *Sexual Racism: The Emotional Barrier to Integrated Society*. New York, Elsevier, 1976

Stowe, Randolph. *Visitants*. New York, Taplinger, 1979

Sunderland, Lynn. *The Fantastic Invasion: Kipling, Conrad and Lawson*. Melbourne, Melbourne University Press, 1989

Taft, Susan (ed.). *Domestic Violence in Papua New Guinea*. Port Moresby, Law Reform Commission of Papua New Guinea, 1985

Thompson, Roger C. 'Making a mandate: the formation of Australia's New Guinea policies 1919–1925'. *Journal of Pacific History*, vol. 25, no. 1 (1990), pp.68–84

Threlfall, Neville. *One Hundred Years in the Islands*. Rabaul, Toksave na Buk Dipatmen, The United Church, New Guinea Islands Region, 1976

Tiffany, Sharon W. and Adams, Kathleen J. *The Wild Women: An Enquiry into the Anthropology of an Idea*. Cambridge, Schenkman, 1985

Timms, Flora A. *Mary McLean: First Missionary of the WMA. A Memorial*. Sydney, Robert Dey, Son & Co., 1943

Trustrum, Myna. *Women of the Regiment: Marriage and the Victorian Army*. Cambridge, Cambridge University Press, 1984

Tucker, Sara W. 'Opportunities for women: the development of professional women's medicine in Canton, China, 1879–1901'. *Women's Studies International Forum*, vol. 13, no. 4 (1990), pp.357–68

van den Berghe, Pierre L. *Race and Racism: A Comparative Perspective*. New York and London, John Wiley & Sons, 1967

———. *The Ethnic Phenomenon*. New York, Elsevier, 1981

———. 'Ethnicity and the sociobiology debate'. In John Rex and David Mason (eds), *Theories of Race and Ethnic Relations*. Cambridge, Cambridge University Press, 1986

van den Boogart, Ernst. 'Colour prejudice and the yardstick of civility: the initial Dutch confrontation with black Africans, 1590–1635'. In Robert Ross (ed.), *Racism and Colonialism*. Hague, Martinus Nijhoff, 1982

van Onselen, Charles. *Studies in the Social and Economic History of the Witwatersrand 1880–1914, Vol 1: New Babylon*. Harlow Essex, Longman, 1982

Ward, Glenyse. *Wandering Girl*. Broome, Western Australia, Magabala Books, 1987

Wedega, Alice. *Listen My Country*. Sydney, Pacific Publications, 1981

Weisbrot, David. 'Integration of laws in Papua New Guinea: custom and the criminal law in conflict'. In David Weisbrot *et al.* (eds), *Law and Social Change in Papua New Guinea*. Sydney, Butterworths, 1982

Wetherall, David. *Reluctant Mission: The Anglican Church in Papua New Guinea 1891–1942*. St Lucia, University of Queensland Press, 1977

Whittington, Vera. *Sister on Patrol: From the Missionary Experiences of Sister Dorothy Pederick*. Rabaul, Trinity Press, 1968

Willis, Paul. *Learning to Labour: How Working Class Kids get Working Class Jobs*. Farnborough, Saxon House, 1977

Wiltgenen, Ralph M. 'Catholic mission plantations in mainland New Guinea: their origin and purpose'. In Research School of Pacific Studies (ed.), *The History of Melanesia*. Canberra and Port Moresby, Australian National University and University of Papua New Guinea, 1969

Wolfers, Edward P. *Race Relations and Colonial Rule in Papua New Guinea*. Brookvale, Australian and New Zealand Book Co., 1975

Woolf, Virginia. *Three Guineas*. Harmondsworth, Penguin, 1977, first published 1938

Young, John. 'Race and sex in Fiji re-visited'. *Journal of Pacific History*, vol. 23, no. 2 (1988), pp.214–22

Young, Michael W. 'Doctor Bromilow and the Bwaidoka Wars'. *Journal of Pacific History*, vol. 12, part 3 (1977), pp.129–53

Glossary

B4s, befores:	expatriates who lived in Papua New Guinea before World War II.
beri beri:	birth celebrations performed by Tabar women.
beri-beri:	disease of peripheral nerves caused by vitamin B1 deficiency and causing paralysis and bodily swelling.
betel nut:	fruit of betel palm chewed in Papua New Guinea with lime derived from burnt coral or shells and hot substances.
bighead/bik het/ bigheaded:	arrogant, self-confident; term usually used to describe a Papua New Guinean who questioned any aspect of colonial rule.
Boi/boy:	colonial pidgin for Papua New Guinean male; combined with nature of work done to describe domestic servants, eg houseboy, cookboy, washboy.
BPs:	Burns Philp Shipping Line, which also owned plantations and trade stores. Between them, BPs and Carpenters held a virtual monopoly on trade with Papua and New Guinea.
bosboi:	Papua New Guinean in charge of other Papua New Guinean workers, for example the labour line.
bush kanaka:	term used by Europeans and Papua New Guineans to describe unsophisticated Papua New Guineans (i.e. those unaware for European customs).
chooks:	Australian slang term for hens.
dimdim:	term for European man used by some Papuans.
doktaboi:	village man appointed by colonial administration to attend to matters of minor health care.

Fuzzy Wuzzy Angels:	Papuans who worked for the Australian armed forces during the Second World War, principally as bearers along the Kokoda Trail.
grillie:	skin disease in which skin becomes pale and appears to be peeling.
hahine:	Motu for 'woman'
kaikai:	pidgin for food.
kanaka:	term commonly used by Europeans before the Second World War to describe Papua New Guineans.
kiap:	patrol officer, the lowest level of colonial administration, who was expected to patrol through his area of responsibility on a regular basis.
kiapa:	carrying basket used by women in Port Morseby region.
kaukau:	sweet potato.
labour line:	workers on plantations.
laplap, lap lap:	length of material worn from waist down, a term more common in New Guinea.
lava lava:	length of material worn from waist down, term used in Port Moresby area.
lemese:	men's house. Papua New Guinean villages were dominated by a men's house in which the initiated men slept and planned their ceremonies.
limbom:	tall slender hardwood palm used as flooring material.
line:	noun and verb referring to Papua New Guinean workers, who might be 'lined'—for example, for medical inspections or to receive daily orders.
longhouse:	house exclusive to initiated males in Papua New Guinean villages.
luluai:	'head man' of village appointed by German and Australian administration in New Guinea to collect taxes and resolve minor disputes.
malagan:	death rituals performed by New Guinean men.
marama:	'mother', wife of Methodist missionary in New Guinea.
masta:	term of address for European males.
medical tultul:	see *doktaboi.*
memsahib:	Indian term of address to European woman.
meri, mary:	pidgin for Papua New Guinean woman.
missus:	term of address for European females.
mumu, mumu blouse, meri blouse:	blouse commonly worn by Papua New Guinean women, usually with puffed sleeves.

Motu, police Motu:	lingua franca of pre-Independence Papua, and spoken by villagers in Port Moresby region.
outstation:	isolated station in colonial administrative area.
panggal:	woven patterned matting used as walls in houses.
patrol officer:	see *kiap*.
pidgin:	lingua franca of New Guinea, now official language of Papua New Guinea as *pisin*.
rami:	Motu word for length of material worn from waist down.
sago:	soft starchy interior of palms and cycads used for cooking.
sak sak:	palm fronds used as roofing material.
singsing:	villagers or church members' gathering to sing and dance.
tabu, tambu:	places sacred or taboo, usually to one or other sex.
talatala:	'father', Methodist missionary in New Guinea.
taro:	tuberous herb, the poisonous root of which is made edible by boiling.
Tolai:	village groups living in Rabaul area.
tultul:	village interpreter and assistant to *luluai*.
yaws:	tropical disease characterised by eruption of raspberry-like excrescences.
wantoks:	members of same clan, ie who speak 'one talk'.

Index

administration, Australian 6, 39, 40–4, 263,
 264 (*see also* colonialism, race
 relations)
  indigenous men in, 187–8
  Papua and New Guinea compared,
   138–40
  and race relations, 4, 123, 138–9, 148–9
  and relations with missions, 55, 142–7
  and relations with private enterprise,
   50–1, 147–58, 239–40
  women in, 1, 2, 10, 44–5, 46–8, 90–1,
   99
    married women's unpaid
     contributions, 44, 233
Andersen, Pat, 5, 25–6, 27–8, 48, 66, 101,
 104, 105–6, 108–9, 124, 142, 173,
 174, 222, 250
Ax, Sr Aquilonia, 6, 23–4, 55, 82–3, 161,
 178, 183–4, 187, 223, 228, 236,
 250–1

Baining Mountains, 15, 68, 97, 104, 106,
 111, 145, 235, 236
base camp system, 41 (*see also* uncontrolled
 areas)
Beale, Dorothy, 5, 21, 22, 79–80, 84, 251,
 265
befores (B4s), 6, 8, 142, 159, 160, 170

Besant, Annie, 6, 231, 243–4
body and mind relations—*see* mind and
 body relations
Bohdana Voros, *see* Voros, Bohdana
Bridgland, Daphney, 5, 13–14, 34, 48, 58,
 59, 65, 70, 78, 101, 116–17, 119–20,
 120–2, 124, 127, 147, 152, 156–7,
 167, 168, 176, 181, 197, 202,
 209–10, 216–17, 218, 220, 232, 234,
 245, 251–2
British New Guinea, 39, 262 (*see also*
 MacGregor)
Bolegila, 8, 196
Booth, Doris, 34, 109, 190, 217
Brown, Rev. George, 9, 35, 76
Brown, Rev. Rodger, 6, 21–2, 54
Butcher, Benjamin, 56, 69, 71, 76, 252
Butcher, Eva, 77, 122, 145, 168, 252
Cheeseman, (Lucy) Evelyn, 2, 26, 74–5, 78,
 93, 96, 99, 100–1, 171–2, 173, 218, 235

childbirth
  dangers for white women, 70–2
  for indigenous women, 76–7
childhood, white in Papua New Guinea,
 124–5, 218
Chinese in Papua New Guinea, 22, 43, 45,
 51, 136, 137, 203

321

white women, *see* women, white

White Women's Protection Ordinance, 42,
    192, 195, 208–9, 247

Wisdom, Brig. Gen. Evan, 39, 139, 141,
    144, 156

women, indigenous (*see also* education,
    gender relations, race relations,
    women, white), 1, 3, 28, 29, 31, 64,
    76, 193, 220, 221–36, 246
  and missions' effects on status, 233
  trained as nurses, 46–7, 225–7, 265, 266
  and treatment by indigenous men, 115,
    147, 211–15, 223–4, 236

women, white (*see also* class relations,
    gender relations, missions,
    motherhood, plantations, race
    relations)
  in administration, 1, 2, 10, 44–5, 46–8,
    90–1, 99
  as feminine face of colonisation, 245
  and movement in uncontrolled areas, 41,
    43, 67
  and racism, *see* racism
  and relations with indigenous women, 4,
    68, 76, 77, 98, 107–8, 110,
    123–4, 130, 131, 228–9, 244–5,
    246, 246–7
    and difference between outstations
      and town, 235–6

and influence of motherhood, 65,
    234–5, 248
relations between white women, 109–10,
    222–3, 227–8, 245
as ruin of empire, 237–49
single, 3–4, 30, 90, 96–9, 191, 231 (*see
    also* lady travellers, missions)
women, white wives, 1, 2, 5, 7, 25–6, 63
  administrator's wife, 2, 5, 233, 234, 249
  and cooking and growing food, 103–5
  and philanthropic work, 11, 75, 91–2,
    231–2
  and tensions with husband's career
    aspirations, 67, 72–3
women's movement, feminism, 31, 140,
    199, 229–30, 240, 247
Woolnough, Mary, 22, 131
work, women's (*see also* administration,
    education, missions, plantations)
  and relations with male colonial rule, 237
  and threat to male status, 87–9, 91, 93,
    99
  married women's, 94

Young, Grace, 5, 22, 55, 67, 104, 110, 111,
    177–8, 220, 260–1